Advances in Experiential
Social Processes

Volume 2

Advances in Experiential Social Processes

Volume 2

Edited by

Clayton P. Alderfer

*Yale University
U.S.A.*

and

Cary L. Cooper

*University of Manchester Institute of Science and Technology
England*

JOHN WILEY & SONS

Chichester · New York · Brisbane · Toronto

British Library Cataloguing in Publication Data:

Advances in experiential social processes.
  Vol. 2
  1. Group relations training
  2. Interpersonal relations 3. Experience
  I. Alderfer, Clayton P II. Cooper, Cary Lynn
  158'.2   HM134   77-22060

  ISBN 0 471 27623 5

Phototypeset by Dobbie Typesetting Service, Plymouth, Devon, England
Printed by The Pitman Press, Bath, Avon

List of Contributors

CLAYTON P. ALDERFER   *Yale School of Organization and Management, New Haven, Connecticut, U.S.A.*

CHRIS ARGYRIS   *Graduate School of Education, Harvard University, Cambridge, Massachusetts, U.S.A.*

DAVID N. BERG   *Yale School of Organization and Management, New Haven, Connecticut, U.S.A.*

DAVID L. BRADFORD   *Graduate School of Business, Stanford University, Stanford, California, U.S.A.*

BARBARA BENEDICT BUNKER   *Department of Psychology, State University of New York at Buffalo, New York, U.S.A.*

DEXTER DUNPHY   *Department of Organizational Behavior, University, of New South Wales, Australia.*

ROSABETH MOSS KANTER   *Department of Sociology, Yale University, New Haven, Connecticut, U.S.A.*

BURKHARD MÜLLER   *Universität Tübingen, West Germany.*

MAX PAGÈS   *Université Paris IX, France.*

PETER B. SMITH   *School of Social Sciences, University of Sussex, England.*

FRITZ STEELE   *Development Research Associates, Boston, Massachusetts, U.S.A.*

BARRY A. STEIN   *Goodmeasure, Cambridge, Massachusetts, U.S.A.*

ROBERT C. TUCKER   *Department of Psychiatry, Yale University, New Haven, Connecticut, U.S.A.*

LEROY WELLS, JR.   *Yale School of Organization and Management, New Haven, Connecticut, U.S.A.*

v

Contents

Introduction to Volume 2   ix

1. **A Design for the Exploration and Development of Interpersonal Space**   1
   Dexter Dunphy

2. **Psychological Defences, System Intervention, and Preventative Mental Health**   37
   Chris Argyris

3. **An Attributional Analysis of Personal Learning**   .   .   .   63
   Peter B. Smith

4. **A Model of Trainer Development**   93
   David L. Bradford

5. **Developing a Theory of Practice for Experiential Learning**   .   121
   Barbara Benedict Bunker

6. **Developing Clinical Field Skills: An Apprenticeship Model**   .   143
   David N. Berg

7. **The Group-as-a-Whole: A Systemic Socioanalytic Perspective on Interpersonal and Group Relations**   165
   Leroy Wells Jr.

8. **Planning for Black Human Interaction Groups**   201
   Robert C. Tucker

9. **Defining and Developing Environmental Competence**   .   .   225
   Fritz Steele

10. **Experiencing Organizational Structure**   245
    Barry A. Stein and Rosabeth Moss Kanter

11. **Consulting to Underbounded Systems**   267
    Clayton P. Alderfer

12. **The Manifesto of Existential Training**   297
    Max Pagès and Burkhard Müller

Index   327

Introduction to Volume 2

The second volume of the **Advances in Experiential Social Processes** continues the pattern of intellectual development presented in the first book. Chapters in this volume identify and clarify value issues, integrate or differentiate theoretical positions, and present technical advances in experiential methods. In addition, the contributions again cover multiple levels of analysis including individual, interpersonal, group, intergroup, organizational, and community. The 12 chapters are ordered roughly by level of analysis, beginning with an individual–interpersonal focus and ending with a community–societal orientation.

The selection begins with Dexter Dunphy's sculptured account of his laboratory design to explore and develop interpersonal space. His work shows how closely related to human values, participant needs, design developments, and behavioural science theory a carefully crafted experiential programme can be. Throughout the history of experiential methods there has been a tension between the laboratory as a countercultural island and 'real' life. An important question has always been to determine the degree of transfer of learning from the laboratory to day-to-day organizational life. Chris Argyris' chapter on psychological defences and system intervention demonstrates the pay-off in terms of improved psychological functioning that can be obtained through interpersonal intervention with the partners and their wives in a professional corporation. Rooted in the theory of action perspective developed in collaboration with Donald Schön, Argyris' analysis also raises basic questions about the theory–practice utility of psychoanalytic theory. Peter Smith then reviews an extensive body of literature on personal learning. With insights stimulated by experiential social processes he is able to propose new theoretical integrations between conventional social psychological theory and experiential theory. Among themselves Dunphy, Argyris, and Smith demonstrate the increasing intellectual exchange that is occurring between theorists schooled without experiential training and those who have included systematic learning from *their* human experience as part of their professional equipment.

As the value of experiential methods has become more clear, there has been a corresponding interest in teaching professionals how to use and to develop experiential techniques. David Bradford presents a clearly charted model of training individuals to lead small groups. Bradford's work is especially useful in identifying predictable patterns in how fledgling group leaders learn and in demonstrating his own dictum that trainers' views of the world must be complex so their interventions can be simple. During the turbulent days of the 1960s many people had 'group experiences' based on the premise that emotional and cognitive functions were opposites and that truly humane learning was decidedly not intellectual. This norm has been shaken in recent years and there is avid interest in how experiential practitioners think. Barbara Bunker provides an empirical–inductive account of the major heuristics used by several of the well-known practitioners in the field. Her work is powerful testimony to the importance of cognitive work in sophisticated experiential practice. The link between laboratory and field once again recurs in David Berg's analysis of the importance of clinical field skills for the practice of organizational behaviour, whether in research or in consultation. Berg shows the critical value of individual and interpersonal learning for people who wish to work with organizations. But he also points out the limitations of learning only at these levels and extends the relevant domain to include group, intergroup, and organizational dynamics.

There is a historical sense in which the most fruitful target for experiential learning has been interpersonal relations. Although the field has greatly expanded its focus since the initial discoveries, many people unfamiliar with current developments associate experiential learning with interpersonal competence. Leroy Wells Jr.'s paper turns the field back on itself. His conceptualization of 'the-group-as-a-whole' identifies interpersonal episodes in which understanding is severely limited if analysis stays at the interpersonal level and in which simple interpersonal competence is ineffective if it is not complemented by group (as a whole) competence. Within the United States in recent years there has been growing recognition of the marked degree to which laboratory education has been a predominantly white male middle-class affair. Robert Tucker's work in this volume identifies the limitations of traditional human interaction laboratories for black Americans and proposes design alterations, including laboratory composition, for making interpersonal learning less hazardous and more useful for black men and women. Tucker's chapter is an important illustration of how experiential practitioners will have to think and act in order for the field to overcome its cultural blinders.

The last four chapters by Steele, Stein and Kanter, Alderfer, and Pagès and Müller focus on experiential methods applied to organizational and more complex levels of analysis. Fritz Steele defines and explores the meaning of environmental competence. His chapter should be consciousness-raising for people who assume that experiential methods are confined to people (not things). Barry Stein and Rosabeth Kanter take on the difficult problem of relating experiential methods to learning about organization structure. Along the way they question the use of experiential methods for this objective, identify some long-standing philosophical problems related to their quest, and propose two designs for teaching about structure. Clayton Alderfer's chapter provides a conceptual foundation for consulting with 'underbounded systems' and illustrates the theory and action implications with case fragments from an urban public school and a top executive committee. Alderfer's work contributes to a theory of organization–environment consultation for groups and organizations and expands thinking about organizational consultation to problems often misunderstood by organization development practitioners. Finally, the last chapter by Max Pagès and Burkhard Müller is a *manifesto* relating the authority dynamics familiar to all competent experiential learning professionals to broad economic, social, and political forces often overlooked by single-culture laboratory activities. The *Advances* series was designed to be a multicultural product. Pagès and Müller's work with French and German youth shows the strength of the cultural dynamics that must be confronted if experiential methods are to be used to promote learning across national boundaries. Their chapter is a fitting conclusion to a book arising from a new and growing field whose limits are unknown and whose limitations must be vigilantly observed.

CLAYTON P. ALDERFER
Bethany, Connecticut
February 1979

Advances in Experiential Social Processes, Volume 2
Edited by C. P. Alderfer and C. L. Cooper
© 1980 John Wiley & Sons Ltd.

Chapter 1

A Design for the Exploration and Development of Interpersonal Space

Dexter Dunphy

University of New South Wales, Australia

INTRODUCTION

In this chapter I want to outline and discuss the design of a personal growth workshop for participants who have not been involved previously in human relations training. This particular workshop design has been developed over several years by a small group of trainers based in Sydney and has been used repeatedly at the University of New South Wales in a postgraduate course 'Experiential Learning Groups' and in an external, non-credit course 'Interpersonal Relations Workshop'.

The aims of the workshop are clearly stated beforehand to participants in the following terms:

The workshop provides opportunities for you to:

(1) *develop more self-understanding*, by recognising a fuller range of feelings, understanding more of how your feelings affect your behaviour, appreciating how others see you and are affected by your behaviour;

(2) *extend your communication skills*, by improving your ability to listen sensitively to what others say and to communicate ideas, values and feelings clearly yourself;

(3) *practice new behaviours*, by extending the range of action available to you in many situations by trying new, unfamiliar and uncharacteristic ways of relating to others. In particular, there will be opportunities to practice the skills involved in bringing about change in yourself and others—skills such as counselling, consulting, leading and implementing change, along with seeking and accepting help, following and learning from others;

(4) *cope more effectively with organizational processes*, by learning to act effectively in such situations as superior–subordinate relations, intergroup relationships, and group problem-solving;

(5) *improve your ability to observe and analyse interpersonal and group behaviour*, by increasing your awareness of the dynamics of interpersonal and group behaviour;

(6) *transfer your learning in the above areas across to situations outside the workshop.*

Participants in the workshops are practising line or staff managers in private or public sector organizations. There is an age range from about 25 to 55 years but the average age would be about 35 years.

The workshop takes place over five days on a residential basis. The design consists of three main phases. Phase 1 is made up of an integrated set of structured exercises designed to clarify interpersonal issues and to provide direction for Phase 2. All participants are physically in the same room for Phase 1 but experience groups of varying size from dyads to simulated organizations consisting of all workshop participants. In Phase 2 participants divide into small groups of eight to twelve which meet in different rooms and operate as encounter groups. Group process is much less structured in this phase. In Phase 3 all participants come together again to participate in further structured exercises designed to increase the transfer of learning to 'back-home' situations.

RATIONALE FOR THE DESIGN

In our view, most experiential groups are dominated by the personal concerns of the trainer: groups run by power-oriented trainers become obsessed by power issues; groups with warm, affectionate trainers work on acceptance and love; and so on. It is not an exaggeration to say that some of the main traditions of group work enshrine such emphases: for example, the Tavistock tradition has centred on power; the Rogerian encounter group tradition on caring; Bach's groups on anger and hostility.

As trainers we are aware that our own experience and awareness are resources we have to offer participants. However, we also know that, particularly where this is the participants' first group experience, our concerns can be highly overdetermining. One important problem we have set ourselves to answer in this workshop is how to create a framework within which participants are free to evolve priorities and we, as trainers, feel free to use our experience to make it easier for them to work on their priorities. In other words, this workshop is designed to maximize the participants' power in determining the focus of learning.

The set of guided group experiences in Phase 1 is designed to minimize the impact of the trainers' or facilitators' personal concerns and to allow group members to identify for themselves areas of growth they would like to explore, to set personal learning goals in these areas, and then to develop or extend relevant interpersonal skills using appropriate methods of behavioural change.

Another task we have set ourselves is to design an approach which encourages as full use as possible of the range of experience and awareness of all those in the workshop who are willing to make these resources available to others. As trainers we model a range of behaviour vital to learning, but we regard this as 'gap filling'. Our aim is to encourage those with skills, knowledge, experience, and other resources to use them. If critical resources are not made available by others in the group when needed and we can fill the gap ourselves, then we will do so. But we try to progressively abandon our initiatives to others.

Another guiding idea behind the design has been to streamline the learning process and make it as efficient as possible. The workshop normally lasts five days, sometimes broken in the middle by two or three weeks. We accept a maximum of 36 participants but occasionally have worked with as few as 12. The second half of the workshop (Phase 2 onwards) is run in small groups of up to 12 participants. We prefer to operate with two trainers for each small group but we have operated with one per group. A fully-fledged workshop therefore operates for five days and has six trainers on staff.

The maximum of 36 participants has been established because when we divide the workshop into subgroups, in Phase 2, we have found it difficult to work effectively in groups larger than 12 participants and two trainers. We also think that the optimum range for the number of trainers in a workshop of this kind is two to six. With six trainers there is a variety of skills, yet the trainer group is still small enough to make coordination simple, to minimize division into cliques, and to prevent planning becoming a satisficing procedure rather than a creative process.

In the time available, we want each person in the workshop to have the opportunity to receive detailed feedback from others on his behaviour, to consider and absorb this feedback and use it to define goals for personal growth, to extend his range of behaviour and to anticipate the consequences, to receive reinforcement for closer approximation to his desired behaviour, and to plan for a self-reinforcing reward schedule that will maintain the learning when the workshop is finished.

We have, therefore, created a design which, while offering flexibility and choice, maintains momentum in learning.

While we initially offer a structured design, we strongly emphasize to participants that this structure is neither inevitable nor immutable. At any point individuals have the right to opt out of an activity, a session or the whole workshop. If there is group pressure or ridicule for such non-conformity, we strongly defend the right of the individual concerned to do what he chooses. We model this ourselves by resting or sleeping if we are tired, or going for a walk if we need a break. In addition, if participants are bored, baffled or rebellious, we stop and consult for preferred alternatives which are then undertaken. As the workshop progresses the level of structure is reduced, although there is a reversion to more structured procedures again in Phase 3.

DEFINING A DIRECTION FOR PERSONAL CHANGE

Underlying the workshop design there is also a concept of personal characteristics which assist learning and of others which inhibit learning—in ourselves as trainers and in the participants. The positive characteristics represent a model to which we aspire ourselves. Similarly, the negative characteristics represent behaviours and attitudes we try to minimize in ourselves because they inhibit learning. As trainers we realize that our most powerful form of influence is our own personal behaviour; others are more inclined to observe and identify with what we do than with what we say. We are also aware that discrepancies between what we say and what we are seen to do can be a source of confusion, doubt, and anxiety for participants.

Exhibit 1 summarizes what we see as the characteristics of the growing person. Exhibit 2 summarizes the characteristics of the 'self-defeating' person, who is unable to learn from his experience and provide the ground for further growth. The workshop is designed to develop *in all participants, including trainers*, behaviours which facilitate learning so that they can continue the learning process more effectively after the workshop is completed.

Exhibit 1 The learning person

Central or core feature: robust self-esteem, consisting of:
(a) self-knowledge, realistically assesses own abilities, aptitudes, motives, etc.;
(b) self-acceptance, affirms the essential validity of own being or reality;
(c) self-respect, respects self regardless of particular achievements or possessions;
(d) autonomy, accepts own need for others but is emotionally independent;
(e) seeks both solitude and company, is willing to spend time with self alone and also with others.

Resultant features:
(f) openness of communication, is non-defensive, willing to express thoughts and feelings simply and directly, to ask for what he/she wants from others while leaving them free to say 'Yes' or 'No';
(g) listens to others and seeks feedback on how he/she affects them. Uses feedback to learn and to modify own behaviour;
(h) active spontaneity and self-expression, a capacity for enjoyment and pleasure, involvement in the present;
(i) willingness to try new ways of relating to others;
(j) sees and accepts others as they are;
(k) wide behavioural repertoire; makes own behavioural choices with knowledge of a range of alternatives and their situational consequences. In particular, can exhibit all the following kinds of behaviour where appropriate:
   power or submission—is able to be assertive or to follow the lead of others;
   affiliation or anger—is able to provide or accept love and support, and to express and 'own' anger;
   achievement or self-expression—has a problem-solving attitude, sets realistic goals, and can postpone gratifying own immediate emotional needs to get a job done; can also relax and express inner feelings openly without fear or embarrassment when he/she chooses to do so.

Exhibit 2 The self-defeating person

Central feature: low or inflated self-esteem, consisting of:
(a) self-misconception, patently misconstrues own characteristics, fails to see self realistically;
(b) self-denigration, constantly criticizes self, regardless of achievements or personal characteristics;
(c) self-delusion, makes an unrealistic overassessment of own abilities, aptitudes, motives, etc.;
(d) dependency, depends emotionally on others, avoids being by himself/herself;
(e) counterdependency, denies need for others and is compulsively a 'loner'.

Resultant features:
(f) defensive communication, diverts or denies own feelings or keeps feelings to himself/herself, projects, represses, denies, etc.;
(g) fails to listen to others and/or distorts their meaning, avoids feedback and prefers illusions;
(h) uptight rigid, has a low capacity for pleasure, enjoyment, and spontaneous self-expression;
(i) routinized, adopts unvarying patterns of behaviour and will not risk changing known ways of relating to others;
(j) criticizes, denigrates others in order to bolster own ego by comparison;
(k) narrow behavioural repertoire, will not or cannot make a flexible response but is overdetermined by past experience or immediate pressures. Is 'locked in' to a particular dimension of human behaviour, such as domination. In particular:
  power–submission—tries to manipulate others by dominant manoeuvres or by dependency;
  affiliation–hostility—is compulsively 'nice' and 'sweet', or relentlessly hostile;
  achievement–self-expression—is achievement-hungry, driven to success and unable to relax, or is self-centred, self-indulgent, and unable to delay immediate gratification for the achievement of longer-term goals.

The central feature of the maturing person is his robust self-esteem. Learning is a form of caring for oneself, of feeding oneself in order that growth may occur. Therefore the workshop is designed, above all else, to nurture the self-esteem of participants rather than to lower it.

The exercises used in Phase 1 are designed and chosen to reinforce a sense of autonomy which is an important part of self-esteem. To thrust the individual into an unstructured situation, with authority figures present, generally creates a high degree of anxiety, leading to dependence and counterdependence. It does not create autonomy. By contrast, we try initially to provide structured situations where the individual must choose from alternative courses of action, confront important interpersonal dilemmas, reflect on his own choice, and take responsibility for the consequences that flow from his choice. We progressively reduce the programmed structure so that the individual then takes increasing responsibility not just for choices within the structure, but eventually for creating the structure itself. At the same time a basic rhythm is created of moving from relating to others to periods of individual reflection, self-absorption, relaxation, and solitude. This rhythm reflects an emphasis on the mature person's ability to be together with or apart from others, and his need to initiate social interaction, learn from it, and then take time out to integrate what he has learned into himself.

From a core of self-esteem flow other features of social behaviour which assist the learning process. Open, non-defensive communication allows the individual to express a full range of thought, feeling, and desire without manipulating others. In turn, an ability to listen with minimal distortion allows him to hear the messages others give him and to use their reactions as feedback. Spontaneity means freedom to explore and enjoy trying new ways of relating to others, and 'seeing others as they are' means suspending the premature evaluation which prevents an appreciation of others as potential resources to be enjoyed, rather than to be exploited and written off. We work towards these personal goals throughout the workshop, but have also chosen the exercises in Phase 1 to develop, illustrate, and reinforce these behaviours.

The final characteristic of the learning person is 'a wide behavioural repertoire'. As a person begins to explore new ways of relating to others, he expands the scope of the behavioural options available to him. To assist us in understanding this process, we have developed a three-dimensional model of interpersonal relations. The three dimensions emerge readily from studies of personal, interpersonal, and small group behaviour and are more thoroughly described in Dunphy's *The Primary Group* (Dunphy, 1972). They are also very similar to the three dimensions described by Bales in *Personality and Interpersonal Behaviour* (Bales, 1970) and correspond roughly with two of Schutz's (Schutz, 1966) dimensions of inclusion, control, and affection. They can be related to the three basic human needs of power, affiliation, and achievement which have been investigated in detail by McClelland (McClelland *et al.,* 1953), Winter (Winter, 1973), and others. We do not regard these three dimensions as exhausting all possible dimensions of human behaviour but rather as covering a large (but incomplete) range. The three dimensions can be seen as comprising a three-dimensional space within which most interpersonal acts can be located with some accuracy and descriptive power. As Bales (Bales, 1970) and Leary (Leary, 1957) have shown, a model of this kind has predictive power, for example a dominant act tends to draw a submissive act in response.

The model indicates that the mature person has the flexibility to choose freely from a wide range of behaviour. The immature person, on the other hand, is usually 'locked into' one or two dimensions or can operate only on one end of a dimension. He acts compulsively rather than exercising choice amongst options. The power-hungry executive, for example, sees all situations in terms of their possibilities for dominating and controlling others—he cannot relax and follow the lead of others or simply enjoy 'goofing off'; the achievement-oriented scientist sees situations in terms of work and goal-achievement—he may fail in his achievement because he is unable to see or handle power relations; The hostile person sees only cues which will allow him to release his anger, and may be unable to respond when others express their affection to him.

In our society people have generally placed a high value on particular ends of these dimensions—they respect the powerful person and despise the submissive; advocate affection and fear to express anger: extol achievement and are suspicious of self-expression or self-indulgence. But in our view *all* the behaviour represented in the interpersonal space is human and valuable. The mature person can lead or follow, express love or anger, work effectively or relax and express his own inner feelings. He moves freely through a wide range of behaviour, choosing the kind he feels is appropriate to his needs and to the situation and doing so with a knowledge of its consequences for himself and others.

The second phase of our workshop, in particular, is designed to allow people to explore and extend their behavioural repertoire. What we have found is that many people seldom or never use areas of the interpersonal space—the behaviour involved is unseen by them, unfamiliar to them, feels useless, inappropriate, phoney or unreal, or is seen as forbidden or 'bad'. Often these 'blanks' conceal a deep hunger and the denial is a source of anxiety—for example the achievement-driven person is yearning to relax and enjoy himself, the dominating person to be dependent and submissive, and so on. But because he has denied so long he has no facility in these areas. This phase of the programme makes a particular contribution to workshop design and intervention theory. As we shall explain in more detail later, it is guided by the learning goals identified by the participants in Phase 1. It provides opportunities to explore feelings, check out others' reactions, and experiment with new or different behaviour.

The third and final phase of the programme provides a basic structure which encourages participants to *review* what has happened, consolidate personal learning, and plan ways of extending and integrating new behaviours and insights into situations away from the workshop.

Traditional 'insight therapies' have tended to ignore the problems of behavioural practice, transfer, and ongoing reinforcement, thinking that insight is enough in itself. Traditionally also, insight therapists have been antagonistic to therapists who used behaviour modification and slow to adopt behaviour modification techniques, partly because of the strong authoritarian flavour of these approaches. However, we regard such techniques as a necessary part of the learning process, provided that the individual himself is allowed the choice of whether or not to deal with the issue and is put in the role of the experimenter or therapist, i.e. rather than 'being modified' by another, he determines his own behavioural goals and builds his own system of reinforcers. Only when he does so has he in a real sense begun to learn to behave differently and ensured that his desired behaviour has some significant probability of persisting. Only in that way can he learn new habits and develop new sets of habitual responses.

I will now examine each of the major phases of the workshop in more detail, indicating what is done and for what reason.

PHASE 1 — TOWARDS SELF-UNDERSTANDING AND SELF-RESPECT

All of us, if we could write the script for our own lives, would invariably create ourselves as perfect beings. Failing to achieve this ideal state, we are left with three choices. We can berate ourselves for falling short of our goal, we can pretend to be better than we are, or we can honestly be ourselves. (Shepard, 1976).

The first phase of our workshop offers participants an opportunity to begin to relate to one another and to receive feedback on how they are perceived and experienced by others. *The feedback is designed to develop and support realistic self-acceptance.* This phase of the workshop consists of a series of structured human relations exercises, chosen to provide feedback on personal behaviour but also graded to develop attitudes, understandings, and skills which provide a base for effective group work in Phase 2.

The sequence of exercises used in Phase 1 has been developed through induction, deduction, hunch, and trial and error. The exercises we now use, and the general sequence in which we use them, create what we visualize as a 'stepped' learning process. Each exercise acts as a building block which is designed to raise the individual's level of awareness about his characteristic ways of relating to others and the consequences of his choices for those developing relationships. Each new exercise in the sequence builds on what has happened before by partially repeating issues and processes dealt with earlier. At the same time learning is extended into new areas. To improve efficiency in learning we have stripped down each exercise into the simplest form we can devise, i.e. we have reduced the exercise to the most basic elements necessary to trigger insight and learning.

In arranging exercises in a sequence we have evolved a number of principles. First, the exercises provide a sequence which moves from the most elementary social group—the dyad—progressively through groups of increasing size until, in the final exercises, the individual occupies one role in a simulated organization which comprises all workshop participants.

Secondly, there is a progression from an emphasis on verbal discussion to the exploration of fantasy and non-verbal behaviour. We see this as a progression from activities which participants see as 'familiar, safe, and cognitive' to those participants see as 'unfamiliar, risky, and more emotionally involving'. While this progression often feels painfully slow to us as trainers, we find that it is not so to many participants. In addition we have found that time spent consolidating a sense of security at this stage saves time in the next phase of the workshop.

Thirdly, exercises are arranged in sequence to create a progressive build-up of personal feedback. Each exercise provides for repetition and reinforcement of prior learning as well as new insights which extend learning. By varying the design of exercises, shifting the immediate social context, and adding new elements such as non-verbal behaviour or fantasy, we allow the individual to see himself over and over again in different situations and with different people. The change of focus keeps interest alive and sets a brisk pace of learning. Participants feel that 'things are happening around here'.

The initial structuring in Phase 1 is used flexibly. Because we know *why* we are using particular exercises, we feel free to change or modify them in response to changing needs, and we are constantly varying the degree of emphasis on particular learnings that flow from them. The informal monitoring system we have developed as trainers is important here. As we work, we maintain communication with each other about how structure can be modified and insights developed.

We will now examine in more detail the kinds of exercises used, indicate why the particular exercises are seen as appropriate, and then outline the aims of the exercises. Examples of participants' statements of their learning then provide some idea of how the exercises actually 'come across' to participants.

Exercise 1: the first presentation of self

The longest journey begins with a single step.

Introduction given by the trainer: 'This is an opportunity for you to consider who you are, how you see yourself, and to decide what you want to convey about yourself to one other person now.'

Typical opening exercises are:
(1) Each participant completes 10 written statements, each of which begins with the words 'I am . . .' (Typical responses would be 'I am married', 'I am a lawyer', 'I am tired'.) Participants then divide into pairs and spend 20 minutes discussing their responses and exploring what they mean.

or

(2) Each participant is supplied with a pencil and paper and draws an outline of his hand. On each of the five fingers he names one significant influence on his current life. (Typical responses would be 'wife', 'father's death', 'university', 'close friend', 'music'.) Participants then form pairs and spend 20 minutes discussing their responses and exploring what they mean.

After (1) or (2) above, the group reassembles for a plenary session in which one trainer leads a discussion of the types of information people chose to disclose or withhold, emphasize or overlook. Typical sequences are also examined, like giving 'safe' information, then venturing something more personal, followed by returning to 'safe' areas.

Reasons for choosing the above as appropriate first exercises:

The first exercise should be brief and simple. There should be three main steps: solitary reflection, then exchange and exploration of personal information with one other person, then group discussion of the self-disclosure process.

Aims

(1) To begin with each person focusing his awareness on his own sense of identity.

(2) To indicate that the responsibility for personal disclosure rests with the individual, who chooses what to disclose and what to keep confidential.

(3) To equalize and maximize participation.

(4) To model the idea that disclosure will proceed by mutual exchange, not by one-sided probing or inquisition.

(5) To reduce threat by simplifying the initial process of relating to others down to a one-to-one exchange, and to form one supportive relationship before moving into the larger group situation.

(6) To provide data for use later, if desired, by an examination in the larger group of the self-disclosure process. Subsequent discussion touches on what kinds of information and inquiry were helpful and unhelpful in getting to know the other person.

(7) To signal that the trainers trust participants to act responsibly without the trainers' immediate supervision.

(8) To signal that the trainers will not adopt an aloof, remote, judgemental role but are prepared to engage in exercises along with other participants.

Such an array of aims may seem a great deal to hand on a single exercise which takes about an hour altogether. However, use of a variety of exercises and other forms of introduction has convinced us that the structure of the first hour plays a decisive role in orienting participants. In most cases, they would not be fully aware of the attitudes they are developing at this stage. Nevertheless the groundwork is being laid on which later exercises and group experiences build. As the participants progress through further exercises, basic principles such as 'mutuality of exchange' are articulated and reinforced.

In the plenary discussion an attempt is made to draw conclusions about the disclosure process and what helps or hinders it. An example of a summary made during this discussion follows:

Summary— 'I am' exercise

(1) Communication with another is an exchange.

(2) Different things can be exchanged:
—generalities and labels;
—information about roles and statuses outside the immediate group;
—specific personal traits;
—personal attitudes and values;
—feelings, both longer-term moods and immediate responses.

(3) The exchange often proceeds roughly in the above order, although it may stop or recycle at any point.

(4) The former items are generally safer, the latter more deeply disclosing.

(5) Relating to others can be speeded up and made more effective by self-disclosure. Simple quizzing the other creates defensiveness.

(6) Early in the process we are searching for 'common ground', i.e. similarities, from which we can build a bridge. Sharing common experiences and feelings can be reassuring.

(7) Later we search for differences to provide interest and to show the availability of alternatives.

(8) In relating to others we often try to exert control over the emerging relationship by holding back information, directing attention away from a sensitive topic, closing up, and withdrawing. We are most likely to do this when we feel we are being pressured by others.

(9) Talking about the 'here and now' is generally more disclosing than talking about the past, future or outside situations because those we are relating to can check on our perceptions/behaviour and point to omissions or to apparent contradictions.

(10) We often inadvertently convey unintended information non-verbally. Non-verbal behaviour is frequently a more reliable source of information about a person than what he says.

It should be obvious at this point that we take care throughout the workshop to develop a conceptual understanding of the process. While we believe that experiential learning is primary, we regard the process of conceptualizing what has been learned from experience as a vital part of the process of generalizing learning from the workshop situation to life outside.

Two statements from participants about this first exercise illustrate how it comes across to those who are involved:

I felt so good when I read Arthur's list, and some of the items—while expressed far more clearly than I had formulated them—jumped off the page at me. I told him that his concerns about study *versus* play time, future career, family *versus* work were similar to mine, and we explored them . . . My anxiety level was reduced considerably by knowing I wasn't alone, and that someone I had reason to believe was competent and successful shared my doubts and fears.

After a relatively short while, I found it easier to talk confidentially to Allan, and in fact we entered into a very interesting discussion during which he confided personal statements which I found quite revealing. I also gained a deep respect for him, emanating from his apparent honesty and sincerity.

It is clear from these statements, which are typical, that anxiety reduction is taking place through personal association as demonstrated by Schachter (Schachter, 1959). Clearly, also there is an attitude of 'you're OK, I'm OK' developing which is strengthening the self-respect of those involved. Exercise 2 allows for these processes to be extended further.

Exercise 2: Extending and consolidating learning about self-disclosure

Introduction given by the trainer: 'You have had one brief opportunity to explore the process of self-disclosure. You will now have a further opportunity to repeat this process in more detail with another person and to try, if you wish to, some of the principles we drew out from the first exercise.'

Typical exercises are:
(1) An encounter with one other using a booklet with unfinished statements, each of which is to be completed orally and alternately by each participant. The booklet begins with statements such as 'My name is . . .' and 'I was born in . . .' and proceeds to statements such as 'What makes me most anxious is . . .' and
'What I like most about you is . . .'. Participants work through the booklet, comparing and discussing their responses. (About 1½ hours).

OR

(2) Drawing or modelling of a 'self-portrait', either realistic, symbolic or abstract, which is first discussed in pairs and then in a subgroup. (About 1½ hours).

There is, of course, a significant difference between these exercises. The first directs the interpersonal encounter along particular paths and sets a basic rhythm to the exchange. The second is much less directed and structured and demands more initiative from participants.

Aims

(1) To extend and consolidate learning about the self-disclosure process.

(2) To build another supportive relationship and/or set of relationships before moving into the larger group situation.

(3) To model a progression from disclosure of more emotionally neutral data to more disclosure of immediate feeling.

(4) To enhance ability to listen effectively to others.

At this stage relatively little time has been spent in a group situation. Apart from one plenary discussion, each individual has spent most of his time developing a dyadic relationship with each of two other individuals. In those two relationships he has had the opportunity to clarify and express how he sees himself. It is our experience that these early one-to-one relationships provide a basic feeling of security as the individual moves into the larger group. It is as if he says to himself; 'I am not alone here. At least one or two other people know me. And I am not likely to be seen as too weird or different.' He is also beginning to realize that the initiative for learning lies with himself. While a basic learning structure has been provided, most of the time he has been left alone to learn for himself.

Some typical responses to Exercise 2 are:

Even if your responses are different from others, others are not necessarily critical of your standpoint, point of view or values. Differences can be sources of insight.

I enjoyed this encounter immensely. My partner and I exchanged a range of information, insights and feelings. We travelled further in a couple of hours than I have moved in most friendships in years. I'm taking home a copy of this booklet to try it with my wife.

I can see now where I have often stopped short in my relationships with others.

The stage is now set for a move into larger group activities which provide feedback to the individual on how others see him and respond to him. This is a potentially more threatening activity, but he moves into these new experiences having had the opportunity to affirm to others some of what he feels about himself and to experience some measure of support from them.

Up to this point, too, the agenda has been structured to make participation and involvement fairly easy. The individual has not had to face much in the way of competition for time and attention, others have not made major demands on him, and he has been operating at a conversational level.

The next round of exercises moves from what has been a primarily verbal and intellectual level to the exploration of 'deeper' psychological processes and more non-verbal interaction.

3. Further exercises: 'Seeing'—the practice of observation combined with giving and getting personal feedback

A sequence of structured exercises is introduced, varied according to the participants' needs as sensed by the trainers. Those listed are typical but are not alternatives as several are generally used. The following are general aims for the whole group of exercises:

General aims for further exercises

(1) To provide the person with opportunities to sharpen his perception of others and to practise giving 'non-evaluative' feedback.

(2) To provide opportunities for each individual to begin to take responsibility for his feelings and behaviour and to accept others' reactions as their responsibility.

(3) To legitimize the expression and exploration of personal reactions and feelings.

(4) To put individuals in touch with the flow of feeling within personal exchanges.

(5) To extend the individual's view of the range of behavioural options open to him in any situation. Participants often feel that what they did was 'inevitable' until confronted with the variety of options explored by others who faced the same situation.

(6) To allow participants to practise behavioural options in a safe learning environment.

(a) *Fantasy feedback*: Participants sit in two concentric circles so that each is facing a partner. The 'inside' partner of each pair begins by making the statement: 'I see you as a . . .' (examples: grizzly bear, worn fence-post, clown). The first association or image that comes to mind is regarded as the best. The person addressed then responds: 'What does a . . . (grizzly bear) do?' His partner then gives an elaboration of the image. 'A grizzly bear is large, cumbersome and heavy and mostly inoffensive or friendly but can become dangerous when enraged', etc. These images are then recorded as sketches, with giver and receiver each keeping a copy. The outer circle then moves on and the same process is repeated until each participant has given and received five images. Participants are then encouraged to search for the common denominator in the images they have been given in order to ask the question: 'How do I come across initially to others?' Then they are asked to examine the five images they have given to others as another source of insight into themselves (projection); the notion is introduced here that we can see others 'through our own eyes' and what we see is at least partially determined by our own characteristics, concerns, and past experiences.

Aims

(1) To explore the fantasy images we create in others' minds through our physical characteristics, dress, voice, movements.

(2) To increase awareness of our own spontaneous fantasies and their impact on interpersonal perception.

(3) To examine how our views of others are affected by our views of ourselves.

(b) *Finger dance:* Participants are seated on the floor in concentric circles in pairs. They place the fingertips of both hands against those of their partner and for five minutes move their hands as they wish. At the end of five minutes they discuss with their partners questions such as:

—in whose territory was most time spent?
—was all the space available used?
—what strategies were adopted and how did they affect the other?
—what feelings were experienced and how did they develop?
—was a flowing, responsive movement developed or did one of the pair frustrate and confuse his partner?

After the discussion, the outer circle rotates and the exercise is repeated with a new partner. The exercise continues until each person has had four partners. Time is then given for each person to reflect on what he has learned about how he takes initiative with others and responds to them. A short plenary session then draws out some of the important principles learned, particularly emphasizing that 'every move we make expresses something of ourselves'.

Aims

(1) To explore our characteristic modes of relating to others.

(2) To examine the reactions these provoke in others.

Some responses to this exercise illustrate its simplicity and power:

What a strange exercise! I wasn't exactly certain what we were supposed to be discovering, but I did find out quite soon that I didn't like to be 'pushed'.

The lessons here for me were about differences across people in the amount they welcome intrusions into private space, the amount they wish to enter others, the amount to which they desire to lead or to be led in various situations, and the need to listen for faint signals as to the desires of others. On this last point, it also seems necessary to acknowledge receipt of these faint signals. We need feedback as to how well we are being understood. This is our guide for further effective communication.

Our experience is that a few participants feel uncomfortable with this exercise, particularly in the early stages. They see little point in it and are embarrassed at touching in this way. This is more often true of men than of women. We use these reactions as a cue to assert again that each person is free to endure his discomfort and participate, or to opt out of the exercise and observe, or to do something else of his choice.

(c) *Mask-making:* Each participant uses coloured cardboard, scissors, string, and paints to create a mask which is 'my current everyday mask'. Each person then dons his mask and moves around, pairing up with others in succession. He responds to the other's mask in two ways. First he attempts to describe the other's mask as objectively as possible, e.g. 'I see a long, blue mask with narrow eye slits and no hole for the mouth', etc. Then he gives his feeling reaction: 'It makes me feel fearful and sad.' In small subgroups participants then discuss what they have learned about their 'defended' selves, the external facades they show to the world; for what, how, and when they use the defence and whether the defence is providing what they want or frustrating them in their relationships.

Aims

(1) To identify defensive 'masks', game-playing, and other potentially confusing, distorting or obscuring behaviour.

(2) To examine the interpersonal consequence of this behaviour. (This includes its real usefulness in self-defence as well as the barriers it creates to meaningful personal exchange.)

At the conclusion of this group of exercises, each individual has gained new insights into his behaviour and has begun to be more aware of and sensitive to variations in the behaviour of others.

(d) *Role-playing in simulated organizational situations:* Most of the participants in our groups are managers from senior executive to supervisory level, coming from both the public and private sectors. In one course they are also mature, part-time or full-time, postgraduate students. Consequently their work situation is vitally important to them. We therefore introduce role-playing and organizational simulations which give increased credibility and relevance as well as beginning the process of relating learning to practical situations outside the workshop. In these exercises the individual gets feedback on how he fills roles and copes with key relations such as the supervior-subordinate relationship.

Organizational simulations are normally more complex and take longer than exercises used earlier. We do not have the space here to describe the exercises we use and, in any case, we vary them to suit the organizational backgrounds of participants. However, we normally use at least one simulation of a role conflict situation. This could be a simple dyadic situation of conflict between a supervisor and a desk clerk, or a more elaborate organizational situation where conflict is created between supervisors, departmental heads, and the divisional head. In this latter exercise, the departmental heads are in the classic situation of the 'man in the middle'. We have found that it is important to have enough people in parallel situations to enable comparisons to be made of their varying strategies for handling conflict. Our emphasis in doing this is to demonstrate that there is a wider range of behavioural options available than any one individual normally envisages, and then to provide behavioural evidence of the consequences which flow from choosing a particular option. Thus conformity to the divisional head's instructions may alienate the departmental manager from his subordinate supervisors, while conformity to the demands of supervisors may alienate the divisional head. We have found that it is useful to obtain simple quantitative measures of such output variables as productivity and satisfaction so that some of the effects of different management styles can be verified.

We also find it useful to conclude with a rather more open-ended simulation which we call 'The Managerial Task'. It creates a number of production organizations which are in competition within a market. The exercise proceeds through a series of stages where we gradually move to build in further features of a real-life organization—beginning with acquiring resources and building a production process and proceeding to competing in a market and making personnel promotions within each organization.

The learning from these situations is not only about interpersonal relations but also about group and organizational processes. In the words of participants:

I concluded that it was the competence of the workers, rather than the management style, that appeared to be the prime variable in determining the finished product. For a competent manager to optimise his output, he should surround himself with competent subordinates and then operate in a participative role.

This exercise illustrated to me the organisational consequences of such common failures as: lack of planning, lack of awareness of the environment in which the organisation is operating, lack of communication between individuals and groups, insularity of thought and reliance on one's own limited value judgements, failure to seek feedback.

The atmosphere of 'playing games' often develops a light mood with a good deal of humour and laughter and many lessons seem not to be absorbed. But the experiences have a power not immediately realized by the participants and often not immediately perceived by the trainers. Later in the workshop, many references are made back to experiences in these exercises. 'The darkness is light enough.'

In addition, new skills are being learned and principles needed for further learning are being developed, e.g.

—differences are OK;

—I will speak for myself and let others speak for themselves;

—I will accept feedback, not discount it;

—to ensure that I have done so, I will summarize and repeat what others say, and check with them that that is what they meant;

—I will speak directly to the person, not about him to others.

Receiving feedback often raises anxiety and creates tension. Because of this, we introduce and intersperse between these exercises, when appropriate, a range of physical relaxation exercises, short periods of contemplation and reflection, and simple introductory exercises in meditation. In some cases we also introduce elements of caring massage, such as massaging one another's hands or feet. All of these exercises are designed to reduce anxiety and produce physical relaxation, to encourage the individual to keep literally 'in touch' with himself and with others, and to allow absorption of the insights provided by the feedback.

At the end of Phase 1, Stage 3, many participants will have formed supportive relationships with one or more others and have participated actively with most other group members in exercises. They will have begun to accept the idea that they alone are responsible for their own learning and that they cannot rely on the trainers to do it for them or to push them into it. They will be beginning to generate and articulate some guidelines for their own learning in this new situation and will be increasingly open with personal information. They will be becoming aware of similarities between the way they see themselves and the way others see them, but they will also discern that there are some puzzling discrepancies or inconsistencies.

On the other hand, other participants may still be relatively isolated and defensive and going through the motions of learning mainly to conform to emerging group norms rather than through any real commitment. One or two may be rejecting the situation as 'artificial' or 'irrelevant', as is shown in the following reaction from one participant:

The environment, a very large room with few chairs and open to the outside world was so artificial, that very soon our normal social patterns of keeping together with fellow workmates broke down.

In the majority of participants these contrasting attitudes will both be present to some degree and they will experience swings of attitude according to the situation. But, as perplexity is the beginning of knowledge, the trainers do not attempt to pressure the 'doubters' nor to reward those who suppress their doubts and reservations. The trainers also actively discourage group members from doing so, stressing that each individual is responsible for his own learning and is free to leave the group, to remain silent and non-participative, to criticize or to participate actively as he chooses.

4. Setting personal learning goals

The final exercise in this phase represents a key link between what has happened so far and Phase 2. Much of the direction of Phase 2 and the allocation of time within it is based on the results of this particular exercise, which we refer to as 'consultation triads'. It is outlined below.

Introduction given by the trainer: 'The next exercise provides an opportunity for you to set personal learning goals to guide you for the rest of the workshop. This exercise is a critical one because we as trainers will work with you to realize these goals, unless you decide to change them. Because of this it is important that the goals are as clearly and simply stated as possible, that they are expressed in concrete behavioural terms rather than as an abstraction, and that they represent something that you regard as practicable to accomplish within the rest of the time we have available. The outcome of this exercise will be one or more goals listed on paper and displayed where we can all refer to them.'

Procedure: Participants divide themselves into groups of three on the basis of who they would like to work with in formulating and clarifying their personal learning goals. Triad members then adopt the roles of client (inquirer), counsellor or observer. The client reviews for the counsellor the following questions:

(1) What have I learned about myself in this workshop so far? In particular, what situations am I now aware of, from this group and/or from other settings, where I have been dissatisfied with the outcome of my own behaviour?

(2) What are the objectives I wish to set for my personal learning in the remainder of the workshop? In particular, what new behaviour (i.e. specific actions) do I wish to learn, or what existing interpersonal skills do I wish to extend, to cope with situations which dissatisfy me?

The counsellor works with the client to assist him in defining as clearly as possible what he has learned and then to clarify his personal learning goals. For instance, the client may have received feedback that he is passive and easily manipulated by others. He recognizes that, while he has defined this behaviour as 'cooperative', others at work and at home have previously given him similar feedback. He decides that he does in fact wish to be more initiating and assertive, particularly in some situations.

Fifteen minutes are provided for each inquiry session and the observer looks in particular for what helps or hinders the inquiry process on the part of the client and counsellor. After the first inquiry session, the observer gives feedback on this to the client and counsellor.

Triad members then change roles so that there is now a new client, and the process is repeated. Then another switch of roles is made so that each member of the triad experiences being client, counsellor, and observer. At the conclusion of the exercise all participants (including trainers) write down their learning objectives on large sheets of paper. These are then displayed around the walls.

Aims

(1) To provide an opportunity for each participant to clarify his personal goals.

(2) To practise key role behaviours needed for the next stage of the encounter process (and useful in organizational settings).

(3) To indicate that the trainers themselves are also still learning.

When this exercise is completed, a basis has been established for the second phase of the workshop. As one participant commented after the programme:

The idea of developing specific behavioural objectives for the weekend from this exercise was very important—Indeed it helped me to focus myself a lot better than I would have, had these objectives not been stated. What's more, I felt that, even if in a limited way, I was able to move positively toward attaining these objectives.

The participants' stated objectives are also of vital importance to the trainers. Trainers work to the stated objectives made by each participant unless he decides to modify or change his objectives. The trainers accept each participant's stated objectives at face value and respond to his behaviour in terms of its apparent compatibility or conflict with his stated objectives. If, for example, an individual states that he wants to learn to empathize, the trainer will work with him on that objective. The trainer will also explore any apparent contradictions or conflict between how the participant actually behaves and how he has stated that he wants to behave. So, for example, if a particular person has said he wants to learn to empathize and yet he appears constantly critical of another who admits feeling helpless, the trainer will point up the apparent discrepancy. We have found that, if we work in this way, we do not attempt to force our values on participants and it is also relatively easy to avoid pressure from some group members to force individuals to conform to group norms. Yet as trainers we can maintain an ethical position in the latent conflict between the participant's right to choose how, when, where, and what to be involved in and the trainer's role of working with resistance and confusion.

PHASE 2—EXPLORING INTERPERSONAL SPACE

We must stop hoping and make it happen. (A participant's comment.)

In Phase 1, participants in the workshop were not divided into definite small groups. In Phase 2, however, participants are divided into small learning groups of 10-12, each group gaving one or two trainers.

We have experimented with different ways of splitting the larger workshop into these smaller groups. For some time we asked participants to divide themselves into groups and then to 'bid' for the trainer pairs available to each group. We used this approach to emphasize the value of participants taking responsibility for their own choices. We have found that this approach works reasonably well with workshops of up to 24 people, i.e. two groups. However, with numbers above that our experience, in these and other programmes, is that we frequently end up with one or two groups having a heavy bias on one or more of the interpersonal dimensions. We have found that the two most frequent combinations resulting from mutual choice are (1) a group of active and passive, hostile and dependent people, who might be labelled 'the resisters'; and (2) a group of initiating, affiliative achievers, who might be labelled 'the enthusiasts'.

In the process of grouping, the enthusiasts rapidly sort themselves into a group which will occupy a central physical position and/or place in the sunlight. The resisters tend to be left behind, caught in their indecision and hostility, and so end up as a 'remainder group', often positioned in a gloomy corner of the room.

In bidding for trainers, the resisters tend to bid on the basis of status and reputation. We suspect that their hidden message is: 'Save us, powerful leader. But, if you can't, we will be justified in our hopelessness because, with all your skill, even you failed to change us.' The enthusiasts tend to choose the trainer whom they like personally. Their message seems to read: 'We are the brightest and the best. We like each other. We like you too. Therefore you will have to like us and do what we want you to do.'

This method of self-selection has proved to reduce the variety of personal resources available to the group for insight. In some cases it also helps build substantial collusive defences which are difficult to loosen. Since our aim is to provide a learning environment where habitual attitudes, values, and behaviours are challenged, we have changed the method of selection into groups.

We now divide participants arbitrarily between groups, with some attention to equalizing numbers on the basis of male/female and younger/older. The principle we are adopting here is that we are trying to achieve as wide a range or as rich a mix of people in each group as possible and to avoid any form of selection that would reduce this. 'Arbitrary' selection is also more efficient;

participants have frequently objected to the 'waste of time' involved in the self-selection process and have failed to see our concern with 'personal responsibility for choice' as relevant.

Phase 2 begins in these groups with the output of the 'learning goals' exercise discussed above. These goals are displayed on the walls and participants talk about what they have identified as personal goals. As discussion proceeds, group members normally begin spontaneously to note recurring issues on the sheets. The trainers actively encourage this process of 'clustering' issue areas. This self-disclosure within the new group provides material to start the group process and the clustering of goals provides direction.

Grouping goals into 'issue areas' provides an efficient base for moving away from structured exercises and into an encounter mode. To deal with each individual's goals would be a time-consuming process and would place the individual in a 'hot-seat' situation which encourages one-way probing rather than mutual exchange. When issue areas are established and assigned priorities by the group, they are then taken up sequentially. The result is that the highest-priority issue is generally one that has been listed by six or eight of the 12 participants. It may be, for example, that five participants want to be more assertive, while two wish to be less dominant at times. The most active of these seven participants then move naturally into sharing their problems and difficulties, echanging viewpoints and giving each other feedback. The high anxiety often aroused by the first moments in an encounter group is therefore reduced for many. Consequently we seldom have the unconscious search for a 'victim' to relieve anxiety which is a frequent result of such situations.

The aims of this review of learning goals therefore are:
—to allow each individual to communicate his personal learning goals to others;
—to create a climate of commitment to learning and a willingness to provide support to others in learning, i.e. a normative system to support learning;
—to consolidate a variety of goals into a smaller number of issue areas which the group can proceed to work on and which the trainers can relate to the 'interpersonal space';
—to create an agreed set of priorities, an agenda, determining the order in which issues of concern to participants are dealt with. This also provides a sense of progress;
—to provide 'company' for the individual as he pursues his learning goals so that he does not feel isolated.

The issue areas are then pursued in the order determined by the group.

Our experience is that issue areas can be readily related by the trainers to the three-dimensional model of interpersonal behaviour described earlier in this chapter. Goals can be readily clustered about the dimensions of power-submission, affiliation-hostility, and achievement-expression, or some combination of these. The trainers use these dimensions to orient themselves to issues raised by participants, who may not be aware that the trainers are operating on such a model.

Typical then, from the trainer's point of view, the group process works through the various dimensions. We will deal with this process in relation to the dimensions in the following order:

(1) domination—submission;
(2) affiliation—hostility;
(3) achievement—self-expression.

Our discussion of the process will inevitably make it appear more systematic and directed than it is. In fact, issues bubble to the surface and participants and trainers relate them back to the individual's stated goals. The process tends to be more encounter-style, with the focus moving from group or sub group discussion to one or two individuals.

In the groups, each dimension is usually dealt with as a whole (e.g. both power and submission together) because we find that those whose concerns lie at the end of the dimension represent a potential source of insight to those who are concerned with the other. Initially, however, those at opposite ends of a dimension represent a source of agitation and challenge to one another which often results in confrontations. The submissive person and the dominant person, for example, have a complementarity of behaviour that is a potential learning resource.

Those participants who have nominated an issue area as relevant normally volunteer to discuss their dilemmas, anxieties, hopes, and experiences and to identify where their behaviour is now and how they would like to change. When this process seems to have bogged down, interest is lagging, or participants are blocking one another's attempts to work, the trainers introduce exercises designed to delineate the issue in behavioural terms. These normally include role-playing, non-verbal, and gestalt exercises. They have a common characteristic: all of them are chosen for their ability to dramatize the key issue being dealt with in the group at that time. The exercises develop a dramatic interplay of interpersonal objectives, with the players in the drama being those group members who nominate the issue as relevant.

As participants work through issues, they are encouraged to set revised, more specific, and more concrete goals. For example, an early goal might be: 'I would like to be able to speak up more in group situations.' This might be revised later to: 'If I really want to be heard, I will try to interrupt others if necessary and persist when they try to talk me down.' But at all times it is a participant's right to decide that he does not want to change his behaviour for whatever reason, although if he does decide not to try to change it is generally because *he* considers the costs of doing so outweigh the benefits of changing.

In the case mentioned above, where one or more participants have reached the point of seeing the concrete behaviour they want to adopt, the trainers may introduce role-playing exercises to help the participant develop the behaviour. In this case role-playing would take the form of assertion training centring specifically about a group situation where there are several dominant, competitive talkers. Frequently the individual is able to acquire some facility with the new behaviour through such practice sessions. However, at times the role-playing reveals some inner conflict such as: 'I would like to be able to talk others down, but I want to continue to see myself as kind and considerate.' In such cases the trainer typically switches to a gestalt activity to externalize the internal dilemma.

Such dialogues frequently expose what Victor Raimy has called a 'misconception' or 'cluster of misconceptions' (Raimy, 1977). In our view, Raimy's notion of 'misconception' is an important and useful one. However, the cognitive flavour of the term ignores the strong affective (emotional) and conative (belief) elements in the basic assumption. We have been forced to ask ourselves often: 'Why does a person cling to a concept that is so obviously inadequate?' The answer lies in the 'psychological pay-off'. If I cling strenuously to the notion that I am inadequate in my work, for example, when everyone around admires my accomplishments, the answer must be that I have an investment in maintaining my conception in the face of overwhelming evidence—an investment that brings a 'return'. We have found it useful to ask the person holding the misconception what catastrophe he fears would flow from accepting a more realistic view, e.g. 'I am competent at my job'. The answer generally comes quickly and clearly: 'If I accepted I was competent, I would have to take on more responsibility and I'm afraid of exercising power. I would rather appear incompetent than openly manipulative.' Generally the misconceptions allow short-term gains which are traded off against long-term losses. For example: 'I won't speak up in the group now as I might say something foolish, even though I know by not speaking up now I am isolating myself further for the future.'

At this stage, the trainer will also frequently pick up critical non-verbal signals which reveal otherwise unexpressed dilemmas. For example, a woman participant opening and closing a large, ornate ring with a hinged top as she discusses a personal problem is able to see that this is the outward expression of her dilemma: 'Do I want to be open or closed about this?' The trainer's sensitivity is critical as the group moves into considering deeper feelings and more powerful dilemmas. The trainer's activity provides a basic pace for the group action in the early part of this phase. As several people explore an issue, the trainer helps them dramatize alternative courses of action, examine consequences, expose personal assumptions, confront dilemmas. The trainers provide support and frustration at critical moments and step back when others can provide insights, are willing to share experiences or move in to be involved with those working through an issue. The trainers also point up defensive behaviour in the sense that Kassorla uses the term:

Defensive behaviour is something we say or do to keep us busy so we won't be able to look at the real problem. In a sense we *defend against* looking at our problems; we don't know how to solve them; so we avoid examining them. (Kassorla, 1977)

As participants substitute new behaviours for old or develop new options to add to their behavioural repertoire, the trainers work to create a climate in which these new behaviour patterns are reinforced by the group, rather than undermined or ignored.

We will now deal with the kinds of issues that are raised as we work through problems connected with each of the key interpersonal dimensions and examine the theory base for understanding the significance of each dimension and the trainer interventions that are appropriate.

The power dimension

Power is a central and important aspect of all social relationships. However, to many behavioural scientists who belong to the 'helping professions' it seems to have become a dirty word. In the group situation the trainer occupies a position of power, however, and must use power if he is to be effective and deal with a range of participant behaviour on this dimension—a range which includes strong and forceful dominance, competitiveness, guilty manipulation, dependency, passivity, and withdrawal. In understanding power we have found the work of Adler (1928), Winter (1973), Schutz (1966), Bales (1970, p.195) and Dunphy (1972) particularly useful in giving a theoretical base for understanding the power motive, in sensitizing us to power imagery, and in providing concrete categories for describing varying forms of power behaviour. I do not have space here to summarize the work of these writers but simply refer the reader to them.

The work of these writers and our own experience suggest to us that all people experience a need for both power and submission. However, some individuals have a particularly strong investment in the behaviour described by this dimension and may express their need by acting at one end of the dimension only. The key question underlying behaviour in this area is: 'how much do I want to, can I, dare I, try to influence and control others? How much do I want others, will I allow others to influence and control me?'

The way the power issue normally manifests itself first in the group is by a division within the group into 'talkers' and 'non-talkers'. This division is frequently remarked on by participants themselves, who seem to recognize intuitively the point established by Bales—that in discussion groups the simplest way to achieve leadership status is to talk the most (Bales, 1970, p.195). Talkers generally despise non-talkers (i.e.the quiet or silent members) whom they characterize, sometimes openly, as 'weak', 'stupid', 'pissy', 'empty', etc. On the other hand, non-talkers often characterize talkers as 'loud', 'manipulative,' 'shallow', 'superficial', etc. Talkers seldom listen to others, compete with one another for air space, and generally think aloud while talking, rather than thinking beforehand and then speaking. This gives them a strategic advantage in seizing the initiative over those who like to think before speaking. Non-talkers are usually better listeners and observers but are resentful of those whom they see as dominating the group. They frequently have low self-esteem based on a cluster of misconceptions that are essentially those of 'depressive neurosis' (see Raimy, 1977, pp100-1). These misconceptions have 'functional value', i.e. there is a pay-off to the person for believing them. The underlying thought is: 'Because I am hopeless, there is no use going through the effort of trying.' The longer the submissive hesitates in participating actively, the more hopeless he feels; the more hopeless he feels, the less energy he is able to generate to try to enter the discussion. To compensate for his feelings of impotence he then begins to indulge himself in grandiose delusions, represented by thoughts such as: 'I am a deeper person than others; I would not indulge in such superficial inanities; I can see through their games and I am above them; I am really superior behind it all.'

When faced with real, concrete, achievable actions which would take him out of his passivity, the submissive will often avoid the effort by constructing 'the false alternative'. He will argue, for example, along the lines: 'You don't think I would want to become a blatant manipulator do you?' He attempts to define the only alternative available as the most far-out form of dominance, ignoring the possibility of merely being more assertive when he wants to be. This latter alternative is the hope that the group can hold out to him—the choice to be unconstrained sometimes by the actions of others, the possibility of expressing himself clearly and communicating with others, the possibility of restoring his self-esteem, gaining the respect of others, and realistically assessing his own capabilities through feedback from others instead of being locked into a lonely, inner dialogue.

The misconceptions of the powerful are usually blatant and more familiar, because more frequently voiced. Typical examples are: 'I was born always to lead. I need no support from others apart from their allegiance. To follow is to be weak.' The hope the group can offer the powerful is the opportunity to relax, to drop perpetually playing power games, to accept guidance and help when it is needed, to learn to listen and observe, to be able to give up manipulation and form open and satisfying relationships. For the powerful, to dare to be vulnerable and to practise being responsive is a healing, wholesome experience.

In working on issues of power, we have found that the biggest problem is to provide the submissives with opportunities to mobilize the energy which they normally dissipate in futile, internal dialogues. We have found that timing is important. The trainer needs to wait until the more vocal members dominate long enough for the submissives' resentment and frustration to build up a critical mass, but not long enough for them to feel totally hopeless and defeated. If necessary, the trainer then legitimizes the expression of this resentment and provides a critical power element in preventing them being overwhelmed and silenced by the powerful. He does this by picking up the submissives' signals of frustration and resentment and turning back to them the decision of what to do. In this way the trainer helps the submissives to act rather than responding to their demand that he defend them or act for them. When backed up in this way, submissives experience a sense of personal power which results from mobilizing their energy and actively directing it outwards rather than using it to crush and denigrate themselves.

From this confrontation can emerge a new understanding by both dominants and submissives of the need to own strength and weakness, of the common anxiety which can lead to dominance in some and withdrawal in others. There can be a new appreciation too of the value of the basic rhythm of living, which requires the channelled use of energy followed by relaxation, appreciation, and reflection. It is important that the trainer himself models the responsible use of power rather than avoiding the issue or exercising power arbitrarily.

Two examples might express more than generalizations. In one group we had a very dominant and vocal man (Jack) whose level of activity and energy in the group was matched by his active participation and excellence in a range of sporting activities outside. He explained (at great length) what a good listener he was but that other people took advantage of this and did not listen to him. When others in the group attempted to ask him questions or express views, he interrupted and talked them down. Finally some group members tried to point out that he did not appear to be listening to them, but he managed to brush their comments aside. Later the trainer introduced an exercise in which group members made cardboard masks of their 'everyday faces' and donned them. The dominant group member made a long mask which was unusual in that it also covered his ears. Part of the exercise consisted of pairing and describing each other's masks. When Jack was paired with the trainer, the trainer began to describe how Jack's mask looked to him. Jack, however, had to interrupt the trainer several times, exclaiming: 'I'm finding it hard to hear you, my mask covers my ears.' Suddenly Jack realized himself what he had refused to accept from others, that he was in fact a poor listener. He decided to experiment with keeping silent for half a day in the group, and discovered that keeping his mouth closed improved his hearing. He began to listen to others and at the same time to sense what they were feeling. His workmates subsequently confirmed that he changed remarkably after the group and was easier to work with.

On the other hand, in another group five members wanted to learn to be more assertive. One of the more dominant members, Bill, volunteered to help them in a role-play in which he would try to dominate them and they would try to develop ways of handling his dominance and assert themselves. They agreed. He then directed them to place chairs for the role-play and sit in particular positions. They complied. When all was arranged for the role-play, the trainer pointed out to the submissives that they had already failed in their stated goal. They were puzzled but Bill quickly agreed with the trainer, saying to them: 'You have already lost but don't realize it.' He had to point out to them that, quite deliberately, he had them running about at his direction. At first they could not believe that anyone would set out to manipulate them so deliberately and, when convinced, their anger was mobilized into a fierce determination to 'beat that bastard at his own game'. They finally succeeded to their own and the group's satisfaction, discovering that they had a real ability to assert themselves in the face of manipulative attempts to control them.

The affiliation-hostility dimension

Love and anger are two enduring human emotions which are expressed in movement towards others and away from them. Love and anger are two poles in any mature relationship. In our culture we extol love and downgrade anger. But anger, like fire, is a cleansing force in human relationships; a source of energy and a lever for change. Together the two emotions are like the tide's ebb and flow.

Our understanding of this dimension has been helped by the works of Schachter (1959), Ardrey (1966), Lowen (1975), Rogers (1970), Bach (1966), Bales (1970), and Dunphy (1972). In particular, the work of Ardrey and Lowen, although not normally connected, provides an understanding of the critical role of sexuality in relation to this dimension. Ardrey's review of ethological studies argues that hostility has a critical role in boundary maintenance and that sexuality is a major force in modifying personal boundaries and overcoming a hostile, defensive reaction. Lowen's study of bodily energies indicates that the form of energy is the same for love and sexuality, but that in love energy is directed upwards in the body while in sexuality it is directed downwards.

To be stuck at one end or the other of this dimension is to be less than fully human. On the one hand, to be compulsively affiliative is to accept the tyranny of having to please everyone and the futile attempt to live up to everyone's conflicting expectations. On the other hand, to be compulsively hostile is to deny one's need for others and to identify with Paul Simon's song 'I am a rock, I am an island'.

The key question that underlies this dimension are: will others accept me? Will I accept others? How close and intimate do I want to be? Can I move away from others if and when I want to? Can I express the resentment, annoyance or anger I feel towards others? Can I handle their resentment, annoyance, anger with me? How will I handle it?

Typically, members of the group who are concerned with this dimension polarize into two camps which I will refer to as consisting of 'overpersonals' and 'counterpersonals'. Overpersonals are all sweetness and light, warmth and friendliness. They express understanding and caring and generally appear optimistic and good-natured. They rush readily into sharing and intimacy, including sexual seductiveness. Counterpersonals, on the other hand, are remote, cold, formal, unfriendly, openly or covertly hostile, resentful and suspicious, quick to anger, and express hostility. The ethos of the encounter movement, particularly in the Rogerian tradition, has tended to support the overpersonal group members to the detriment of understanding and appreciating the onesidedness of the overpersonal position and the potential contribution which can be made by the counterpersonals.

We have found that, as issues relating to this dimension are raised, the overpersonals deny their own anger and hostility, particularly when challenged by the counterpersonals. The overpersonals see anger and hostility as 'bad' impulses and become sweeter, more sugary as they become angrier but suppress their feelings. They try their habitual mode of manipulating others, which is to please and to reward with affection, which they fake if necessary. The counterpersonals, for their part, deny their own need to reach out to others, to give and take love and support from others.

Both overpersonals and counterpersonals share a strong anxiety about losing friends but they handle the anxiety differently. The overpersonals try desperately to establish and maintain relationships by making heavy downpayments of affection and thus building up an implied obligation to return it. (What would be called in international economics a 'positive balance of trade'.) They are afraid that if they express their anger and frustration and fail to please the other they will lose the relationship. They see anger as bad and destructive. They believe they should love and like everyone however the other may treat them. They hope to be liked by showing liking, to be given to because continually giving. In fact they are often seen as 'generous' and taken for granted or exploited, with resultant feelings of being empty, unloved, and resentful because 'used' by others. They create this situation themselves since, while they present themselves as giving much, they accept little. In this way they maintain a position of advantage over others and appear, to themselves and others, to be morally superior. However, their generosity often appears forced, as the gestures of giving increasingly reflect what they feel they ought to do rather than what they want to do. By withholding their feelings of anger they are giving as little of themselves as the counterpersonals, since they are saying essentially: 'You aren't worth getting angry about!'

Counterpersonals, on the other hand, handle their anxiety by trying to ensure that they have nothing to lose. They act as if the resources of love are in very short supply and must therefore be used sparingly, if at all. They do not believe in 'displaying' positive feelings because to do so cheapens the feelings. They feel that there is no point in expressing affection because others should 'know' that they are loved and cared for without them expressing those feelings. They readily give out resentment and anger, however, and do so partly to test the reality of others' love and concern for them. The (usually unexpressed) thought is: 'If you really love me, you should continue to love me whatever I do. In fact the way I test your love is to use you miserably. If you stick around, then you are genuine.' Therefore the counterpersonal often treats his friends worse than he treats his enemies, fearing that if he invests in a relationship, he may lose the relationship and be hurt. If the friend does in fact abandon the relationship out of emotional starvation or hurt, the counterpersonal can then justify his own lack of giving by saying to himself: 'Lucky I didn't give; see how untrustworthy he was.'

We have found that certain simple exercises and activities provide insight into the nature of these dilemmas and can lead to acceptance of the need to experience and express both caring and anger. One such exercise involves giving each group member a handful of buttons (or any other varied objects) which he is told 'represents all your resources'. Group members are then told that they can use their resources in any way they wish, as in life. Some give all or part away, others trade competitively or steal, others guard them jealously, some join with others in making patterns, and so on. After 15 minutes or so, the group discusses how resources were used by each member, and this reveals clearly the basic modalities of withholding, giving, and taking adopted by each person. As participants express wishes to be able to show more caring or more anger (or both), it is then natural to move into activities like Indian wrestling, fighting with sponge batons, pounding a punching bag or, on the other hand, caring massage. In addition, practice in vocalizing feelings on this dimension can be had by group members inviting feedback and being given it in sentences beginning 'I like/enjoy/appreciate your . . .' and 'I resent/dislike your . . .'.

Non-verbal behaviour is particularly important for this dimension as so much of our interpersonal feelings is expressed physically. Therefore group members who wish to be more expressive are encouraged to discern and adopt loving and angry postures. Often there is need also to develop and practise new internal messages such as: 'I have a right to my feelings of love or anger regardless of who is the object of them. I don't have to feel guilty or apologetic about my feelings for others whatever those feelings may be. There are no "right" or "wrong" feelings—the real issue is how I express my feelings.'

As this dimension relates to sexuality, there can be a high level of anxiety about traditional taboos, like members of the same sex touching each other. We have found that male-to-male physical contact in a caring way is particularly anxiety-provoking in our culture. Underlying this anxiety is the false premise: 'If I allow myself to enjoy touching another male, I am a homosexual, and homosexuality is bad, dirty, etc.' One of the advantages we find from introducing massage is that it raises these issues and can provide a legitimate way of restructuring these attitudes and assumptions.

Exercises which allow participants to experience feelings of love, anger, and sexuality provide groundwork in being open and direct in relationship with others. Participants learn that honesty is important in intimacy and that it is possible to be close to others while reserving the right to say 'Yes' or 'No' without our behaviour being dominated by fear, guilt or remorse. It is an exhilarating feeling for many people to feel close to others while remaining autonomous and free. There is often a great sense of relief to learn that anger is a natural response to frustration and rejection—that it is an integral part of being human, of experiencing one's own strength, of keeping alive a gutsy feeling of vibrancy and zest for life. Anger is an act of self-affirmation and therefore an important ingredient in self-esteem. Unaccepted and unexpressed, it becomes cold, quiet, mechanical, devious, and destructive.

The achievement-self-expression dimension

The underlying logic of this dimension is not so immediately self-evident as with the others we have discussed. But basically the dimension can be summarized as 'goal-directed, structured activity' *versus* 'unplanned and spontaneous expression of inner feelings'. Our society strongly rewards achieving behaviour, i.e. the setting of task goals and postponement or repression of immediate need satisfaction in favour of 'getting on with the job'. We admire the person with 'get up and go', who 'gets things done'. McClelland *et al.* (1953) have catalogued the development and shape of this drive-determined behaviour. It is important in our society that we can establish the self-discipline involved in achieving. However, many individuals have an insatiable hunger for achievement which destroys their capacity for enjoying the fruits of their labour and will not allow them to relax and enjoy 'being' rather than 'doing'.

The other side of this dimension is self-expression. We might more aptly call it 'self-indulgence' if that term did not carry such an overload of moral judgement. The mature person can achieve but he can also respond spontaneously to his inner moods and feelings. He seems alive because he laughs, jokes, weeps, trembles, dances, becomes elated or wistful. Self-expression of this kind is an important part of the development of all art forms, but it is only a beginning. The creation of a final art product also requires achievement behaviour. Part of the rhythm of artistic creation is a movement from concern with inner feeling (self-expression) to a disciplined process of channelling feelings into a finished form (achievement). But the same kind of rhythm can be found in many aspects of life. For example, decision-making groups normally swing from task-oriented behaviour to joking and laughing as the meeting (and the task) is completed; a tense football match shows the same swing from concentrated, goal-directed activity to a frenzied shouting, running, hugging, and leaping when the final whistle blows. The expressive end of the dimension is also the world of sensuality, of fun, feasting, fighting and fucking for their own sakes, not as a form of communication with others (as in the affiliation-hostility dimension) but as personal indulgence—the experience and expression of pleasure and pain in particular.

Issues connected with this dimension polarize group members into two factions which I shall refer to as the 'achievers' *versus* the 'expressors'. The achievers are sometimes characterized as 'greasy grinds' or 'workniks' by group members and the expressors as 'playboys' or 'goodtimers'. Their mottoes might be characterized as 'rigour' *versus* 'fun'. If the issues are not raised directly from the lists of learning goals, they emerge spontaneously when the group has been working long hours and the sun (or moon) is shining, the flowers nodding or the beer waiting. There is often simultaneously a strenuous but obvious effort to maintain progress on the defined task combined with a rise in fantasy level and a feeling of escapism. Led by an expressor, a proposition is innocently put to the group such as 'It's a lovely day, why don't we meet outside?' or 'Why don't we finish early and get drunk?' Or a run of jokes may start; or horseplay breaks out. The achievers sense immediately this may lead to subversion of the group's commitment to its task. Often the trainer also feels he ought to treat it this way (although, God knows, he could do with a break too). In fact it may be appropriate for the trainer to follow the use of spontaneity into joke-telling, expressive dance, music, impromptu drama, horseplay, clowning, a fantasy trip.

Once again, we have a dialectic between two important elements within each of us—a dialectic that is externalized into a dramatic exchange between those who identify with one side or other of this particular dimension. The achievers take themselves so seriously that they believe the task has value beyond themselves; the product becomes more important than the process. As a result they lose their sense of joy in working but continue to work on with a grim sense of determination and a readiness to make not only themselves but others suffer too. The expressors, on the other hand, are ready to indulge themselves at the slightest excuse. They cling to the spontaneity of childhood like a security blanket, trying to recreate the innocence of Eden long after adulthood has closed the gates. So the resultant dialogue often reads like a parent-child, child-parent transaction in transactional analysis terms, or a 'topdog-underdog' exchange in gestalt terms. The achievers can readily switch from a sensible goal commitment to an authoritarian and tyrannical, parental or topdog stance and, in doing so, very effectively draw a naughty child or rebellious underdog reaction.

The trainers can develop insight by introducing both achievement and expressive exercises such as goal-setting, life and career-planning, quoit-throwing, and problem-solving (achievement); and body movement, dance, painting, rhythm, music, and clay modelling (expressive). Ultimately the aim is to move towards behaviour which combines creativity and achievement, and this often leads to a final phase of sustained, creative work by group members. Where the other two dimensions have been worked through successfully beforehand, this stage of the group can provide a model of what a deeply human world could be like—a flexible combination of leading and following, support and confrontation, spontaneity and achievement. From the trainer's point of view it is important to keep faith with both work and fantasy, if only to ensure his own sanity. But for many in our work-orientated society the deepest insights come from regaining a spontaneous flow of feelings. As Lowen says:

But the body has feeling, and it alone can experience pleasure, joy and ecstacy. It alone has beauty and grace, for apart from the body these terms are meaningless. Try to define beauty without referring to the body and you will see how impossible it is. (Lowen, 1975, p.121).

PHASE 3—CONSOLIDATION AND CLOSING OFF

In our view the traditional opposition between insight therapies and behaviour modification therapies is false. Growth depends on reinforcement of new behaviours which must themselves be grounded in insight. Insight therapies traditionally ignore the need for consistent practice of new behaviour, adaptation of the new behaviour to a variety of social settings, and construction of a reinforcement schedule to maintain and consolidate new behaviours and insights.

Ideally, support for behavioural changes made in the workshop would be continued over into work and private life. However, since our workshops are usually 'stranger' workshops, many participants do not maintain relationships developed there. Despite the myth that relationships in encounter groups are 'transitory', our experience is that a substantial minority of participants do form relationships which last for months and, in some cases, years. In most cases these relationships help participants maintain behavioural changes. In addition, we have provided two-day 'continuation workshops' which are well attended. But our main stress has been on encouraging participants to develop clear, concrete, achievable plans for behavioural change in significant relationships and on designing a reinforcement schedule for themselves that will support these changes. This is done in the final phase of the workshop.

The encounter-group setting of Phase 2 is terminated and the workshop assembles as a whole again. The reason for this is that we wish the individual to experience, within the workshop setting, some loss of support as group ties are dissolved, and to learn to state and maintain his learning with others from outside the group. We work through the following sequence of activities in this phase:

(1) Reflection session—participants are asked to review in silence what were for them the main events of the group sessions.

(2) Summary of personal learning—participants summarize on paper their main learnings and then add a statement of how they intend to behave differently in specified relationships at home and/or at work.

(3) Pairs discuss the products of Step 2 above. Each participant chooses a partner who was not a member of his own group and they discuss what they learned and how they plan to modify their behaviour. Each person is asked to check the reality of the other's plans by asking himself the following questions: Are his aspirations clear and unambiguous? Are they concrete and specific? Are they practical? Is he attempting too much or too little? Where will he start? When? What will be the likely consequences of making such changes? How can he anticipate and cope with these consequences?

(4) Individuals then take their plans and revise them, if they wish, on the basis of this critique. After this, each individual asks himself the following questions: whom do I think will reward me in these changed behaviours? Whom do I think will punish me for these changed behaviours? How can I reward myself for these changed behaviours? How can I prevent myself from extinguishing these changed behaviours?

(5) Each individual then returns to the pair established for (3) above and tries to establish a reinforcement schedule for the changed behaviours which provides adequate rewards to maintain the behaviour. For example: "I want to be more spontaneous in expressing feelings to members of my family:
   —therefore I will stop telling myself 'Don't do that—you will look stupid' and do it anyway;
   —I will begin with Joan, who is most likely to accept and enjoy my spontaneity;
   —I will start with small things like romping on the floor with Jimmy and touching Joan when I'm feeling close to her, rather than buying tickets for a holiday abroad;
   —I will shout myself a chocoloate-malted milkshake each time I risk being spontaneous, whether I come through embarrassed or awkward or whatever;
   —when I feel I have really made progress, I'll dare to try being spontaneous with those at work."
The pairs are then brought together to make a small group of four who then share and assess each other's plans and reinforcement schedules.

The workshop then assembles for a final exercise to close off the programme. The closing session often evolves spontaneously but we have found that three needs predominate: (1) the need for people to make final communications to each other; (2) the need for physical contact to express closeness; (3) the need to express joy and sorrow at having experienced much together and to be parting.

CONCLUSION

For most participants the overall experience has been a useful and moving one; for some a critical experience which leads them to make or remake some central life decisions. Most also have generated a wealth of insights: as one participant in a recent workshop stated, 'I have learned more in five days here than I learned in five years in university'. But, most significantly, participants leave with a heightened feeling of self-awareness and the sense of personal responsibility that flows from self-knowledge. This is perhaps best expressed in Moustakas' words:

The presence of the self, the valuing of my own being, the awareness of who I am and what I believe, ensures an awakening, a clear sense of my own feeling and thinking and an implicit faith in my own experience to guide me and move me forward in my growth. The valuing of myself is precisely the source of my power, the unique sense that no-one can take away . . . (Moustakas, 1977)

ACKNOWLEDGEMENTS

I wish to thank particularly Barry Larkin, Bryan Burke, Beverley Dunphy, Suresh Mukhi, and Rudi Weber for their contributions to the development of this design. The ideas expressed in this chapter, however, do not necessarily represent their views.

REFERENCES

Adler, A. (1928) 'The psychology of power', *J. Indiv. Psychol.*, 1966, **22**, 166-172.

Ardrey, R. (1966), *The Territorial Imperative*. London: Collins.

Bach, G. (1966), 'The marathon group: intensive practice of intimate interactions', *Psychological Reports*, **181**, 995-1002.

Bales R. F. (1970) *Personality and Interpersonal Behaviour*. New York: Holt, Rinehart & Winston.

Dunphy, D. C. (1972) *The Primary Group*. New York: Appleton-Century-Crofts, pp. 102-17.

Kassorla, I. (1977) *Putting It All Together*. New York: Circus Books, p. 40.

Leary, T. (1957) *Interpersonal Diagnosis of Personality*. New York: Ronald Press.

Lowen, A. (1975) *Pleasure—A Creative Approach to Life*. Baltimore: Penguin.

McClelland, D., Atkinson, J., Clark, R. and Lowell, E. (1953) *The Achievement Motive*. New York: Appleton-Century-Crofts.

Moustakas, C. (1977) *Turning Points*. New Jersey: Prentice-Hall, p. 69.

Raimy, V. (1977) *Misunderstandings of the Self*. San Francisco: Jossey-Bass.

Rogers, C. (1970) *Carl Rogers on Encounter Groups*. New York: Harper & Row.

Schachter, S. (1959) *The Psychology of Affiliation*. Stanford, California: Stanford University Press.

Schutz, W. C. (1966) *FIRO: A Three-Dimensional Theory of Interpersonal Behaviour*. Reprinted as *The Interpersonal Underworld*. Palo Alto, California: Science & Behaviour Books.

Shepard, M. (1976) *Fritz*. New York: Bantam, p. 221.

Advances in Experiential Social Processes, Volume 2
Edited by C. P. Alderfer and C. L. Cooper
© 1980 John Wiley & Sons, Ltd.

Chapter 2

Psychological Defences, System Intervention, and Preventative Mental Health

Chris Argyris

Harvard University, U.S.A.

During the last decade, the author has participated in interventions where 'deeper' mental health factors have surfaced; where individuals became mental health resources for each other and the systems in which they worked. At the same time, the research and theory that informed the intervention practice raised several possibilities about the nature of the (so-called) deeper psychological factors, about clinical practice, and about ways to design and improve preventative mental health activities. For example, the deeper the relevant factors the more likely it is assumed that intense individual or small group therapeutic experiences are needed to overcome them. The more such intense experiences are required the less likely that we can (1) design educational programmes for 'average citizens' to learn to become mental health resources to each other or (2) mount such efforts in the world of work or home where many adults would be reachable.

This chapter suggests an approach to overcome some of those limitations in the world of work and at home. It is organized into two parts. The emphasis in the first part is upon the data gathered, with some running commentary. In the second part, we focus on the implications for the concept of psychological defence and the relevance to preventative mental health activities.

THE CONTEXT OF THE RESEARCH

The data come from a long-range study of an intervention involving three partners, their wives, and the organization in which the partners are embedded. The three partners of this young and growing professional organization have met three times a year during the last two years to discuss business problems, especially the difficult and long-range ones. The author was present to help them diagnose and overcome ineffective problem-solving conditions that might arise due to individual, group, or organizational factors. More recently, sessions have been added where the wives joined the husbands. The agenda included the impact of the firm on the families as well as the exploration of long-range strategy for the firm. All the sessions were tape-recorded. The episodes included are taken from these recordings.

The substantive issues during the first session related to ownership and compensation of the partners. John* began by stating that he doubted that Robert and Bill wanted to involve him as an equal in a genuine partnership. This resulted in a long, intense discussion about what, in John's view, Robert and Bill did to lead him to infer that he would never become an equal partner. During the discussion a theme of inconsistencies appeared in John's position. They will provide the data from which his defensiveness was inferred.

The remaining three episodes occurred during the two-day session of the partners and their wives. In Episode II John displayed similar inconsistencies, only now he was dealing first with the interventionist and then with his wife. By Episode III John had received adequate data to suggest that the pattern of defensiveness was real and not random. This led him to self-inquiry. The first step was the development of a 'thought experiment' which, if not disproven, would prove that he should not change. John carried out his experiment. The result was that his hypothesis was disconfirmed in a way that led him to conclude that the next step was to begin to alter the defensive reaction. At that point, he not only designed rules to keep him aware of his learning in the future but became more open to feedback from his peers (partners and wives).

EPISODE I

The first episode (among the three partners) occurred during a meeting whose purpose was to identify and correct long-range problems of the firm. One of these problems was the growth of the firm and the integration of new partners into the 'executive office' or the top officer group. John, who had been a member of the executive office for about a year and a half, began by describing the difficulties that he was having in becoming integrated with the other two partners. Indeed, he had reached the conclusion that the firm was a two-person firm and not, as was contemplated, a firm of six to nine partners. 'It is very difficult to break into the relationship between you two (Robert and Bill).'

---

*All names are fictitious. The chapter focuses on John because the data available makes his case the easiest to describe here. The choice is not meant to imply that he was substantially different from the other participants.

Below are excerpts from the tape recordings and notes made by the author while the action was going on and later upon listening to the tapes.

Dialogue	*Interventionist's thoughts or feelings*
John: I'm wondering if this firm will ever be something more than a good little company. Robert and I have started to have some real problems in the last few months . . . Also the way compensation and ownership are handled, I wonder if newer partners like myself can break into the inner circle of you two.	
Robert: (in response to John): I don't understand that. I don't think we're having real difficulties. I think we have a couple of personalities that can go 'bang'. I think that's inherent in very strong characteristics that each of us has.	Robert appears to play down the personality and interpersonal issues. If John continues his view, how will Robert react?
John: Yes, you like to control. You like to be in control and the easiest person for you to work with is somebody that will be controlled. I don't want to be controlled. We can't have equality among partners if you are in control all the time.	John is correct. Equality is not congruent with unilateral control. Is he implying that Robert is unaware of this? If so, it would not be confirmed by the data all of us have about Robert's confrontability. I predict that Robert is feeling hurt, bewildered, and probably angry.
I know that you think this is my problem but I do not think it only me.	
Bill: It is the characteristic of our jobs that we deal with people who desire to have control. We need to be in control.	Bill finds causes for interpersonal problems that are valid *and* that distance people from their personal responsibility. As Bill has pointed out in the past, he dislikes interpersonal hostility.
Int. (Interventionist): Would you like to respond, Robert?	
Robert: No, I'm more interested in hearing Bill's views.	Robert seeks data from Bill before he responds. *Note:* Later we learned that Robert felt very angry and he deferred to Bill in order to remain calm. None of us detected overt signs of anger on the part of Robert.
Bill: Well, yes, let me back into it. I would agree that all three of us like controlling the (consulting) situation . . . We never give up anything among each other without a difficult fight.	As Bill has often stated, he hates interpersonal conflicts. He now is able to 'back into' them.

The dialogue continued with John giving examples of how oppressive Bill and Robert had been during certain meetings. Bill confirmed the descriptions, although questioned if John had not magnified Robert's oppressive behaviour, but then added:

Bill: I think that during the first two years Robert was oppressive. Starting the company caused him a lot of emotional problems . . . Robert may have thought that he had to make it work but could not admit his uncertainties to others.

I can confirm Bill's evaluations partially because Robert has stated that he was anxious and kept it to himself during the early years of the firm.

John said he sought a relationship where he would not be continually checked upon by Robert or Bill. Bill listened attentively throughout the dialogue. He spoke several times only to ask questions about John's description.

Int: Robert, how did you react to John's comments?

Robert: I was angry. A flush of anger that I have not felt for a long time. I felt that John's description was really unfair. (He selected specific things seen only from his point of view with no consideration for other views.)

Robert appears to be describing his feelings candidly; he is stating his desire not to have his motivation and behaviour distorted; he is accepting some of the responsibility.

I think you're angry that you're not getting paid what you think you're entitled to. But I believe that you are earning more than we committed to you.

How does he know this is the case? Is he going to test this attribution?

John: Money is not the issue, Robert.

Robert: But you keep coming back to the same scenario. I am so controlling and I take unfair advantage of you. It's articulated in terms of last-minute changes, unfair expectations, perfectionist, unbelievable demands, etc.

I don't see (the problem) as me; I see that as you *and* me. I don't see you as seeing it as you and me.

Again Robert accepts responsibility; asks John to accept his part of the problem.

John: You don't see it as just my problem?

Robert: Absolutely not.

John: I don't see it as your problem alone either; I see it as our problem. So I see it the same way.

I heard nothing so far that indicated that John was accepting a share of the responsibility. I am glad he owns up to the mutuality of the problem because that increases the likelihood of learning.

Robert: OK. Because I hadn't heard you say that before.

John: I see it as together, both of us.

Robert: My concern is if you can't see that I was making contributions to you (and my trying to help you) then I despair if you will ever (understand me).

Robert is becoming more candid about his feelings of despair due to the number of times this type of episode has been repeated. Are his actions also punishing of John?

(Robert then gave examples of ways that he helped John. Bill was able to confirm most of them.)

Yes, I do like to be in control of things in a way of a defence. I think you, John, also like very much to be in control.

Robert owns up to his controlling when he feels defensive and attributes the same to John.

John: Uh-hmm.

Robert: And personally I find you much more controlling than I find myself. (Gives examples.)

There is a quality of counterattack. But the examples were confirmed by Bill and largely agreed upon later by John.

(Later)

(What it all adds up to is that) we don't care about the money; our passions come from (the feelings) that you value me, and all the work I put into it.

Robert owns up to his seeking being valued and places Bill and John in the same domain.

This discussion led the partners to conclude that in order to be valued one must be successful in the business *and* not ask for help. All agreed that they hated to ask for help from each other or from others.

John wondered about what concrete actions they might take in order not to have these pressures reoccur (e.g. better scheduling of meetings). He guided the conversion in the direction of seeking solutions that were mechanical and did not deal with all the inconsistencies just produced (e.g. being on time for meetings, keeping to the agenda).

After they had agreed on a 'solution' to schedule meetings more effectively, I noted that they had made such promises before. Also, I could not see how such actions would reduce the problems that they had identified. Bill then said that he would not doubt that a new partner would come in and say to himself: 'Look, I'm as good as they are. I'll show those son-of-a-bitches that I can produce as well as they do. I'll never ask for help.'

John: Yes, as soon as I say to myself I can't do this and I can't do that I am afraid that you guys will say that he can't make it.

John describes his fears about being seen as a failure.

Robert: I wish we could figure out a way to resolve this issue (we think the world of your performance. You keep underrating your performance and competence).

As Robert points out, they have told John that he is highly valued. I heard John's performance described in glowing terms by Robert to John and to the Board (John was present at all times).

John: I am reluctant to ask for help because I was afraid that you, Robert, would see that as *really* weak . . . I'd rather not do that.

There is plenty of evidence that Robert has made himself available to help other partners when they are pressed.

Also, a fourth partner, who had not been producing well, was kept on longer than John would have done, because Robert wanted to give that partner as much opportunity to correct his performance.

Int: And what has Robert said or done that he would interpret such a request as weak?

John (pause): I guess it's a standard of the firm. If you can't that's defined as a failure.

Note that in describing important organizational issues John also made public important personal feelings. Both men, especially Robert, responded to John's feelings about the organization and about them. Simultaneously they expressed their feelings about John. The feelings were not skin-surfaced or trivial.

A few minutes later John thought out loud that maybe he was not appreciated 'on a sustained basis'. I wondered if such a request might lead Robert and Bill to see John as 'weak' because he needed to be complimented all the time. Such a consequence would be counterproductive to John's desire that he should not appear weak.

It appears reasonable to hypothesize from the above that John was feeling pressed, frustrated, and fearful of being in a situation in which he might not succeed. He was in a double bind. If he asked for help, he would feel failure. If he did not ask for help, he ran the risk of failing.

Int.: It may be, John, that Robert is not your only problem. You seek to be successful and you make commitments that overwhelm you. You then hate like hell to ask for help—because of the attribution you make about Robert and Bill's reactions to such requests. But, you may also get angry at yourself for placing yourself in a position where you will see yourself as weak.

Note: This is an edited version of a much longer comment. I was unclear and repeated my idea several different times.

John: Say that again?

Int.:   You do not like yourself when you place yourself in situations that you have to admit you are overcommitted and need help. You get anxious when you are not in control.

John: Yes. I don't like to ask for help.

Bill: Me too. It drives me up the wall.

John: (I believe when you are under pressure) grit your teeth and run through the line and hope you don't get your ass busted. So (I blame others) when I'm really overloaded because I don't know how to ask for help.

Int.:   Or you do know how to ask for it, but are embarrassed to do so.

John: I hate to look weak. Who the hell wants to look weak!

Robert: I wonder if we have created a group norm for hours and volume of work which is too high. And secondly, a norm of never asking for any help.

John: Never show weakness would be the general statement. Asking for help would be an expression of that.

Robert: If so our organizational norms will become rigid because they are undiscussable.

Bill: And the people in the firm use the same rules and demonstrate the same rigidities.

Reflecting on the data collected (some of which have been illustrated in the transcripts), and focusing only on John, we may note the following themes:

John asserts that Robert and Bill distance themselves from him. Their actions prevent him from feeling that they want him to become a fully integrated partner in the firm.	Robert (and later Bill) had recommended these sessions to help develop genuine integration among the partners.
John says that Robert sees John's sense of being left out as being only John's problem.	On several occasions Robert acknowledges that he tends to control and to pressure, especially when he is tense and anxious about the quality of their service to the firm.
John states that Robert controls and pressures others through his high standards and a compulsion for work.	John also states that he too has high standards and that he is often blind to the effect that his persistent work has on others.
John asks for greater autonomy.	John asks to be appreciated on a more sustained basis.

The interventionist's strategy throughout the episode was to focus on the quality of the learning processes that the participants were creating. We see, for example, that he noted Robert's downplaying of the interpersonal issues and wondered if John would become angry. Both of these activities would inhibit learning. He also noted that a series of attributions John made about Robert were accurate but also described 'negative' features that applied to John. The interventionist was able to make these evaluations of John's attributions because he had direct experience in observing the partners during their everyday business meetings and during board meetings (as well as listening to tape-recordings of meetings that he could not attend).

As the inconsistencies developed into a trend, the interventionist placed more attention upon keeping the problem-solving process facilitative of learning. He noted, for example, that Robert did take on such a responsibility (he did not, for the most part, counterattack John and he owned up to his responsibility). John and Bill also owned up to their responsibilities. All three were able to agree on features to be blamed on the company. The episode ended with John saying that he hated to feel weak and hence rarely asked for help. The others agreed that this was true of them.

Throughout the dialogue the interventionist kept 'testing' the validity of the participants' assertions about each other's actions and motivations against his own directly held knowledge. He also attempted to test publicly his inferences. Such tests helped to serve two purposes. One was to encourage confrontation of his views. The other was to provide a model for the clients as to how it is possible to make statements that are publicly disconfirmable.

He was prepared to intervene whenever he saw actions that would inhibit the learning, but waited to see if the participants took on such a responsibility. Since they did take on such responsibility, the interventionist did not have to intervene as much as might be the case in groups where the problem-solving process is less effective. In the few times that the interventionist took action it was to provide Robert with an opportunity to respond to John; to ask for data he needed and had not heard (Robert, how did you react to John's comments?); or to ask a participant for data to illustrate a key attribution that he was making (what has Robert said or done that you would interpret such a request as weak?) All of these interventions helped to inform the interventionist and the partners, and hence to reinforce an effective problem-solving process.

The same interventions also helped the interventionist to realize that John, during these episodes, was invalidly adding to and subtracting from reality; that the invalid additions and subtractions appeared rational to John if he could blame Robert, and Bill or the organization, for qualities that he also held and reinforced. The latter were, in effect, second-order invalid additions which, for John, made the first ones rational. But, since the second-order additions were disconfirmable by data jointly held by the interventionist and the partners, and since John espoused that he wished to learn (and behaved in ways that supported his view), the interventionist was able to deduce that the second-order additions were covering up information that John held about himself that was tacit and not in his immediate awareness. Hence the interpretation that he made (it may be, John, that Robert is not your only problem . . .).

EPISODE II

John, Robert, and Bill plus their wives (Mary, Jill, and Judy) were having a dinner prior to the first session together. The objective of the session was to discuss interpersonal problems that they were having, especially those related to the dominant role 'the firm' played in their lives.

John said that he would begin the session early by raising (during dinner) a serious question with interventionist. 'Four months ago you asked us to complete a case. Then three months ago you asked us to write another case. Tonight I thought that you were to start the session during the meal and now you seem to be uncertain how to start it. I'm beginning to wonder about you. You have our lives in your hands and I'm not sure that you can be trusted.'

The interventionist asked how others felt. Mary, John's wife, expressed annoyance at having to write another case. The others did not agree with John. They presented relatively directly disconfirmable data to illustrate their disagreement. For example, they recalled that the request for the different cases was made three months ago and that the interventionist had told them that they could, if they wished, use the original cases. They recalled that the interventionist suggested the new format because recent research showed it to be more productive. John agreed with these recollections. The interventionist then added that the reason he did not want to begin the session during dinner was because the dinner had started late; they all had a heavy meal; the planned lecturing mode would be counterproductive; and he was concerned about how tired everyone was (especially because of the hassles some had experienced in the city traffic).

This appeared to be another example of John fearing that the interventionist was confused and weak, becoming upset, and placing the blame on the interventionist. The form of the blame was to see the other (interventionist) as weak and confused. Assigning the 'bungling' behaviour to the interventionist appeared to make it possible for John to express his fears because he was not aware that these features could be attributable to him.

The reaction of the interventionist was to test this attribution about John. It could be that the intervention was a distortion to protect himself. His view of reality was supported by the others (and this inference, in turn, is subject to test by having an independent observer listen to the tapes). He did not proceed further because the hour was late and it was the first session with this group. He wanted to assess the capacities of the group members to learn, so that he could decide if raising the issue could lead to a fruitful discussion. He soon learned that the group was quite able to deal with this issue and raised it during the episode the next day.

EPISODE III

John was describing the goals he set for his wife Mary. He wanted her to spend much of her life taking care of the children and to prepare herself for an increasing autonomy and time as the children grew up.

John (to Mary): Look, your major job now is to pour into the three children all the good things (that you can). You can't change adults. But you have a real opportunity to change three young children. You ought to pour it all in, and you shouldn't be diverting your activities to other things. But that's a definite period of time. It's going to be over. And you want to make sure during that period that you're building something so that when they grow up you're not feeling lost.

Int:	Do you feel that Mary would not grow unless you put the pressure on?
John:	Yes . . .
Jill:	What's the evidence for that?
Mary:	Yeah, why would you think that I wouldn't grow unless you prodded me to grow?
	(Short silence)
Judy:	Maybe you want her to grow in a different way?
John:	No, I do not wish to control her . . .

The purpose of the interventionist's question (about Mary) was to generate data, to test if Mary was indeed as dependent and helpless as John's strategy implied. If not, then the hypothesis that John was being defensive would not be disconfirmed. If she was, then the interventionist could be distorting, and that required exploration in the group setting.

John appeared to be controlling Mary but blind to this fact. I recalled the previous episode and wondered if this was not another example of John being controlling while feeling frightened. This time he saw his wife as weak; that she needed to be controlled and managed. One way he could prevent being in a situation that he disliked (a wife with nothing to do that reminded him of Mary's mother's situation) was to attempt to design parts of Mary's life. I asked him, 'What is it that suggests that Mary would not grow unless you keep a kind of optimal pressure on her?'

John responded that he was 'planting seeds as opposed to pressuring. I don't thing that I am turning the screw down.' Mary said, 'It is stressful though.'

Int.: Could you be unaware of the stress that you are creating?	If he is willing to own up to this unawareness, I should like to ask him to surface his feelings if his wife 'failed'.

John: OK?

Int.: How would you feel if 15 years from now Mary turned out to be like her mother?

John: I would feel very unhappy because I'd know my life is going to be tough. I know it would be stressful for me. I wouldn't like that one bit.

Int.: (recalling the episode above and describing it quickly to the wives): This appears to me to be like the previous case. When you get anxious you place the blame upon others and see them as weak.

Mary: Yeah. I'll agree with that.

John: Got that. Is there some learning I can get from that now that you've clearly identified the way I act?   Is this interpretation that new to him? Did I state it incorrectly? Does he hear it but not believe it?

Int.: Well, first, does all this make sense to you?

John: Yes, it does.

Before I could respond, a long and involved discussion occurred between John and the three wives. They saw him as controlling Mary. It led John to think out loud about the possibility that the wives also hated to admit that they had inadequacies but that it would be difficult for them to admit this to husbands who disrespected weakness in themselves and others. The wives agreed with his insight.

Int.:   A while back you asked me what can be done with the insight. What is the insight as you now see it?

John: Whenever I get anxious I look for some factual information to pass that anxiousness to somebody else. Then I can cleanse myself of it and don't have to get uptight myself.

Mary: He passes the responsibility on to somebody else.

John: So that I can abdicate the responsibility. So what you're saying is that one of the characteristics is to systematically screen out information . . . for my benefit.

Int.:   When you are anxious—not in every situation.

(Later)

John: Let me tell you another insight I am having. When I want an issue discussed and I am not sure that it will be, I add to it—magnify it—to make sure it is difficult to ignore.

John now appears to recognize some new inconsistencies. On the one hand, he describes himself as willing to get his ass busted while plunging through the line. On the other hand, he acknowledges that when he gets anxious he strives to pass the responsibility on to someone else. Also, he now appears to realize that he magnifies problems so that the others involved will find it more difficult to ignore them. However, if the others were not to agree with the magnification, then he may have created a new set of problems for himself.

Some readers may point out that John is not really learning or, if he is, it is at the intellectual and not at the emotional level. They might say this because John deals with interpretations that he accepts as valid by immediately asking for action recommendations. This could be an indication of too quick agreement, a possible sign of resistance.

It could be resistance to learning. But our perspective suggests another interpretation. John values highly his theory of effective action. He is not going to make paradigmatic shifts in this theory until he is relatively certain that his present theory is inadequate. His behaviour is similar to that of most social scientists dealing with evidence that appears to disconfirm their theories. He resists altering the theory until he has tested it further.

John understandably conducts a series of thought experiments to disconfirm the new information. If he succeeds, then he will not have to make a paradigmatic shift in his theory. If he does not, every experiment will provide insight into what aspects of this theory require changing. Let us look at an example of such a thought experiment.

EPISODE IV

After the episode above, John explored various implications of the insights with his wife. He designed a thought experiment which, when performed, suggested to him that the insights he was getting could be counterproductive to his effectiveness. But the thought test has to be carried out in front of the people who had generated the evidence that was threatening his theory-in-use.

John began by repeating the insights that he had learned about distorting reality and simultaneously finding an appropriate person or system upon which to place the blame, thereby not coming into contact with his fears of probable failure, desire for help, and possible weakness. He then said:

John: I guess that I'm the kind of person who likes to win and doesn't like to lose. I don't like to admit that I'm weak and I don't like to admit that I might lose. And the actions that I take are predesigned to reduce the chance of losing.
If I lost, that would lower my self-esteem. Hence, the solution is that I have to lower my self-esteem. And there's going to be some benefit to that which is ill-defined.
I have trouble in seeing the benefit of losing more often and reducing my self-esteem.

Mary: You see why I wanted him to bring this up. I've been sitting here for an *hour* hoping he'd bring it up.

Robert: I don't think you appreciate yourself as much as others do. You have a nationwide reputation in your field. If you felt as confident about yourself as others do there I think you would be able to take the defeats or losses *in stride*. No problem.

Don't reduce your self-esteem. Let it rise to a realistic level.

Jill: You ask what you'll get out of it. Well, you won't require other people to take on your anxieties. People will feel less defensive with you and that will enhance the relationship.

Bill: The only person you're protecting on that scoreboard is yourself. You've lost with the other person (if you continue your present defensive strategy). If your only strategies are either to win or to lose, I would accept neither.

(Later)

Int.: You started by saying that you hate to lose. We are now suggesting that with your old strategy you will only lose. The other person may not tell you that is the case.

Also, you say that you do not want to appear weak and frightened. Yet (in all the episodes above) I experienced you as frightened and so weak that you were distorting reality. You speak of self-esteem. One criterion of a person with a high self-esteem is that he can create conditions for others to enhance their self-esteem.

Your old strategy did not help you or the others. Your new projected strategy would be equally counterproductive. To use your language, you would be playing a losing game.

John: I guess I see. I'm pretty slow in this area. I have a lot to learn. Is this something I have to solve by myself or is this something that I can expect and ask for help from others?

The group members responded that they all felt they had much to learn. One of the purposes of the group was that the members could become resources to each other. For example, Bill and Robert could alert John when he was going into a counterproductive cycle at the office or with a customer. The wives could help in the home setting. The interventionist agreed and added that learning such as this was not a one-shot affair. It would take time; it should take time. The key is to be open to learning and to have resource people. 'I see both of the conditions.' John smiled and said 'Fine!'

Perhaps the above is adequate to set the stage for the examination of the concept of defence. I turn to a brief discussion of this.

THE ESTABLISHED VIEW OF DEFENCE

A defence is usually defined as '. . . a protective action or attitude directed against danger', while a defence mechanism is a specific technique used by the ego to ward off inner or external dangers (e.g. projection, denial, repression) (Wolman, 1967, pp.109-10).

According to Kroeber (1963), defences have been viewed as having adaptive as well as pathological features. Freud spoke of the differences between 'moral' and 'pathological' defence mechanisms, but as Anna Freud pointed out, Freud's primary interest was in the pathogenic features of defences (Freud, 1937, p.4).

Kroeber (1963) attempted to view the pathogenic and the adaptive features as part of the mechanisms of the ego. He described the former as defensive behaviour and the latter as coping behaviour. Defensive behaviour (a) is rigid, compelled, channelled, (b) is pushed from the past, (c) essentially distorts the present, (d) involves a larger component of primary process thinking and partakes of unconscious elements, and (e) permits impulse gratification only by subterfuge or indirection (p.184). Coping behaviour, on the other hand (a) is flexible and involving choice, (b) is pulled towards the future, (c) is oriented to the reality requirements of the present situation, (d) involves a larger component of secondary process thinking and partakes of conscious and preconscious elements, and (e) permits impulse satisfaction in open, ordered, and tempered ways (p.184).

If we examine John's behaviour before the interventions began, it approximated to the defensive features of being rigid, inflexible, pulled from the past, and distorting the present situation. The task of the author was to help John to shift his behaviour so that it could become more like coping behaviour. In cases like this, although John's behaviour may have been pulled from the past, it is not necessary to identify it as part of primary processes and partaking of unconscious elements. Another possible explanation is, as we shall see, that it involved secondary thinking processes and preconscious elements.

A fundamental assumption of much of present practice is that the maladaptive aspects of defences can be corrected if insight can be obtained into the distortive processes that are peculiar to each defence. Another basic assumption is that a dialogue between client and therapist, managed by the latter, can lead to insight into the distortive processes (Kanzer and Blum, 1967, pp. 109-10). The dilemma embedded in these assumptions is that the therapist must depend upon the reconstructive capacities of the client, yet these involve the very inference processes that are distorted, and include the processes that keep the actors blind as to how the distortions operate. When people recollect, they are reconstructing what they have already constructed. Hence the recollections tend to be distanced from the context of action in which the therapist and the client are trying to understand.

Therapists recognize these dilemmas. They strive to create, in the present therapeutic situation, conditions that could surface these distortive capacities as well as insight into when they may have begun. For example, transference is utilized in this manner. Transference is '. . . the experiencing of feelings, drives, attitudes, and defences toward a person in the present which do not befit that person, but are a repetition of reactions originating in regard to significant persons of early childhood, unconsciously deplaced onto figures in the present' (Greenson, 1967, p.171). The task of the therapist is to surface the issues and objects that act as symbols to trigger off the defensive reactions and divest them of their anxiety-producing potential (Hobbs, 1968, p.17).

PSYCHOLOGICAL DEFENCES: A THEORY OF ACTION PERSPECTIVE

A theory of action perspective assumes that human beings appear to be the naive scientists that recent social and cognitive psychologies suggest (Heider, 1958; Wegner and Vallacher, 1977). But the theories humans test have fundamentally different purposes from those held by most social scientists. In the jargon of normal science, they are always theories of application.

The theory of action perspective has been described elsewhere in detail (Argyris and Schön, 1974, 1978a; Argyris, 1975, 1976a,b). According to this perspective, human beings are meaning-creating organisms, continually striving to achieve their goals (intended consequences). They do this by constructing their own meaning to reality, through the use of a theory that specifies the *behavioural strategies*, the *values the behaviour is to 'satisfice', and the consequences that flow from these*. The theory (theory-in-use) is like an executive programme, which people use to design their micro-theories-in-use (subroutines for designing and implementing their actions in any given situation). The ultimate test of theories-in-use is their effectiveness in bringing about the intended consequences, in such a way that future effectiveness is not impaired.

In most cases studied, therefore, there has been an incongruity between espoused theory and theory-in-use. This means more than that people do not behave according to what they espouse. It means that *people are unaware of the theories they use to design and to carry out their actions*. One reason for the unawareness is that the theories-in-use have become tacit. The reason that they have become tacit is that given our information-processing capacities, this is the only way the human mind can store and retrieve the complexity of information required to design and implement actions. As the literature of skill research shows, skills are tacit programmes. Indeed, an operational criterion for skilful behaviour may be the effortless performance of actions without conscious attention to the activities required (Argyris and Schön, 1978b; Reason, 1977). All theories-in-use are tacit.

Let us now return to John in the cases above. There are four features of his actions that are relevant. First, he added to and subtracted from reality. The validity of these additions and subtractions was publicly disconfirmed. For example, his attribution that Robert, and less so Bill, were responsible for his potential failure to feel included, and that they saw him as a failure, was disconfirmed by data that Robert, Bill, and the interventionist produced and that John agreed were valid. Second, John made requests that were mutually contradictory. He asked for more autonomy and more sustained signs of being appreciated. Third, John surfaced feelings about himself that eventually he realized were unacceptable to him (I hate to ask for help) yet were necessary for effective performance in roles he valued highly.

The fourth feature was that John appeared unaware of the disconfirmability, inconsistency, and mutually contradictory characteristic of his actions. The minimum result of these four features acting in unison was to make it highly unlikely that John would be able to detect and correct the error caused by this behaviour while remaining unaware that this was the case.

Defensive action may be defined as any invalid addition to and subtraction from concrete reality that inhibits the detection and correction of error as well as the detection of the unawareness that the actions are defensive. Defensive actions are therefore error-enhancing, learning-inhibiting actions about which the individual is usually unaware.

There are actions that individuals may use to 'defend' themselves which do not inhibit learning or enhance error. Individuals may differ with others; they may strive to correct incorrect attributions about their views or their psychological motivation. As long as these 'defensive' actions are implemented so that there is no invalid addition to and subtraction from reality and the action does not block learning, then such actions may be viewed as protective but coping (Kroeber, 1963).

Robert exhibited coping behaviour when he maintained that he was not the only major cause of John's problems; when he provided relatively directly observable data (concrete examples) to illustrate his views; and when he asked Bill to speak in order to reduce his anger at John so that he could remain open to learning. I would prefer to call these actions defensive and the previous ones protective. However, this would reverse the presently accepted definition of defensive action, use of which appears to be so widespread that the switch in meaning would probably make misunderstanding highly likely.

Following established practice, therefore, I view defences as reactions to danger or vulnerability, and I infer vulnerability must exist when human beings behave in ways that will inhibit effective learning.

It is not necessary for our perspective to explore the origins and ideology of defences nor to categorize them according to their specific mechanisms. For example, John could be ejecting something from within his self-representation into another person; hence projection. Or, John could be displacing his feelings and fantasies from an object or object representation into the past to one in the present (Greenson, 1967, p.175). All we need to show is that the actions invalidly add to or subtract from reality and that they prevent awareness of the fact.

Nor is it necessary to view defences that inhibit learning and appear to be pulled from the past as unconscious ways to deal with anxiety. People may be unaware of their defences because they are skilful, complex micro-theories-in-use whose effective execution requires that they be tacit. This does not mean a defence could not also be associated with trauma. John's distortive capacity could be related to an early traumatic event. Perhaps it is not necessary to seek to surface and understand the trauma. The rule is to first consider the so-called 'unconscious' factors as factors that are simply tacit. If they are tacit, they are part of skilful behaviour. Skilful behaviour can be surfaced by interrupting it. John had his defensive behaviour (now read as skilful behaviour that invalidly added to and subtracted from reality) interrupted because he was in a learning environment where he was trying to acquire an additional theory-in-use whose learning required contradictory governing variables to those of Model I (e.g. seek to produce valid information).

Why the divergencies? One answer is that we are not dealing with highly pathological defences, because all our clients are operating relatively effectively in their everyday life. If this is so, then this case illustrates how John's non-learning behaviour can manifest both maladaptive and adaptive features. To use Kroeber's terms, John's actions lead to defensive and coping features. The former are related to the lack of learning; the latter to John's superior performance. It may be, for example, that John designs his life to reduce the probability of fear, hence he works very hard to be a superior performer, and hence is highly successful at his job (which, however, does result in his resisting asking for help).

A more important reason, I believe, for the divergencies is that we obtain the information about John's defences as he is presently manifesting them and do so with relatively directly observable data. Hence we are not dependent on the actor's reconstructions and all the potential for distortion noted above. Nor, therefore, do we require transference-type relationships, because we are able to observe at first hand any invalid attributions of motives, feelings, and values by the actor towards others. Or, to put it another way, we are able to observe John participating in transference relationships with Robert. Robert, being the president, could be an authority figure to John, hence an appropriate target for transference.

In our approach we seek:

(1) To place the clients in situations that approximate as closely as possible the conditions under which they appear to get into trouble.

(2) To observe the conditions and the trouble with minimal dependence upon the clients' recollections.

(3) To examine and reexamine these conditions by relatively constant replay (e.g. tape-recordings).

(4) To invent and produce new courses of action which can then be tested for their effectiveness.

(5) To have the situations that are required for the repeated tests created in non-contrived events.

These conditions imply that (1) the actors' capacities for learning are not so distorted that they cannot learn from colleagues or a professional; (2) the actors are motivated to learn and to experiment; (3) the critical situations required for the tests are repeatable in non-contrived ways; (4) opportunities can be created to reflect on the experiments; and (5) the therapists have models of inquiry and action that the clients find easy to understand and are capable of learning to use.

If the clients are so vulnerable that they cannot permit themselves to learn, then perhaps the 'deeper' therapies are required. But before this conclusion is accepted we must partial out the fact that the meaning of 'deeper', at the moment, is partially defined by the same theory the therapist uses to construct his reality. The deeper features may appear because of the processes by which they are discovered. Deeper features usually mean that they are discovered later rather than earlier, or as the defences are unpeeled. But the unpeeling process is a function of the theory of therapy used and the learning conditions created.

For example, Fenichel (1954, p.138) differentiates between transference resistances and character resistances. The latter are 'deeper' and more rigid than the former and they occur in many different situations. One could make the case, I believe, that John's defence was a characterological one because it appeared in many situations over time and resisted change. However, the surfacing of the defence was relatively easy and straighforward. But, the sceptical reader may ask, what about the resistance to changing defences? It is possible that the resistance was due less to threat and more to the number of thought and action experiments John wanted to create in order to validate the insights and make a paradigmatic shift in his theory-in-use. People without any signs of deep emotional problems have taken two or three years to make such transformations (Argyris, 1976a). The reasons for the time required may be the inherent difficulties in learning these activities; others do not know how to help, and opportunities for non-contrived experiments where reflection almost immediately afterwards is possible are not frequent (Argyris, 1976b). Another reason is related to the primitiveness of our learning technology.

To the extent the conditions that we seek to create hold, then learning about psychological defences will occur through the use of skills human beings already have to build and test theories. These skills therefore may be more easily taught than are the skills involved in traditional therapies. We may be able to take advantage of this fact by helping the people with whom the clients work become ongoing resources for learning.

The assumption embedded in the above is that individuals can 'work through' their anxieties and decrease the automaticity of their defences by repeated learning experiences in the present. If John required more love than Robert and Bill can give, and if John can see that the requirement is inconsistent with his need for autonomy and/or can inhibit his effectiveness as an executive, then the hypothesis is that he will alter his behaviour without having to work through the original causes of the defence.

We can make the prediction therefore that John (with the help of others) will decrease the number of times that he automatically distorts reality (denies or projects or displaces); that he will design and use new behaviour that is effective; and finally that if he returns to defensive behaviour he will be aware of it and be able to own up to that fact. These predictions are subject to disconfirmation because we have continued access to samples of John's work and home life. If the prediction is not disconfirmed then our belief that John is indeed working through 'deeper' defences by more socially available and useable educational techniques would not be disconfirmed.

To illustrate, we turn to A (Nutt, 1978) (in a different seminar) who presented the case of Joe (his subordinate) who was performing poorly. During the discussion he became aware of the anger that he had suppressed towards Joe. During the following session (one week later) he became aware that he had suppressed his feelings of anger towards himself (for not confronting Joe with his poor performance and lackadaisical attitude). He also began to see that these were not unrelated.

'I now recognize', he wrote in his analysis of the tapes, 'that I was angry at myself. I wrote down a heuristic: When you experience anger, you are often angry at yourself as well as the other person.'

Several weeks later, A Became angry at his wife. He thought of the 'automatic angry response' and the heuristic. For several days he tried to figure out what he might be angry about in his own behaviour. He finally recognized that he hated to have his competence questioned.

He explored, with his wife, what it was about her questioning that led him to interpret it as a threat to his sense of competence. He concluded that the difficulty was that he held an unrealistically high expectation about his performance. Indeed, if he followed his expectations he would have to be perfect; anything else would be failure. Under those conditions even 'innocent' questions were experienced as threatening.

A then reported that he developed two heuristics which he has found helpful in other situations. They are: 'The anger you experience at yourself may be related to (1) an unrealistically high sense of personal expectation of yourself or (2) an unrealistically high sense of personal responsibility to the system in which you are involved.'

Hence we see an individual becoming aware of his feelings of anger towards others, relating them to anger at himself, and relating the self-anger to an unrealistically high sense of responsibility. As he began to develop a more realistic level of aspiration, he became more accepting of himself and of others. As he did that, he found it easier to confront poor performance in himself and others more effectively.

The sequence of events embedded in the cases described above appears to be as follows:

(1) A (actor) constructs reality and makes public the assertions that follow from his construction. The presentation is usually about a central (rather than peripheral) problem.

(2) The problem is stated in front of the people involved. The statements are tape-recorded so that the same relatively directly observable data are available to all parties.

(3) Several directions then become possible:

(a) The others disconfirm or cannot confirm A's assertions. They then present additional data and/or show A that he is interpreting the data incorrectly.

(b) If A does not agree they enter into a joint process of inquiry that produces more data and/or that leads to an agreement on who is or is not making correct interpretations.

(c) Assuming that inquiry results in A's becoming aware of his share of the distortions, then he must be helped to see that the responses to these stressful situations are not only defensive, they are automatic. Automatic responses indicate programmes or rules in people's heads that are so well learned that they are tacit. Responses that are informed by tacit rules cannot be corrected until after they are made explicit. Hence, for a while at least, the actor will be in a situation where he will be responding incorrectly and becoming aware after the fact.

RELATING THE THEORY OF ACTION PERSPECTIVE TO OTHER PERSPECTIVES

We may now relate our perspective to some recent work by clinical psychologists who also share an information-processing bias. Wexler (1974, pp.62-69) suggests that individuals may be vulnerable when they have no rules to organize the information and thus lose it in their short-term memory (denial), or when their rules are not adequate to organize all the information they have (distortion).

This means that reducing defences will require that individuals become aware of the rules that they use to make automatic responses that are counterproductive; the rules they hold to hide the first rules from their awareness; and the consequences of holding such rules (e.g. the inconsistencies that are created).

For example, John may be said to have, at least, two rules in his head: (1) ignore my feelings of weakness, which if I became aware of would lead me to become angry and fearful of myself, and (2) remain unaware that I (John) have such a rule.

But John is not willing to hold rules that lead to positions that he cannot knowingly defend to himself or to others. He holds a third, more general rule therefore, namely, all constructions that he makes of reality should neither be inconsistent nor counterproductive, and he should be able to advocate his case successfully to others as long as they too hold the rule that they do not wish to be inconsistent or counterproductive to generating valid information.

The first two rules cited above violate the third rule, because John is unlikely to be consistent and to create valid information if he ignores important and relevant information.

(4) With these new awarenesses the actor has now differentiated his life space to include more information than was previously acceptable. He now needs rules to integrate this information (Wexler, 1974). But integration is a slow and difficult process.

(a) The initial steps are usually designed to maintain the old rules. For example, as soon as John became aware that he distorted reality he asked the interventionist for solutions. John's request made 'sense' if we keep in mind the old rules. For example, if John's rule was do not accept weakness and if the new awareness led him to feel weak, then if he can correct it he will no longer be weak. But the difficulty is not only that John does not have a solution, he cannot even invent one. The reason that he cannot invent one is that he is operating under the old rules.

(b) A next step is to conduct experiments to attempt to disconfirm the consequences that the actor must change. For example, John blamed the organization for his fears. Part of the blame was accepted and corrected by the partners, but that did not solve John's problems.

The individual may also conduct private thought experiments. For example, John developed an analysis of how he would lower his self-esteem if he reduced the defences. As a result of inquiry he learned that his analysis was faulty and that continuance of the present strategy would be counterproductive.

The experiments designed to delay integration also created the conditions for integration. The experiments provided new information that made it even more compelling for the actor to integrate. Every one of John's experiments 'proved' that it was in his best interest to integrate the new awareness. Also, every experiment helped to provide information that could be used to design new cognitive maps of integration (Wexler, 1974, p.71).

(5) The next step may be called active or planned integration. It can occur

privately or publicly. A, in the case above, developed two rules. They were (a) do not trust your existing construction whenever you get angry at others who appear to you not to be performing adequately, and (b) if you become angry at others (as he did with his wife), ask privately what the other said or did that might have been a threat to you. Do it privately so that you are not seen by others as incompetent because that will trigger the old rules.

Once A was able to see that he was angry at himself for not performing effectively *and* for having unrealistically high levels of aspiration about performance, then he could go public and discuss the episode with his wife. He was now able to appear as aware and in control. This, in turn, reduced the likelihood that the old rules would operate.

The time it will take to internalize or to make the new rules tacit will vary with individuals, the intensity of the threat, and the context. One can facilitate the learning by increasing the number of private and public experiments in two of the most important segments of the individual's life, namely, work and family. The experiments will not be contrived but come naturally. In John's case this will happen whenever he is under stress or pressure. Hence they may come once a month or even less frequently. But whenever they come he has the resources available to help him interpret the data and to develop and practise new skills.

A second research programme with which we may learn is the recent work by Havens (1976) on therapeutic intervention strategies. Havens reexamined the interpersonal perspective of Harry Stack Sullivan. He not only has developed new theoretical insights about personality theory but has connected these to clinical practice. A key strategy in the new perspective is to help the clients look at their defences by the use of a 'counterprojective' screen. The purpose is to move the clients' projections '. . . out of the medium between therapist and patient onto the space on the screen before them'. The goal is to encourage the clients to see their distortive processes (Havens, 1976, p.101). A second key strategy is to create conditions where the clients can share their feelings and acknowledge the reality of their distortions. The goal is to reduce or disavow the distortive actions (p.103).

If we examine the conditions illustrated in this chapter, they tend to create the screens that Havens recommends. First, the organization became a counterprojective screen for the partners when they were talking about their human problems. They could surface and project the causes of the distortive processes partially because they could blame the organization. For example, John's defensive actions became apparent as the partners were trying to discuss ownership of the firm and the structure of the executive office. Bill created a screen because he hated emotional conflicts. Every time John attacked Robert or owned up to his feelings about admitting weakness, Bill was able to show that the same processes were also caused by the requirements of starting up a business and of maintaining it in a highly competitive world. The wives helped John by exploring the way their husbands pressured them. Finally, the interventionist created appropriate screens by relating John's actions to organizational dynamics within and outside the firm. Diagnosing systemic defences may make it easier to reflect on and own up to one's own defences because one can see that the organization is partially responsible *and* that in surfacing them one helps the organization. Finally, any diagnosis about systemic defences that is confirmed by others makes it easier for the individuals to explore the personal defences that appear to be triggered by systemic issues.

There is another body of literature to which our efforts relate. It may be called cognitive-behaviour-modification, where the emphasis is upon integrating the cognitive and behaviour aspects into a unified perspective (Meichenbaum, 1976). Our perspective appears to overlap with Beck's (1970), where the focus is upon the distortion in thought patterns. We frequently focus, as he does, on arbitrary inferences, magnification of the meaning of an event, disregard for important aspects of the problem, oversimplified thinking, and generalizations beyond what the data allow. Whereas Beck explains these distortive capacities as having become overlearned and involuntary, our perspective is that they are involuntary because they are skills. Skilful behaviour is activity based upon a tacit programme, that achieves intended consequences in an apparently effortless manner (Argyris and Schön, 1978a).

On the other hand, we have not found it useful, as does Ellis (1961), to explore the aetiology of the irrational premises that people hold. If their premises are irrational, their irrationality is explored in the here and now. For example, John's view about having approval from others and controlling others' behaviour is congruent with what Ellis considers the end state of rational therapy (1961). That is, John is able to accept himself when others do not, and John does not seek to coerce people continually. He is less flexible in making errors, but he does not believe that he must never make errors. Hence, John would be seen as operating effectively by Ellis (1961).
Yet John was having the difficulties described above.

Our perspective appears closer to that of Meichenbaum (1976), who combines the focus on reducing distortions in thought with the development of skill programmes to help people become more effective in problem-solving and coping with stress.

There are two fundamental differences between our approach and all those we have explored in the congitive-behaviour therapy domain. Firstly, they focus on educating people to become more competent in the world as it is (which from our perspective means Model I). The second characteristic of all their programmes is that they teach skills that are sanctioned and rewarded by society. This means that the subjects either have the skills to follow the programmes designed for them by the cognitive-behaviour therapists or they can learn them easily. It also means that, once learned, the skills can be reinforced in everyday life.

The differences with our approach are best seen in studies published elsewhere (Argyris, 1976a, b). We focus on teaching double-loop skills, which means that the individual and societal theories-in-use are questioned. This, in turn, means that people do not have the skills for the kind of learning required and they tend to be unaware that this is the case. What skills they do have act to prevent them from realizing that they are producing the wrong behaviour (even when they know what behaviour they wish to produce). Skilled educators can help them to see their errors after the fact. Whenever they receive help from untrained peers the feedback tends to be accurate in substance but stated in ways that are defensiveness-producing and hence inhibiting of learning.

Finally, our subjects are faced with the challenge that the double-loop skills they are learning, although valued at the espoused level, are seen as deviant, if not dangerous, skills at the level of theory-in-use. To use and to maintain their new skills requires changes in the society (the social system that makes it up). This is why individual and organizational change appear to us to go hand in hand if we are to design and implement preventative mental health programmes.

IMPLICATIONS FOR PRACTICE AND THEORY

If defences are distortions of reality that can be dealt with in everyday life as deficiencies in learning, if it is possible to ignore their aetiology and hence make it unnecessary to deal with them differently, and if the processes to correct them may be similar to the cognitive processes used to correct any theory-in-use, then a wider range of human beings can be taught skills for preventative mental health. More people could become resources for their own and others' learning.

For example, skills in obtaining and giving directly observable data, in making one's inferences from the data public, in subjecting them to public verifiability, in identifying inconsistencies and incongruities, and in reflecting on one's actions can be taught to people in large groups. Moreover, these skills are versatile in the sense that they are at the basis of much liberal arts and professional education. Hence the skills learned to enhance individual mental health may be relevant to increasing the effectiveness of work and systems.

Since work and mental health factors are now combined, it is possible to conceive of individual preventative mental health becoming a foundation for group and organizational development. For example, after we generated maps of the individual partners' theories-in-use, we were able to generate maps of the group dynamics that would result when the partners interacted. The procedures used to develop these maps were also used to develop maps of the organizational learning systems. We were able to show that the competitiveness among the partners could lead to the subordinates being placed in competitive situations. In larger organizations we have found this to lead to destructive intergroup dynamics (crisis and wars) that made systemic double-loop learning highly unlikely.

We have also found that individual, group, and organizational level maps are highly stable and permit robust predictions. For example, we have predicted that the destructive intergroup rivalries in a large newspaper would not be overcome by creating a rational financial reporting system. On the contrary, the human dynamics would eventually distort the financial system. Most of the executives rejected this possibility on the grounds that they could reduce the destructive intergroup processes if they set their mind to it. Two years later those that rejected the prediction admitted that it had been confirmed (Argyris, 1974). People have developed their types of maps as a basis for understanding the complexity in their home or work life. They have also been used for designing and evaluating change.

REFERENCES

Anderson, W. (1974) 'Personal growth and client centered therapy: an information-processing view'. Wexler, D. A. and Rice, L. N. (eds.) *Innovations in Client-Centred Therapy*. New York: Wiley-Interscience, pp. 21-48.

Argyris, C. (1974) *Behind the Front Page*. San Francisco: Jossey-Bass.

Argyris, C. (1975) 'Some dangers in applying results from experimental social psychology', *American Psychologist, 30*, No. 4, April.

Argyris, C. (1976a) *Increasing Leadership Effectiveness*. New York: Wiley-Interscience.

Argyris, C. (1976) 'Theories of action that inhibit individual learning', *American Psychologist*, **31**, No. 9,pp. 638-54.

Argyris, C. and Schön D. (1974) *Theory in Practice,* San Francisco: Jossey-Bass.

Argyris, C. and Schön D. (1978a) *Organizational Learning*. Reading Mass.: Addison Wesley.

Argryis, C. and Schön, D. (1978b) 'On learning skills', Mimeograph.

Beck, A. (1970) 'Cognitive therapy: 'nature and relation to behaviour therapy', *Behaviour Therapy, 1*, 1970, 184-200.

de Charms, R. (1968) *Personal Causation*. New York: Academic Press.

Ellis, A. (1961) *Reason and Emotion in Psychotherapy*. New York: Lyle Stuart Press.

Fenichel, O. (1954) *The Collected Papers of Otto Fenichel*. New York: Norton.

Freud, A. *The Ego and the Mechanisms of Defence*. London: Hogarth Press.

Greenson, R. R. (1967) *The Technique and Practice of Psychoanalysis,* Vol. 1. New York: International University Press.

Hammer, E. F. (1978) *Use of Interpretation in Treatment*. New York: Grune & Stratton.

Havens, L. (1976) *Participant Observation*. New York: Aronson.

Heider, F. (1958) *The Psychology of Interpersonal Relations*. New York: Wiley.

Hobbs, N. (1968) 'Source of gain in psychotherapy' In Hammer, F. (ed.) *Use of Interpretation in Treatment*. New York: Grune & Stratton.

Kanzer, M. and Blum, H. P. (1967) 'Classical psychoanalysis since 1939'. In Wolman, B. B. *Psychanalytic Techniques: A Handbook for Practicing Therapists.* New York: Basic Books.

Kelly, G. A. (1955) *The Psychology of Personal Constructs.* New York: Norton.

Kroeber, T. C. (1963) 'The coping functions of the ego mechanisms'. In White, R. W. *The Study of Lives.* New York: Atherton, pp. 178-99.

Maruyama, M. (1963) 'The second cybernetics: deviations-amplifying mutual causal processes', *American Scientist,* 5, No. 2, 164-79.

Meichenbaum, D. (1976) 'Toward a cognitive theory of self-control'. In Schwartz, G. E. and Shapiro, D. (eds.) *Consciousness and Self-Regulation.* London: Plenum Press, pp. 223-60.

Nutt, S. (1978) 'Reflections on my learning', Harvard Graduate School of Education.

Reason, J. T. (1977) 'Skill and error in everyday life'. In Howe, M. J. A. (ed.) *Adult Learning.* New York: Wiley.

Rice, L. N. (1974) 'The evocative function of the therapist'. In Wexter, D. A. and Rice, L: N. (eds.) *Innovations in Client-Centred Therapy.* New York: Wiley-Interscience, pp. 289-312.

Scheff, T. J. (1977) 'The distancing of emotion in ritual', *Current Anthropology,* December.

Wegner, D. M. and Vallacher, R. R. (1977) *Implicit Psychology.* London: Oxford University Press.

Weick, K. E. (1969) *The Social Psychology of Organizing.* Palo Alto, Cal.: Addison-Wesley.

Wender, P. H. (1968) 'Vicious and virtuous circles: the role of deviation amplifying feedback in the origin and perpetuation of behaviour', *Psychiatry,* 31, No. 4, 309-24.

Wexler, D. (1974) 'A cognitive theory of experiencing self-actualization and therapeutic process'. In Wexler, D. A. and Rice, L. N. (eds.). *Innovations in Client-Centered Therapy.* New York: Wiley-Interscience. pp. 249-58.

Wolman, B. B. (ed.) (1967). *Psychoanalytic Techniques: A Handbook for the practicing psychoanalyst.* New York: Basic Books.

Advances in Experiential Social Processes, Volume 2
Edited by C. P. Alderfer and C. L. Cooper
© 1980 John Wiley & Sons, Ltd.

Chapter 3

An Attributional Analysis of Personal Learning

Peter B. Smith

University of Sussex, England

Striking changes have occurred in the form of experiential training since the tentative beginnings of both T-groups and Tavistock groups in the mid-forties. As Benne (1964) among others has documented, these changes have included a continuing diversification of different approaches and an increasing emphasis on the individual rather than the group as the primary focus. This changing emphasis is unlikely to be explicable simply in terms of processes inherent in experiential training. It is much more likely that the changes are reflections of broader social changes in society. The forms of experiential training which achieve currency at a particular time can be seen as those which focus on concerns salient to many of us at that time. The early forms of small group training stressed democratic processes, group decision-making, communication skills, and the potential irrationality of group process. While all of these emphases still occur in some contemporary approaches, additional goals which are now equally frequent include self-knowledge, self-acceptance, bodily awareness, and the taking of important decisions in one's career, working relationships or personal life. This chapter does not attempt a socio-historical analysis of why 'self' has become so central to some forms of experiential training. It considers first of all the manner in which research studies of groups have mirrored the changes alluded to above. It then examines models of the change process in groups and seeks to show that those focusing on self-awareness have some promise. A model is presented which draws on attribution theory in attempting to predict the circumstances under which experiential training should generate lasting changes in self-concept. Some studies are described which test various aspects of the model.

CHANGE AFTER EXPERIENTIAL TRAINING

Small group training methods have been seen as controversial at almost all stages in their development. Controversy has generated a substantial number of research studies, but as in so many fields it often turns out that protagonists of group approaches see no compelling need for research data to substantiate that which they already know to be worthwhile. Likewise, sceptics are well versed in rehearsing the fallibility of measurement in the field. The role of researcher has thus been that of a contributor to a debate rather than a provider of final answers to focused questions.

Early studies

The earliest studies made in T-groups were almost all concerned with the analysis of processes occurring within groups (e.g. Stock and Thelen, 1958; Stock, 1964). Where it *was* seen as important to assess the overall effects of a group experience, control group data were frequently not obtained so that firm conclusions could not be drawn. Early work on Tavistock groups was descriptive in nature (Trist and Sofer, 1959). One of the earliest substantive studies was that by Miles (1960). Miles studied the effects of a 10-day Bethel T-group laboratory programme on 34 elementary school principals. Two control groups were also employed. Respondents were asked to describe any changes they had noted in themselves eight months after the training programme. Job associates of trainees and controls were also asked to report on changes. A system of content analysis was devised, based on scoring of 'verified changes', i.e. those reported independently by two or more respondents. Miles found verified changes for 72 per cent of trainees but only for 17 per cent and 29 per cent of his two control groups. The areas in which verified changes were most markedly greater for trainees were: 'the areas of increased sensitivity to others, equalitarian attitudes, skills of communication and leadership and group and maintenance skills' (Miles, 1965). Significant correlations were found between those who scored high on verified change and those whom the trainers had seen as changing most at the close of the group.

The methods developed by Miles were employed in several subsequent studies by other investigators. Bunker (1965) obtained data on 229 participants in T-group laboratory programmes conducted at Bethel for comparison with 112 controls nominated by the participants. Verified changes in follow-up behaviour were found among 67 per cent of participants and 33 per cent of controls. Bunker developed a more complex set of content analysis categories than Miles. He found significant differences in change rates in 11 of his 15 categories. Categories showing the greatest differences were 'sensitivity to others', 'acceptance of others', 'tolerance of new information', and 'receiving communication'. The variance in reported changes for trainees led Bunker to the view that the effects of experiential training should not be interpreted as the imposition of a particular pattern of response on trainees, but rather as the acquisition by each individual of skills and learning appropriate to his or her current need. Boyd and Elliss (1962) studied training within a Canadian utility and obtained very similar results. They found verified changes among 64 per cent of trainees and 23 per cent of controls. These authors also stressed the individual variance in changes reported and suggested the metaphor of the cafeteria, i.e. each trainee is seen as selecting from a broad range of possible changes. Valiquet (1968) also studied trainees in an in-company programme. He found verified changes among 73 per cent of trainees and 20 per cent of controls. In this population the categories in the Bunker content analysis system showing greatest difference between trainees and controls were different. The largest differences were obtained for 'increased interdependence', 'insight into self and role', 'functional flexibility', 'acceptance of others', and 'risk-taking'. A final study using the same methods was that by Moscow (1971), who studied T-groups in England and Holland. Verified change was again greater for trainees than for controls. The categories showing greatest change were 'sending communication' for the Dutch groups and 'tolerance of new information' and 'relational facility' for the British groups.

In reviewing research in this field during the sixties, Campbell and Dunnette (1968) concluded that the verified-change studies provided the strongest evidence available at that time that T-groups do have lasting beneficial effects. At the same time they pointed to the evident flaws in this type of research design, such as potential bias of observers, who know perfectly well who attended groups and who did not. Further difficulties are the unorthodox manner in which control groups were recruited and the use of measures collected only after training. The early studies of groups thus provided persuasive but not conclusive evidence that change did occur after group participation. The changes found were seen as diverse but were focused particularly around work relationships. The categories showing highest change mostly centred around collaboration, openness to new ideas or other people, flexibility, and so forth.

Recent studies

The explosion of interest in small group training in the late sixties triggered a much greater volume of research into the effectiveness of groups. While all the studies described so far examined the effects of residential T-group programmes, the more recent research encompasses a much wider range of methods, locations, and participants. The availability of a greater range of studies permits the establishment of more demanding criteria against which to judge the studies. Smith (1975) surveyed 100 studies of the effects of sensitivity training.

The studies included all had control groups and all employed a measure which was applied before training as well as afterwards. All studies were based on at least 20 hours of training time. Therapy groups were not included. While the 'verified-change' researchers were able to adopt an inductive approach to the study of change, the use of pre-post measuremen requires that the researcher has some firmer hypotheses as to the changes he anticipates. Since experiential group methods are now employed for a very wide range of purposes, it follows that different researchers might anticipate quite widely varying effects. The detection of change on a particular measuring instrument should not imply that experiential groups could *always* generate such a change, but only that such methods *could* generate the change where there was an appropriate match between training goals, training methods, and participants' goals. The wide range of measures employed by researchers can therefore be seen as consistent with the emphasis placed by the verified-change researchers on the diversity of change arising from group experience.

Such diversity may be appropriate but it poses a challenge to the reviewer. Smith (1975) grouped the measures employed into eight categories. An updated version of the findings is shown in Table 1. The table indicates that despite the more demanding criteria adopted, evaluation studies continue to detect changes not found among controls. The proportion of studies showing change is substantially higher on measures completed immediately after training than it is for follow-up measures, but a considerable number of studies did detect effects which persisted. It is of particular interest that the rate of detected change in organizational behaviour is actually higher at follow-up than immediately after training. Measures of organizational behaviour are normally only available where groups who have participated in training together remain in contact subsequently. Other types of measures are much more likely to be employed with groups who separate when the group terminates.

Some of the categories in Table 1 are fairly close to the types of change reported by the verified-change researchers. For instance, orientation towards participative behaviour, changes in prejudice and open-mindedness, and improvements in organizational behaviour all appear consistent with the earlier findings. The newer emphasis on self which has characterized many aspects of the encounter movement is represented in the table by the first two categories. Included in 61 studies, or more than half the total, these investigations show a more striking pattern than is apparent from the summary table. The great majority of studies of self-concept change have employed one of three measures: semantic-differential type ratings, Fitts' (1965) Tennessee self-concept scale (TSCS), and the personal orientation inventory. Of the 19 studies which have used the semantic-differential or similar types of ratings 17 (89 per cent) have detected significant changes not shown by controls. Of the 14 studies using the TSCS only 2 (14 per cent) show positive change. The most plausible explanation of this puzzle is that TSCS does not measure those aspects of self-concept which are most salient in groups. The test does include specific items concerning for instance one's

Table 1 Changes found after sensitivity training (revised from Smith, 1975)

Type of measure	Changes immediately after training			Changes at follow-up		
	Intended effects found	Total N	Per cent successful	Intended effects found	Total N	Per cent sucessful
Global self-concept	24	43	56	6	9	67
Self as the locus of causality	10	18	56	1	3	33
Prejudice and open-mindedness	12	24	50	2	5	40
Orientation towards participative behaviour	15	23	65	2	9	22
Other aspects of personality	10	20	50	2	5	40
Perception of others	5	13	38	1	2	50
Others' perception of trainees	18	23	78	2	4	50
Organizational behaviour	10	13	77	11	12	92
Total sample	85	108	79	23	33	70

Note: A number of studies with major design flaws are omitted from this table. Total sample comprises less than the sum of the preceding columns because many studies included more than one measure.

family relations and one's moral values, which would be less likely to change during a group since they are descriptive of events or feelings outside the group. Lang and Vernon (1977) have recently questioned the validity of the TSCS in its present form. The apparent contradiction between studies using ratings and studies using psychometric tests such as the TSCS might thus be resolved by concluding that, after a group, trainees do not see their social space or their role within that space all that differently, but they do feel more warm and accepting of themselves.

The third measure of self-concept which has been frequently employed is the Shostrom (1966) personal orientation inventory (POI). This test is described as a measure of self-actualization. Its principal scale is labelled inner-directedness and the items focus on the degree to which respondents see themselves as reaching their own decisions in life rather than being governed by externally imposed moral or social sanctions. Of 12 studies using POI, six (50 per cent) found significant change not obtained for controls. Three more of the studies found changes among both trainees and controls. The implicit values of the POI test appear well attuned to the values of the new encounter-oriented approaches to experiential training. Successful learners in such groups would be those who were well aware of their feelings in a particular setting and used them as a basis for taking decisions as to how to act. The fact that significant changes have sometimes been found also among controls suggests either that the act of completing the test has been sufficient to induce reflection and change, or else that concern about changing values towards 'inner-directedness' in recent years has been sufficiently widespread to induce changes outside groups also. Five further studies have employed the conceptually similar Rotter (1966) locus of control scale. Four of the five studies found movement towards belief in internal locus of control among trainees but not controls.

The evidence concerning change in self-concept after group experience thus suggests that many group members finish the group feeling more warmly towards themselves and more personally able to control their life-choices than previously. Unlike the verified-change studies reviewed earlier, these effects were obtained immediately after training. Table 1 shows that only a small proportion of these studies also obtained follow-up data as to whether these changes persisted. However, the studies carried out did show that in some cases the changes do persist. The percentages cited cease to be of much meaning when such small numbers of studies are being considered, particularly since the likelihood of detecting change has been shown to be strongly dependent on whether one employs ratings or the TSCS as a criterion measure.

The availability of so much evaluation data concerning the outcome of experiential training encourages a movement towards reformulating research questions. It is no longer all that interesting to ask whether groups achieve the effects they intend. Both the verified-change studies and the more recent and better controlled studies have frequently found significant effects of training. By examining which measures do detect change and which do not, we can tighten our thinking about the effects which groups can and cannot achieve and start to think about why that might be. One worry that quickly arises where some studies detect change and others do not is whether this divergence is due to differences between groups or whether it is due to differences between measures employed in the different studies. The study by Lieberman *et al.* (1973) goes some way towards reducing the ambiguity here. By employing a wide variety of measures in their study of 18 encounter groups at Stanford, they were able to show that some measures detected change while others when completed by the same trainees did not. For instance, they found significant change on semantic differential ratings of self but not on the Rosenberg self-esteem scale. Such a finding lends support to the proposition advanced above that ratings detect a global change in self-evaluation, while psychometric tests such as the TSCS or the Rosenberg scale miss this effect because they are more specifically focused on existing social relations. The alternative possibility would have been that somehow researchers using semantic differential ratings had chosen to study successful groups while those using TSCS had picked on unsuccessful groups.

The models of personal learning which have guided researchers in this field have varied widely. Three of the most popular views will be examined in the light of the data now available.

MODELS OF PERSONAL LEARNING

Individual skill learning

According to this model experiential training provides a 'laboratory' within which the trainee can develop and test out new skills in relating to others. Skills which are successfully learned may then be transferred to non-training settings. The origins of this model lie in Lewinian theory and it was espoused by many of those active in T-groups in the sixties (Miles, 1960; Bradford *et al.*, 1964; Schein and Bennis, 1965). One of its central concepts is that the creation of an adequate laboratory for learning requires a temporary setting or 'cultural island' upon which a set of social norms conducive to learning may be established. Once the norms are established, individual trainees are expected to obtain for themselves the feedback available in reaction to this or that behaviour. The leaders do not seek to impose a particular pattern of learning upon participants, and what is expected is that each individual will take out of the experience feedback or learning appropiate to his or her needs. The resemblance to the 'cafeteria' model of learning espoused by many of the verified-change researchers is clear.

The individual skill learning model is clearest about what happens to the trainee while he or she is *on* the cultural island. The journey home and the initiation of change in work or personal relations are seen as 'application' or 'transfer of training', and by implication less problematic than the creation of learning in the first place. During the sixties many critics and quite a few practitioners of T-groups for initial strangers concluded that, whatever effects they might achieve in the short run, these effects rarely lasted. This change in belief certainly did not stem from a reading of the verified-change studies. The widely read and frequently misquoted review by Campbell and Dunnette (1968) may have had something to do with it. Most likely, what Campbell and Dunnette wrote keyed in with a realization by many at that time that participation in T-groups might indeed generate appreciable changes, but that those changes were nowhere as radical or as far-reaching as had been anticipated. Campbell and Dunnette's particular contribution to this was to point out that although the verified-change studies showed that trainees *did* change, there was very little evidence as to whether the changes achieved benefited the trainee's employing organization or not. Not everyone would want to argue that the only type of change worth achieving is that which serves the employer's ends, but there has been a long-standing linkage between T-groups and management training. Many of those who espoused the individual skill model earlier are now committed to the view that organizational development provides a more secure road to lasting change.

The recent studies cannot be seen as wholly supporting or contradicting the individual skill learning model. The fact that many studies have obtained significant overall changes on various standardized scales implies that change after groups cannot be entirely idiosyncratic. Certain types of change must be more frequent than others. On the other hand, changes have been detected on such a wide variety of measures that it would be equally misleading to describe the outcome of groups as uniform or standardized. In one sense the proposition that learning in groups is 'individual' constitutes a type of null hypothesis. It is up to researchers who believe that the variability of training outcome is explicable in terms of this or that variable to show that this can be achieved. In the absence of such hypotheses, the individual learning model provides a diffuse but not misleading characterization.

One researcher who sees continuing virtue in the individual skills model is Lennung (1974). He made a study of a residential T-group programme within a Swedish company. Trainees were assigned to training or control group status at random. It was found that there was no overall tendency for ratings of various aspects of work activity to increase, decrease or move to the mean. On the other hand, trainees showed far more individual variability in their scores than did controls. Lennung suggests various reasons why recent research showing increases or decreases overall on various scales may have arisen from the manner in which the scales were formulated and the type of population sampled. An alternative view of his work is to see it as evidence of how much of the data to be explained is lost when findings are expressed simply in terms of overall mean changes.

Learning how to learn

The first model presented implied that learning was a unitary process. A number of theorists have argued at various times that it is fruitful to differentiate different types of learning. Schein and Bennis (1965) presented a model which laid some stress on individual skill learning, but which stressed in addition the trainee's prior need to 'learn how to learn'. By this they meant that before trainees could start to increase their skills in the training setting it was necessary for them to understand the bases of learning in that setting. For instance, they must learn that paying attention to feelings and to the here and now behaviour of others is important, as well as taking risks in seeking and in giving feedback to others. These aspects are referred to as the 'metagoals' of training. The distinction between metagoals and learning is in some ways a helpful one since it helps to clarify some of the confusion surrounding the

individual skill model. Somehow, under the individual skill model, the trainee's learning was seen as free and unconstrained and yet at the same time dependent upon adherence to the 'rules' of the cultural island. The Schein and Bennis model clarifies this by acknowledging that the meta-goals are provided by the staff rather than arising spontaneously.
As they put it:

. . . we must distinguish between norms which concern *how to learn*, and norms that concern *what will be learned*. The staff creates a setting which in effect *imposes norms of how to learn*, but such norms do not prejudge what will actually happen in the groups, what observations will be made, what feelings will be revealed, and therefore *what will be learned*. (Schein and Bennis, 1965, p.290, their italics.)

Schein and Bennis analyse in some detail the reasons why it is likely that these metagoals will be accepted. They differentiate factors in the situation which are likely to encourage the participant to seek out new learning methods and factors which are likely to make those which are provided by the staff acceptable. They see the search for new models as engendered by the *disconfirmation* of existing models in the training setting and the acceptability of the new models as resting on the *psychological safety* they provide.

The Schein and Bennis model provides a challenging characterization of experiential learning. Regrettably, very few researchers have conducted their studies with its hypotheses directly in mind. Most usually learning how to learn has been seen as an 'intervening variable', whilst the researcher's task is seen as that of assessing the substantive learning achieved once the learning how to learn is accomplished. This way of formulating the problem is inadequate since it implies that learning how to learn and actual learning are somehow logically separate, so that what is learned is not in any way affected by the prior learning of how to learn. A specific example will indicate the unlikelihood of this. Suppose a participant attends a group with the prior intention of achieving increased skills in working with others. If the participant learns in the group that he or she frequently ignores the feelings of others, and that much is to be learned from attending closely to here and now behaviour, those learnings are likely to provide the major basis for change after the group. In other words, in this instance and probably in many others the learning how to learn is not a precondition to learning, it *is* the most substantive learning arising form the experience.

Perhaps the most distinctive feature of the Schein and Bennis model is its emphasis on the manner in which learning how to learn precedes actual learning. While this dichotomy may not have proved wholly fruitful, Schein and Bennis' analysis of the preconditions for such change—disconfirmation and safety—has elements in common with Harrison's (1965) model. Harrison argues that learners require both support for their old orientations and also dissonance or confrontation by new phenomena which cannot be integrated within the old system. Thus Harrison's model resembles Schein and Bennis' model in that it delineates two elements of learning. It differs in that it lays greater emphasis on the cognitive nature of the changes induced. As he puts it:

> . . . for integrated cognitive growth, a person should at all times have both a 'castle' and a 'battlefield'. By a man's 'castle' we mean that area of his life in which his cognitive equipment is viable and effective. By the 'battlefield' we mean a set of experiences in which the individual is confronted with disconfirming and dissonant phenomena. (Harrison, 1965, p.105)

Both Schein and Bennis and Harrison lay some stress on how change occurs where both factors are concurrently present. Harrison's model is more specifically focused and has proved more attractive than that of Schein and Bennis to researchers. Their work will be considered later in the chapter.

If learning how to learn is considered to be the major achievement of experiential training, one should not anticipate the broad diversity of learning envisaged under the individual skill model. There should instead be movement towards the values and goals of trainers who transmit the skill of learning how to learn. While such a match may exist in the research data, there is no very adequate way of judging how good it is. This is partly because of the diversity of research criteria employed and partly because it is not wholly clear to what degree trainers do have a unified set of goals.

The process of learning how to learn may also cause participants to relabel their previous behaviour patterns, with resulting confusion for the researcher. For instance, Walker *et al.* (1972) found nuns to be less self-disclosing after group experience, Zand *et al.* (1969, found less perceived trust after an organizational development programme, while Cooper (1974) found that social workers scored higher on neuroticism after a group. In each of these studies the researchers were troubled by the fact that they appeared to have detected adverse effects of training. In each case they sought additional data to clarify the meaning of their findings and finished up concluding that what they had detected was an increased willingness to concede negative judgements about themselves or others which was not associated with any decrease in effectiveness in relating to others. In other words, they may be seen as concluding that the obtained effects were side-effects of the process of learning how to learn and were not 'real' in the sense of actual increases in neuroticism, distrust or secretiveness.

Golembiewski *et al.* (1976) also argue the case for differentiating types of change. They differentiate types termed alpha, beta, and gamma. Alpha change is change along a stable scale, while in beta change some recalibration of the scale employed occurs during the change effort. In gamma change there is a major redefinition of the manner in which change shall be evaluated, such that an entirely new scale would be appropriate. Golembiewski *et al.* are primarily concerned with organizational development, and they cite a study of an organizational change which appeared to fit the gamma pattern.

The learning how to learn model is provocative in that it has stressed the occurrence of a ' category shift' in learning during experiential training. This has not induced researchers to seek differentiable types of learning, which might be separately assessed. However, it has provoked some enquiry into the processes whereby such a category shift occurs. In terms of the three models of personal learning presented in this chapter, the learning how to learn model is clearly intermediate. The first model presented stresses participant autonomy and the learning of individual skills. The third model rests on a normative view of learning. The division within the second model between learning how to learn and the actual process of learning gives it elements of both the others. The hypotheses it generates about the processes inducing the 'category shift' in learning are directly comparable to those arising from the third model.

Learning personal responsibility

While the first two models derive primarily from the T-group trainers of the sixties, the third is associated with various facets of the encounter movement. The central element in this model is the conceptualization of learning as the creation of experiences in which the trainee accepts responsibility for his or her feelings and behaviour. It derives most clearly from Perls and the gestalt therapists, but has increasingly also characterized the approach of Schutz and other encounter leaders of the Esalen school. As Perls, *et al.* (1951) put it:

One cannot on any ground take responsibility for what one is not in contact with. This applies to happenings in distant places, of which perhaps one has never heard, but it also applies equally to events taking place in one's own life if one is not aware of them. If one makes contact with them and becomes intimately aware of what they are and how they figure in one's functioning, then one becomes responsible for them—not in the sense of now having to assume some burden which was not there before, but rather in the sense of now recognising that it is oneself who determines in most instances whether they shall or shall not continue to exist.

The procedures employed to teach personal responsibility are a good deal more direct than those envisaged in the learning how to learn model. Although there may be much in common between the essence of learning how to learn and the taking on of personal responsibility, the participant who is learning how to learn mostly has to rely on indirect teaching, whilst the client in gestalt therapy receives very direct guidance once he or she has accepted a contract to 'work' with the therapist. For instance, the client may be told to attend to present feelings, to accept non-verbal behaviours or body postures as expressions of feeling, to say 'I' rather than 'we', 'it' or 'one', to say 'and' rather than 'but', and 'won't' rather than 'can't'. In all such ways the taking of personal responsibility for one's present responses is encouraged.

The personal responsibility model differs from the models discussed previously in that it lays no stress on the acquisition of specific skills. Change is seen as a personal therapy rather than training in skills appropriate to a particular setting. Those advancing the personal responsibility model are much less closely associated with management training.

At the heart of the personal responsibility model lies a paradox: the goal of experiential training is seen as increase in responsibility for my actions, and this goal is to be approached through the acceptance of explicit instructions from others. If I *do* accept responsibility for my actions, there is no particular reason why I would wish to continue accepting instruction. If I do not accept responsibility, I am more likely to carry out instructions, but the instruction will have failed in its purpose if I do so. Of course, I may just enjoy working within gestalt ground rules, in which case, to adapt Perls' much-cited 'gestalt prayer', I do my thing, the therapist does his, and if perhaps we meet, it is beautiful. Such a convergence in therapist and client goals postpones but does not evade the paradox to be confronted. Sooner or later, if I am to accept responsibility for my behaviour, I must assert the difference between my priorities and those of the therapist.

The delineation of the paradox at the centre of the personal responsibility model in no way diminishes its potential usefulness. It may very well be that the sharpness with which this model is formulated permits the identification of a paradox which underlies all approaches to experiential training. Even where the learning model utilized does not provide for such direct teaching by the group leader, the leader's very presence and role in creating the learning setting implies that that setting is somehow more real or more important for learning than is everyday experience. The trainee must then wrestle with the paradox that the setting is both real and artificial. If I see my group as more real than the rest of life, I make it artificial by separating it from those other aspects of life. If I see the group as artificial and unlike life, I deny the reality of potential learning implied by the leader's presence.

A number of theorists have argued that the experience of paradox underlies therapeutic change (Frankl, 1971; Watts, 1961; Watzlawick *et al.*, 1974). According to this view the juxtaposition of mutually incompatible propositions concerning oneself forces a reappraisal and choice as to how to behave. Watzlawick *et al.* in particular argue for a psychotherapy built around the construction of 'therapeutic double binds'. A therapeutic double bind would comprise a carefully constructed combination of injunctions from therapist to client designed to make difficult the continuance of a previous behaviour pattern. Instances might be instructing a client to behave in a manner which he or she had previously been trying very hard to avoid, or responding to a client's fears or fantasies as though they were literally true.

The role of experienced paradox in inducing change is only now beginning to be explored. Its importance in evaluating the personal responsibility learning model is that it provides a potent source of hypotheses as to why that model might induce change. In discussing the learning how to learn model it emerged that some workers within that tradition also have identified the presence of contradictory elements as a central element in change.

Some studies were reviewed earlier concerning the personal orientation inventory and the locus of control scale. These indicated that where researchers *have* looked for evidence that trainees see themselves as increasing in responsibility for their feelings and behaviour, they have mostly found such evidence.

Comparison of the models

The three models of learning presented can be seen as representing three different phases in the evolution of experiential training theory. They reflect a shift, already noted in training practice and research findings, from a skill-oriented group focus to a therapy-oriented personal focus. Not everyone would agree that this shift either in theory or practice represents progress towards a more desirable state. In terms of the three models, however, there do appear to be some advantages with the more recent formulations. It was suggested earlier that the individual skills model represented a kind of 'null hypothesis' about learning processes. If later theorists cannot explain adequately the diversity of experiential learning, the individual skills model stands. If they can, it becomes superceded. The personal responsibility model does offer such a unifying hypothesis: the variety of personal changes shown after training can all be seen as instances of enhanced personal control over behaviour. Direct tests of the hypothesis are of course required, but the model is rather clear as to what would need to be measured in order to provide these.

The learning how to learn model is clearly intermediate to the other two. Its division between learning how to learn and the actual content of subsequent learning gives it a more substantive focus than the individual skills model. However, there are grounds for doubt that the two processes are as readily separable as Schein and Bennis proposed. In reading their theory one is reminded of the writings of experimental social psychologists at about the same time, arguing that all that the experimenter does is to establish the research setting without in any way influencing people's subsequent behaviour. Group trainers, like experimenters, are powerful figures and there is no reason to believe the arguments they advance that they do not influence their clients or subjects. Indeed, there is now substantial evidence linking the trainer's behaviour to group outcome (Psathas and Hardert, 1966; Hurley and Force, 1973; Lieberman *et al.* 1973; Smith, 1980). The most plausible hypothesis is that the leader is influential both in transmitting norms as to how to learn and in affecting which particular facets of themselves group members learn about.

This analysis of three learning models thus concludes that the personal responsibility model currently hold most promise. Its promise lies both in its specificity and in the manner in which its emphasis meshes in with a growing focus of research and practice: awareness of self.

THE SELF AS OBJECT

Study of one's awareness of self has a long history both within psychology and outside it. Carl Rogers is said to have made the concept of self a central component in his theory of personality because clients so frequently referred to their selves in the course of talking with him (Pervin, 1970). Others from James (1890) onwards have argued that a coherent psychology of self requires some initial conceptual distinctions. James himself distinguished the 'I' who experiences the stream of consciousness from the 'me' who is cognisant of 'I' experiences and is able to stand apart from them and be aware of the person it is who experiences them. In Rogers' analysis of childhood experience the 'me' or self-concept gradually becomes alienated from the 'I' or objective bodily experience as a result of the conditional reactions of parents and others. We learn to tell lies to ourselves and others about our experience in order to sustain a self-concept consonant with the demands placed on us. Such a self-concept will have both positive and negative facets.

With adolescence and adulthood further complexity arises. Using the framework of attribution theory (Kelley, 1967), Jones and Nisbett (1971) have pointed out how in perceiving others' behaviour, especially that of strangers, we are often aware of an individual's behaviour only in one setting. If that behaviour differs from the behaviour of others in the same setting, it is easy for us to attribute that behaviour to the individual's personality. By contrast, in perceiving our own behaviour we are all too aware of how we have behaved in numerous previous other settings. If there are differences between our behaviour in the different settings, as there frequently are, we are likely to attribute the differences to the varied settings. In this way we should come to see ourselves as having weak or inconsistent personality, since our behaviour varies with the circumstance. By contrast we should see others as having definite and consistent personality, since we observe how their behaviour differs from that of others in a particular setting. This erosion of the conception of self which we form, at least in stable childhood experience, is likely to be more acute the more varied is life. It should also occur more at times of transition.

Our capacity to reflect upon our own behaviour is a source of both strength and weakness. If reflection leads us to think about aspects of ourselves associated with past failures, we may seek to minimize this by living lives which are as invariant as possible, or at least by avoiding settings in which it has been particularly hard to sustain our prior self-concept. We may also anticipate that others will evaluate us as negatively as we may do ourselves, and try to conform to their expectations in order to give them as little reason as possible to judge us harshly.

Duval and Wicklund (1972) go so far as to postulate that objective self-awareness (i.e. the awareness of oneself as an object) is an aversive state. In a series of experiments they showed that simply placing a mirror on the wall of a psychology laboratory made it more likely that subjects would blame themselves for failures in various hypothetical circumstances which the experimenter asked them to evaluate. This increased tendency to blame oneself did not occur when the experimenters distracted subjects' attention from themselves by concurrently giving them other tasks to perform. Duval and Wicklund's formulation has required some subsequent revision with regard to the aversiveness of objective self-awareness. Wicklund (1975) acknowledges that where positive feedback is given, objective self-awareness may be a pleasant state, although he believes this to occur only rarely. Davis and Brock (1975) showed that when subjects were in front of mirrors or cameras positive feedback enhanced the degree of self-focus. With negative feedback there was no more self-focus than in the absence of cameras or mirrors. Duval and Hensley (1976) present evidence suggesting a strong link between focus of attention and the attribution of causality. In other words, their proposal is that where we attend to our own behaviour we see ourselves as causal, whereas when we attend to the environment we do not see ourselves as causal.

Jones and Nisbett's (1971) proposal is of course rather close to this hypothesis. There are a number of relevant empirical investigations. In an ingenious study, Storms (1973) made videotapes of conversations between two people (whom he termed actors). Each actor was observed by a separate observer. Storms found, as the Jones and Nisbett theory would predict, that the observers were much more certain in their ratings of the actors' behaviour than were the actors themselves. The observers saw the actors' behaviour as caused by the actors' personality, whereas the actors saw their own behaviour as caused by the situation they were in. Storms then created a reversal of the experimental situation through the use of videotape. In this situation, each actor was asked to watch the video of himself, while each observer was asked to watch the video showing the conversation partner of the actor previously observed. Under these circumstances the pattern of ratings was reversed. After the actor had watched himself on video, he saw his behaviour as more personally caused. After the observer had watched the video of the conversation partner, he rated the situation as more important in determining how the actor had behaved. Thus by a reversal of the attention of actor and observer Storms achieved a complete reversal in the perceptions of causality about the actor's behaviour. His study supports the view that one way to enhance people's sense of personal causality is to make them more aware of their own behaviour. Of course in Storms' experiment the actors had little choice but to attend to their videotape. In more natural settings, people may only be willing to attend to their own behaviour if that turns out to be a pleasant rather than an unpleasant experience. Taylor and Koivumaki (1976) asked people to make ratings as to why they themselves or various others might behave in particular ways. They found strong support for the view that favourably evaluated behaviours are seen as personally caused whereas unfavourably evaluated behaviours are seen as situationally caused. Thus one might expect the effect obtained by Storms (1973) only to hold where the experience was a pleasant one.

The foregoing analysis suggests some reasons why we may frequently avert attention from ourselves. We may do this in order to avoid the pain of acknowledging our failure to live up to our own or to others' expectations. More simply, we may do it because there are many events external to us which compel our attention. The point of the analysis is to argue that the consequence of this diversion of attention is the loss of our conception of ourselves as able to cause events. To the extent that we focus attention outside ourselves, we will come to see ourselves as spectators of other people's worlds. Of course, someone who is totally self-absorbed is also unlikely to be able to sustain effective interchange with others. But the path by which such self-absorption is reached may frequently involve incomprehensible reactions from others, as Laing (1960) and others have suggested.

If attention is mostly focused on things which are pleasant and successful, the individual's awareness will encompass a further dichotomy between self and others. While the individual is often able to witness others' successes and the feelings which arise from them, others' feelings of failure are less frequently made visible. In contrast, the individual's own feelings of uncertainty or inadequacy are readily available, whereas success, at least in fields where it is socially defined, is dependent on the availability of feedback from others. The field is thus full of potentiality for the creation of faulty attributions. One may readily learn to see oneself as having more of almost any negative trait than others. Clinical applications of attribution theory (Strong, 1970; Valins and Nisbett, 1971; Storms and McCaul, 1976) mostly explore the manner in which clients blame themselves for failures or deficiencies which they see as uniquely caused by their own inadequacy. The treatment favoured by these theorists consists of enabling the client to discover that others frequently experience a similar difficulty when faced with the same circumstances. Thus a perception of personal causality of negative traits is decreased by encouraging clients to attend to the *context* of their behaviour and to note the reactions of others to similar circumstances.

This excursion into theories of self and of causal attribution leads to the conclusion that the experience of self as causal rests on two circumstances: (1) that individuals be aware of their successes, and (2) that individuals be aware of the context of their failures.

We turn now to an examination of evidence from experiential training to see how far it is able to provide these circumstances. In looking at the evidence we shall need to see not only whether training can provide the experience of enhanced personal responsibility but whether it can provide it in a form which persists after the experience is over.

THE SELF AS CAUSE

In reviewing theories of experiential learning it was concluded that some of the more promising formulations were built around the notion that the experience of paradox is central to change. The discussion of attribution theory which followed makes it possible to examine the experience of paradox more fully. Participants in experiential training will seek to make sense of that experience by attributing their behaviour during training to some cause or other. Following the Jones and Nisbett model, we should expect that initially trainees will attribute their behaviour to situational circumstance. Training mostly occurs under non-routine circumstances, and if one's initial behaviour is in any way unusual it would seem self-evident to most people that the unusual behaviour was due to the unusual circumstances. Different aspects of the unusual circumstances might include the physical locale, the group leaders, or other group members, all of whom might be invoked as causal.

One of the most predictable effects in experiential training is the growth of warmth and cohesion in the group. After a while, the participant may feel accepted by the group, and be behaving in a manner somewhat different from usual. There is still no attributional dilemma for participants—their behaviour differs because this is an exceptionally nice bunch of people. Now suppose that one or more group members behave in a way which *challenges* other participants. The challenge need not necessarily be an overt challenge or a hostile reaction; it might just be another group member successfully carrying through a behaviour which some participants would like to be able to perform but cannot. Participants will now be aware of simultaneous messages from others *both* that their behaviour is acceptable as it is *and* that it would be good to change it. There is a state of safety plus disconfirmation (Schein and Bennis, 1965), support plus confrontation (Harrison, 1965), or paradox (Watzlawick *et al.*, 1974). Whatever they do there will be a good reason why they could just as well have done the opposite. Since there are good external reasons for acting in either way, it becomes a great deal harder to see one's behaviour as the product of external circumstance. One has to choose.

Learning episodes in groups will vary in the degree to which they can be seen to provide a truly paradoxical set of injunctions to the participant. At one extreme would be an episode in which participants receive two logically contradictory messages from the same source, demanding that they both do and not do something. More frequently one of the messages will be explicit while the other will be implicit, either in non-verbal cues accompanying the first message or in the previously existing relationship between the two parties. In these circumstances it would most often be impossible for an observer to judge whether or not the messages were *logically* paradoxical. The relevant point in these circumstances would be whether or not the recipient of the messages experienced conflict or confusion as a result. Still other types of learning episodes in groups would not involve concurrent and contradictory messages at all, but the hypothesis of this chapter is that there is no reason why these should create changes in perceptions of oneself as causal.

Kiesler (1973) has argued that many of the effects of T-groups are the product of their short-term nature and that leaders should devote more time to the need to train participants to attribute these effects to the changed situation which a group provides. In one sense she is clearly right. The experience of paradox such as the hypothetical one just described is a creation of the group. It would not occur if the group had not taken place. But to dismiss the effect as situational because of this would be to throw out the baby along with the bathwater. By experiencing such a paradox participants may learn that they *can* choose between two behaviours. It is for them to test out in how wide a range of settings that proposition remains true.

Klemke (1977) provides a fine instance of the type of change under discussion. He asks students to write a short essay entitled 'This is me' before and after sensitivity training. Before training one student wrote briefly and described himself entirely in objective terms. His description began:

I was born in Spokane, Washington at an early age. I lived there for 18 years and then spent 2 years in the Navy . . .

Afterwards, he wrote:

Four months ago, I recognized the fact that I had many feelings and ideas. I suppose everyone realizes this fact as soon as they become a rational thinking human being. I also recognized the fact that many of these feelings were hindering me in my effort to become a 'fully-functional' human being. These were feelings of insecurity and resentment. I have always been able to hide these feelings from others, and to a great degree from myself. I have spent many uncomfortable moments wanting to bring these feelings out and really examine them, but was never able to conquer the fear which surrounded them. This class has given me a start in this direction. What I do with this start is now almost entirely up to me, but the desire for this type of mental growth is certainly there . . .

Oshry and Harrison (1966) used an allied method but with a more substantial sample. They asked participants in T-groups to describe a current work problem which they faced before training and again after training. Content analysis of the problems revealed that subsequent to training trainees more frequently saw themselves as having a causal role in the creation of the problem, and presumably therefore also in its solution.

TYPES OF CHANGE

The preceding section has differentiated two types of change, change which the participants attribute to the effect of others and change which the participants see as caused by themselves. While both types of change will coexist within the group, once the group is over the distinction becomes crucial. Changes attributed to the effect of others have no reason to persist, since the others are no longer present. The prospects for persistence of changes which are self-attributed are much greater.

One theorist who has proposed a similar differentiation of types of social influence is Kelman (1958). He distinguishes three social influence types, compliance, identification, and internalization. Compliance is said to occur where A has means control over B. B goes along with A's demand because if he does not A will withhold rewards or administer punishments. Identification is said to occur where A is attractive to B. B goes along with A's preferences so as to sustain a rewarding relationship with A. Internalization is said to occur where B makes a change in behaviour because he sees that that change would have some personal utility. B derives the idea of making the change from A, who is observed to have goals which are congruent with B's goals but who is seen as able to achieve some of these goals more effectively than does B.

The processes of compliance and identification are clearly instances of change attributable to others. Kelman foresees that change based on these processes will be severely restricted by the reactions of others outside the group. Only where pressures for change both within and outside the group concur will change persist. By contrast, internalization is formulated in terms of B's *choice* to change. The prospects for the continuance of change outside the original setting are much greater.

Smith (1976) reports a study which uses these ideas to examine the persistence of sensitivity training effects. Measures were collected of the patterns of social influence relationships experienced by participants during training, and of reported levels of change at the end of training and five months later. In order to test predictions it was necessary to classify participants as falling into one or other influence type. This was achieved through the use of measures of confrontation and attractiveness. These measures were selected because they derive from the various two-factor theories of learning already discussed. Using these terms, compliance occurs where the participant is influenced by those who confront him or her with the need to change but who are not attractive to him or her. Identification occurs where the participant is influenced by those who are attractive but not confronting. Internalization occurs where the participant is influenced by those who are *both* attractive *and* confronting. The definition of internalization thus reflects the two-factor learning models discussed earlier. The use of the term confrontation in the definition of internalization requires some explanation. What is envisaged is not the type of overt demand which might characterize compliant influence. The confrontation is an *intra*personal one in which the individual is aware that there is some goal which he or she would like to achieve and which some other member of the group does achieve. Andrews' (1973) use of the term challenge might better capture its essence.

The subjects of the study were 199 participants in five-day residential sensitivity training programmes held in England. At the close of the week they were asked to rate how much each of the others in the group had influenced them, how much each of the others liked them, how much they trusted each of the others, and how much each of the others behaved in a way which made them feel tense. The ratings of liking and trust, which were strongly correlated with one another, were employed as the measure of attractiveness. The ratings of tension were employed as the measure of confrontation. Planned correlations were computed for each individual between their ratings of influence and the other three ratings. Where all three ratings were positive the individual was considered to be an internalizer. Where influence-tension was negative and the other two correlations positive the individual was considered to be an identifier. Where influence-tension was positive and the other two correlations negative the individual was considered to be compliant. This procedure yielded five participants showing a compliant influence pattern, 53 showing an identifying pattern, 108 an internalizing pattern and the remainder unclassifiable. The compliant and the identifier participants were combined into a single category and referred to as externalizers.

The incidence of change in this study was assessed by ratings of 'benefit' on a seven-point scale. The rating was completed with regard to self and each other member of the T-group. Ratings were also made by the trainers. Additional ratings on the same scale were obtained by mail five months after training with regard to oneself. In part of the sample two close associates of the trainee were also asked to make ratings of benefit five months after training. The findings are summarized in Figure 1. It can be seen that at the close of the group those who had shown the internalizer pattern and those who had shown the externalizer pattern did not differ either in their evaluations of how much they themselves had benefited or in the evaluations made by other members. However, the trainers saw internalizers as having benefited more ($p < 0.05$). After five months the ratings of benefit for externalizers had sharply decreased both for self-ratings ($p < 0.01$) and for ratings by others ($p < 0.01$). In contrast, the much smaller decreases for internalizers show no significant change from the ratings made at the end of the group. The findings of the study are thus entirely as predicted—both types show changes during the group experience, but externalizers show significant fade-out whereas internalizers do not. The fact that the trainers are already able to discern at the end of the group which people's changes will persist must presumably be due to their greater experience of sensitivity training and consequent awareness that not all perceived change in a group is likely to be durable. Miles (1965) also found that trainers' ratings of change at the close of the group were predictive of follow-up change, whereas participants' ratings were not.

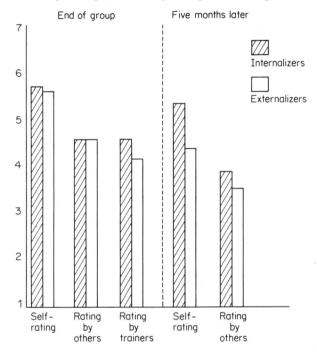

Figure 1   Ratings of benefit by internalizers and externalizers.
From data in Smith (1976)

This study provides a firmer test of two-factor theories of experiential learning than hitherto available. This is because it includes follow-up data. A number of previous studies, mostly provoked by the Harrison (1965) theory, have tested hypotheses linking the presence of support and confrontation to criteria of learning within the group. Harrison and Lubin (1965) showed that groups composed for support and confrontation were more likely to generate learning. Pollack (1971), Reddy (1972), and Smith and Linton (1975) all obtained results consistent with this view. Andrews (1973) found that T-groups most highly evaluated by trainers were those with the most 'high-challenge' pairings. Frankiel (1971) showed that where there were two trainers one tended to become more supportive while the other was confronting, which was detrimental to the level of learning achieved.

The findings of the Smith (1976) study underline the hazards of using participant ratings obtained during the training programme as criteria of learning. Some previous studies such as Andrews' (1973) did employ trainer ratings and may therefore have successfully differentiated internalized change from externalized change. Others, which have used participant ratings, are more likely to have confused the two types of change. One weakness of the Smith (1976) study is that it used post-only ratings. This type of design fails to exclude some possibilities which might also explain the results. For instance, the measure of internalizers may for some reason detect not persons who benefit particularly from experiential training but those who are prone to report high levels of change from all their life-experiences. To test more rigorously the explanations advanced by Smith (1976), a further study was required which also obtained control data as well as measures of how participants attributed the changes they observed in themselves.

Attributing the causes of change

Smith (1978) studied two further sensitivity training programmes in England with a total of 70 participants. The design was an own-control one, such that each participant was asked to make ratings of changes experienced prior to training, as well as during the experience and after it. Data were collected on the first and last days of the programmes and by mail five months later. The previous measure of 'benefit' was not employed, but was replaced by separate ratings of the amount of change perceived and an evaluation of that change. The first rating asked respondents to rate on a seven-point scale how much they had changed over the past few months. The verbal anchors on the scale ranged from 'Not at all' to 'In many extremely important ways'. A second scale asked for evaluations of these changes on a nine-point scale ranging from 'Entirely for the worse' to 'Entirely for the better.' The third scale asked what had been most important in generating these changes. A nine-point scale was used which ranged from 'Others and/or external circumstances have been the sole cause' to 'I have been the sole cause'. At the end of the week ratings on these scales were again obtained, except that they now referred to changes during the week. The final ratings were collected five months later and once more referred to changes over the past few months.

The findings are shown in Figures 2, 3, and 4, which are based on the 38 participants who did respond to the follow-up questionnaire. It can be seen that the amount of change reported after training is greater than that reported beforehand ($p < 0.005$). The evaluation of change is also more positive after training than before ($p < 0.02$), although there is some fallback from the even more positive level achieved during the training. The perception that the changes occurring were personally caused is higher after training than before ($p < 0.05$), but this change is not apparent until after training. Subdivision of this small sample into those classified as internalizers and those classified as externalizers reveals that, as anticipated, internalizers show significantly more increased evaluation of change ($p < 1.001$) and increased perception of personal causility ($p < 0.02$).

This study lends further support to the attributional model of personal learning. The own-control design makes it clear that the rate of change and evaluation of change reported after training *are* increased from the pre-

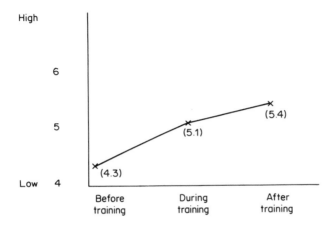

Figure 2   Ratings of change at each time. From data in Smith (1978)

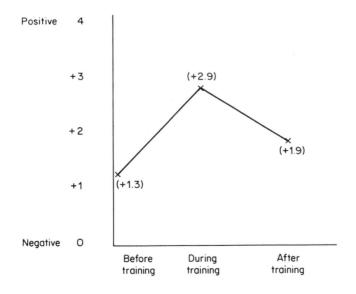

Figure 3   Evaluation of change at each time. From data in Smith (1978)

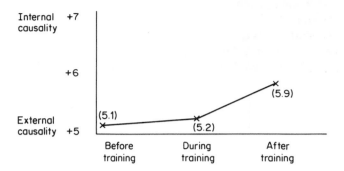

Figure 4   Individuals' perceptions of causes of their change
at each time. From data in Smith (1978)

training level. Furthermore, as predicted, the changes are associated with increases in perceived personal causality. The major puzzle posed by these findings is that the enhanced personal causality experienced by internalizers is found only after training, and not in relationships with group members during training.

The most likely explanation of this anomalous finding lies in the confusing circumstances which a participant experiences at the close of the training programme. As Kiesler (1973) has reminded us, the achievements of experiential training *are* in one sense situationally caused. They would not arise if the training programme had not taken place. At the same time, successful learners in the training programme will be aware of an enhanced sense of personal causality *within* the programme. Faced with a rating scale which treats personal and situational causality as opposites, they may well feel like ticking both ends of the rating scale. Indeed, one or two respondents did just this. In contrast, when the pre-and post-ratings are completed no major situational change has necessarily occurred and the rater has a less confusing task. If this analysis is correct, the failure to obtain changed ratings for personal causality at the end of the week is due to the inadequate rating scale employed. Taylor and Koivumaki (1976) have recently reported data showing that where subjects were permitted to make independent ratings of personal and situational causality, their responses on the two scales were only weakly related. A valid test of this aspect of the attributional model of personal learning will therefore require further empirical study.

The finding that the change which persists after training is that which is associated with an enhanced sense of personal causality is of course central to the model. Further data relevant to this point are provided by the chapter by Allen in the study reported by Lieberman *et al.* (1973). Allen found that those encounter group participants who succeeded in maintaining change stressed the taking of personal initiatives, thinking out what one wanted to do and so forth, as might be expected of internalizers. Those who had failed to maintain change laid greater stress on the reactions of others subsequent to training, which is the pattern one might expect for externalizers. The search for further empirical data relevant to the model is frustrated by the fact that so many studies of experiential learning are *either* evaluations of outcome *or* studies of process during training. The linkage between process and lasting outcome is often enough written about, but rarely studied systematically.

Enhancing personal causality

There is thus some evidence that personal causality may be enhanced through experiential training. It is by no means clear yet what are the implications of the finding. The determination of the *objective* causes of events is rarely practicable outside a laboratory. The changes found are changes in individuals' subjective conception of themselves. The linkage between objective causality and subjective causality is not certain and may sometimes be at odds. But an increase in subjectively perceived personal causality must also make likely an increase in objective causality. Those who do not believe themselves to be causal are unlikely to take initiatives to influence events. On the other hand those who do see themselves as causal will do so, and consequently will at least sometimes *be* causal. To some degree one's belief in personal causality is a self-fulfilling prophecy.

In this chapter a belief in personal causality has been presented as a unitary trait. Such an oversimplification may be necessary in order to present a viewpoint, but it is unlikely to provide more than a crude summary of the individual's awareness of self. Most individuals are likely to be quite confident that they can cause certain events such as perhaps greeting another person amicably, but much less certain that they are able to take responsibility for their behaviour in other settings, such as sustaining a physical assault for instance. Enhancement of personal causality after training might therefore be seen as an increase in the *range* of behaviours the individual feels able to cause.

It was suggested earlier that enhanced personal causality would occur as a consequence of increased awareness and increased success. The two variables were seen as interacting since we are more likely to attend to success than failure. Consequently the behaviours about which we develop an enhanced sense of personal causality should be those which generate success within the training experience. Such success might include expressing feelings or behaviours towards others which achieve their intended effect. They could also include sharing with others negative aspects of oneself and failing to receive the anticipated rejection, as well as the discovery that others also experience similar negative feelings.

Enhanced personal causality should not be thought of as a delusion of omnipotence. The causality referred to concerns only the individual's success in creating a particular behavioural act, not the ability to guarantee others' response to that act. No studies have been reported of the effects of experiential training on perceptions of others' causality. Insofar as trainees spend a good deal of time in groups attending to others rather than to their environment, one might speculate that perceptions of others' personal causality might also rise. Such an effect might not prove too reliable, however, as at least some groups also encourage members to share information about back-home environments in a manner which might lead one to see the other as less personally causal rather than more so. It may be that the learning of enhanced personal causality does indeed rest on individuals learning to differentiate more sharply between self and others, i.e. between those experiences which they can and cannot personally cause. The directive teaching of gestalt therapists, such as the injunction to say 'I' rather than 'we', 'one' or 'it', is very much directed towards this point.

The personal responsibility model has been presented as arising primarily from the newer encounter-oriented modes of experiential training. While the model's emphasis on awareness of self underlines this parentage, it should prove equally applicable to other modes of experiential training. Organizational development programmes do not typically focus on the same aspects of self as do encounter groups composed of initial strangers. They do nonetheless provide a sustained focus of attention, typically through the use of off-site meetings. Such attention may be focused on the working relationships of a team or it may be focused on that team's relations with others. In either case, a similar dynamic might be foreseen whereby the salient issue receives sustained attention in an atmosphere of trust and support and the issues and differences are confronted. There may be a good deal less trust and a good deal more confrontation than in some stranger groups, but the effective organization development consultant will seek to diagnose an appropriate balance. Where he fails to do so the personal responsibility model predicts that it is much less likely that individuals will take on a continuing responsibility to behave in new ways. However, a lesser level of commitment may be adequate since, particularly in team development, the other participants will continue to be around and can provide external incentives to one another to sustain change.

The creation of an experiential learning setting rests on numerous variables, whose effect is as yet little understood. In the Smith (1976) study, the proportion of participants classified as internalizers in each of the 20 T-groups included in the sample ranged from 25 per cent to 86 per cent. Such a substantial variation in a series of training programmes which are evaluated highly by participants and well respected in the field indicates how far we are from an adequate understanding of training practice. The possible sources of such variance must include participant personality, training design, emergent group climate, and trainer behaviour. Each of these received some attention in the study by Lieberman *et al.* (1973). However, the fact that they studied only one group per leader meant that it was difficult to disentangle the different sources of variance. Most probably each of the four variables *can* exert a crucial influence on whether or not the conditions for enhancing personal causality are established. How often they actually do so is a separate question. Logically, it would appear that the trainer's behaviour must be preeminent as a cause of outcome. This is because if trainers continue to take responsibility for their actions until the end of the programme, opportunities remain to influence outcome. In contrast, participant personality and training design are likely to be fixed by the start of the programme and group climate is much more likely to become fixed during the programme than is the behaviour of any one individual. How far trainers are actually able to adapt their behaviour to that required in particular groups has been little studied. Smith (1980) studied three trainers each leading three five-day T-groups and concluded that they did adapt their behaviour to each group, particularly in the degree to which they were confronting. However, he also found marked consistencies between their roles in each of their groups. Much more work is required to elucidate the processes whereby trainers decide how to adapt their behaviour to the context of their groups. Only when they are found to take such choices can they be said to be modelling the exercise of personal responsibility in groups.

ACKNOWLEDGEMENTS

I am grateful to Matthew Miles and Clay Alderfer for their comments on an earlier draft of this chapter.

REFERENCES

Andrews, J. D. W. (1973) 'Interpersonal challenge: a source of growth in laboratory training', *Journal of Applied Behavioural Science*, **9**, 514-33.
Benne, K. D. (1964) 'History of the T-group in the laboratory setting'. In Bradford, L. P., Benne, K. D. and Gibb, J. R. (eds.) *T-Group Theory and Laboratory Method*. New York: Wiley.
Boyd, J. B. and Elliss, J. (1962) *Findings of Research into Senior Management Seminars*. Toronto: Hydro-Electric Power Commission of Ontario.
Bradford, L. P., Benne, K. D. and Gibb, J. R. (eds.) (1964) *T-Group Theory and Laboratory Method*. New York: Wiley.
Bunker, D. R. (1965) 'Individual applications of laboratory training', *Journal of Applied Behavioural Science*, **1**, 131-48.
Campbell, J. P. and Dunnette, M. D. (1968) 'Effectiveness of T-group experiences in managerial training and development', *Psychological Bulletin*, **70**, 73-104.
Cooper, C. L. (1974) Psychological disturbance following T-groups', *British Journal of Social Work*, **4**, 39-49.

Davis, D. and Brock, T. C. (1975) 'Use of first person pronouns as a function of increased objective self-awareness and performance feedback,' *Journal of Experimental Social Psychology*, **11**, 381-8.

Duval, S. and Hensley, V. (1976). Extensions of objective self-awareness theory: the focus of attention-causal attribution hypothesis'. In Harvey, J. H., Ickes, W. J. and Kidd, R. F. (eds.) *New Directions in Attribution Research*. Hillsdale, N. J. Erlbaum.

Duval, S. and Wicklund, R. A. (1972) *A Theory of Objective Self-Awareness*. New York: Academic Press.

Fitts, W. H. (1965) *Manual for the Tennessee Self-Concept Scale*. Nashville: Counselor Recording and Tests.

Frankiel, H. H. (1971) 'Mutually perceived relationships in T-groups: the co-trainer puzzle', *Journal of Applied Behavioural Science*, **7**, 449-65.

Frankl, V. (1971) *The Will to Meaning: Foundations and Applications of Logotherapy*. London: Souvenir Press.

Golembiewski, R. T., Billingsley, K. and Yeager, S. (1976) 'Measuring change and persistence in human affairs: types of change generated by OD designs', *Journal of Applied Behavioural Science*, **12**, 133-57.

Harrison, R. (1965) *Cognitive Models of Interpersonal and Group Behaviour: A theoretical Framework for Research*. Washington, D.C.: National Training Laboratories.

Harrison, R. and Lubin, B. (1965) 'Personal style, group composition and learning', *Journal of Applied Behavioural Science*, **1**, 286-301.

Hurley, J. R. and Force, E. J. (1973) 'T-group gains in acceptance of self and others', *International Journal of Group Psychotherapy*, **23**, 166-76.

James, W. (1890) *Principles of Psychology*. New York: Holt.

Jones, E. E. and Nisbett, R. E. (1971) *The Actor and Observer: Divergent Percentions of the Causes of Behaviour*. Morristown, N. J.: General Learning Press.

Kelley, H. H. (1967) 'Attribution theory in social psychology'. In Levine, D. (ed.) *Nebraska Symposia on Motivation*, **15**, 192-240. Lincoln: University of Nebraska Press.

Kelman, H. C. (1958) 'Compliance, identification and internalization', *Journal of Conflict Resolution*, **2**, 51-60.

Kiesler, S. B. (1973) 'Emotion in groups', *Journal of Humanistic Psychology*, **13**, 19-31.

Klemke, L. W. (1977) 'Sociological perspectives on self-concept changes in sensitivity training groups', *Small Group Behaviour*, **8**, 135-46.

Laing, R. D. (1960) *The Divided Self*. London: Tavistock.

Lang, R. J. and Vernon, P. E. (1977) 'Dimensionality of the perceived self: the Tennessee Self-Concept Scale', *British Journal of Social and Clinical Psychology*, **16**, 363-72.

Lennung, S. A. (1974) *Meta-Learning, Laboratory Training and Individually Different Change*. Stockholm: Swedish Council for Personnel Administration.

Lieberman, M. A., Yalom, I. D. and Miles M. B. (1973) *Encounter Groups: First Facts*. New York: Basic Books.

Miles, M. B. (1960) 'Human relations training: processes and outcome', *Journal of Counselling psychology*, **7**, 301-6.

Miles, M. B. (1965) 'Changes during and following laboratory training: a clinical experimental study', *Journal of Applied Behavioural Science*, **1**, 215-43.

Moscow, D. (1971) 'T-group training in the Netherlands: an evaluation and cross-cultural comparison', *Journal of Applied Behavioural Science*, **7**, 427-48.

Oshry, B. and Harrison, R. (1966) 'Transfer from here and now to there and then: changes in organizational problem diagnosis stemming from T-group training', *Journal of Applied Behavioural Science*, **2**, 185-98.

Perls, F. S., Hefferline, R. R. and Goodman, P. (1951) *Gestalt Therapy*. New York: Julian Press.

Pervin, L. (1970) *Personality: Theory, Assessment and Research*. New York: Wiley.

Pollack, H. B. (1971) 'Changes in homogeneous and heterogeneous sensitivity training groups', *Journal of Consulting and Clinical Psychology*, **37**, 60-6.

Psathas, G. and Hardert, R. (1966) 'Trainer interventions and normative patterns in the T-group', *Journal of Applied Behavioural Science*, **2**, 149-69.

Reddy, W. B. (1972) 'Interpersonal compatibility and self-actualization in sensitivity training', *Journal of Applied Behavioural Science*, **8**, 237-40.

Rotter, J. B. (1966) 'Generalized expectancies for internal versus external control of reinforcement', *Psychological Monographs*, **80** (Whole No. 609), 1-28.

Schein, E. H. and Bennis, W. G. (1965) *Personal and Organizational Change through Group Methods*. New York: Wiley.

Shostrom, E. L. (1966) *The Personal Orientation Inventory: An Inventory for the Measurement of Self-Actualization*. San-Diego: Educational and Industrial Testing Service.

Smith, P. B. (1975) 'Controlled studies of the outcome of sensitivity training', *Psychological Bulletin*, **82**, 597-622.

Smith, P. B. (1976) 'Social influence processes and the outcome of sensitivity training,' *Journal of Personality and Social Psychology*, **34**, 1087-94.

Smith, P. B. (1978) 'Changes in personal causality and sensivity training experience', submitted for publication.

Smith, P. B. (1980) 'The T-group trainer—group facilitator or prisoner of circumstance?', *Journal of Applied Behavioural Science*, In press.

Smith, P. B. and Linton, M. J. (1975) 'Group composition and changes in self-actualization in T-groups, *Human Relations*, **28**, 811-23.

Stock, D. (1964) 'A survey of research on T-groups'. In Bradford, L. P. Benne, K. D. and Gibb, J. R. (eds.) *T-Group Theory and Laboratory Method*. New York: Wiley.

Stock, D. and Thelen, H. A. (1958) *Emotional Dynamics and Group Culture*. New York: New York University Press.

Storms, M. D. (1973) 'Videotape and the attribution process: reversing actors and observers points of view', *Journal of Personality and Social Psychology*, **27**, 165-75.

Storms, M. D. and McCaul, K. D. (1976) 'Attribution processes and emotional exacerbation of dysfunctional behaviour'. In Harvey, J. H., Ickes, W. J. and Kidd, R. F. (eds.) *New Directions in Attribution Research*, Vol. 1. Hillsdale, N. J.: Erlbaum.

Strong, S. R. (1970) 'Causal attribution in counselling and psychotherapy', *Journal of Counselling Psychology*, **17**, 388-99.

Taylor, S. E. and Koivumaki, J. H. (1976) 'The perception of self and others: acquaintanceship, affect and actor-observer differences', *Journal of Personality and Social Psychology*, **33**, 403-8.

Trist, E. L. and Sofer, C. (1959) *Explorations in Group Relations*. Leicester: Leicester University Press.

Valins, S. and Nisbett, R. E. (1971) *Attribution Processes in the Development and Treatment of Emotional Disorders*. Morristown, N. J.: General Learning Press.

Valiquet, M. (1968) 'Individual change in a management development programme', *Journal of Applied Behavioural Science*, **4**, 313-25.

Walker, R. E., Shack, J. R., Egan, G., Sheridan, K. and Sheridan, E. P. (1972) 'Changes in self-judgements of self-disclosure after group experience', *Journal of Applied Behavioural Science,* **8,** 248-51.
Watts, A. (1961) *Psychotherapy East and West.* New York: Pantheon.
Watzlawick, P., Weakland, J. H. and Fisch, R. (1974) *Change: Principles of Problem Formation and Problem Resolution.* New York: Norton.
Wicklund, R. A. (1975) 'Objective self-awareness'. In L. Berkowitz (ed.) *Advances in Experimental Social Psychology,* **8,** New York: Academic Press.
Zand, D. E., Steele, F. and Zalkind, S. S. (1969) 'The impact of an organizational development programme on perceptions of interpersonal, group and organization functioning', *Journal of Applied Behavioural Science,* **5,** 393-410.

Advances in Experiential Social Processes, Volume 2
Edited by C. P. Alderfer and C. L. Cooper
© 1980 John Wiley & Sons, Ltd.

Chapter 4

A Model of Trainer Development

David L. Bradford
Graduate School of Business
Stanford University, U.S.A.

T-groups and trainers have constantly to deal with the paradox between simplicity and complexity. Although the process in a T-group is intricate, the goals are relatively simple. What trainers need to know about interpersonal and group theory and about themselves is vast, but frequently the most effective intervention is just a few words. Even though trainers need to spend years in developing their understanding and skills, the ultimate goal is to be able to have such knowledge sufficiently integrated to be consciously ignored but used in an authentic fashion. However, the trap for the developing trainer is frequently the reverse of these paradoxes. The danger is in having an overly simplistic view of the world that leads the trainer to use overly complex interventions.

At one level, what could be simpler than developing the ability to interact in an increasingly authentic fashion? But the ability to recognize one's own feelings, accept the vulnerability of sharing them, and take the risk of becoming fully engaged with another person is far from easy. Likewise, building norms that support risk-taking without irresponsibility, supportiveness without protectiveness, and confrontation without destructiveness is a major task. Even though at the end of a T-group experience members frequently are amazed at how easy their open interaction has become, they often forget the pain and struggle that built the conditions where such behaviour could take place.

Similarly, being a trainer—a good trainer—in such a process is incredibly complex yet appears so simple. Participants sometimes jokingly comment on what a soft job training is: 'You don't have to prepare; you don't have to lead; you are silent most of the time and when you do talk, half the time you either say "How do you feel about that?" or "Is there something more you want to say?" — and they pay you for that!' What they fail to recognize is that keeping silent is harder than talking, and knowing when to talk (and what to say) so that comments help rather than hinder the process requires sophisticated training.

How difficult for the trainer to learn that frequently the best response to a complex situation is to remain simple because only by so doing can the complexity work itself out rather than be distorted by an artificial order imposed by the trainer. Several years ago I commented to a colleague that no good intervention was longer than 25 words. Now I wonder if any comment, other than a summary intervention that provides cognitive clarification, ought to be that extensive! But knowing what few words to say—and when to shut up so that a member will say it minutes later—is a very difficult decision process.

Learning to become a trainer is a process of moving into greater complexity and greater simplicity at the same time. Trainers need to develop a firm grounding in the applied behavioural sciences, learn an array of intervention and design skills, and gain more insight about their own personal and interpersonal dynamics. But equally important, the trainer has to discover how such complex knowledge, skill, and insight can lead to greater simplicity in training style with less reliance on complicated exercises, elaborate designs, and intricate interventions. This knowledge, once properly integrated, can allow trainers to use themselves as the major training resource in a direct and simple way.

This chapter will deal with these paradoxes by presenting a model of trainer development which describes three stages that I think most advanced trainers go through. The first stage is 'trainer as a role', in which the novice trainer is learning a theory of training and appropriate intervention skills. The second stage is 'trainer as being', in which the trainer moves from primary cognitive reliance ('training out of one's head') to a greater intuitive reliance ('training out of one's guts'). The final stage is 'training as process', in which the trainer can be sufficiently in tune with what is occurring in the group for the process to largely determine the trainer's actions.

The importance of cognitive and affective skills has been recognized from the earliest writings about the training process (Tannenbaum et al., 1961). What has not been fully explored is the pattern in which these are learned. Although it may appear that I am suggesting that trainers learn cognitive material in Stage I, the affective in Stage II, and an integration in Stage III, the world is not that tidy. An interaction between conceptual and emotional issues exists in all three stages. Furthermore, the third stage is not only an *integration* of both the cognitive and affective but an *internalization* so that trainers stop focusing on their own thoughts and feelings and focus more on the group.

Each stage has its strengths and pitfalls. Because the three stages contain crucial learnings, each one is necessary and should neither be by-passed nor hurriedly travelled through because to do so would deprive the developing trainer of important knowledge and skills. While I believe the third stage is likely to be more effective than the preceding two, trainers can be productive working primarily out of either of the other two stages as long as they are aware of and can compensate for the major problems of each stage.

The following sections of this chapter will describe the three stages, the types of learning each can offer, their limitations and potential pitfalls, and the conditions that lead to the transition from one stage to the next. The chapter will then close with a discussion of the implications of this model of trainer development for an effective training-of-trainers programme.

These thoughts are not based on any rigorous quantitative research but instead reflect observations I have made over the last decade. Some of these observations were made as a staff member in various trainer development programmes sponsored by the NTL Institute, as a supervisor with student trainers in the Graduate School of Business at Stanford University, and from observing myself and others as we struggled to learn and grow. Since they are primarily my observations, the reader should be warned that they may reflect my biases more than objective reality.

Before describing the stages, I would like to delineate the type of training this chapter describes. Definitions of T-groups may range from highly instrumented training programmes that have a feedback component to a totally unstructured group with a personal growth focus. While the points being made in this chapter may apply to all such groups (and also might be relevant to the teacher in a traditional classroom and the therapist with a client), my primary focus will be on the basic NTL laboratory with either an interpersonal or group emphasis. Although exercises and other structured activities may be part of the general laboratory design, within the T-group itself the major learning component is the unstructured group with members learning from their own interactions.

Another important distinction in this chapter is between a T-group as a laboratory for inquiry and a T-group as skill training. The initial T-groups in the late forties and early fifties were very much of the former type (Bradford, 1974). It was still an emergent field and the leaders had only a vague idea about what could occur. The uncertainty required joint inquiry among participants and staff to discover, by examination of their own process, the dynamics of interpersonal and group behaviour. But as time went on and the same 'lessons' emerged in group after group, T-groups tended to become a workshop for skill attainment rather than a laboratory for exploration. Even worse, as Back (1972) points out, trainers sold a set of predetermined solutions to participants under the guise of scientific examinations. This was often accompanied with a 'true believer' orientation in which strong conformity pressures emerged to accept certain beliefs and values. The trainers had achieved order in a complicated world by a simplistic view of how people should act and groups should operate.

While not advocating the reinvention of the wheel, I am disturbed by the loss of true inquiry in a T-group. What trainers started to confuse was the *process* necessary for learning to occur and the *outcomes* from that learning experience. For example, in a T-group it generally holds that more learning will occur if people disclose their feelings about another's behaviour rather than making an attribute of the other's motivations. While that is an important method of learning in the T-group (and outside as well), it is a means for people to learn about themselves. But when such a process variable becomes rigidified into 'the 10 rules to T-grouping' and then generalized to all situations, it distorts the fullness of human interaction.

If a T-group can truly be a learning laboratory, then participants can discover under what conditions reporting feelings is valuable and when raising questions about the intentions of others is appropriate. Not only can an inquiry model build a more sophisticated and contingent view of the world, but conclusions based on here-and-now events are more likely to fit the member's personal and interpersonal style. Furthermore, a true inquiry model can serve as an important safeguard against the pitfalls that may occur in each of the three developmental stages. Conversely, T-groups which have become skill training workshops limit the extent to which members can develop the skills to learn from their experience (because the trainer has been 'training up the group' to get them to act 'appropriately'). Not learning how to learn limits the participant's ability to build other learning settings at work and at home.

THE THREE STAGES

Stage I — Training as a role

The beginning trainer, even if he or she has participated in several groups and has co-training experience, still finds the notion of leading a group unsettling. This is understandable given the demands of the task. Using one's knowledge of individual, interpersonal, and group processes to help members build a learning group where they can examine and learn from their own experience is a complicated process. The trainer has to help the group identify what is occurring (but not determine it) and assist the members to grapple with and learn from the major issues (but not force the outcome).

Not only is this task more complicated than in the traditional classroom or training workshop (where goals and processes have been clearly delineated beforehand), but the power held by teachers and workshop leaders is removed in the T-group. Regardless of whether the group has an interpersonal or group focus, the formal authority to set the agenda, guide the discussion, and determine the procedures is in the hands of the group, not the trainer. Furthermore, the trainer does not hold the high degree of expertise power of a teacher or workshop leader since the group can and should be encouraged to rely on its own evidence. Although this undercuts participants' reliance on an authority for determining 'the answer', it does not necessarily decrease the trainer's feelings of personal responsibility for the success of the group. The trainer may say 'this is our group' and 'we have shared responsibility for its success', but nevertheless members look to the trainer for answers, and the trainer in turn frequently feels special responsibility for the outcome.

Thus the primary concern of the beginning trainer is that of survival. 'How am I going to open the group meeting?' 'How will I answer when they say 'You've been through this before, what should we be doing?' 'How do I respond when people question my competence?' Beginning trainers frequently desire a cognitive theory of training, a clear description of the trainer's role, a set of predetermined goals and objectives, a list of interventions and exercises, and sure-fire responses to the dozen of dilemmas they fear will occur. These concerns are legitimate, since participants are perplexed about how to behave in this strange type of group and naturally will turn to the trainer for answers.

I believe it is a legitimate and important function of the supervising trainer to provide a cognitive map of this strange and forbidding territory. At first I found it difficult to respond to the needs of the novice trainer for solutions. When asked how to handle certain situations, I would respond that 'it depends' and then list a dozen contingencies that I use in determining my response. But it soon became clear that I was moving too far too fast. After all, the process of education should complicate the learner's world only to the point where the complexities can be integrated, and not further. Then, at a later time when more knowledge can be given, what were truths now become clichés. While definitive answers to all training problems cannot be given, the supervising trainer can provide a boundary as to what are, and are not, the major characteristics of a T-group (as contrasted with a traditional classroom discussion section or a therapy group), a rough description of the trainer's role (as contrasted with that of participant, process observer, or traditional task leader), and a set of suggested norms and procedures that have worked well in the past.

In addition to providing useful information, such knowledge also gives a necessary reassurance. People do not operate at their best under excessive anxiety and the starting trainer needs this information to keep the stress level low enough to be able to use other internal resources. Such support to the trainer is also necessary if members are to maximize their learning. It is unrealistic to expect high involvement and personal risk-taking from participants if they feel their trainers do not know what they are doing.

The first stage then is a process of learning the role of trainer. How should one act? What should one do (and not do)? What are the areas of responsibility? After more than 30 years of experimenting, the field has developed a vast amount of knowledge that can be quickly transmitted but would take years to learn on one's own. In this first stage, trainers should be well grounded in the research and theory of the applied behavioural sciences, have a well-developed theory of the training process, have a range of intervention skills (including the ability to develop and conduct different types of structured and unstructured exercises), and be able to design different laboratories for different learning populations.

In addition to acquiring this cognitive knowledge about training and the behavioural sciences, it is also important in this first stage to help trainers identify their own personal 'Theory' of training. I believe that all of us develop our own theory based more on experience than on formal instruction. We develop a set of assumptions about individual, interpersonal, and group behaviour. In most cases this theory is more implicit than explicit and reflected more in our behaviour than in our verbal statements. It is important that our 'theory-in-use' be made explicit so that it can be examined for flaws, discrepancies, and internal contradictions. It can also be examined to see what assumptions we are making about others based on their sex, race, and age. As our society struggles with issues of sexism, racism, and ageism, it is important that we, as change agents, make conscious our assumptions and preconceptions on these issues.

Finally, from the beginning the trainers should become increasingly in touch with their feelings. Because of the central role that emotions play in the learning process, trainers need to understand not only what their own feelings are but how to use them as interventions. Learning about emotions and learning about training theory can be closely intertwined. I have found that one of the best ways to learn content is through exploration of feelings. By asking developing trainers how they felt about particular incidents in their group, the supervising trainer can then examine how expressing (or not expressing) that emotion is congruent with the theory. But even when the trainers in Stage I use their feelings, it is usually very much of a cognitive process. The trainers try to understand the feelings, think about how that fits in with the dynamics of the group, and then decide whether or not to share these emotions. It is still too early in their development to automatically trust their internal responses.

For all those reasons, the first stage is not one for trainers to hurry through. In fact, for many types of learning situations there is little need to move beyond Stage I. If one is conducting a rather structured programme with lectures interspersed with exercises, then the knowledge and skills described in the first stage would be sufficient. Also, even in an unstructured T-group, trainers with this approach can do an effective job in helping participants learn. (In fact, some top trainers, particularly those who learnt in the early years of training before emotionality was as highly stressed as is presently the case, operate primarily out of this conceptual mode.) Thus trainers should not feel stigmatized for staying in Stage I if they make full use of their knowledge. To be able to understand cognitively the various interpersonal and group phenomena occurring in a T-group is indeed a valuable skill. Trainers who develop within this stage can become increasingly perceptive about the internal dynamics of the group (as well as their own internal reactions) and use that awareness to determine what interventions are most appropriate.

Benefits from Stage I

This knowledge can expand the world of the beginning trainers. Most people initially view behaviour in the group as deriving from 'personality' factors ('he is uptight', 'she is willing to take risks,' 'she has a hard time with anger'), completely ignoring interpersonal forces (e.g., how one person's self-disclosure is influenced by another's). Even more rare for the beginning trainer is the ability to perceive on the group level of analysis . But to be able to understand how the group's dynamics (norms and standards, leadership and power, stages of development, etc.) influence individual behaviour is to begin to understand fully the world of the T-group. Theories, concepts, and categories can provide the cognitive glasses which allow the beginning trainer to see so much more and thus be able to make sense out of the vast array of data that is constantly being produced within the T-group. Unless trainers can begin to observe and understand the experiences within the group, they will be severely limited in building a laboratory where participants can learn from their experience.

This cognitive understanding also assists the trainer in helping participants generalize their learning to other settings. A T-group may be a 'cultural island', but unless participants can understand how to transfer the lessons from the T-group to their work or home, there is little of lasting value from the experience. Making that transfer requires, for example, that the trainer have an appreciation of family and organizational dynamics. Just as there are many types of successful marriages (other than the intense 'everything is shared and we are constantly growing together' form), so too there are a variety of ways to operate successfully in the organizational world. Unfortunately, many trainers have an overly simplistic view of the way organizations should be. Leadership should be Theory Y; decision-making should be participative; relationships should be collaborative; and one should be open and trusting. But practioners know that the desired world (let alone the present one) is more complex. There are times for participation and times for autonomous decision-making, times for collaboration and times for competition, times to trust and times to be guarded. What we, as behavioural scientists, have to offer is a knowledge of the conditions under which each is appropriate. But insofar as we have stunted our own cognitive development, we are limited in helping participants make the connection between what they have learned in the T-group and how it can be applied to other settings.

A cognitive understanding of the training process also provides the criteria for trainers to assess success (and therefore their own personal competence).

Without a sophisticated understanding of the various ways people learn (and the even more varied types of learning a T-group can provide), it is too easy for trainers to use members' approval as a measure of how well they are doing (which can hinder the trainer's willingness to take personal risks or confront). Or the measure can be the number of new and flashy exercises and interventions used. Schutz (1971) has nicely captured this dilemma:

I fear being dull, repetitive, and disappointing to people . . . This leads me to sometimes overdo flamboyance or to be over dramatic. I feel a desire to be always new, original, and to not do things like other group leaders, even including not doing things like in my own book *Joy*. This does have the virtue of impelling me onward toward new things, but there is a somewhat compulsive quality about it that I find I must fight. It comes up when people are just talking in the group. Even though talking may be exactly the right thing to do at that point, I feel some push that must be suppressed to make the actions more exciting. Often fantasies of the Flying Circus members intrude here, thoughts that they would be doing something more dramatic, and I'm just going back to my old, tired, T-group . . . techniques. (p.228).

There can also be the danger of using emotionality as a measure of success. There is a story, perhaps apocryphal, of two trainers who were running groups in a growth centre in Southern California. Meeting in the hall after their sessions, one said: 'My group went very well today; three people cried.' His colleague responded: 'That's nothing, one of mine threw up.' While it may be difficult to have groups where significant learning occurs without much feeling, it is certainly possible to have high emotionality without much learning.

Problems in Stage I

What happens when Stage I is slighted? One common outcome is for the trainer not to treat the group as a learning laboratory but as a workshop to learn specific skills. If the trainers' limited awareness prevents them from appreciating all that is occurring within the group, they tend to turn to gimmicks. Rather than being able to recognize and utilize the group's inherent complexity, they think they must add complexity through new types of exercises, activities, and interventions. An extreme example is a trainer I know, who has a travelling van complete with games, records, a portable massage-table, pillows, musical instruments, and bongo drums! Although entertaining, does this approach really help participants learn from their own experience?

Conversely, problems can emerge for the trainer who does develop fully in Stage I. Although a conceptual understanding can be a powerful approach, it is analogous to one channel in a stereo system. Since one of the overall goals of laboratory education is to help participants discover how they can be 'more themselves', it is poor modelling to have trainers constantly in their head (even though such conceptual statements may include reports of the trainer's emotions). Participants are faced with the incongruity between the trainer's verbal statements and the trainer's behaviour. ('Should I act more spontaneously as the trainer suggests or should I think things through ahead of time as the trainer does?') Furthermore, as rich as words are, participants can often gain a greater understanding of new behaviour by seeing it demonstrated by the trainers.

A second difficulty with using only one channel of the stereo is that it can overload the system. The events that are occurring between members of a group (and the resultant feelings within the trainer) are many and varied. How is the trainer to determine which ones are central and which ones peripheral? No matter how knowledgeable and self-aware the trainer might be, the ability to think logically through all that might be occurring is very difficult. Not only can this lead to a mechanical 'doing it by the book' style of training, but it throws off timing because often we can intuit long before we can cognitively understand.

In a sense, Stage I trainers are a victim of their own success. The problem of being overloaded with options and knowing how to select among the alternatives increases the more the trainer has learned. But successful completion of the first stage can provide the support for moving on. Having as a base of strength increased confidence about their abilities, trainers may be willing to take risks that would have been overwhelming before. They now know that the lessons have been well enough learned to be recalled in an emergency.

Perhaps co-training with a senior trainer who gives permission to 'be more oneself' may be the stimulus that leads the trainer to venture into Stage II. Others may decide to move after being confronted by participants with the discrepancy between their advice to members and their own behaviour in the group. For still others, the stimulus may come from experiencing increasing dissatisfaction with the limits of training as a role. This can occur in the situation when the developing trainer begins to experience all the rules and theory not as enabling, but as constraining. An example is the trainer who after a group session bemoans the fact that the role has kept him from really saying what is on his mind. 'Boy, if only I were a participant, would I tell Joe exactly how I feel.' One of the ways to help such a trainer move on to Stage II is to assist him in exploring what he would say. Assuming that the trainer stuck with feelings (and did not give an interpretation of the other person's motives or intentions), it usually turns out that the feelings would be the perfect intervention.

The transition to Stage II is not an easy one. Up to that point, the trainer has relied on theory and sets of rules to determine appropriate behaviour. Often this cognitive map has included the messages not to be too intrusive, not to get in the way of the process, not to do the group's work for it. Now, the trainer is told to 'listen to oneself, respond to one's feelings, be spontaneous, don't think through everything ahead of time'. Not only is this a rather fundamental shift in orientation but it removes the security that the cognitive map provides. Now the trainer is thrown back to an ambiguous and scary world which forces that person into an area of undeveloped competence with increased vulnerability. Little wonder that so many choose not to listen to this suggested change in training style and instead stay in Stage I.

Stage II — Training as being

In the first stage, trainers see leading a group as fulfilling a role, but in this second stage, they see it more as a process of *being*. This involves trusting oneself and knowing that listening to one's feelings, impulses, reactions, and hunches is likely to be appropriate. It also involves a willingness to be wrong, to make mistakes, and to be 'messy' along with the participants. This trusting of oneself has several related but separate components. One is a greater reliance on expressing emotions. Comments that tend to be more 'I feel . . . ' rather than queries about what others might be feeling. The second component is an increasing willingness to act impulsively, to speak without thinking through all the possible implications, and to raise an issue even though unsure how it will turn out.

In Stage I the developing trainer could not fully trust the self. Now, in Stage II, trainers internalize the cognitive models they used as a guideline for interventions and rely on the self as the primary resource. This means that the major distinction between the first two stages is *not* between thoughts and feelings but rather the extent to which one can rely on oneself. In Stage II, the trainer is willing to set aside the conscious cognitive 'quality control' that was developed in the first stage and act on impulse, whether that impulse be to share a thought or a feeling. The second stage is not a rejection of the first stage but rather its internalization.

The movement towards greater trust of oneself, more reliance on hunches, first impulses, and 'what seems right' is felt as a freeing and exciting process. To find that one's self is not an enemy but an ally, not a burden but a resource, is a powerful discovery. Similarly, to learn that one can show anger without destroying participants, inadequacies without being devalued, needs without controlling the groups, is an exhilarating step.

This process of more fully trusting oneself means more trainer self-disclosure. This disclosure not only includes feelings about members and what is occurring in the group but also sharing of doubts and concerns about performance. These doubts have always existed but during Stage I were more likely to be surfaced outside the group with the co-trainer or the supervisor during post-meeting sessions. Now, with a greater sense of competence, the trainer can risk expressing feelings of low competence! Doing this, however, is often felt as a great risk (as it well can be), and often is done only after much hesitation.

This dilemma was illustrated for me recently by an incident with a friend of mine. Carl is very bright and his tendency to stay at the conceptual level is reinforced by being a professor in academia. The following incident occurred during the Monday evening session of a one-week laboratory. His group was a bit slow getting going and Carl, although impatient to have things develop, held back from providing strong direction, hoping that members would take the initiative. But they waffled through the evening and at the end expressed disappointment with Carl's 'performance' and wondered why the other group was doing so much better. While expressing their dissatisfaction, they also started to share what they wanted from the group and from each other and laid plans for more disclosures in the morning. In spite of this, the evening session ended in a decidedly down note—if not so much for the group members, certainly for Carl.

Carl went back to his room for a drink and solitary contemplation. During those ruminations, he developed an elaborate theory about what was occurring in the group. The more he worked on it, the more excited he became both because of the potential learning for the members and because of the support it provided for his decision to keep quiet. He planned to share this theory in a 15-minute lecture at the beginning of the next morning's group.

At breakfast Carl happened to mention his plans to me. In discussing the previous night, it became clear to both of us that he was sitting on a lot of emotions: pain, feelings of personal inadequacy, sense of not being appreciated, fear that he had let me down, and competition with the other trainer. Fortunately, upon my urging, Carl agreed not to share his theory but instead to disclose his feelings. With much trepidation, because he did not know what would happen but feared that such disclosure would cost him status, respect and effectiveness in the group, Carl did so. It was exactly what the group needed. His disclosure of feelings deepened the level of intensity, modelled self-disclosure around here-and-now concerns, helped the group explore its own process, and demonstrated (in a laboratory focusing on leadership theory) that competent leaders can express self-doubts and get help from subordinates. Carl, by being willing to take the risk of moving from Stage I to Stage II, became a vastly more effective trainer.

The order of Stages I and II

But why the sequence of first learning a set of rules and then setting them aside to just be oneself? Why not a high degree of spontaneity and sharing of feelings (including feelings of self-doubt and failure) from the beginning? Could not the problems of Stage I be avoided (or at least reduced) if we urged trainers not to see training as a role but as a process of just being themselves?

This would be difficult because each stage deals with different processes. Stage I concerns the *acquisition* of new knowledge and skills. Time is required for such information to be understood, integrated, and assimilated into one's behavioural repertoire. Only when such knowledge is assimilated can a spontaneous *utilization* occur. The ability to 'trust thyself' in Stage II can only occur when there is a developed self to trust! Otherwise, if trainers in the initial stage were to listen to impulses and feelings, they would frequently experience a contradiction between what they (and the supervising trainer) thought should be said and their initial impulses.

The reason for the contradiction in Stage I is that the concerns, and therefore the emotions and reactions, of most neophyte trainers, are with themselves: 'Am I doing all right?' 'What do they think of me?' 'What does that person's comment say about my position in the group?' This concern with acceptance, esteem, and influence makes it difficult for the trainer to focus on anybody else. Running through all of this is a preoccupation with doing the job correctly and fear of not being adequate (which are reality-based concerns since these trainers are at the beginning of their professional development). Thus any intervention based on feelings comes out of the *trainer's* needs rather than those of the group. Such self-disclosure would almost always focus members' attention on the trainer—an alternative most participants would welcome because it removes the attention from them.

A final reason why these first two stages should be separate is that most group members would not react as benignly to an untrained leader who operated only out of personal concerns, as occurred in Carl's group.

Participants are also worried about the process. This anxiety makes them ambivalent about the trainer; while they don't want an omnipotent God, they do want someone upon whom they can rely. Imagine what would happen to members' anxiety level if they perceived their trainer as having little confidence (or competence) and only a preoccupation with personal adequacy. One of the reasons why Carl's disclosure worked so well is that the members had already experienced his high degree of knowledge and training skill.

But there are some developing trainers who do not start with a highly cognitive training style but whose comments from the very beginning come out of their intuition. They respond, when asked why they made a specific intervention, 'because it just felt right'. But even with these trainers, it can be useful to start with a heavy conceptual component in a trainer development programme. Such knowledge helps them understand what they are doing even if they do not (and should not) use that cognitive information as the major determinant of what interventions to make.

Psychological health of the trainer

Clearly the ability to move effectively into Stage II requires that the person be psychologically healthy. We are telling the trainer to internalize the cognitive control and trust the self. But a 'self' that is seriously flawed is a problem, not a resource. If trainers have overly strong needs for acceptance and approval, control and power, intimacy and affection, then it is these needs, not what is occurring within the group, that will determine the trainer's response. An example of this was the case of Paula. Although a licensed counsellor and therapy group leader, she found it very difficult to respond accurately on the feeling level to events in the group. She had such strong needs for approval and validation that any confrontation from a member was interpreted by her as indicating non-acceptance. She was a much better trainer when she did not use her feelings but instead relied primarily on her analytical skills and stayed in Stage I.

The thrust of a training-of-trainer programme during Stage II is self-exploration. While additional training theory can always be useful, more crucial is helping trainers develop greater insight into their feelings, their motives for training, and their 'crazy areas'. By the last, I mean the parts in all of us which, when triggered by an external stimulus, move with their own energy and cause us to overreact. For some of us this may be when our authority is questioned, for others when we do not feel accepted and approved, and for still others when our masculinity/femininity, competence, authenticity, is challenged. The area in which I tend to overrespond is when a person, usually a woman, acts dependent and then blames me when I don't fulfill her expectations — I get hooked and not infrequently react in a rejecting and punishing manner.

Given the power of the role and the fact that the trainers rarely have their own 'trainer' in the group to help them clarify their feelings, if they are to be encouraged to trust and respond to their feelings it is important that they be aware of situations where their reactions should be suspect. A second reason to identify personally loaded issues is that the loading can lead the trainer to over- or under-emphasize such phenomena in the group. There are some trainers whose groups never have conflicts, while other trainers always have a high percentage of 'counterdependent' members. Likewise, there are some trainers whose groups always focus heavily on issues of sexuality, while for others this never seems to be the members' concern. This means that the intensity of the issue is not determined by the extent to which it reflects the members' needs but the trainer's. Again to quote Schutz (1971):

Another phenomenon that it is essential to be aware of is the tremendous influence of the leader on the course of the group . . . Whatever I was interested in at the moment turned out to be exactly what the group happened to focus on. If I was exploring nonpermanent relations, behold, they were exploring the limits of marriage. When I had just had an insight about the nature of competition, my groups were wrestling . . . ' (p.229).

The goal in this self-exploration is not for the trainer to resolve all personally loaded areas; that is asking too much. No person, not even the most highly skilled professional, will have all parts in order. Show me a person where that is the case and I will show you a person who has trouble letting go of control and taking personal risks! But at the very least, the trainer should be able to identify these personally troubling issues, know what situations are likely to trigger them, and at such a time be able to move away from trusting impulses and use the more cognitive style developed in Stage I.

This phase of starting to deal with problem areas and aspects of the self has its own excitement. To examine oneself, explore old (perhaps dysfunctional) patterns, reassess values and priorities, and explore new options opens up a new world and is probably the period of greatest personal growth. This self-exploration can know no boundaries. What first started out with an examination of the self in relation to the trainer's role now moves into other aspects of the trainer's life: work; marriage; other relationships; and one's priorities in life. Often 'training can be harmful to your mental health', with work and marital stability frequently the casualties during this period. Insofar as this process is a natural occurrence in Stage II, we can begin to understand why relatively few people are willing to open the dungeon doors of the inner self and fully enter this second stage.

Where best should this personal learning occur? In some cases the trainers can appropriately raise these issues in the group they are leading. This models the learning process for members and shows that learning is a continuous process — even for those who are fully trained. But there is a fine line between working out one's own issues in a way that helps the group and working them out at the expense of the group. The latter necessitates other learning settings.

Clearly one of the most important places can be the trainer development programme itself, particularly if a major component is a trainer's T-group with an intrapersonal, self-exploration focus. Developing trainers who want to work on personal issues are not caught in the bind between 'working the issue' and 'facilitating the process'. Removing the responsibility for being the trainer allows the person to fully grapple with the issue itself. Still other trainers find it useful to make a much more complete commitment to self-development, which may mean participating in personal growth groups, going into therapy, or even temporarily dropping out of training to get their internal house in order. But regardless of the place or manner in which such personal learning occurs, this is the crucial learning task of the second stage.

Problems with Stage II

Assuming that the developing trainer is able to move into Stage II and can effectively train from this modality, what are the dangers and pitfalls that can occur? One is in making the erroneous leap from 'trust yourself' to 'trust yourself at all times on all things'. There is more to training than 'being authentic'. This orientation is particularly dangerous when there are parts of the self that are destructive but the rationalization of 'I am only being me' serves as a defence against dealing with these dysfunctional parts.

Trainers who move into Stage II can become seduced by the excitement of their personal discoveries and can want to spread the message to the unenlightened. Where in the previous stage the trainer was likely to say 'do what I say', in this state it can be 'do what I do'—or even 'be what I am'. It is one thing to model another way of relating so that participants have more options than they previously thought, and another to move into the guru stage to convey that this is the *only* way to be. The former is enabling while the latter is constraining.

An example comes to mind that illustrates this danger. Dan was a mathematician by training who took his first T-group with a great deal of scepticism. The feedback from group members was loud and clear; they told him that his aloof, put-down style impressed no-one, but that the warm, caring Dan that he sometimes let slip out was much more attractive. Another T-group experience followed and then a co-training experience, both of which reinforced his message. Then in the next T-group in which he co-trained, Dan became a 'true believer'. He was constantly coming out of his feelings and pounding others over the head if they did not follow his example. Out of the best of intentions, he wanted others to have the learning he had gained. But in the process his groups changed from being a freeing place where people could discover their own learning to an indoctrination programme—to learn certain predetermined truths.

Trainers who move into Stage II experience a contradiction between what the supervising trainer is presently recommending and what was suggested in Stage I. Previously there was the warning against overcontrolling the group by assuming too much responsibility or doing the group's work for them and against forgetting how potent the trainer's feedback could be to members. Now in Stage II how do trainers handle the possibility that something they say might harm members or be dysfunctional for the group? Rather than living with (and learning how to manage) the tension in this dilemma, some trainers rationalize away the problem by denying the fact of social influence and pushing a belief system that says individuals are totally responsible for what happens to them. An extreme example is the following quote from a trainer who announced at the beginning of a laboratory:

I'd like to state first that, whatever happens, you are responsible for yourself. That is, if during the course of these things you want to become physically injured, then you can do that if you want to; if you want to bow to group pressure you can do that. If you want to not bow to group pressure, you can also do that. But I want to underline clearly at the outset that you are responsible for whatever happens to you here. (Back, 1972. p.226)

Even though it can be a learning for participants to 'take responsibility for their lives', to deny peer pressure and group conformity is to deny reality. This is another example where ideology replaces objective inquiry. Seeing the world in simplistic extreme terms may make training easier but it denies the potential richness of the T-group in learning how to reconcile the sometimes contradictory forces of individual rights and group responsibility.

Another difficulty that can arise in this period of high personal growth is the paradoxical fact that the more successful trainers are in exploring the inner self, the more their 'centredness' may be undermined. The process of exploring new, underdeveloped (or conflicting) aspects can make the 'self' (which is the strength of Stage II) suspect. For example, if the trainer has discovered that acknowledging and expressing anger is a 'crazy area' and starts to explore the reasons why that is the case, he or she is likely to see anger in most situations. Furthermore, being in the middle of experimenting with how to express negative feelings can lead to responses that are too extreme. Thus the process of dealing with one's self may make that self a less reliable resource.

Another problem I sometimes see in Stage II is the paradox of 'constant exploration to *avoid* the self'. These are trainers who appear to be growing and experimenting, but each year sees a new technique, a new theory, that is championed as the answer. Such people throw themselves into the new approach and say that they are gaining great personal learning in the process, but I am left with the impression that such individuals are no closer to their core issues than they were before. The involvement with the cause prevents an involvement with the self; again an example of adding on complexity rather than moving into one's own simple, yet basic, essence.

How can these potential problems be handled? Are they inevitable or can precautionary measures be taken that will lessen their severity? Clearly, an important safeguard is to have a core part of the Stage II training-of-trainer programme contain a learning setting where the developing trainer can raise these issues. Trainers working them through with their peers (and under the guidance of a senior staff member) can increase the probability of successful resolution without the danger of damage to participants in their T-group. Another safeguard is for the trainer to be sure to utilize the inquiry model in the T-group he or she is leading. Such an orientation counters any tendency of the trainer to impose personal values and style on the group since members can now examine how the trainer's message fits the reality they are presently experiencing. Also, a laboratory for learning means that everybody, including the trainer, is open for feedback and confrontation. One of the richnesses of the learning process in a T-group (as compared to a traditional classroom and a therapy group where there are structural and normative barriers against feedback to the leader) is that the trainer is potentially open to the same process as participants.

Finally, a sophisticated theory of training learned in Stage I can cushion the potential excesses of Stage II. An understanding of individual development indicates that several paths and timetables for learning exist (and not just the one chosen by the trainer). A theory of learning places emphasis on the process (not on any one outcome). Knowledge of group behaviour provides a more complex view of the world by acknowledging interpersonal and group forces in addition to individual dynamics. Finally, a thorough conceptual knowledge can serve as a set of guideposts trainers can use when they are exploring new personal areas and cannot fully trust the self.

Transition to Stage III

What leads the trainer to make the transition from Stage II to Stage III? As with the first transition, there can be many reasons. The trainer can grow satiated on such a rich diet of constant personal growth. Or many of the trainer's personal issues may be reaching resolution and he seeks a balance to put the personal into perspective with the conceptual. But a third cause is similar to what happened previously: the learning in Stage II has provided such a rich complexity that now a simplifying mechanism is needed. The very success of Stage II has provided an awareness of the vast array of possible emotional responses—so vast that the trainer can no longer just 'listen to his guts'.

This last point refers to the case where a specific incident produces many rather than just a few emotional responses. For example, let us take the situation in which the group has been progressing slowly, members have not been disclosing their reactions, and the trainer has several times unsuccessfully intervened. About two-thirds of the way through the session a member who has systematically blocked any explorations of feelings by other members accuses the trainer of not performing adequately. Think of the range of reactions that trainer is likely to have: *defensiveness* at being attacked; *anger* that it was this specific person, of all people, to make that point; *annoyance* at other members for their complacancy; feelings of *inadequacy* for not having been able 'to do magic'; *competitiveness* with the other trainer whose 'group is doing better'; *worry* at what the supervising trainer will say upon hearing of this incident; *fear* of being rejected by the group; *concern* that fully expressing the anger will blast the attacker away — and most of all a lot of *pain*!

Now what should the trainer say? If we answer 'trust yourself', which of these many parts is the trainer to trust? If the person shares everything at one time, it will be overwhelming to the group. As with the first stage, the very success of Stage II has produced such increasing complexity that the trainer is again in need of a simplifying decision mechanism.

Stage III — Training as process

The third stage is difficult to describe so the reader will have to bear with me as I try to tease out its essence. Initially it is felt as a synthesis between the cognitive and the emotional and between the controlled and spontaneous. This may be felt, internally, as a dialogue between the parts with neither dominant for long. A thought is checked against a feeling, a hunch is analysed, a spontaneous act examined, an emotional state explored. Sometimes this dialogue is carried out publicly, more frequently privately, and probably most commonly at a preconscious level.

But Stage III is more than just a balance, an integration, of the two preceding stages. In both Stage I and Stage II the trainers were focusing on themselves: in the first stage on their cognitive processes and in the second stage on the intuitive. But in the third stage the trainer is able to move beyond focusing on the self and can pay primary attention to the process. It is now the *process* (what is happening between individuals and in the group itself) that determines the trainer's response. The trainer *reacts* rather than acting *because* of his/her reactions. The self (both cognitively and emotionally) has now become so fully developed that it can be largely forgotten—the trainer can become truly selfless because the self has been previously attended to. The trainer does not have to say: 'What am I thinking?' 'What am I feeling?' 'What should I do now?' 'How am I reacting to what is occurring?' Instead the attention can be on the group and on the interaction among the members.

Let me try some analogies to explain. The first stage saw the trainer as conductor—standing away from the events and doing things *to* members to make things happen. The trainer 'helps', 'enables', 'causes', 'facilitates', 'unfreezes', and 'produces'. All of these are important and valuable acts but all are of an instrumental nature. In the second stage, the trainer is in the middle of the river—splashing around, urging others in, showing them that the water is not that deep nor the current that fast. But in the third stage it is the river, not the trainer, that is central. The river will flow regardless of what the trainer does, and the task of the trainer is to assist—not produce—that flow. This may mean gently drifting with it, moving slightly ahead to point out the way, assisting participants in removing a log that is slowing progress, pointing out different beds the current can flow in so that members can decide the appropriate channel for them. In this third stage, the trainer is not larger than life—as was the case in the two preceding stages—but part of life itself.

In placing the group's process as the dominant focus, the trainer uses himself or herself (both cognitively and emotionally) to help that process develop. This may mean keeping out of the way and letting the current flow by itself or making a simple comment that helps clarify what is occurring. It may mean pointing out the dilemma the group is wrestling with or sharing some feelings that allow others to understand their own emotions. It is truly a 'facilitating' role. The advantage of having the process dominant is that it is the best way to make sure the T-group will be a learning laboratory. If the trainer can truly stay with the process and not determine it, then the emergent learnings will result from the members' interactions.

Naturally, such a condition is not easy and requires a thorough development of the preceding two stages. It also demands a high degree of psychological health and self-awareness, more so than in Stage II. In the second stage, personal needs had to be dealt with so that they would not seriously distort the trainer's reactions. But in the third stage, the trainer has to be further centred so that he or she does not use the group as an important source of personal gratification. One has to satisfy needs for acceptance, approval, prominence, influence, and affection elsewhere. It also means that the trainer has to be willing to let go of control, to be willing to let the group develop out of the members' interactions. Now that is not to deny that trainers have needs in the group nor that they would be bothered if attacked, disapproved of or rejected. What I am saying is that the trainer has to have such needs well enough resolved not to control the process. If they do come up as issues in the group it is because the process has provoked them, not the trainer.

This ability to be congruent with the process appears similar to Massarik's (1972) definition of the Utopian training state where a perfect correspondence exists between the trainer's needs and the needs of the group. While Massarik points out that such a condition is not possible, I want to go a step further and claim it is not desirable! To seek perfect correspondence between one individual and the dynamics produced by 12 interacting others is to lose one's individuality (which is hardly an attractive role model for participants). If one of the desired outcomes is to build a group where members' differences and uniquenesses can be expressed and accepted, then the trainer and members need to learn how to manage the dynamic tension that is constantly occurring between the needs of the individuals and the requirements of the group.

As I observe trainers in this stage, most of the time they are very congruent with what is occurring in the group. They become part of the process rather than force the process to fit the trainer. This congruence may have occurred in Stage I by the trainer wrenching the group from its present activity and turning it 90 degrees in another direction to fit what the trainer thought was the appropriate path. Congruence was achieved in Stage II as the group followed the trainer's personal path. In Stage III it is the trainer who is following the process — not producing it. Now this congruence does not mean that the trainer is totally immersed in the process. Instead a sense of 'detached involvement' exists which has evolved from the two preceding stages: an involvement from Stage II because one's self and one's feelings are in tune with the group, and a slight detachment from Stage I because the knowledge allows perspective.

Another characteristic I observe in Stage III trainers is a greater sense of authenticity, of humanness if you will. This is in contrast to the analytical nature of Stage I and the 'guruness' of Stage II. Some of the excesses found in the two preceding stages have been modulated. Comments are short, to the point, and lack the jargon frequently found before. A better sense of perspective develops: a realization that T-group training will neither save the world nor cause radical transformations of all members. This produces a lighter tone. Interventions are not felt as such but more as comments made by somebody perhaps more knowledgeable and skilled than the participants but still of the same flesh and blood. Best of all, congruence develops between being a trainer and the rest of one's life. Training is not seen as a role to be enacted or a religion to be embraced.

Difficulties with Stage III

I do not want to imply that Stage III is the point of completion, the stage where one has 'arrived'. This is not a state where all issues are resolved and the trainer has but to relax and be. One of the greatest difficulties I find is concurrently caring what happens in the group but staying detached enough to give up controlling the group's direction. In the previous states, the trainer was frequently in control, although such control was often subtly expressed. Trainers in Stage I had a conceptual map of how the group should act and where it should move. Trainers in Stage II, had a personal form of control, believing that 'as I go, so goes the group'. But in trusting the process, trainers become naked for they give up trying to predict or influence the future and instead stay fully in the present. Golden (1972) has vividly captured these concerns:

Each training group is for me like another combat flying mission, another encounter with the contingencies of the firing line. I sweat out each group because I am never really certain of myself. I do not know definitely whether my being present in a group serves any genuine purpose. Often during a group, I experience feelings of loneliness, uncertainty, and inadequacy. A training group in a sense is a happening, and so is flying at the critical moment. All the planning one has done, all the skill one has developed, all the conceptualization of strategies may or may not prove adequate to the situation one faces. Indeed there are times when I say to myself, 'Why are you taking on this responsibility? Do you know what you are getting into? Who do you think you are, God?' And similarly, at other points in the process, I find myself asking, 'What are you doing? Where is your blueprint? Are you aware that you are letting it happen and that you seem to have no plan or strategy? Come on, face it. Just what do you do in a group?' (p.14).

I had an experience recently that painfully brought to my attention the difficulty of staying fully with the group and the cost when I impose my own process. It was in the T-group course that we teach a Stanford. The class is composed of 36 students divided into three groups that each week meet twice in class plus one evening session. Two-thirds of the way through the 10-week term the class goes off-campus for an intensive weekend where professional trainers are brought in to lead each group.

The group that I was to join had been bogged down in the last two weeks with a major conflict between A1 and the rest of the group. A1 was constantly in his head making cognitive observations about the interactions in the group. Even though he wanted to be helpful, his comments were often felt as judgemental and not at all self-revealing. The group had several times given him such feedback but A1 swatted each comment away with a logical justification of his position. This cycle of feedback-defensive response-further feedback had continued until A1 felt isolated, rejected, and misunderstood (but would not acknowledge any of those feelings). These reactions were based on reality, because several group members, when they found that I was to be their trainer, told me that if A1 made another of his defensive comments they were ready to ask him to leave the group.

Even before the weekend started, I was wishing it were over. I had a thousand things to do in the office and a friend of mine was very sick. I was not looking forward to the emotional involvement that I knew was likely to occur, but I had a job to do and set off the the weekend resigned to my responsibilities as a trainer.

True to form, 20 minutes into the first session on Friday night, A1 attacked the group for their lack of caring and perceptiveness. This was countered with a vicious attack by two members and then silence. As this was going on, I was forcing myself to empathize both with A1 and with his attackers. What must A1 be feeling since he was thinking he was trying to help the group and only getting rejected in return? How frustrated the other members must feel being bogged down and fearing that the weekend was going to be wasted in this useless cycle of attack and defense. I used my knowledge and feelings to get A1 and others into their emotions so that in 20 minutes, through a process of asking questions, sharing my feelings, making several perceptive cognitive clarification statements, I was able to have the issues cleanly on the table. A1 finally realized and expressed his feelings of hurt and others were able to hear and empathize with him. A1 and another were crying, and the issue was soon resolved. Veritably I had done magic—and in the process ruined the group for the weekend!

There was little energy in the group during the next two days. While members raised important issues which led to many valuable learnings, most of this was at a cognitive, analytical level. None of us left the weekend with high feelings of excitement or of personal satisfaction. It was only in next week's evening meeting that the members discovered what had occurred. After they had struggled for two weeks with this problem and been ready to give it up as hopeless, I had come in and solved it in 20 minutes. What a personal defeat and how inadequate it made them feel! In addition to producing feelings of low interpersonal competence, I had robbed them of the opportunity to develop their skills in resolving the problem. Instead, the meta-learning I provided was that one needed an expert around.

What went wrong? On the surface, it was a model of skillful trainer intervention because I had, through sharing my feelings and using my cognitive knowledge, resolved an issue that was blocking the group. Not one of my comments was irrelevant; the statements were a model of brevity, pinpointed the problem, and helped the group move. Why is this not desired training? The answer, obviously, is that I confused the journey with the destination. What was important was not only that this problem be resolved so that the group could progress, but that members learn how they got into that dilemma in the first place and then learn how *they* could get out. I completely by-passed their learning needs and instead focused on problem resolution. I moved too far ahead, ignored the process, and forced them to follow the path I was initiating.

When one has been through numerous groups, it can be an easy trap to use one's knowledge and skills to move too quickly towards the destination and forget that the crucial learning arises from an examination of the journey. (This is a particularly likely trap for the trainer who stops seeing a T-group as a laboratory for learning and instead sees it only as a skill training activity.) But if the trainer can focus on the process, there can be the realization that it is the struggle that is paramount. The trainer may realize the value of expressing feelings, but it is the participant taking the risk of trying this out and testing the validity of the concept that is important. What the trainer needs to do is support the participant in that struggle, not determine the outcome for that person.

Even within Stage III there is a developmental process. But while the development in the two preceding stages was towards increased complexity, the development in Stage III is towards increased simplicity. At the beginning of this chapter, I pointed out that the process in a T-group is disarmingly simple. For example, in many cases the basic, but most difficult, learning is how to relate in a more authentic fashion. 'How can I just share myself?' 'How can I say what I want, for me?' 'How can I reach out to you?' — these are all very simple, basic acts (that any six-year-old can bring off but which are difficult for us as sophisticated adults, living in a spohisticated world). What the trainer learns in Stage III is how to help participants find their own answers to these basic questions. He or she learns how to use the vast reservoir of knowledge, skills, and self-awareness to become increasingly direct, and almost primitive, in his or her interactions.

The discussion thus far has carried the implication of three distinct stages. But, in reality, a great deal of overlap exists between these three. Even in Stage I trainers are attempting to identify and express emotions (even though the decision of which ones to express is frequently a cognitive process). Likewise Stage II is not a state of constant impulsivity, and, as I have pointed out, Stage

III is not one of perfect congruence. In any one of these stages trainers may be operating primarily out of their theory of training, out of their intuition, or out of following the process. Effective trainers use all three and have the flexibility to move back and forth as the situation requires.

The second point to keep in mind is that implicit in the discussion of these three stages are clear value preferences. Almost everybody would prefer to be in the second stage rather than the first, and the third stage rather than the second. This can lead the developing trainer to pass quickly through these preceding stages (or pretend to be in Stage III when that is not the case). Yet each stage has crucial learnings that many trainers have not fully absorbed. Supervising trainers have to spend as much time slowing people down in their rush to 'become professional' as they have to help people develop from one point to the next.

IMPLICATIONS OF THIS MODEL

Conditions for trainer excellence

I think this way of conceptualizing the trainer development process helps explain why, given the many thousands of people who lead experientially based groups, there are only a few hundred that are truly excellent. With all the cognitive, skill and personal knowledge that training demands, it is little surprise that relatively few people are able or willing to make the journey. Without legal requirements to become accredited or having to periodically upgrade one's skills, it is easy to stop by the wayside and rationalize that one has 'arrived', when that is not the case. (This is particularly easy in Stage II, when trainers can do magic to produce adoration and acclaim.) Thus it is unreasonable to expect that the quality of the field will advance if we rely solely on people's desire to learn.

This model of trainer development can also explain why there has never been a fully developed training-of-trainer programme. Such a programme would have to last over several years (with quite intensive mentor contact over that period), would have to be quite differentiated in terms of allowing people to progress at different rates, and would probably be prohibitively expensive. While more attention should be paid to providing quality training programmes for people at different stages in their career, this alternative, by itself, will not solve the problem of developing excellent trainers.

The third alternative, in addition to individuals planning their own development and formal training programmes, would be an apprenticeship model. This is a frequent approach and allows the individualized attention that provides personal learning. The drawback can be in having only one role model. That condition can lead the apprentice to be 'made in the master's image', which can also make the mentor less objective and critical. Ideally several models would be available because learners have different needs at different stages of their development. A friend of mine mentioned the following important differences in his two mentors:

While both were superb, the trainer who was in Stage One was easier for me to learn from initially because her model was clear, her interactions definable and reproducible, her goals easy to conceptualize and she taught it well. As a beginner, I saw the Stage Three person as being almost a magician. I watched what she did but couldn't apply it. It was only later I could begin to learn from her. Her moves all came out of incredible preceptiveness of the group (an intuitive integration of the cues, awareness of feelings in herself and the group) none of which she conceptualized until later.

Perhaps the solution to the problem of how to develop quality trainers is not to rely on any one of these three approaches but to realize that while all three are necessary, no one is sufficient. There is the need for several mentors who can demonstrate an array of approaches and also can give personal attention, feedback, and support. There is the need for standardized programmes that provide a heavy dose of conceptual and skill development and, by bringing together a number of learners, can provide peer feedback. And there is the need for trainers to see learning as a continuous process and not to equate completion of a certain training programme with completion of their learning.

There are a few signs that trainers and organizations are acting on the last orientation that learning for professionals is continuous. IAASS has a review process every three years for members who are accredited, NTL Institute has recently introduced a few advanced programmes just for its professional membership, and individual trainers have frequently attended various advanced growth programmes on their own. While important steps, these are still a far cry from a strong norm that expects all trainers to assess their learning needs on a regular basis and to seek feedback from colleagues about their strengths and weaknesses. Also needed is a norm that makes it appropriate for professionals to confront each other. Too frequently we avoid confronting colleagues on their behaviour by defining collegial support as staying silent with the excuse that 'everybody has his own style'. Of course, it is one thing to say that such norms should be developed and another be able to do so. But if our business is being able to build learning settings where interpersonal feedback can occur, it would do no harm if the training field were to treat itself as the client!

Thus, part of my trainer development, be it a mentor relationship or a more standardized workshop, should contain constant and clear feedback to developing and developed professionals on the present limitations of their style. I cringe when I think that most participants after a two-week trainer development programme will go out to lead groups. While they may do so irrespective of what we say, it is unethical to give them false confidence. We can both reduce their pain from future training disasters and lessen the potential damage to participants by giving clear feedback on the type of training they should and should not consider, the areas they are likely to have trouble with, and further development they should undertake. It may be necessary to suggest to some developing trainers that they do not lead an unstructured T-group but stick to more structured workshops, or to suggest to others that they consider not training at all until they are able to resolve certain personal issues. Such feedback is painful but a necessary process for both the supervising staff and the trainers.

One of the reasons why such feedback is difficult is because participants frequently come to a training-of-trainers programme as much for validation as for learning. Certainly they wish to acquire new theory and some techniques (particularly if those can be acquired easily without making them vulnerable) but frequently they also want to find out how good they are. These conflicting forces have always existed but the tension increases the further the trainer progresses. Not only is the training role more central to the experienced trainer's occupational self-identity but personal self-identity is now involved. The issue is not only 'How good am I as a trainer?' but 'How am I as a person?'

This need for validation can interfere with learning. It is indeed difficult to explore new areas, be willing to look at one's mistakes, and be open to inadequacies when the learner wants a guarantee of success ahead of time. This means that the participant processes each activity on two levels: the first is the specific learning contained in that activity (which the developing trainer is more willing to learn from) and the second is the more general conclusion about present and future competence (which is more strongly resisted). It is one thing to learn four ways to handle personal attack, but what if the developing trainer discovers basic personality difficulties with anger? It is crucial, however, that participants receive feedback on the more general as well as the specific level.

Who should train

This model of trainer development also provides clues as to the person who should be encouraged to go into training. What are the characteristics of a potentially effective trainer? Obviously, a necessary but not sufficient condition is high intelligence. If one is to be able to handle all the relevant knowledge about personal, interpersonal, and group process, then a high degree of intellectual skill is necessary. We are talking about intelligence, not knowledge. The latter can be increased while the former is fixed. Thus I pay less attention to people's previous knowledge or skill level if I feel that they have the ability and interest to learn.

While the ability to learn is important, equally necessary is the potential for self-awareness (and the ability to use that awareness). Again, I pay less attention to the extent to which the novice trainer is presently in touch with and expresses his or her feelings and am more concerned with the potential. There are several reasons for this. First, not infrequently there are cases where the person who appears to be the ideal participant turns out to be far from the ideal trainer. What led to high self-disclosure, awareness of own feelings, willingness to take risks as a participant, came out of some non-healthy dynamics.

Nancy is an example. Basically she is a very lonely woman whose self-esteem is highly dependent on the approval of others. (This condition is not helped by the fact that she is going through some severe marital and work readjustments.) Recently she participated as a member in a group in which she was 'the star of the group' (as reported by her and the trainer). She was constantly in her feelings, pushing herself into some painful areas and confronting others. As she was doing this, she received increasing approval from the trainer and other group members which led to even fuller self-disclosure and risk-taking. At the end of the session, the trainer was so impressed with Nancy that he asked her to co-train in the next group. One shudders to think how her needs for acceptance and approval will interfere with her ability to be an effective trainer.

Another difficulty with using 'being in touch with your feelings' as the major criterion for picking potential trainers is that there are people who might be in touch with themselves but are unwilling to learn further. They feel they have arrived and will do nothing that shakes this self-perception. This unwillingness is not only the worst possible modelling for participants but it also is a good predictor that the trainer will start to see the group as a place to teach predetermined answers rather than a place to explore and discover.

In contrast, there are people who are initially out of touch with their inner state but have the potential for such self-discovery (Dan, the mathematician, was one example). Note that there are two components to the criteria being suggested: one is the ability and the other is the willingness. The former refers to not having major personal issues which interfere with the person's willingness to risk self-examination. (Paula, with her strong needs for acceptance and approval, would not put herself in the position of moving into new areas that might lead to personal failure.) Likewise, there are people who are potentially able to learn but unwilling. This unwillingness may come from many sources: a need to be in control and thus difficulty with the ambiguity of a learning situation; a difficulty in giving up the rewards of established behaviour patterns; an unwillingness to suffer the pain and threat that new learning demands; or an unwillingness to have certain values and beliefs questioned. An example of the last is Ralph, who had strong religious convictions that made him unwilling to look at certain values or even to open himself up for treating the group as a laboratory for learning out of fear that the conclusions from any sort of here-and-now data collection might conflict with his belief system. (Fortunately, he decided not to continue training.)

But most of all, being willing to look at oneself and one's motives can be very painful. Exploration is not only of weaknesses but also of strengths. Doing either may move a person into new areas, because not infrequently we operate as much out of fear of success as fear of failure. Remember also that the transition from one stage to the next occurs because the trainer has been very successful in the previous stage and is now able to let go. But to be able to give up what has paid off in the past and move into a new and uncharted territory is difficult. Fritz Perls' comment that 'to be willing to suffer one's own death and be reborn is not easy' is as true for trainers as it is for participants! But the process of training demands a repeated willingness to suffer the loss of old approaches, beliefs, and behaviours.

In addition to intelligence and the ability for self-awareness, a third characteristic I look for in potential trainers is their motivation to train. There are many persons who found the first group experience an exciting one and want other such experiences. But they should participate in advanced laboratories, not train. Other people have found 'the answer' and want to spread the gospel to the unenlightened, but 'helping the hell out of others' is a dangerous motivation. Still others have found something in the T-group experience that compensates for what is lacking in their personal life and like the 'groupie' who participates in laboratory after laboratory for a monthly fix, this person needs the group for strong personal reasons. While these reasons are operative to some extent in all of us, if they are the primary source of satisfaction then our potential effectiveness is seriously limited.

The motive I think is most important is the *desire to learn*. That may sound a reiteration of the second characteristic but the latter dealt with the *willingness*. One can be receptive without being desirous. The desire to learn concerns the question of the major rewards the trainer receives from leading a group. When this desire is the primary goal, a greater chance exists for the T-group to be a laboratory for learning, a greater chance that the trainer will be open to self-exploration and feedback from others, and a greater chance that the trainer will see learning as a continuous process and not something that stops once one finishes a training programme. But perhaps most important of all, if this desire is primary there will be the willingness to let the process be supreme and to follow where it goes. Only in doing so can one concurrently appreciate the complexity of human interaction and also seek to become more simple, more authentic, and more human in one's training and one's personal life.

ACKNOWLEDGEMENTS

I would like to thank Clay Alderfer, Jacqueline Becker, Leland Bradford, Allan Cohen, Roger Harrison, Murray Horwitz, Jerry Porras and Suzanne Besunder-Stier for their helpful comments on an earlier draft of this chapter.

REFERENCES

Back, K. M. (1972) *Beyond Words*. New York: Russell Sage Foundation.

Bradford, L. P. (1974) *National Training Laboratories. It's History: 1947/1970.*

Golden, W., Jr. (1972) 'On Becoming a Trainer'. In Dyer, W. G. (ed.) *Modern Theory and Method in Group Training*. New York: Van Nostrand Reinhold.

Massarik, F. (1972) 'The natural trainer: A systematic-normative view'. In Dyer, W. G. (ed.) *Modern Theory and Method in Group Training*. New York: Van Nostrand Reinhold.

Schutz, W. C. (1971) *Here Comes Everybody*. New York: Harper & Row.

Tannenbaum, R., Weschler, I. and Massarik, F. (1961) *Leadership and Organization: A Behavioural Science Approach*. New York: McGraw-Hill.

Advances in Experiential Social Processes, Volume 2
Edited by C. P. Alderfer and C. L. Cooper
© 1980 John Wiley & Sons, Ltd.

Chapter 5

Developing a Theory of Practice for Experiential Learning

Barbara Benedict Bunker

State University of New York at Buffalo, U.S.A.

INTRODUCTION

1947 is usually the date cited for the birth of the T-group, that progenitor of what has commonly come to be called 'laboratory education' or 'experiential learning'. In the three decades since this seminal social invention, authors have chronicled the subsequent developments (Bradford *et al.*, 1964; Golembiewski, 1973; Schein and Bennis, 1965), described the social movements it has spawned (Back, 1973), and differentiated it from other forms of education (Benne *et al.*, 1975; Bennis *et al.*, 1969; Bunker *et al.*, 1977).

Few, however, have attempted to define it rigorously or to conceptualize the various types of experiential learning (see Lennung, 1978, as an exception). Yet there are literally thousands of practitioners who use these methods in classrooms, organizations, and training sessions for executives, managers, volunteers, and other professionals.

An experiential learning design can vary from one session of only an hour to a laboratory several weeks in length. Practitioners of experiential learning, therefore, are engaged in a very diverse set of decisions in their practice.

How do they know what to do? What knowledge do they have which guides their practice? In the early days (1950s) the social scientists who engaged in laboratory education often collaborated in designing the 'exercises' that were employed to help clients reach their learning goals by the experiential method. For years these exercises were passed around among trainers as part of their lore. More recently they have been organized into mammals where both old and newly created training exercises are described so that other practitioners may use them (Pfeiffer and Jones, 1977). Bunker and Solomon (1978) created a planning framework for selecting exercises that describes major characteristics of experiential learning exercises. This framework is given in Figure 1. Usually, these exercises are organized by their content focus, e.g. conflict, trust, although, as Bunker and Solomon suggest, other types of organization are both possible and potentially useful. An examination of Figure 1 makes clear the complex nature of the process of creating and selecting experiential learning exercises.

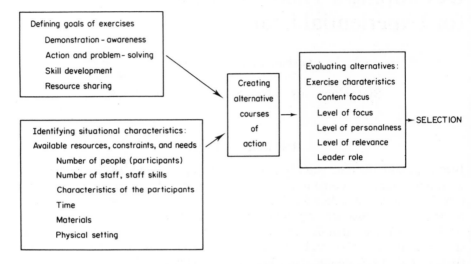

Figure 1   Planning framework for selecting exercises

Exercises were initially viewed as a supplement to the centrepiece of laboratory education, the T-group. Another supplement was the theory session, in which the social scientist reviewed or elaborated the concepts that were being experienced in the T-group or exercise. From the basic human interaction laboratory including T-groups, skill practice, and theory sessions, other types of training events with different foci have proliferated, e.g. conflict laboratories, communication workshops, team building events. They vary greatly in the degree of structure which is imposed. Some are 'instrumented', i.e. preplanned completely in great detail from start to finish. Others, more loosely structured, are changed and redesigned as events occur. The process of selecting a structure, of organizing a series of experiential events into a learning system, is referred to by practitioners as *designing*. It is a central skill of the accomplished practitioner.

There are many highly effective practitioners, applied behavioural scientists, who design and implement workshops and training events around a set of objectives agreed upon with a client. The effectiveness of the practitioner depends on two important competencies. We have already mentioned the skill of designing, the selection or creation of a series of structures, groupings, conceptual inputs, which help the participant achieve the objectives of the workshop, e.g. greater awareness of male-female issues, increased skills in problem-solving, running meetings or conflict management, etc. The other major competency is in managing, supporting, and intervening in the experiential learning system so that it is maximally effective. These are the skills of *intervention* or implementation.

At one time, these skills were all learned by the apprentice method. Now programmes have been developed to train 'trainers', though it is not clear whether these programmes are more than a group of apprentices to one staff. In most programmes students learn by doing, and in some there is work with real clients.

Again the question: what is it that these practitioners know? How do they know how to organize such events? What principles and assumptions guide decisions about design and how they behave when they lead these events? Is there a theory of practice of experiential learning? This is the question that this chapter addresses.

We have almost no written attempts to explicate these issues, and yet among practitioners there is a rich oral tradition of assumptions and 'rules of thumb'* which apprentices learn in their training with experienced professionals.

Argyris and Schön make a useful distinction between one's 'espoused theory' and the 'theory-in-use'. An espoused theory is a verbal declaration of what I intend to do. A theory-in-use is inferred from an examination of what I actually do.† In this project, we collected the espoused 'theories' of practice of a number of practitioners in the form of rules of thumb and assumptions about what works in experiential education. Since this was a preliminary investigation, field observation of working practitioners was chosen as the method of data collection.

METHODOLOGY

Highly competent practitioners with strong backgrounds in applied be-havioural science were observed working with their real clients. They were interviewed prior to the event about their plans and expectations, during the event about what was occurring, and at the conclusion of the event for their views about outcomes. The criteria used to select practitioners were that they were well known and well regarded in the field, that they were conceptually oriented with the kind of behavioural science background that would permit them to describe their espoused theory, and that they would be willing to have

*Assumptions are beliefs about effective behaviour which guide action. Rules of thumb are proscriptions or principles telling how to act.
†The original idea for this distinction comes from Kaplan's (1964) distinction between 'logic-in-use' and 'reconstructed logic'.

the author watch them work with a real client population in a setting in which time demands permitted conversation before, during, and after the event.*

Rules of thumb and assumptions were separated out and individually identified from the field notes about these conversations. Then an organizing framework was created in which to place them.† These frameworks will be presented in greater detail ln the body of the chapter. For the moment it is sufficient to say that many, if not most, of the assumptions collected fell into two major categories. The first was rules about how to *design* or create experiential learning events. The second was rules about *intervention*, i.e. what the practitioner should do to forward the learning. During the course of the project about 10 different workshops were studied in this manner. They varied in length from one to five days. In this chapter we will present the assumptions of two pairs of practitioners in different types of training events. All events had between 40-50 participants, were three-day events, and employed two staff persons (a man and a woman) who were equal colleagues. The participants were both men and women coming from a large parent organization. The goals of the workshops were interestingly different. In one case the programme was to increase the competencies of personnel in the recreation centre of a large government department; in the other it was to increase the awareness of men and women working together in organizations about their differences and commonalities as men and women. The author was able to study each set of practitioners in two workshop settings.‡

The focus of the skills development workshop was on increasing skills for both planning and doing the job. In this workshop the two staff worked with 40-50 persons and provided resources through the design and through individual contact. Many of the exercises used to develop skills could also be used in the work setting of participants. Different levels of skill among participants were acknowledged and the more skilled often helped the less skilled. This use of participants as resources to each other enlarged the staff function. Staff made new conceptual material available to all in general sessions while much of the skill development was done in highly structured small groups of participants.

Although the male-female awareness workshop had about the same number of participants as the skills development workshop, the senior staff selected two associates to work with them. Thus four staff were always available. Groups usually had 12 members and one staff person. Most of the workshop

*Because the author is herself a well-known practitioner, this was probably easier to arrange than many research efforts. Also, since this was an anthropological expedition, the author could occasionally do things which increased her acceptance by the client population and minimized the intrusiveness of the research into the training setting, e.g. give a short theory session, make a comment, etc.
†Jeanne Solomon was an able associate in this phase.
‡The author is grateful to Ronald O. Lippitt and Eva Schindler-Rainman and to Harold N. Kellner and Edith Whitfield Seashore, who were the practitioners studied, for their willing cooperation, stimulating substantive contribution, and supportiveness during the project.

was spent in either same-sex or mixed-sex groups, although there were also general sessions at which concepts and ideas were presented and discussed. Each participant was in both a same-sex and a mixed-sex group. An underlying assumption of this staff was that the exploration of issues of gender is a highly sensitive and somewhat vulnerable area for most persons. As a result, the design, while crucially important in producing the data with which to work, must be implemented by the staff with concern for supporting participant exploration and protecting them from group pressure. In short, the intervention skills of the staff are crucial to an effective design, especially at points where blockage may occur. For this reason, intervention principles become quite important in this workshop.

When we had completed coding the rules of thumb espoused by the practitioners in both workshops, some interesting quantitative differences emerged. The workshop on skills development produced 50 principles of design but only 13 principles of intervention, while the male-female awareness workshop produced 12 principles of design and 17 principles of intervention. Differences may be a product of the subject-matter of the workshops, the values and interests of the practitioners, or both. In this research design it is not possible to distinguish them.

FINDINGS: PRINCIPLES OF DESIGN

We turn now to a discussion of the principles that emerged in the interviews with the practitioners who designed and ran these workshops. In Table 1 there is a list of the categories created by studying all the design assumptions that were collected. In this section each category will be explained and illustrated with rules of thumb and assumptions from these workshops. Intervention assumptions will be discussed in the same way in a subsequent section.

Table 1   Categories for important principles of design

(1)	Initial activities
(2)	Establishing a collaborative relationship between staff and participants, among participants.
(3)	Levels of participation.
(4)	Maintaining energy.
(5)	Maximizing sources of positive psychic income and minimizing resistance.
(6)	Factors which increase the probability of design effectiveness:
	(a) Size of groupings
	(b) Who is grouped with whom
	(c) Flow (e.g. self-disclosure, what follows what)
	(d) Conceptual inputs
	(e) Transfer of training and action-taking
	(f) Giving instructions
(7)	Time allotments in meeting design objectives
(8)	Debriefing structured experiences.

Initial activities

Many practitioners have theories about the importance of the opening activities of an experiential training event. Assumptions include beliefs about the psychological state of participants and the meta-messages delivered by early events. These practitioners believe that the opening events are used by participants as models of what the rest of the workshop will be like. In particular, they create expectations about activity level and the staff role.

For the skills development staff, the implication of these assumptions is that opening sessions should be similar in structure to the rest of the programme (not, for example, a long lecture or explanation). They also assume that the psychological state of people in new settings tends to be overloaded and stressed. Because of this, entry activities are harder to get into than later activities. Therefore start-up activities should be easy to do, reasonable in light of stated objectives, and legitimate in terms of the client population norms. A third principle collected was that people who come on time and have to sit and wait for a late start become hostile and passive. To avoid the development of these feelings, this staff created activities that could be started on arrival. This process they dubbed 'the raggedy start-up'.

The male-female awareness workshop opened with a sharing of data that participants had collected in structured interviews with others before the workshop. The staff believe that these interviews energize people before the session begins and create an opening session around a common experience, thus making entry easier for people. The staff also believe that whenever participants are asked to do work in preparation for a training event, the design of the training event should reflect or use the product. Thus, staff take seriously requests they make of participants and a mutual relationship is established. The initial events are, therefore, very important in the development of a collaborative relationship between participants and staff, a topic to which we now turn.

Establishing a collaborative participant-staff relationship

An assumption which would probably be shared by many practitioners is that the way staff relate to clients has effects on the psychological state of readiness to engage in learning during an experiential event. With this in mind, the skills development staff believe that those who are 'planned for' need to have an important part in influencing, replanning, and evaluating the learning they are receiving. Action or design implications of this assumption might be regular periods for participant input to the design. A corollary assumption is that, at the beginning of an event, participants may be only partially aware of their learning needs. As they engage in the workshop their needs may clarify and change. Good designs are able to be responsive to these changes and regularly reassess the participants' own sense of whether their learning goals are being adequately met in the workshop design.

The male-female awareness staff were no less concerned about their relationship with participants. The nature of the task, however, i.e. developing awareness in areas where many participants were initially unaware of what could be learned, led to different rules of thumb for creating collaborative relationships between participants and staff. There were design structures that were shaped in response to the staff's sense of participants' needs. General theory sessions, seminars, and other types of inputs were selected after staff diagnosis of the stage and needs of the workshop as a learning system-sometimes even in response to specific participant requests. Collaboration was built primarily, however, in the relationship which was developed between staff and participants in the ongoing small groups. That relationship will be described in more detail in the section on intervention, since it is a part of making the planned structure work effectively.

Levels of participation

Practitioners of experiential learning make a number of assumptions about the effects on participants' learning of being actively engaged (participating) in the learning process. The theory espoused is that people learn better if they take active responsibility for their own learning. A design prescription that logically follows is that maximum choice should be created whenever possible, e.g. workshop members in both workshops selected what they wanted to read from a table of readings. Thus choice permits more relevant learning.

There are also assumptions around levels of activity, participation, and commitment. Rule of thumb from the skill development staff: the more work participants do themselves in a given activity, the more commitment to the activity. For example, when participants are asked to generate some implications of feedback data they have received, they develop more commitment to the subsequent action steps than if the staff did it for them. Or, if participants vote their top priorities in a goal-setting process, when the work on the top priorities occurs they are apt to be more committed to it. Several unarticulated assumptions may underlie this rule of thumb. In its simplest form, activity (involvement, choice) is believed to increase commitment to the learning structure which then leads to better learning or implementation. It may also be that to the degree that people avoid difficult or anxiety-provoking learning, active involvement and an increased sense of control over the task decreases the resistance arising from anxiety. Currently, our theories about participation appear overly simple. Only as we can begin to examine the unarticulated assumptions will we approach a more complete explanation.

Maintaining energy

One very central concern of many practitioners is often articulated in terms of managing the 'energy' of the training event. Learners are seen as needing to maintain some optimal level of arousal for effective involvement. There is, in fact, a substantial data base in social science research to support this assumption (Bruner, 1966; Knowles, 1973; Walker and McKeachie, 1967). The rules of thumb which flow from this assumption often are prescriptions about how to keep energy mobilized. According to the skill development staff: 'Energy is created by physical movement, by varying or changing the activity, by groups with new people. When the physical system is low, for example after lunch, a highly involving activity such as brainstorming should be scheduled as a re-energizer.' As a matter of fact, the practitioners in this workshop instructed their clients to monitor their energy needs, to take their own breaks, to get coffee and juice from the 'nurturance centre' whenever they needed it.

It should also be acknowledged that some of the same activities which are seen as creating energy, e.g. physical movement, new groupings, also use up energy. In other training settings we have heard assumptions about creating structures that can drain energy. For example, there is a rule of thumb that crossing too many boundaries, i.e. having to interact in too many groups of people consecutively, can be dysfunctional for effective experiential learning.

In the male-female awareness workshop the staff were also interested in the management of energy. It is their view that much of the energy for learning and change is located in one subgroup of the population (the women). Whenever this is the case, they believe, the design must energize and enable this subgroup to share their experience and to engage others. As those who are less engaged with the issues begin to understand and experience the isues with those who are more affected, the assumption is that they will become energized about their own learning. Thus energy is created from new information about the experiences of others coupled with an empathic perception of how they feel about their experience.

Maximizing sources of positive psychic income and minimizing resistance

Closely related to the prescriptions about the maintenance of energy is the notion of how to increase positive psychic income for participants. These are several examples from the skill development workshop: (1) Immediate products give people a sense of reinforcement for work accomplished. If there is a ditto machine nearby which can make results immediately available, this is useful. (2) Methods that locate and use the clients' resources and competencies are gratifying. One example would be an exchange of practices design. (3) It is useful to create occasions to celebrate achievements on the way to a longer-term goal. Thus people do not have to wait indefinitely for reinforcement when they are moving in the direction of a goal. In this way, it is what has been accomplished that is salient, not how far I have yet to go to the goal. The underlying assumption here appears to be that reinforcement (positive psychic income) helps learners sustain or stay engaged with the learners task.

Learning structures which increase resistance while at the same time moving a participant towards a change are seen by the skills development staff as ineffective. For that reason they reject problem-solving or personal change strategies where diagnostic methods focus on what is wrong, thus increasing depression, impotence, and a sense that it is hard to change anything. Rather they prefer methods that ask people to consider how they would like things to be, what positive changes would be gratifying, and what scenario of the future would be pleasing. The change images then are psychically positive.

These same principles were used by the male-female awareness staff in the pre-workshop interviews. Participants were assigned interviews with a set of heterogeneous others. Attitudes which they found in others like their own may have provided support for acknowledging their own attitudes in the workshop, while attitudes which were different from theirs could cause difficulty in believing that everyone is the way I am.

Increasing the probability of design effectiveness

As we move to this next category the principles we are working with become very specific. This category represents the lore about how to get the most out of training designs and the specifics of good designing.

Assumptions about *size of groupings* have to do with the optimal number for certain types of activities. The following are some examples from the skill development practitioners. Behavioural skill practice is best done in three-person groups. This gives plenty of time to practise and reduces anxiety about being observed. Brainstorming should be done in groups of three to eight. This permits enough air time for everyone's ideas and yet includes enough people to maximize the stimulation of creative new ideas. Groups that are going to use each other as resources to exchange ideas or practices should be from eight to 10 persons in size. Again, this balances need for air time and enough people for a good exchange.

How does a staff decide about *groupings*, for example, whether to have people work individually or in groups? When the following four conditions obtain, groups are in order: more ideas are needed, the social facilitation of others is needed (reduction of risk), the social enjoyment of others is needed, diffusion of responsibility is needed (creativity and craziness are associated).

The male-female awareness staff consider some of their assumptions about groupings crucial to understanding the effectiveness of their design. They believe that the different levels of awareness and readiness for change should be reflected in the laboratory groupings. When you provide people with an opportunity to be with others who are like them, they can strengthen their identity and receive support from that group, while in heterogeneous groupings confrontation and change may occur. Therefore in this workshop same-sex group meetings usually occurred immediately prior to mixed-sex groupings.

The decision about *what design elements flow appropriately from what* is also a category in which rules exist.

The groupings used in the male-female workshop often were assigned discussion tasks or topics. When decisions were made by the staff about what an appropriate topic would be, rules of thumb about the flow of self-disclosure emerged. In the beginning less intimate subjects were selected, e.g. how role models in your family affected your sex role image. Later the same group was asked to discuss how people in this group behaved around sex role issues. The progression was from less to more intimate subjects. The assumption is that people disclose more easily about themselves on controversial topics if they have first talked with the same group of people about more objective or less risky topics. This assumption is very congruent with much of the research about patterns of self-disclosure in our culture (Jourard, 1971; Altman and Taylor, 1974).

How should *conceptual inputs* be organized? The skill development staff believe that theory sessions are best delivered in small chunks of not more than about five minutes, followed by a chance for questions, discussion of a focused question, or reactions. This prevents too long a period of passivity and the accompanying energy loss.

Conceptual inputs occurred in many contexts in the male-female workshop. In seminars conceptual inputs were often illustrated by exercises demonstrating the substantive material. In the same-sex and mixed-sex groups, staff pointed out examples of group behaviour which illustrated concepts from theory inputs. In this workshop the emphasis appeared to be on increasing participants' ability to recognize concepts when they were occurring.

Another set of assumptions is about how to increase *transfer* from the training setting to the work setting. In a skill practice where participants were attempting to respond more effectively to a situation they identified as needing improvement, a trio first generated a list of responses which could be made and the learner wrote them all down. Then the learner selected the ones to try out in the practice session. However, the list could be taken home and reconsidered later. Thus writing down the list was a design idea that was used specifically to increase potential transfer effects.

Another version of the concern with transfer is the emphasis in planning processes on implementation decisions (Who will do it? When?). The rule is: 'If planning is to be effective, follow-up must be part of the planning process.' A similar rule is that public commitment to an action step increases the probability of change occurring. Here is an interesting example of a rule which has entered the practitioners' lore direct from social science research (Lewin, 1947).

The male-female workshops were made up of people from the same large company but no-one who worked immediately with anyone else. The staff believe that having peers from the same system, but not the same company, increases the probability of back-home transfer.

Finally a category was created for those rules which govern how-to's in *giving instructions*. For example, we are told that if a broad range of responses is legitimized by the form of an evaluation question (e.g. What were the *strengths* and *weaknesses* of this workshop?) we are more apt to receive the full range of responses including the more negative ones. Or, the more specific a task you give to a group, the higher probability that the discussion pay-off will be good. Therefore, instead of just handing people an article to read, one might ask them as they read it to select one concept to share with others, or decide what they would most like to tell someone back home about this reading.

Time allotments

Prescriptions about the use of time fill the next category. There is a lore about how much time it takes for certain types of groups to develop fully, to do certain tasks, etc. One prescription that we found in both workshops was that if you want people to do something, there must be a place for it in the official schedule. If your really want people to read, you need a scheduled reading period; if you want them to write a journal, writing and reflecting time must be planned.

Another assumption was about the amount of small group time that is necessary to build the experience base for people to engage with each other in the here and now, give feedback, etc. The male-female awareness practitioners believe that three and a half days are needed for the experience to occur fully. At the same time they hold another assumption which is somewhat contradictory. It is the inverse of the old dictum that 'work expands to fill the time allowed'. Their dictum was 'participants will reach laboratory goals in the allotted time, regardless of the amount of time'. In other words, they will manage to reach the goals in whatever time you give them. These conflicting assumptions about time point to a need to probe further the relationship between perceptions of time available and learning tasks.

Debriefing structured experiences

Since there are many simulations and exercises which have been created to help people learn experientially, it is not surprising that there are accompanying rules about the best way to structure learning from these experiences. Role-playing was a frequently used method of the skill development practitioners who have clear assumptions about how it should be debriefed. Specifically, the most involved persons (the central role players) should be allowed to discuss their feelings and reactions first, before any observers make comments. This will maintain the perspective of the role players uninfluenced by observers' comments and allow the most affectively involved to make the needed transition from intensive participation to active conceptualization. Subsequently, less affected participants can contribute their reactions and insights.

Sources of design assumptions

In considering this collection of practitioner assumptions, it is difficult to resist speculation about how they developed and where they came from. Some ideas have moved into the practitioner's lore directly from social science research. An example which emerged with the practitioners was the rule about the importance of public commitment in change processes. Lewin's early experiments made this point clear. It is not surprising that it has become accepted as a generally true principle. In the same way Bunker and Knowles' (1965) study of T-group effectiveness produced evidence that the amount of transfer from experiential laboratories was a monotonic function of the amount of laboratory time given to back-home consideration. On many occasions trainers have been heard invoking this principle without, of course, referencing the original source.

A second source of design principles is experience. Initially it is the experience of others. I well remember as a young trainer listening with great attention to the pronouncements of the established members of the field that 'we need to schedule at least 15 hours of T-group time if we expect these groups to develop adequately in this lab'. Having no experience of my own, I incorporated these rules as a substitute for my own experience. Gradually as experience grows practitioners develop their own prescriptions. The understandings collected about how to design and intervene in the sensitive area of male-female awareness were developed as these practitioners designed and ran dozens of workshops. The previously mentioned 'raggedy start-up' was the solution to a training dilemma: waiting for people to arrive and watching those who came promptly sit and lose energy.

A third and perhaps the most interesting source of assumptions comes from a general concern with what makes experiential learning effective. Many assumptions concern the state of the participant: the amount of resistance or defensiveness, the energy level, the psychic income. It is as if there is truly an optimal state which, if reached, will permit the participant to engage the learning available. This implicit learning theory has been translated by some into a set of strongly held espoused values. They are often heard in this form:

'Participants must be responsible for their own learning.' 'We always start where the client is.' When they take a value form as contrasted with an hypothesis, the potential for a discrepancy between espoused theory and theory-in-use increases. It is not uncommon to run across those who espouse the doctrine of participant responsibility, but plan and run sessions that make it difficult to be responsible for one's own learning. Creating a learning structure which enables participants to feel in charge and energized about their learning is a complex art. It cannot be equated with any single set of variables, for example the amount of participant design choice. It requires practitioners who are clear about and capable of using their expertise in design and intervention skills. Perhaps the strong value stance so frequently heard is really an attempt to achieve a security which cannot yet be provided by a clear theory of experiential learning. The current state of the art is that the phenomena are complex, the theory is not clear, and practitioners make many decisions by rule of thumb or intuitively. This leaves them in the difficult situation of uncertainty about what works.

FINDINGS: PRINCIPLES OF INTERVENTION

When the staff have decided upon and organized the learning structures (design), there still remain the issues of effective implementation. What roles shall the staff take? What relationship shall they establish with the client system? What effects do they wish to have on the processes which occur during the workshop? We have organized the data that address these questions as principles of *intervention*. Interventions are those acts of the staff (verbal and behavioural) which effect, direct, and change the processes that are occurring in the designed structure. They are intentional acts aimed at increasing learning effectiveness. They occur in small groups, in interpersonal relationships, and in the total workshop community.

Work has been done by Cohen and Smith (1976) on how to select an intervention. They propose that the important factors controlling the selection of interventions are: the level (individual, group, etc.), the desired intensity, and the type (experiential, conceptual, structural). Their work is, however, mainly aimed at intervention into the processes of small groups. The concern of this section is far broader; it is for intervention at any level of workshop functioning. The principles of intervention which were collected are organized into the types of intervention roles that staff might take in any experiential learning event. Table 2 presents the six roles which are the organizing principles of our current work.

Teacher-Guide

When staff intervene as teachers they usually give concepts, bring in material from outside sources, point out how concepts are being embodied in current

Table 2   Intervention roles of staff in experiential learning events

(1) Teacher-guide.
(2) Director of design events or exploration, design manager.
(3) Process intervener.
(4) Blockage identifier.
(5) Norm sender, reinforcer, or shaper.
(6) Role model for participants (model member).

laboratory processes. An intervention that occurred often in the male-female awareness groups was staff taking what had just happened in the group and pointing out how it illustrated a concept or idea already presented. When men in a mixed-sex group, for example, took the lead in intiating most of the discussions, it might be pointed out as the traditional male sex role pattern.

A principle about how to use teaching interventions was also proposed. When a diagnostic concept which describes group members' behaviour is given, it is effective to suggest an action step that could be taken if they wished to try new behaviours rather than simply leaving them with the diagnosis. For example, if the group process is that women who take initiatives are not supported by others and their contributions are ignored, an action step might be to experiment with supporting women's ideas even if you do not agree with them, in order to get them discussed.

A different way of teaching involves the art of using what *is* happening to let the group know what *could be* happening. In one group a participant made a really significant and rather risky disclosure. There were no direct supportive responses, and the next speaker referred to the disclosure but went off on quite another tack. Rather than let that process go unnoticed, the practitioner turned to the second speaker and said with quiet humour. 'Well, I'd say you get five points for support but none for relevance'. The group laughed and began to interact with the risky discloser.

In the male-female awareness workshop, staff intend to develop a particular kind of expert-learner collaboration to assist the developing awareness of participants. They believe that learners need to choose how far they wish to go in the development of their own awareness. The staff role is to provide resources, to offer to point out areas of unawareness, to provide some sense of security, to protect those who choose not to explore, and to support whatever is selected by participants for their own study. This is a more clinical model of the staff role than the one adopted by the skills development staff.

The skills development staff did some of their teaching in a daily analysis of the workshop design. As they reviewed each exercise, event, or process, they pointed out how it could be used in the work settings of the participants. They believe that increasing awareness of workshop processes will increase the potential transfer of the training.

Director of design events

Since much of the work was done in small groups in the awareness workshop, the prescriptions about process management (sometimes referred to as 'traffic directing') had more to do with the small group than with the larger design. One rule of thumb which was found in both settings is: when there are several competing agendas, the leader should help the group select the one where there is the most group energy. Another was that if a group member disrupts an ongoing process because of, or as a way of managing, personal anxiety about that process, the trainer may intervene to support the group continuing to work and not permit the member to distract it.

Not surprisingly, the skill development staff had many assumptions about the staff role as managers of the design. One of the most interesting was a set of rules about how to relate to subgroupings in a design where there are not enough staff for each group to have a staff person. They see four role choices: (1) leave the groups alone; (2) observe them, listen in while floating around; (3) float, listen, and participate where it seems appropriate, e.g. clarify the task if there is confusion; (4) join a group and stay with it as a staff contributor. There were specific assumptions about what the appropriate role is, depending on how far into the workshop one is. At the beginning, small groups should be left alone to get themselves together. Staff presence may bring out dependency and the need for direction and evaluation ('Are we doing it right?'). If there are not enough staff to be present all the time, groups need to develop a sense that they can operate alone. After the start-up, however, session leaders should actively listen so they can know what is going on. Once established, groups will be able to tolerate this without being disrupted. In the next phase, staff will be able to move in and out, contributing and clarifying, without the expectation that they will remain with any one group.

Another interesting prescription concerns the effective management of large groups by a small staff. When instructions are given, for example, the task will go more smoothly if people anticipate the problems they may have. Thus in brainstorming, directions like, 'If you get tired of recording, hand the pen to someone else', or 'Don't worry about spelling', or 'Don't be afraid of the silences, someone usually thinks of something really creative, so enjoy them', all help the process by helping people cope with the stumbling blocks. (They also reduce the possibility that these problems get used in the service of task resistance.)

Another rule of thumb is the three-minute warning or pre-transition signal. When working in small subgroups, there are always transition points to new tasks, groupings, etc. The rule is that people need some warning ahead of these transition times to wind up and get closure on the situation they are in, so that they are psychologically ready to move on.

Finally, the way the staff give direction, especially in workshops which involve moving large numbers of persons, has important effects on the learning climate. When people are invited to join groups rather than told to do it 'army fashion', the climate is more collaborative. If they are to use the learning environment well, people need support, to be listened to; not to be ordered about, punished, or ignored.

Process intervener

A number of these rules of thumb might also be considered process interventions in that they affect the processes of the group or workshop. In our scheme, however, we shall use this term somewhat more narrowly. Specifically, the process intervener helps participants look at the experience they are creating, the data they have generated, so that they may learn more from it. For example, if in the male-female awareness workshop the group members are talking about an issue in the 'there and then' and the trainer believes that these same issues are present among the members, a comment suggesting that the group may want to look at the same issues 'in this group' is a process intervention. Another type might occur when someone dramatizes a feeling in a way that overlooks contrary evidence within the group. An effective process intervention here would be to point out the data that contradict the assertion.

The practitioner pays attention to the whole group process. If a subset of the group is discussing an issue of high interest, the trainer may check in with the less verbally involved so that they do not become disengaged. This in turn heightens the whole group's awareness of involvement dilemmas.

Another form of intervention that helps the group stay with its own data may occur near the end of a group when there is a strong pull to evaluate the experience. If the discussion is global the trainer may ask people to be very specific and concrete about 'this particular group and the people in it'. The implicit assumption here is that global evaluations which occur towards the end of training events often arise from the group's need for closure and a positive termination. Continued learning can be encouraged by a realistic appraisal of what did and did not happen to individual participants. It also leaves the learning system realistically thinking about next steps rather than relaxing in the warmth of good feelings.

Blockage identifier

When processes that impede learning occur out of the awareness of participants, it falls to the staff to clarify what is happening. In this sense, identifying blockages is a specific form of process intervention. One example regularly occurred in the mixed-sex groups whose task was to become more aware of processes between men and women. When a subset of the group was actively disclosing, the rest of the group stopped listening to the disclosure, labelling it 'insignificant?' The staff clarified what was occurring so that the disclosing subset was not discouraged about trying to communicate and others became more aware of the impact of their inattention.

Another form of blockage is the group collusion. For example, if the whole group is behaving as though it is impossible to bring women into certain roles or into particular units of the company, the trainer might ask 'Why don't you bring in six women?'. In other words, if there were a critical mass, not just a token, would we still be assuming 'It can't be done', or 'It won't work', rather than 'How can we make it work?'.

Norm sender, reinforcer, or shaper

An important way that staff work with groups is to send reinforcing messages about certain behaviours, sanctioning messages about others, and shaping messages about still others. These messages are read by participants and shape the norms of acceptable behaviour in training groups. Reinforcing messages occur regularly when staff approve, point out the value of, or simply repeat a participant behaviour. In the awareness workshop the staff wanted to encourage people to respond to each other's contributions. If there was no response, a trainer might say 'Are you alone in this? Does anyone else feel this way?' to the whole group, thus eliciting responses and responding herself. If there was a response the trainer might immediately point out how helpful it had been to hear from another person, sending a reinforcing message to the responder and a normative message to the entire group. A prescription we found in the awareness workshop is that it is very important to reward all efforts to express awareness, not just the ones which are congruent with staff views. In this way the leadership supports the norm that all attitudes are available for awareness and exploration.

We saw negative reinforcement occurring when members tried to force change on each other. The staff intervened quickly if an exploration of a particular issue turned into a session where many doctors tried to cure 'the patient'. The staff might point out the pressure the person was being subjected to or they might agree with the 'patient's' hesitancy about continuing the discussion. At whatever level they intervened, the message was that pressuring others to change will be challenged by the staff.

Shaping messages were sent about the exploration of male-female issues. A rule of thumb in use in the awareness workshop was: whenever people risk and move to explore a new issue, the leader can be very supportive and interested in that contribution, call attention to it, and help the contributor explore it. Shaping differs from reinforcement in that the staff actively help, suggest effective steps, react to behaviour rather than simply endorsing it. The staff of the male-female workshop used this type of intervention a great deal in support of the overall design.

There also was evidence of *norm sending* behaviour in the skills workshop staff. If participants opted out of an event, the staff did nothing to try to legislate attendance. They might physically be available but no move was made to enforce participation. This was seen as a way of ensuring that the message about participant responsibility for own learning was clear.

Sometimes social processes which are negatively valued in the general culture are studied, e.g. conflict. Here in particular, norm sending behaviours may help participants' willingness to work with these processes and then make their own judgements about whether the cultural values are correct.

Role models for participants

Anything the staff do can be an intervention if participants use it as a model for their own behaviour. The skill development practitioners believe that participants will mirror staff energy; if the staff 'run down' so will the participants. Therefore the staff need to be energetic.

A different kind of modelling occurs when the staff intervene to demonstrate how something should be done. This staff often demonstrated the role-playing that they were asking groups to do in order to clarify the procedure and demonstrate that the staff are willing to participate, to be vulnerable.

REVIEW AND DISCUSSION

The purpose of the work to date has been to study practitioners in their natural settings, to explore the notion that there is an as-yet unorganized but nonetheless existing espoused theory of practice of experiential learning in the minds of practitioners. This chapter has proposed a framework for organizing the guiding assumptions of these practitioners and has presented a full set of assumptions as examples from the work of several of the most experienced professionals in the field.

Any review of what we have been able to do in developing a theory of practice quickly turns up a number of issues. First, it is clear that the organizing categories in both the design and the intervention sections are not necessarily discrete. The reader may have wondered from time to time why a particular rule of thumb was in one category rather than another. In some cases the categories fit well and are discrete. In others it is apparent that the prescribed actions do several things at once. For example, reviewing the design activities is probably both a teaching intervention and a process intervention. These categories, therefore, can only serve as a preliminary form of organization.

Second, the rules of thumb and assumptions used by these practitioners sometimes contradict each other. In several cases where we examined the contradictions, it appears that the problem occurs especially where the principle is global. What is needed is a more careful examination of the limiting conditions in order to develop more specific rules of thumb. Many of the espoused principles which appear correct in the circumstances in which they were collected might be altered for other situations.

An even more productive method of dealing with contradictions among assumptions may be to identify underlying themes which occur across categories. When we look, for example, at intervention assumptions now organized around practitioner roles, there appear to be several underlying themes running through them. One has to do with how the staff handle their own expertise effectively.

Managing expertise is important because its overuse creates a dependency that interferes with participants' felt responsibility for their own learning and thus reduces the effectiveness of individual learning. The underlying assumption is that some forms of dependency are dysfunctional, while appropriate forms are useful. This is a complex issue that involves how individuals manage their relationships with authority figures. Clearly the staff are authorities and an effective learning system helps people relate to expertise without denying their own resources. For this reason these staff made an effort to help learners be clear when the resources for a learning event were in other participants and when they were in the staff. A collusive process that sees all of the resources as in the staff seldom results in maximally effective learning.

What are the areas of staff expertise? One clearly is in the skills of design. In no case in these workshops was collaboration with participants taken to include asking them to design. (It is, of course, conceivable that if the workshop objectives were to teach design skills, participants would be involved in designing with the staff.) Another area of expertise is in how to learn from the data produced in the workshop. A third is in certain substantive areas where the staff have knowledge or awareness not available to participants. It appears then that organizing the several principles collected that have to do with effectively managing the expert-learner relationship is a potentially interesting alternative formulation of the framework.

Another theme that underlies a number of the intervention categories is the building or shaping of a learning climate that enables people to comfortably do what may be uncomfortable. When people are encouraged to learn they may try out new behaviours at either skill or awareness levels that, like any new experience, may make them feel awkward, anxious, etc. Therefore a number of rules of thumb concern support, responsiveness to others, creating a feeling of security and protection that permits people to risk. These assumptions concerning the learning climate could also be part of a possible alternative formulation developed from underlying themes.

This is a somewhat lengthy way of acknowledging that the current framework, while useful as a first approximation, should not be codified. It is a good descriptive organization for these workshop events, but there are significant omissions. For example, it does not deal with questions such as 'What controls the intensity of an intervention?', 'How can a practitioner avoid being either too obvious or too threatening in what he calls attention to?', 'How are decisions made about level of intervention?'.

In short, our framework is an important and useful first step which requires more study if we are to develop the theory fully. Future work can go on at several levels. First, more data collection of assumptions is needed, and empirical work to demonstrate the generality of the various assumptions would be helpful. Second, when the theoretical framework is more secure, we need to look at the actual behaviour of practitioners and compare their espoused theories with what they in fact do. Finally, in a much later stage, it is hoped that the causal links between practitioner behaviour and participant learning can be specified and tested so that our understanding of this most compelling but complex set of processes will be clarified.

REFERENCES

Altman, I. and Taylor, D. A. (1974) *Social Penetration: The Development of Interpersonal Relationships*. New York: Holt, Rinehart & Winston.

Argyris, C. and Schön, D. A. (1976) *Theory in Practice*. San Francisco: Jossey-Bass.

Back, K. W. (1973) *Beyond Words*. Baltimore, Md.: Penguin.

Benne, K. D., Bradford, L. P., Gibb, J. R. and Lippitt, R. (eds.) (1975) *The Laboratory Method of Changing and Learning*. Palo Alto, Cal.: Science and Behaviour Books.

Bennis, W. G., Benne, K. D. and Chin, R. (1969) *The Planning of Change*. 2nd Edition. New York: Holt-Rinehart.

Bradford, L. P., Gibb, J. R. and Benne, K. D. (1964) *T-Group Theory and Laboratory Method*. New York: Wiley.

Bruner, J. S. (1966) *Toward a Theory of Instruction*. Cambridge, Mass.: Belknap-Harvard.

Bunker, B. B., Bender, B., English, L. D., Solomon, J. L. and Exiner, H. (1977) 'A study of two components of experiential learning', Mimeograph.

Bunker, B. B. and Solomon, J. L. (1978) 'A framework for choosing or creating experiential learning exercises', Mimeograph.

Bunker, D. R. (1974) 'Social process awareness training'. In Milman, D. S. and Goldman, G. D. (eds.) *Group Process Today*. Springfield, Ill.: Thomas, pp.51-62.

Bunker, D. R. and Knowles, E. S. (1965) 'Comparison of behavioural changes resulting from human relations training laboratories of different lengths', *Journal of Applied Behavioural Science*, 3, 505-523.

Cohen, A. M. and Smith, R. D. (1976) *The Critical Incident in Growth Groups: Theory and Technique*. La Jolla, Cal.: University Associates.

Golembiewski, R. T. (1973) *Sensitivity Training and the Laboratory Approach*, 2nd Edition. Itasca, Ill.: Peacock.

Jourard, S. M. (1971) *Self-Disclosure*. New York: Wiley.

Kaplan, A. (1964) *The Conduct of Inquiry*. San Francisco, Cal.: Chandler.

Knowles, M. (1973) *The Adult Learner: A Neglected Species*. Houston: Gulf.

Lennung, S. (1978) 'A classification of experiential social process: A European perspective'. In Alderfer, C. P. and Cooper, C. L. (eds.) *Advances in Experiential Social Processes*, Vol. 1. London: Wiley.

Lewin, K. (1974) 'Group decision and social change'. In Newcomb, T. and Hartley, E. (eds.) *Readings in Social Psychology*. New York: Holt, pp. 330-44.

Pfeiffer, J. W. and Jones, J. J. (1977) *Reference Guide to Handbooks and Annuals,* 2nd Edition. La Jolla, Cal.: University Associates.

Schein, E. H. and Bennis, W. G. (1965) *Personal and Organizational Change Through Group Methods: The Laboratory Approach*. New York: Wiley.

Walker, E. L. and McKeachie, W. J. (1967) *Some Thoughts About Teaching the Beginning Course in Psychology*. Belmont, Cal.: Brooks/Cole.

Advances in Experiential Social Processes, Volume 2
Edited by C. P. Alderfer and C. L. Cooper
© 1980 John Wiley & Sons, Ltd.

Chapter **6**

Developing Clinical Field Skills:
An Apprenticeship Model

David N. Berg

Yale School of Organization and Management, U.S.A.

INTRODUCTION

A developing profession must struggle with the task of designing and implementing its own training programme. Without the transmission of knowledge, skill, and values across generations there would be no profession, for the term implies the accumulation of knowledge and skill that is conveyed to each member of the profession as the basis for competent practice. As a result, it is imperative that professions find ways to provide entering members with the requisite skills and values and to update established members on the rapidly changing aspects of the field. Particularly for a fledgling profession, however, the development of a training programme is often a difficult process. The difficulties are rooted in the differing opinions and beliefs concerning the substance and method of the training programme. The very nature of a new professional enterprise means that theory and technique are still being developed, tested, and revised. At best one can make only provisional commitments to both theory and practice. In spite of this 'provisional' atmosphere, the profession must make some difficult choices that define the knowledge, skills, and values necessary for professional work. An inability or refusal to do this can result in the death of the profession itself.

Applied social scientists in the field of organizational behaviour are in the midst of this process. Organizational behaviour practitioners (those field researchers, consultants, in-house OD specialists and consultants/researchers who attempt to use the theories and concepts of applied behaviour science to guide and inform their professional activities) are a new breed of professional. They are struggling with a variety of professional needs (information networks, accreditation procedures, continuing education programmes, professional authority structures) including the need for competent professional training programmes. Currently these training programmes are designed and administered by universities, training organizations, corporations, and individuals, and there is little coordination. As a result, the following questions are seldom posed, discussed or answered. What should be the content of a professional training programme in organizational behaviour? How much standardization should there be and in what areas or methods? Is there a theory of professional education in the field of OB? How much fieldwork, course work, and supervision should be involved?

This chapter offers answers to some of these questions in an attempt to stimulate discussion within the profession on the topic of professional training programmes. The first section states and defends the contention that clinical fieldwork is an important professional activity for all OB practitioners and that the skills required to carry out competent fieldwork should be core elements in OB training programmes. The second section describes a conceptual framework for understanding basic clinical field skills, and the final section proposes a model for the development of clinical field skills that is based on this conceptual framework.

THE NEED FOR CLINICAL FIELD SKILLS

Clinical field skills refer to a set of skills required when one is involved in direct observation, interaction, and/or intervention in a human system. These skills are not important if one is a theoretical mathematician or a concert pianist, but they are crucial if the success of one's work depends on the quality of one's relationships with the members of a human organization. Academic researchers, organization development practitioners, and other 'interventionists' with a variety of orientations and backgrounds all depend on their relationships with others in doing their work. This 'dependency' is usually complex. The OB practitioner depends on *people* for information about the organization or for their participation in specific activities. Researchers and consultants may depend on their *relationship* with the system to alert them to important events, critical decisions, and sensitive issues that arise. Relationships with system members can provide practitioners with feedback about the nature of the client/practitioner partnership (e.g. Do people mistrust the OB practitioners? Are there significant disagreements, conflicts or strong emotions influencing the client/practitioner activities?). Clinical field skills provide the OB practitioner with the expertise to manage this 'dependency' in the service of the mutual goals of the client and the practitioner.

It is therefore not controversial to suggest that all OB practitioners whose professional work includes fieldwork (clinical activity of any kind) should receive training in clinical field skills. More controversial is the contention that clinical fieldwork plays such an important role in the professional lives of most OB practitioners that *all* should receive training in this area. Without clinical field skills the quality of professional work in OB is seriously compromised. In order to examine this contention we will consider two cases, the academic researcher in organizational behaviour and the internal organization development (OD) consultant. An analysis of these two types of OB practitioners illustrates the central role of 'clinical activities' in the work of two very different organizational behaviour professionals (Alderfer and Berg, 1977).

Academic researchers

Academic researchers in the area of organizational behaviour are constantly concerned with at least two extremely important issues. First, how to 'keep in touch' with the phenomena they study, thereby ensuring that their theories are related to practical issues. And second, how to make sure that their theory-building is based on data that are both valid and collected in an ethical, non-expliotative way. Failure to resolve the first issue can lead to the development of a conceptual base for the profession that is estranged from the realities of organizational life. Failure to resolve the second can result in the development of theories that are contaminated by invalid data (the product of mistrust, deception or incompetence) or by a polluted pool of 'subjects', i.e. organizations whose previous experience with researchers has been exploitative and unethical. Consideration of these concerns leads to the conclusion that OB researchers must spend time doing 'fieldwork' and must learn to do this work competently and ethically. Only by doing research in organizations can researchers stay in touch with organizational behaviour and ensure that their theories and concept are anchored in the realities they purport to understand. Only be developing the field skills necessary for collecting valid data in ethical ways can researchers hope to translate their field experience into meaningful theories of organizational behaviour.

In spite of this apparent centrality of fieldwork in OB research, there are many powerful influences on academic researchers to keep them out of organizations and away from fieldwork. Specialization is one such influence. As the field of organizational behaviour becomes more complex and more differentiated, the individual researcher feels increasing pressure to specialize in order to be able to master a manageable intellectual domain. More and more of these 'areas of specialization' involve little or no direct contact with living systems (e.g. survey research, multivariate statistical techniques). In some universities it is entirely possible to complete a doctorate without seriously pursuing any fieldwork at all. While some may argue that this is a desirable state of affairs, it creates a 'class' of professionals in organizational behaviour who are simultaneously unable to do primary research in ongoing organizations and unable to work with organizations in the utilization of scientific knowledge.

Another factor that discourages OB practitioners and students from doing fieldwork and learning the skills necessary to do it completely is the lack of quality training experiences. While statistics, multivariate analysis, and research methods are *all* required areas of expertise in most Ph.D. programmes (and they should be), it is the rare programme that requires (and hence puts resources into) the development of expertise in the field skills necessary to do field research. As a result, high-quality training experiences are hard to find and the process of comparison, evaluation, and cross-fertilization across university programmes is woefully inadequate.

A third factor which similarly discourages the development of field skills is the personal self-scrutiny that is a necessary part of such programmes. In order to understand and manage field relationships, the OB practitioner has to understand what he or she brings to these relationships (values, biases, idiosyncracies, personal characteristics and proclivities, etc.). This is often a difficult and uncomfortable undertaking and one that we are reticent to *require* of professionals in organizational behaviour. We collude with students' unwillingness to examine themselves by labelling self-scrutiny experiences (and training) as 'optional' or 'not necessary'.

Finally, some argue that the field of organizational behaviour already has more than enough unanalyzed data and that the goal for the immediate future should be more thorough and rigorous data analysis. While this statement is undoubtedly true from the perspective of the number of variables and cases in data banks around the world, it is equally true that the absence of competent field skills in many organizational research projects raises serious questions about the advisability of devoting more time, money, and effort to future secondary analyses.

In summary, competent fieldwork can (1) decrease measurement problems and invalidity that arises from mistrustful or suspicious client-researcher relationships, (2) increase the researcher's sensitivity to the *dynamic* nature of organizations, (3) increase the number and quality of exploratory studies, a research component particularly important in a relatively new field, (4) increase the information available to the researcher during the *interpretation* phase of even highly structured research activities (how does one interpret a 'factor' or a 'cluster' without clinical field experience?), and (5) increase the role of the human brain in understanding and conceptualizing the complex nature of human organization.

An analogy with a medical researcher may serve to illustrate the dangers of having a trained OB researcher/practitioner who has few 'clinical field skills'. In medicine, the doctor is trained to collect 'clinical' data during patient interviews and examinations. He or she is also trained to use and rely on this information to augment and inform the numerous test data which can also be collected. But gathering 'clinical' information is difficult. It involves knowing what to ask about and what to look for as well as how to get the patient involved in the diagnosis itself, including the disclosure and the description. Especially with new or rare problems or diseases, this 'clinical' information is crucial for an accurate and useful diagnosis. Like the academic researcher, the medical researcher must collect this 'clinical' information if he or she is to understand and diagnose the situation.

Internal OD consultants

Internal OD consultants depend heavily on their relationships with organizational members for information. They strive to initiate and maintain relationships that are trustful and non-exploitative in the interest of valid information exchange and joint problem-solving. But the internal OD practitioner is less concerned about 'keeping in touch' with organizational life than about being able to understand and learn from the constant contact that is part of the job. The issue for the internal OD practitioner is how to conceptualize his or her experience in a way that guides and improves future actions and decisions. The critical 'field skills' for these OB practitioners involve the conceptualization of field experiences and the ability to step back from ongoing experience and search for patterns and relationships among events; a basic and critical field skill.

As with the academic researcher, there are strong pressures operating on internal OD consultants that make it difficult to develop these field skills. As in academe, there are pressures towards specialization. Becoming an expert in one technique or one approach to organization or human development is often the road to high visibility and promotion. Distinguishing oneself may require linking one's name with a specific technology or service. Organizational life also brings with it the realities of a strict hierarchy. Internal OD consultants sometimes feel immense pressure to use the 'theories' already subscribed to rather than those that might emerge from their own experience. In addition, the organization's 'fast track' may be reserved for employees who demonstrate quick successes. Developing meaningful concepts and theories requires time for reflection and opportunities for repeated experimentation and observation. The internal OD consultant who chooses this path may be jeopardizing his or her career in the organization. Finally, there is the shortage of quality training programmes for these OB practitioners, too, particularly programmes that benefit from a dialogue with the academic side of the profession. At best, internal OD consultants can attend evening courses and summer workshops or 'labs'. Although these programmes can be of considerable value, they cannot provide the kind of comprehensive training available for people who can devote themselves to full-time education.

The professionalism of these particular OB practitioners depends on their ability to augment their knowledge and skill by developing concepts and theories from their own experience. If they merely apply the techniques and theories of others they run the serious risk of misapplying them, or worse, of prescribing a cure that is in their kit rather than one that fits the disease.

To return to our medical analogy, the internal OD consultant *without* clinical field skills is like a general practitioner (MD) during a patient examination who cannot ask the right questions and who searches for indications of diseases that he or she is familiar with while missing symptoms or patterns of symptoms that, although readily observable, are outside his or her area of expertise.

CLINICAL FIELD SKILLS: A DESCRIPTION AND CONCEPTUALIZATION

Clinical field skills enable OB practitioners to establish, manage, and learn from relationships with human organizations. Whether these relationships centre on research or on intervention, the skills required are very similar. They include at least three major areas of emphasis: (1) personal/emotional skills (i.e. understanding and managing the personal factors that constantly exert an influence over one's relationships with client systems); (2) relationship management skills (i.e. understanding and managing complex relationships with individuals, groups, and larger social systems during research or consultation); and (3) diagnostic skills (i.e. collecting data and drawing inferences from data while directly involved with an organization). The following paragraphs describe each of these sets of skills in more detail.

Personal/emotional

Personal/emotional skills refer to the ability to analyse and understand one's own behaviour; to struggle with a constantly changing and developing identity that includes both professional and personal elements; to learn from mistakes and failures as well as from achievements and successes; to confront one's own strengths and weaknesses, ambitions and fears, emotional and intellectual character. Among the most important emotional skills is the ability to live with ambiguity and anxiety (Wells, 1979). In doing fieldwork, the OB practitioner is constantly faced with ambiguous and uncomfortable situations and choices. Stepping into the field means surrendering control, and with this diminished control comes increased uncertainty. A practitioner who cannot tolerate either ambiguity or anxiety is forced to make decisions based on his or her own internal dynamics rather than on those of the client system. An ability to live with these emotions and others like them is an important field skill. Without such skills, the OB practitioner cannot begin to understand what needs and values or she brings to a professional relationship. A lack of personal self-awareness necessarily obscures one's insight into the needs, values, and actions of others.

Personal/emotional skills are constantly in use in the case of the competent OB practitioner working in the field. With each new situation, each success or failure, each interview and project, one has the opportunity to learn more about oneself. Capitalizing on these opportunities allows the practitioner to refine his or her theories and practice. In addition, the 'steady diet' of self-scrutiny provided by the OB practitioner's work also invites personal growth and development, a process that inevitably enhances professional life.

Relationship management

Managing field relationships competently is the second major category of clinical field skills. A mismanaged relationship can be more destructive than no relationship at all. A mistrustful client/practitioner relationship can distort information and sabotage well-intentioned actions by either or both parties thereby adversely affecting either the organization and its members or the validity of social science knowledge and the effectiveness of those who use it. The following paragraphs describe four types of relationship management skills: interpersonal, intra group, intergroup, and project level skills.

Interpersonal

Clinical fieldwork is defined by direct contact with others. Often the OB practitioner seeks to establish a trusting, mutual relationship with system members in which the information and skills of each can be used in the service of the primary task that brings them together. These relationships are often characterized by complex emotional dynamics rooted in the interaction of professional and client.

Managing these emotional dynamics so as to ensure that the professional services provided meet the needs of both the client and the practitioner is a crucial field skill. For example, the OB practitioner viewed as an expert may elicit deferential, dependent responses from organization members, responses that can minimize the value of interaction for both parties. What should he or she do? Implicit in most relationships are questions of hidden agendas, sexual attraction, and trustworthiness. For many OB practitioners an uncomfortableness with conflict, or a projection of the uncomfortableness onto system members, prohibits the exploration of sensitive or difficult issues that should be explored if the practitioner/client relationship is to bear fruit. In all of these interpersonal interactions the OB practitioner is faced with managing complex emotional dynamics in which he or she plays an active part.

Consider as a final illustration of the difficult interpersonal situations that the OB practitioner often encounters the classic case of the data collection interview that transforms itself into a psychotherapy hour. The respondent decides to open up to an 'apparently' trustworthy outsider and the

OB practitioner not wanting to jeopardize the open, honest, relationship with a system member, does not intervene. This unsettled situation, which meets neither an individual's need for professional assistance/reactions/guidance nor the practitioner's need to provide professional service requires that the OB practitioner be trained to manage such situations in ways that meet rather than frustrate both parties needs.

Intragroup

It has long been accepted that group skills are an important ingredient in training OB practitioners who do work in the field. Understanding and being able to manage group processes is one of the foundations of competent behavioural science work in organizations (see Schein and Bennis, 1965; Bradford, Gibb, and Benne, 1964). Specifically, managing authority relations in groups in which the OB practitioner is a member, and understanding these issues in the groups that one observes is crucial to accomplishing research or consultative objectives. Similarly, issues of power, communication, participation, scapegoating, and the dynamics of splitting and projective identification (see Wells's chapter in this volume) are easily ignored or mismanaged to the detriment of the work at hand.

Once again, consider the case of the OB practitioner at an introductory meeting with an organizational group where he or she is explaining the rationale and goals of a particular activity (research or consultation). In response to a call for questions he or she receives silence except for murmurings of 'sounds OK' and a few nodding heads. What should be done? Now suppose one young man asks a confronting question and is reassured by the supervisor at the meeting. What should be done at this point? Although many of us may know the answers *now*, we probably did not the first time and we probably learned the hard way.

Intergroup

Managing intergroup relations in a field setting is an immensely difficult and hazardous undertaking (Lewicki and Alderfer, 1973; Berg, 1977) and perhaps the most important. The politics of organizational life often refer to the power relations among organizational groups: labour/management, line/staff, production/marketing, men/women, black/white, etc. Intergroup relations are characterized by their own unique dynamics (Coser, 1956; Sherif, 1962; Blake and Mouton, 1962; Alderfer, 1977a). Intergroup conflict and the dynamics of ethnocentrism can embroil the OB practitioner as he or she begins work (Berg, 1977), in the middle of his or her professional activities (Argyris, 1958), or at the end of a project (Walton, 1975). The OB practitioner's affiliation or identification with one or a number of groups brings with it the attributions of outgroups members (usually negative), and an unwitting involvement with a group that is in conflict with other groups can foredoom any effective professional activity. Low trust, resentment, and restricted information flow are the consequences of mismanaged intergroup relations.

As an example of the complex intergroup events the OB practitioner might be called upon to manage, take the case of the external researcher who proceeds with a top-down entry process only to discover that the top of the organization is heavily populated by family members and the bottom of the organization is non-family personnel. An understanding of intergroup relations might have alerted the OB practitioner to the hostility and rejection he or she later experiences, and some experience in managing intergroup relations [e.g. establishing and developing a liaison system (Alderfer, 1977b)] might have enabled him or her to establish a relationship with the entire organization from the outset of the project.

In this case, as in the other two, relationship management skills involve both intellectual understanding and the practical experience of applying this understanding. In all three cases, neither understanding nor uninformed experience alone would have been sufficient to productively initiate and sustain important organizational relationships.

Project

Finally, the OB practitioner must learn a set of skills related to managing a project or programme in an organization. These skills include negotiating entry, developing a 'contract' that outlines the needs and responsibilities of all the parties involved, establishing and maintaining confidentiality, managing relationships with the organizational authority structure, and developing ethical guidelines for the feedback, future use, and (where applicable) publication of information gathered during the practitioner's work.

Diagnostic

One of the OB practitioner's primary tasks in a field setting is to produce an accurate *diagnosis* of system dynamics. This system diagnosis can serve as the basis for theory construction (as in the case of the academic researcher) or for intervention activities grounded in existing theories (as in the case of the OD consultant). Arriving at an accurate diagnosis of a human system with which one has direct and ongoing contact requires diagnostic skills. Unlike the laboratory where one is able to control and specify the variables and hypotheses under examination or the computer terminal where one can restrict oneself to a specific date set, the fieldworker must learn how to 'diagnose' a system in which he or she is an actor (Mills, 1976; Mann , 1974).

Although there is no clear line between data collection and conceptualization activities, there are skills that fit more easily into one or the other category. As with all clinical work, the sequence of data collection followed by conceptualization is an iterative one; data influence concept and theory-building, which in turn direct the search for new data to refine one's conceptual understanding, and so on. An *accurate* understanding depends on this iterative process and on the skills that enable OB practitioners to carry it out (Alderfer, 1979).

When the OB practitioner is in direct contact with the organization, data collection skills include (1) mastering a wide variety of clinical data collection techniques, (2) learning how to make choices about what data to collect (from among the uncountable pieces of information available each hour), and (3) learning how to counteract one's own inclination to impose order on unfamiliar events and situations as quickly as possible.

Data collection techniques for fieldwork are an established part of the literature of organizational behaviour, but fewer and fewer OB practitioners actually receive training in participant observation, interview design and conduct, unobtrusive data collection, sociometric data collection techniques, structured observations, effective 'field note' technique, the pros and cons of organizational informants, organization-specific questionnaire design, group interviewing, liaison systems, etc. (McCall and Simmons, 1969). Each of these techniques has been designed to contribute (in specified circumstances) to a researcher's or practitioner's understanding of a social system. They are the clinical field skills that enable the OB practitioner to choose the right 'tool' for the specific organization.

Another important part of the data collection process is knowing what to look for and how to make choices about the use of one's time and energy. Direct contact with a human system can be energizing but it can also be overwhelming. Once the OB practitioner is overwhelmed he or she can easily lose energy, perspective, and the ability to function effectively. Overwhelmed, the clinically untrained might (1) retreat into a defensive posture that could seriously compromise the 'examination' or (2) rely on the security of a diagnosis conceived and constructed outside the client system or (worse yet) in flight from it. Organizing a field project so as to guard against these hazards is a major skill in and of itself. Data collection methods must be selected, modified, sequenced, and augmented in the face of a growing familiarity with and sensitivity to organizational members, events, problems, and goals.

Finally, data collection involves the ability to effectively use oneself as a reliable and uniquely valuable resource in the data collection (and later in the conceptualization) process. As numerous clinical researchers have noted (Rogers, 1961; Mann , 1974; Mills, 1967), being able to use oneself as a data collection 'tool' requires training, commitment, and the ability (developed over time) to tolerate the tensions and conflicting emotions that come with being an involved researcher. Without involvement, these writers argue, one loses the rich sources of data that are available only to the diagnostician who can identify or empathize with the group or social system in which he or she works. Learning to trust one's involvement and at the same time learning to mistrust the potential distractions of this same involvement is a critical clinical field skill.

The conceptualization aspect of a system diagnosis is defined by those skills that are required to build a formal, systematic understanding of a human system. Glaser and Strauss' (1967) work has given its name to this process, the development of grounded theory, or, in other words, the development of an understanding of a living system that is rooted in clinical fieldwork and validated through it. The theory-building skills described by Glaser and Strauss (1967) and others are guidelines for developing concepts, generating hypotheses, and building theories from clinical information gathered through direct contact with an organization on an ongoing basis. Their work details a critical skill, the skill involved in conceptualizing experience. Along with data collection, the ability to conceptualize and to build theory are the conerstones of the diagnostic process (Argyris and Schön, 1974).

A HIERARCHY AMONG FIELD SKILLS

These three sets of skills have a distinct hierarchical relationship. Understanding the dynamics of one's own 'internal life' is a necessary precondition for managing complex relationships with individuals, groups, and large social systems. The ability to understand and manage these relationships is a necessary precondition for conducting a diagnostic process. Put another way, without relationship management skills diagnostic skills cannot be learned or practised and without personal/emotional skills relationships cannot be managed or understood.

The evidence for this hierarchy is empirical as well as intuitive. Experience and research in a variety of social science disciplines suggest that the individual's awareness and understanding of his or her psychological characteristics is directly related to the quality of his or her relationships with others. In psychoanalysis, the analyst must understand and manage countertransference reactions in order to successfully establish a working therapeutic relationship in which the patient's analysis can proceed (Greenson, 1967). Rogers (1961) makes a similar point about helping relationships in general when he emphasizes the importance of self-awareness and self-acceptance in working with others. Storr (1961) describes two 'fears' that influence an individual's ability to enter into a trustful relationship with others. A fear of being abandoned can result in a collection of superficial relationships, while a fear of being overwhelmed can lead to no meaningful relationships at all. Finally, psychological defence mechanisms such as projection and projective identification are further indications of the ways in which intrapsychic dynamics can shape and distort interpersonal and intragroup relations (Ichheiser, 1949).

This research attests to the influence of psychological and emotional characteristics on the individual's ability to establish and manage relationships with others. Only with significant self-understanding and self-awareness is one likely to establish relationships relatively free of distortions and projections.

Just as personal awareness is the basis for managing relationships, the ability to establish and manage relationships is necessary for effective diagnostic fieldwork in human systems. In the extreme, no relationship means no diagnostic work. In many cases, relationships with client systems are begun but terminated prematurely due to relationship management problems. Lewicki and Alderfer (1973) describe a labour-management consultation project that ended prematurely because the authors were unable to manage the complex union-management intergroup relations. Nadler (1978) describes a 'quality of work life' intervention in which the first consultants were fired because of their inability to spend enough time with system members. Other studies in the area of organization devevlopment document projects that were terminated or withered away because relations with top management were not competently handled (Bennis, 1977; Walton, 1975).

In still other cases diagnostic work continues in form but its validity is suspect because of mistrustful or hostile practitioner—client or researcher—client relationships. Alderfer (1968) found that the validity of a questionnaire improved significantly when the instrument was preceded by interviews. From one perspective this is simply a data collection sequencing issue, but the author demonstrates that the validity on the diagnostic questionnaire improved, at least in part, because the interviews helped establish a more trustful *relationship* between respondent and researcher.

In summary, the view of clinical field skills presented in this section emphasizes two points. First, clinical field skills can be divided into three major areas: personal/emotional, relationship management, and diagnostic. Second, the three component areas of clinical field skills are hierarchically related, i.e. diagnostic skills depend on relationship management skills, which in turn depend on personal/emotional skills. A model for training OB practitioners in these skill areas must address both of these points. The next section proposes such a model.

DEVELOPING CLINICAL FIELD SKILLS

The approach to developing clinical field skills that is presented here is based on an apprenticeship model. *Apprenticeship* is a term that dates back to the twelfth century [although apprenticeship relationships are mentioned in the Code of Hammurabi (2100BC)] and refers to the learning of a trade, craft or other professional calling by practical experience under the guidance of a master with an agreement (often legal) defining the relationship between master and learner and the duration and conditions of their relationship. The central characteristic of the apprenticeship relationship is that the apprentice learns by doing, and through practice with and under the guidance of the master hones his or her skills.

The apprenticeship model was chosen as a basic framework for two major reasons. First, apprenticeship denotes experiential learning, an educational process in which experience precedes and fosters conceptualization (Kolb, 1974). For a profession that is part craft and part science with a strong commitment to practical application, an experiential learning approach emphasizes the intellectual and practical components of fieldwork as well as the important connection between the two. A more traditional didactic classroom approach to education runs the risk of overemphasizing the intellectual component by ignoring the practical, and experience without conceptual development would err in the opposite way. Experiential learning approaches not only address both the conceptual and practical elements of professional activities, but also the link between them.

The second reason for using the apprenticeship model is that the *relationship* between teacher and learner provides a medium for learning many of the personal and relationship management skills that are central to clinical fieldwork. A significant relationship that develops over time is more likely to be characterized by mutual trust and respect than one that exists for only a semester. Shared experience coupled with developing trust and respect provide the basis for teacher and learner to explore difficult personal and and interpersonal issues, a process that serves the learning goals of the relationship.

The apprenticeship model, however, merely describes a structural framework for professional training in organizational behaviour. The next step in designing the training programme is a description of the characteristics of an apprenticeship aimed at developing clinical field skills. Specifically, how are (1) personal/emotional, (2) relationship management, and (3) diagnostic skills learned in an apprenticeship framework? The following five characteristics of a specialized apprenticeship model address this question. Each of the characteristics is designed to promote skill development in at least one of the three major skill areas.

Personal/emotional

Characteristic 1: identity development

An explicit feature of this apprenticeship is the attention to the development of the trainee's professional and personal identity. As described earlier in this chapter, fieldwork cannot be undertaken competently without an awareness of the dynamics of one's own personal and professional identity. This awareness is cultivated within the relationship through a constant attention to the adult developmental process that is at the core of entering a profession. It is neither easy nor comfortable to focus on one's strengths *and* weaknesses, to seek greater insight into one's values, beliefs, and idiosyncracies, and it is particularly difficult to risk the vulnerability implicit in enlisting another's help in these tasks. Yet, this is precisely what this model asks of both the teacher and the learner. It is assumed that both have things to learn, and while the specific developmental or professional identity issues may be different for each of them, the road to increased self-understanding is hazardous for both.

The *mentoring* relationship (Levinson *et al.* 1978) catures the essence of this aspect of the apprenticeship. The mentor helps the mentee develop both professional competence and a professional identity. Especially between the ages of 25 and 35, the mentee is concerned with choosing an occupation and defining a Dream, a vision of what he or she would like to accomplish in life. The realization of one's Dream requires guidance by someone who knows the ropes, can teach the skills required to function effectively in one's occupation, and is willing to help the mentee develop a self-image or identity that is consonant with his or her occupation and Dream. It is most critical that the mentor be able to help the mentee with the deep emotional struggles that are part of the development of a professional identity: Who am I? What can I be? What are my strengths and weaknesses? Am I good enough to succeed? Am I as good as my mentor? The ability to help with these questions is what distinguishes the mentor from the sponsor (Kanter, 1977), for while both provide the trainee with information, contacts, and access to the profession, the mentor also takes on the task of providing emotional guidance during the transition from student/learner to adult professional.

Perhaps the most crucial element of this component of the apprenticeship model is the ability of the relationship to accept and learn from mistakes and failures (Mirvis and Berg, 1977). Inevitably, a training relationship will experience failure, either perceived or real, and the way in which these events are managed is central to the successful emotional, personal, and professional development of the trainee. If the teacher and learner can accept and work through the difficult emotions involved in failure and proceed to use the experience as an opportunity to learn, the trainee will gain not only valuable knowledge, but experience with a valuable process as well. Particularly with respect to failure, the skill and understanding required of the teacher is immense. Managed poorly (or not at all), failure experiences during training can cripple the trainee's future development. The intensity of the feelings surrounding such events (for both teacher and learner) makes it difficult to manage them well.

Relationship management

Characteristic 2: Ongoing examination of the teacher-learner relationship

The most important element of the apprenticeship model is the attention given to the examination of the teacher-learner relationship as it evolves and develops. This relationship is a rich source of experiential data that, if examined, can increase the learner's self-awareness and help him or her develop important relationship management skills. The supervisory relationship in clinical psychology serves as a paradigm. Ekstein and Wallerstein (1958) in describing the supervisory relationship identify two major tasks: overcoming learning problems and overcoming problems in learning.

Learning problems arise as the trainee is faced with difficult clinical material from the patient or is confronted with difficult decisions in diagnosis, disposition or treatment. How to conduct initial interviews, manage termination or fit together clinical material so as to understand and treat the patient are all examples of learning problems. These conceptual and practical problems arise because of the trainees' lack of experience and knowledge. In the conceptual framework proposed in this chapter, these could be called 'diagnostic' problems.

The phrase 'problems in learning' refers to problems encountered in the supervisory relationship that make the task of 'learning' (professional training) difficult. These 'problems' include the personal, intrapsychic problems of the trainee, relationship issues between supervisor and trainee (dependency, counterdependency, intellectual and emotional insecurities or inhibitions), feelings of incompetency or inadequacy, countertransference reactions (i.e. feelings the trainee has towards the patient that originate in his or her unconscious and are transferred onto the patient), and others. The supervisory relationship struggles to surface, understand, and work through these problems in learning for two reasons. First, 'solutions' to these problems will enable the trainee to be a better therapist. Second, these problems and the struggle to understand and solve them are analogous to the problems and struggles faced by the patient. Thus, supervision not only deepens the trainee's emotional understanding of the therapeutic process but also, through the 'mirroring' phenomenon, helps the trainee learn the skills necessary to treat and manage these problems in his or her own future practice.

In the tradition of the supervisory relationship, the apprenticeship model requires the examination of the training relationship in the service of developing a number of important skills.

(1) An implicit (if not explicit) part of the teacher-learner relationship is an

entire range of authority dynamics: the relationship of novice to expert, issues of dependency, counterdependency, and the emotions associated with each; feelings of helplessness, powerlessness, and loss of pride; etc. These are issues which are also part of the client-practitioner relationship and are 'mirrored' in the teacher-learner relationship. An examination of these issues and feelings from inception to termination provides invaluable and intensely personal insight into what it means to be a client seeking help, advice, training or information.

(2) Inevitably the teacher-learner relationship will encounter conflict. Again, this conflict is often a mirroring of actual or latent conflict in the client-practitioner relationship in which the teacher and learner are jointly involved (Alderfer *et al.*, 1978). An examination and resolution of this conflict within the teacher-learner relationship can provide insight into the causes and dynamics of the conflict while at the same time modelling a process for resolving it.

(3) The examination of the teacher-learner relationship also provides a setting for exploring the trainee's 'problems in learning' in ways that are similar to Argyris and Schön's (1974) Model II learning. The constant reexamination of the entire learning process not only improves the learning outcomes, but also provides a vehicle for a continuous examination of the learning process itself. This final benefit means that the learner is participating in a model that can be used in other learning relationships in other settings, be they teacher-learner, client-practitioner or colleague-colleague.

Characteristic 3: Multiple learners for each teacher

The apprenticeship model advocates multiple learners (four or five) for each teacher. This is done for two reasons. First, multiple learners mean that trainees can participate in the education of their peers. In this way, they begin to learn how to teach as well as how to learn. Peers can also provide support for each other during the difficult emotional periods (failure, struggles towards self-awareness, feelings of inadequacy or incompetency). Even the hazards of multiple learners for each teacher (sibling rivalry and competition, jealousies, etc.) provide opportunities for learning about these dynamics as they occur in all bureaucratic organizations. Second, the 'learners' group' provides a setting for an in-depth experiential analysis of small group dynamics. Much as 'group supervision' has become a component of clinical psychology training because of the insight into group dynamics that it affords, 'learners' groups' could be used to teach (in an experiential, self-analytic way) critical skills and concepts in the area of group dynamics.

Diagnosis

Characteristic 4: Joint activities

In an apprenticeship the teacher and the learner undertake clinical fieldwork together. This does not preclude the learner from taking on his or her own projects, but the training programme must include joint work by teacher and learner. The opportunity to work with an experienced OB practitioner provides the learner with a chance to watch a professional at work and to gradually develop his or her own skills under the careful and continuing tutelage of a competent teacher. Without this joint work, it is doubtful that the learner would have an opportunity to observe, first hand, the pragmatics of applying theories and techniques to live, ongoing projects. This observation, coupled with the opportunity to practise diagnostic skills learned, provides the basis for sound experiential learning (Kolb, 1974).

In addition, joint work begins the trainee's education in (1) the ethics of clinical fieldwork (through observation of and discussion with the teacher as ethical issues arise) and (2) the difficult but often necessary process of working *with* someone in one's professional work. These tasks are best undertaken (at least initially) in a professional relationship in which there is a growing sense of trust and a common pool of experiential data. Working together provides common experiences that can be analysed and discussed, and while there is no way to guarantee a trustful relationship, a constant examination of the potential sources of mistrust (described above) including competition and exploitation can be significant steps in that direction.

Finally, when teacher and learner work together, they form a professional group' (of a kind) and their relationship with the client system provides an opportunity for learning about intergroup relations (client-practitioner). As they are 'outsiders', the phenomena characteristic of ingroup/outgroup relations almost always assert themselves and thereby provide experience and data for learning.

Characteristic 5: Conceptual work

The final characteristic of the apprenticeship model is the centrality of intellectual learning. Hand in hand with fieldwork goes constant intellectual and conceptual development. Included in this educational component would be (1) examination of theories of intervention (e.g. Argyris, 1970), research (e.g. Glaser and Strauss, 1967), and diagnosis (e.g. Alderfer, 1979); (2) exposure to the intellectual and conceptual history of the profession; and (3) classroom activities that not only provide opportunities to practise a range of diagnostic techniques but also explicitly discuss the theories behind them.

A crucially important aspect of the intellectual learning component of the model is regular and frequent written work by the trainee aimed at developing his or her conceptual skills. If OB practitioners are to possess the conceptual skills necessary to analyse and understand the social systems on which the work, the training must start early. The apprenticeship model borrows from clinical supervision the belief that only through regular attempts at organizing and analysing data within a conceptual framework can the trainee develop facility in conceptually based action. As a result, the learner in the apprenticeship model is periodically asked to 'write up' a project on which he or she is working or comment on a case write-up or research article done by others. Regularly scheduled activities of this sort (with feedback) are included in the model so that the trainee can develop the intellectual and conceptual competencies that are a necessary companion to the practical competencies developed through fieldwork.

Sequencing

As discussed earlier, the three skill areas are hierarchically related. Ideally, a training model sensitive to this 'nesting' of skills would have two features: (1) it would begin with personal/emotional learning experiences, move on to relationship management training, and conclude with the development of diagnostic skills; and (2) it would examine the interaction of these three areas, periodically, as the sequential learning process evolved. A training model with the first feature only would not take into account that learners *change* as they learn! This dynamic quality of human development means that the ideal training programme must have the second feature as well. It must accommodate and encourage the development of personal/emotional skills during work on relationship management and the development of both personal/emotional and relationship management skills during diagnostic training.

The apprenticeship model proposed in this chapter describes a relationship that can be flexible enough to include a sequential learning process and prescriptive enough to require continuous attention to the interaction of the three skill areas. This model also assumes that it is more important to address all the areas on a continuing basis than to adhere to a rigid learning sequence. (This assumption translates into the *absence* of a prescription for 'sequential learning'.) The reason for this is simple. If the skill areas are hierarchically related, diagnostic skill development *cannot* occur until some personal/emotional and relationship management skills have been acquired. If the seqeunce is reversed in the training programme, little or no learning is the likely result. If training is undertaken in all three areas simultaneously, the result is a *de facto* sequential learning experience, since diagnostic skill development will not occur in great depth until after some personal/emotional learning has taken place.

Implications

To seriously consider using the apprenticeship model for training organizational behaviour professionals, one must assess the implications of the model. First, it is a costly one. One teacher working collaboratively and in the 'field' with four or five learners is as expensive as it is intensive. Such a model is even more expensive than the clinical psychology supervision model since the teacher must spend fieldwork time *as well as* supervision time with the learner.

Second, the apprenticeship model relies heavily on teachers who are competent supervisors, masters, and mentors. This brand of competency is not necessarily a natural by-product of a career of competent research, consultation or teaching. It requires special skills, special knowledge, and perhaps even the special sensitivity that comes with having been through the process as a trainee. Finding qualified trainers may be the most difficult aspect of implementing an apprenticeship training model.

Third, an apprenticeship model and the commitment to developing clinical field skills that it implies would mean restructuring most of the educational programmes in organizational behaviour. Courses would have to be added and requirements reconsidered.

Finally, an apprenticeship model for professional training runs the risk of promoting 'fiefdoms' within the profession. Although competent teachers should encourage learners to develop their own professional identities, the apprenticeship model can easily be abused in the service of oversized egos or perceived political realities. Nothing would subvert the goals of the apprenticeship model more than for it to degenerate into a collection of personal 'fiefdoms' cut off from a professional community and kept alive to serve their own insulated interests. Such a state of affairs would stifle the development of the field by reinforcing tightly knit groups of like-minded practitioners.

CONCLUSION

It has been the intent of this chapter to propose a model for training organizational behaviour professionals in the area of clinical field skills. The chapter began by stating and defending the contention that the ability to manage and learn from direct contact with human systems is a crucial skill for *all* OB professionals. The middle section described three types of clinical field skills that enable OB practitioners to establish, maintain, and learn from their relationship with an organization and discussed the relationships among them. The final section described an apprenticeship model for developing these skills, a model that integrated aspects of the clinical supervision relationship in psychology, the apprenticeship relationship in craft training, and the mentoring relationship in occupational development.

If there is an overriding point to this discussion it is that the development of clinical field skills is a crucially important and extremely difficult and time-consuming process. In our continuing efforts to train competent professionals in a new and emerging field, we cannot afford to settle for less than a standard of excellence.

ACKNOWLEDGEMENTS

The author would like to thank Clayton Alderfer for his helpful comments on an earlier draft of this chapter.

REFERENCES

Alderfer, C. P. (1968) 'Comparison of questionnaire responses with and without preceding interviews', *Journal of Applied Psychology*, **52**, 335-40.
Alderfer, C. P. (1977a) 'Group and intergroup relations'. In Hackman, J. and Suttle. J. (eds.) *Improving Life at Work*. Santa Monica, Ca: Goodyear.
Alderfer, C. P. (1977b) 'Improving organizational communication through long-term intergroup intervention', *Journal of Applied Behavioural Science*, **13**, 193-210.
Alderfer, C. P. (1979) 'The methodology of organizational diagnosis', *Professional Psychology*, In press.
Alderfer, C. P. and Berg, D. N. (1977) 'OD: The profession and the practitioner'. In Mirvis, P. and Berg, D. (eds.) *Failures in Organization Development and Change*. New York: Wiley-Interscience.
Alderfer, C. P., Brown, L. D., Kaplan, R. and Smith, K. (1978) Unpublished manuscript.
Argyris, C. (1958) 'Creating effective research relationships in organizations'. *Human Organization*, **17**, 34-40.
Argyris, C. (1970) *Intervention Theory and Method*. Reading, Mass.: Addison-Wesley.
Argyris, C. and Schön, D. A. (1974) *Theory in Practice: Increasing Professional Effectiveness*. San Francisco: Jossey-Bass.
Bennis, W. (1977) 'Bureaucracy and social change: An anatomy of a training failure'. In Mirvis, P., and Berg, D. (eds.) *Failures in Organization Development and Change*. New York: Wiley, pp. 191-216.
Berg, D. N. (1977) 'Failure at entry'. In Mirvis, P. and Berg, D. (eds.) *Failures in Organization Development and Change*. New York: Wiley-Interscience.
Blake, R. R. and Mouton, J. S. (1962) 'The intergroup dynamics of a win-lose conflict and problem solving collaboration in union-management relations'. In Sherif, M. (ed.) *Intergroup Relations and Leadership*. New York: Wiley.
Bradford, L. P., Gibb, J. R. and Benne, K. D. (1964) *T-group Theory and Laboratory Method*. New York: Wiley.
Coser, L. (1956) *The Function of Social Conflict*. New York: Free Press.
Ekstein, R. and Wallerstein, R. (1958) *The Teaching and Learning of Psychotherapy*. New York: Basic Books.
Glaser, B. and Strauss, A. (1967) *The Discovery of Grounded Theory*. Chicago: Aldine.
Greenson, R. R. (1967) *The Technique and Practice of Psychoanalysis*. New York: International Universities Press.

Ichheiser, G. (1949) 'Analysis and typology of personality misinterpretations'. *American Journal of Sociology*, **55**, 27-31, 40-3, 47-9, 51-3.

Kanter, R. M. (1977) *Men and Women of the Corporation*. New York: Basic Books.

Kolb, D. A. (1974) 'On management and the learning process'. In Kolb, D., Rubin, I. and McIntyre, J. (eds.) *Organizational Psychology*. Englewood Cliffs, NJ: Prentice-Hall.

Levinson, D. J., Darrow, C. N., Klein, E. B., (1978) Levinson, M. H., and McKee, B. *The Seasons of a Man's Life*. New York: Knopf.

Lewicki, R. J. and Alderfer, C. P. (1973) 'The tension between research and intervention in intergroup conflict'. *Journal of Applied Behavioural Science*, **9**, 423-68.

McCall, G. J. and Simmons, P. (1969) *Issues in Participant Observation*. Reading, Mass.: Addison-Wesley.

Mann, R. D. (1974) 'The identity of the group researcher'. In Gibbard, G., Hartman J. and Mann, R. (eds.) *Analysis of Groups*. San Francisco: Jossey-Bass.

Mills, T. M. (1967) *The Sociology of Small Groups*. Englewood Cliffs, NJ: Prentice-Hall.

Mirvis, P. H. and Berg, D. N. (eds.) (1977) *Failures in Organization Development and Change*. New York: Wiley-Interscience.

Nadler, D. A. (1978) 'Hospitals, organized labour and quality of work: An intervention case study'. *Journal of Applied Behavioural Science*, **14**, 366-81.

Rogers, C. (1961) *On Becoming a Person*. Boston: Houghton-Mifflin.

Schein, E. H. and Bennis, W. G. (1965) *Personal and Organizational Change through Group Methods*. New York: Wiley.

Sherif, M. (ed.) (1962) *Intergroup Relations and Leadership*. New York: Wiley.

Storr, A. *The Integrity of Personality*. New York: Atheneum.

Walton, R. (1975) 'The diffusion of new work structures: Explaining why success didn't take'. *Organizational Dynamics*, Winter, 3-21.

Wells, L., Jr. (1979) Personal communication.

Advances in Experiential Social Processes, Volume 2
Edited by C. P. Alderfer and C. L. Cooper
© 1980 John Wiley & Sons Ltd.

Chapter 7

The Group-as-a-Whole:
A Systemic Socio-Analytic Perspective
on Interpersonal and Group Relations

Leroy Wells Jr.

Yale School of Organization and Management, U.S.A.

INTRODUCTION

This chapter presents concepts that are central to understanding interpersonal processes and group relations in an organizational context. Emphasis is placed on interpreting interpersonal relations from the group level using what may be labelled a 'systemic socio analytic' perspective. Several case studies are used to examine interpersonal relations from the systemic socio analytic perspective. Heuristics are delineated which help agents of organizational change to better understand, interpret, and intervene in interpersonal and group relations.

AIMS AND PRINCIPLES

The present theoretical framework for understanding group and organizational processes has been heavily influenced by work of writers from the Tavistock Centre for Human Relations in London. These scholars have greatly influenced the author's conceptual development and largely account for the biases that colour his understanding of group and organizational phenomena.

The 'systemic socioanalytic' perspective for understanding organizational processes integrates:

(1) Current thinking regarding the application of open system theory to group and organizational behaviour (Alderfer, 1976; Baker, 1973; Mant, 1976; Reed *et al.*, 1978; Wells, 1978b; Singer *et al.*, 1975; Astrachan, 1970).

(2) Concepts associated with Kleinian psychoanalysis (Klein, 1932, 1955; Klein and Riviere, 1964; Jacques, 1955).

(3) Principles articulated by the psychoanalytic group psychology tradition (Bion, 1961; Gibbard et al., 1974; Gibbard, 1975; Colman and Bexton, 1975).

Through the integration of these perspectives and their concepts, a more cogent framework is formed from which the complexity of interpersonal processes can more readily be discerned.

Traditional experimental and social psychological views of interpersonal relations represented by Cartwright and Zander (1968), Thibaut and Kelly (1959), Krech et al. (1962), Newcomb (1961) and Lott and Lott (1965) are eschewed in this discussion* This does not suggest that traditional social psychological perspectives are not useful in understanding interpersonal relations, but that the perspective utilized here is novel for *most* applied behaviour scientists. The aim of this chapter is to provide another vantage point from which organizational processes can be understood.

On the other hand, work from the psychoanalytic group tradition (Gibbard, 1975; Bion, 1961) is often written in a form that is alien and meaningless to the reader who is 'untrained' in psychoanalytic concepts and concomitant jargon. Thus, the contribution that psychoanalytic group concepts can make to a better understanding of group processes goes unrecognized or is diminished. This chapter is an attempt to present psychoanalytically derived concepts in a schema that is helpful for organizational diagnosticians who are not familiar with the analytic tradition.

ORGANIZATIONAL PROCESSES

Organizational processes refer to actual working activities, formal and informal relations, and psychosocial phenomena that occur among individuals and groups in organizations. Groups and organizations are considered open living systems that exchange energy, material, and information with the environment (Miller and Rice, 1967; Alderfer, 1976; Baker, 1973). They are vehicles through which a variety of goals can be pursued.

Alderfer (1977a), using an open-system perspective, defines a human group as:

. . . a collection in individuals: a) who have significantly interdependent relations with each other; b) who perceive themselves as a group by reliably distinguishing members from non-members; c) whose group identity is recognized by non-members; d) who have differentiated roles in the group as a function of expectation from themselves, other members and non-groups; and e) who as group members acting alone or in concert have significantly interdependent relations with other groups.

Moreover, Singer et al. (1975) and Alderfer (1976) have described three

---

*An excellent discussion on interpersonal relations from the traditional social psychological perspective can be found in Albanese (1975, pp.525-38).

levels of group processes. These perspectives provide the theoretical background for further discussion of group and organizational processes.

Wells (1978b) has described (extending the Singer *et al.* (1975), Alderfer (1976), and Astrachan (1970) models) five levels of organizational processes. They are: (1) intrapersonal; (2) interpersonal; (3) group-level (Group-as-a-whole); (4) intergroup; and (5) interorganizational (see Figure 1).

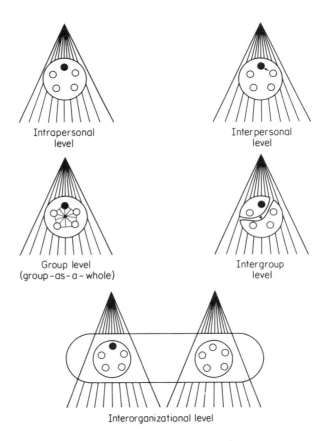

Figure 1   Five levels of organizational processes

(1) *Intrapersonal processes* in an organizational context refer to the co-actor's relatedness to him/herself. Analysis of *intrapersonal* processes focuses on the personality characteristics, character traits, mode of ego defence, ego ideal, and various need levels of the co-actors. In short, an intrapersonal analysis assumes that the behaviour emerges from the internal life or from within the co-actor (Astrachan, 1970).

Personnel departments and assessment centres typically evaluate behaviour of their employees or clients from an intrapersonal perspective. Personnel departments usually use a battery of psychological tests (MPPI, TAT, IQ, Sanford-Binet) to evaluate aspects of their employees' personality. Little attention is paid to processes that occur outside or between individuals. Emphasis is placed on the employees' personality, knowledge, and skills.

Additionally, gestalt therapy and personal growth groups focus on and use the intrapersonal level of analysis as the foundation of their work (Perls, 1970; Yalom, 1970; Weir and Weir, 1978).

(2) *Interpersonal processes* refer to *member-to-member* relations. The focus is on the quality and type of relationships that exist between co-factors. Emphasis is placed on communication patterns, information flow, level of conflict and trust, and relating styles of co-actors (Astrachan, 1970; Argyris, 1962). Interpersonal processes examine how well or poorly individuals relate to their peers, subordinates, and supervisors. Emphasis is placed on how well individuals listen and establish meaningful and viable alliances.

The 'T'-group examines interpersonal processes and focuses on increasing participants' level of social relating skills and interpersonal competence (Argyris, 1962).

(3) *Group-level processes* refer to the behaviour of the group as a social system and the co-actor's relatedness to that system. The focus is on the group-as-a-whole (supra-personal) (Bion, 1961; Gibbard, 1975; Rioch, 1970).

The unit of analysis is the *group* as a system. Groups can be considered more or less the sum total of their parts. Hence, group members are considered interdependent subsystems co-acting and interacting together *via* the group's life mentality. Group-level analysis assumes that when a co-actor acts he or she is not only acting on his or her own behalf, but on behalf of the group or parts of the group. Co-actor behaviour from a group-level perspective cannot be simply examined by assuming that the motivation and genesis of the co-actor is merely a function of his or her idiosyncrasies. It must be viewed as a synthesis of and interaction with the *group's* life and mentality. Simply stated, the co-actor is seen as a vehicle through which the group expresses its life. (An in-depth discussion of group-level phenomena follows.)

Tavistock small study groups use the group-as-a-whole as the unit of analysis (Rice, 1965; Klein and Astrachan, 1972). Miller and Rice (1967) also use group-level analysis for work redesign strategies and autonomous work groups.

(4) *Intergroup processes* refer, in part, to relations among various groups or subgroups. The intergroup processes derive from the group memberships that co-actors carry with them into groups and their behaviour towards other groups. The basis for intergroup relations can develop from hierarchical and task position, sex, race, age, ethnic identities, and ideological differences

(Alderfer, 1977a). Intergroup relations: (1) determine in part how we treat and are treated by others; (2) profoundly colour our perception of the world; and (3) play a critical role in determining how co-actors form their personal sense of reality (Smith 1977). Experiential simulations are sometimes used to study intergroup phenomena (Wells, 1978c; Oshry, 1978).

(5) *Interorganizational processes* refer to relationships that exist between organizations and their environment and concern the set of organizations that make demands of, or have impact upon, the focal organization (Evan, 1966). Interorganizational analysis focuses on the ecotone and the causal texture of the environment (Emery and Trist, 1973).

Each of the five levels described above refers to behavioural systems conceptually different from, but not unrelated to or without connection to one another. Analysis of organizational processes at these levels moves towards a comprehensive view of individual and group dynamics.

Since behaviour is multidetermined, organizational processes can be examined and understood in terms of any or all of these levels. Organizational processes are analogous to a radio broadcasting band. If one tunes into 107.5 FM, this does not mean that 96.0 is not broadcasting, but rather that one has just amplified a particular station. Thus, if one focuses on interpersonal processes, it does not mean that group-level processes are not occurring, but only that one has selected a particular level of organizational process for attention. For the purposes of this chapter group-level phenomena are elucidated. In other words, group-level processes are amplified.

GROUP-AS-A-WHOLE (GROUP LEVEL) AS A UNIT OF ANALYSIS

Using a group-level perspective, a group is conceptualized as being more *and* less than the sum total of the individual co-actors (members) and their intra-psychic dynamics. Group life exists above and below that of individual group members, and the group has a life of its own distinct from but related to the dynamics of the co-actors who comprise the group membership.

Groups are living systems and group members are interdependent co-actors (subsystems) whose interactions form a *gestalt*. That *gestalt* is the *'élan vital'* of the group, and becomes the object of study from the group-level perspective.

In this connection, Bion (1961) has postulated that a group's mentality*

*Bion's concept of group mentality and the concept of the group's *élan vital* (its quintessence, its existential core) are related in a very fundamental way. They both assert that there is a phenomenon that exists above or below that of individual group members. These concepts postulate that a group life exists distinct from the individual group members. Yet, Bion's group mentality and its conceptual cousin, basic assumption group, are helpful but often confusing (Sherwood, 1964). (For an excellent review of Bionic theory, see Gibbard, 1975.) In their present conceptual form they leave too many unresolved and knotty theoretical issues which cloud rather than clarify.

For conceptual simplicity, I will refrain from their use here. I will offer an alternative heuristic concept (projective identification motif) by which to understand the group-as-a-whole phenomenon.

exists beyond that of the individual group members. He suggests that the group's mentality connects (bonds) group members by an 'unconscious tacit agreement'. Gibbard (1975) suggests that the group's mentality is best understood as:

> . . . a process of unconscious collusion . . . 'a machinery of intercommunication' . . . which is at once a characteristic of groups and a reflection of the individual's ability or even his propensity to express certain drives and feelings covertly, unconsciously, and anonymously. (p.7)

At this point it would be helpful to consider the following series of questions:

(1) Of what substance is the group's *élan vital* made?

(2) Using the group as the unit of analysis, why are co-actors considered interdependent? And, why are all of their behaviours conceptualized as mere manifestations and representations of the group's existential core?

(3) Do individuals have ultimate control over determining what they say, think, and do in groups?

These questions are only a sampling of the myriad that could be raised. The material below attempts to answer them and describes the theory upon which a group-level analysis using a systemic socioanalytic perspective is founded.

GROUP-AS-MOTHER

Competent individuals often behave as though they were deskilled, non-rational or lobotomized. When brought together in a group to perform tasks, capable human beings often lose their problem-solving facilities, become emotionally segregated, and blame others for their failure, Their behaviour in these instances is marked by an infantile, regressed quality.

Groups and group members can behave in effective problem-solving ways; yet, all groups regress at some point in their life. It is the group's *regression* to which this chapter addresses itself.

Bion (1961), Gibbard (1975), and Scheidlinger (1964) assert that the central issue for individuals, when joining or participating in groups, is the tension generated by the unconscious fear of being engulfed, obliterated by the group (fused with) at one extreme and becoming a person-in-isolation (estranged/separated) from the group at the other extreme. Both extremes are severely undesirable. This tension creates strong ambivalent (love/hate) feelings towards the group situation. The individual is conceptualized as possessing conflicting feelings about the same object (i.e. group situation) simultaneously. Moreover, these strong ambivalent feelings unconsciously return the adults to their infant roots.

An infant, too, struggles with ambivalence. On the one hand he seeks to be engulfed and fused with mother, while on the other he seeks to become separated from her. Indeed for the infant's survival both options are undesirable ends. Given this tension, the infant has strong ambivalent feelings about mother. In a word, infants have both conflicting love/hate feelings about the same object — mother. The infant's struggles with mother and the individual struggles with the group parallel. Bion (1961) states that the group-as-a-whole 'approximates too closely in the minds of individuals comprising it very primitive fantasies about the contents of the mother's body'. In short, the group represents the *primal mother* for the individual.

This tension and ambivalence experienced by the infant and individual-in-group create an unbearable psychological state of affairs. There is a need to resolve these ambivalent feelings, thus relieving the frustration about the same object—for the infant it is mother, for the individual-in-group the group.

Object-relations theory suggests (Klein, 1946; Mahler, 1972) that an infant initially is unable to make a distinction between what is inside the self and what is outside the self. Thus, the infant has no 'ego' to differentiate self from the world; he or she experiences self as the world; and to him or her everything *is* self. Concomitantly, the infant experiences self as omnipotent. This onmipotence is reinforced by continuous meeting of the neonate's needs. As time passes, the infant matures and some needs are gradually frustrated. Greatly troubled by the frustration, the infant develops a strategy to cope with this condition by projecting 'good' and 'bad' feelings onto outside objects. Rice (1965) suggests:

So far as it excites him and gratifies him, it is a 'good object' which he loves and on which he lavishes his care; so far as it frustrates or hurts him, it is a 'bad object' which he hates and which he vents his rage on. In his struggle to deal with these contradictory attributes he splits objects into good and bad, which represents their satisfying or frustrating aspects.

What complicates matters more is that the infant learns that the same object (typically mother) sometimes satisfies and sometimes frustrates—hence the same object is both good and bad. Yet, the infant wants to lavish the good object and wants to destroy (eschew) the bad object.

This condition creates a major problem for the infant—to take in the good object (mother), the infant also takes in what is bad—thus threatening to destroy what he wants most to preserve, i.e., good object. In this confusing state of affairs the infant is unable to cope with simultaneously conflicting feelings about the same object—then splits off the bad parts into others . . .

The infant both loves and hates object/mother. Unable to cope with the overwhelming ambivalent feelings, the infant uses splitting and projective identification to maintain psychological equilibrium and to cope with life-threatening anxiety generated by having both bad and good in the same object. Often the infant's solution to this ambivalence is to have a good mummy and bad daddy. As infants progress, their solution then becomes good parents—bad strangers. Infants always act to maintain an *autistic pre-ambivalent state*. They seek an autistic state akin to intrauterine life.

Splitting is a primitive psychological mechanism used where individuals disown parts of self that are undesirable. *Projective identification* is a psychological mechanism by which individuals unconsciously identify with an object (person, event, attitude) by externalizing (projecting) split (disowned) parts of themselves.

Melanie Klein (1946) introduced the term projective identification to indicate a process by which parts of self are split off and projected into an external object or part object (Malin and Grotstein, 1966). Hanna Segal (1964), a colleague of Klein, remarks:

Projective identification is the result of the projection of parts of the self into an object. It may result in the object being perceived as having acquired the characteristics of the projected part of the self, but it can also result in the self becoming identified with the object of its projection.

Jacques (1955) suggests that adults in institutional and group settings often use infantile coping strategies, i.e. projective identification, to cope with over-whelming ambivalent feelings generated in the course of social relations. Illustrating the concept of projective identification, he states:

. . . the soldiers who take their leader for their ego, are in effect projectively identifying with or putting themselves into him. It is this common or shared kind of projective identification which enables the soldiers to identify with each other. In the extreme form of projective identification of this kind, the followers become totally dependent on the leader because each has given up a part of himself to the leader.

He goes on to cite Freud's (1922) case of how Assyrian soliders became totally confused and acted as though they were brain-damaged. They retreated in confusion upon hearing that their leader, Holofernes, had had his head cut off by Judith. For not only had the commonly shared external object (the figurehead) binding them all together been lost, but the leader had also lost his head. Thus, every soldier had lost his head because each was inside the leader *via* projective identification.

Groups (families, work groups, classrooms, experiential learning laboratories) elicit strong ambivalent feelings in their members. Groups both nurture and scold. Groups are needed, yet resented, by individuals. Groups are experienced as both bad and good simultaneously. Groups create feelings of bliss and despair. Groups, like mothers, create strong, conflicting ambivalent feelings of love and hate.

Gibbard (1975) aptly states:

The natural psychological habitat of man is the group. Man's adaptation to that habitat is imperfect, a state of affairs which is reflected in his chronic ambivalence towards groups. Group membership is psychologically essential and yet a source of increasing discomfort. (p.33)

Bion (1961) declares that:

The individual is a group animal at war not simply with the group, but with himself for being a group animal and with those aspects of his personality that constitute his 'groupishness'. (p.131)

Ambivalence is central for infant-mother relations and for individual-in-group relationship. Groups create the same range of feelings that are created in the infant-mother relationship. Moreover, both infants in relation to mother and individuals in relation to groups use projective identification and splitting to cope with overwhelming tension and ambivalence. Hence, the concept of group-as-mother is established.

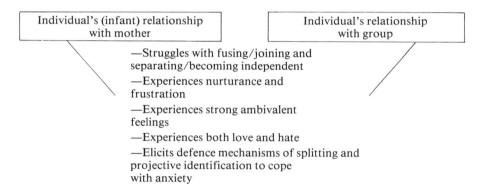

Individual's (infant) relationship with mother	Individual's relationship with group

—Struggles with fusing/joining and separating/becoming independent
—Experiences nurturance and frustration
—Experiences strong ambivalent feelings
—Experiences both love and hate
—Elicits defence mechanisms of splitting and projective identification to cope with anxiety

It is the *group-as-mother* paradigm that underlies the group-level analysis. The interplay between projective and introjective identification* and splitting that brings group members together is being analysed in the group-as-a-whole approach. Moreover, it is the dynamic unconscious pattern or matrix shared by the group members that provides the substance of the group's *élan vital*. Thus, individual group members are considered connected to each other by an unconscious or preconscious tacit alliance.

This unconscious (tacit) alliance allows each member to use other members as objects to express split parts of him/herself. The unconscious alliance and

---

*Introjective identification is a psychological defence by which the individual identifies with an external object by taking the object into him/herself.

concomitant motif begins when the group members experience tension and ambivalence created by the struggle between engulfment or enstrangement by the group. This struggle unconsciously returns the adults to their infant roots—therefore to the infant-mother dyad, concomitant dynamics, and coping strategies used by the infant, e.g. projective identification.

Group-level analysis is an important perspective in understanding group and interpersonal relations. The integration of system theory and Kleinian concepts provides a helpful vantage point from which organizational processes can be discerned. Projective identification, role differentiation, and scapegoating are common manifestations of these dynamics.

PROJECTIVE IDENTIFICATION, ROLE DIFFERENTIATION, AND SCAPEGOATING IN GROUPS

Projective identification, role differentiation, and scapegoating in groups are defined and discussed in detail in this section. The premise is that excessive projective identification leads to rigid role differentiation which ultimately can cause scapegoating (a special and destructive form of role differentiation) in groups. Particular attention is given to analysing interpersonal (member-to-member) relations in groups from a socioanalytic perspective. Understanding these concepts and their relationships is central to the 'systemic socioanalytic' approach.

Projective identification

The term projective identification was first proposed by Melanie Klein (1946) to describe a psychological process by which individuals project split parts of self into an external object. Zinner (1976) states:

Projective identification is an activity of the ego that modifies perception of the object and, in reciprocal fashion, alters the image of the self. These conjoined changes in perception influence and may, in fact, govern behaviour of the self toward the object. Thus, projective identification is an important conceptual bridge between an individual and an interpersonal psychology, since our awareness of the mechanism permits us to understand specific interaction among persons in terms of specific dynamic conflict within individuals.

Thus, projective identification provides us with a way to understand the psychosocial matrix that exists between individuals and groups.

Klein (1946) further defines projective identification as 'a combination of splitting off parts of the self and projecting them onto another person'. In her later work (Klein, 1959), she describes projective identification as the 'feeling of identification with other people because one has attributed qualities or attributes of one's own to them'.

As indicated earlier, projective identification is a coping mechanism—a defence—that infants use to manage anxiety and ambivalence that is generated in relation to the mother for being both a good (nurturing) and a bad (frustrating) object. Wanting only the good-nurturing object, the infant splits off bad parts and projects these out to others (non-mother). Hence, projective identification is the primary psychological defence mechanism employed by infants to cope with life-threatening bad objects. Projective identification entails some distortion of reality. It simplifies one's emotional life, e.g. making mother into an 'all good' object.

Zinner (1976), Jaffe (1968) and Malin and Grotstein (1966) all remark that projective identification is closely related to Anna Freud's description of Edward Bibring's concept of 'altruistic surrender'. Anna Freud (1946) describes 'altruistic surrender' as when the 'self finds a proxy in the outside world to serve as a repository for the self's own wishes', where the self can experience vicarious gratification of the projected impulse. There is an implicit willingness by the object to collude in providing vicarious gratification for the subject.

Malin and Grotstein (1966) suggest that projection cannot occur without identification with the object upon which the projection is thrown. They assert:

When we start with the projection it is necessary that there be some process of identification or internalization in general, or else we can never be aware of the projection. That is, what is projected would be lost like a satellite rocketed out of the gravitational pull of the Earth. Eventually, all contact with the satellite will be lost. Although the satellite has left Earth, it must remain under the influence of Earth's gravitational pull to remain in order for it to maintain some contact with Earth. A projection of itself, seems meaningless unless the individual can retain some contact with what is projected. That contact is a type of internalization, or, loosely, an identification. (p.27)

In short, a projection has an object with which the individual must identify, often unconsciously. The individual identifies with the object through projection. Projection implies an identification.

In further refinement, Zinner (1976) describes four ways in which projective identification operates within interpersonal and group relations. He states: (1) the subject perceives the object as if the object contained elements of the subject's personality; (2) the subject can evoke behaviour or feelings in the object that conform with the subject's perceptions; (3) the subject can experience vicariously the activity and feelings of the object; and (4) participants in close relationship are often in collusion with one another to sustain mutual projection, i.e. to support one another's defensive operations and to provide experiences through which the other can participate vicariously (p.285). Zinner (1976) further states:

For projective identification to function effectively as a defence, the true nature of the relationship between self and its projected part must remain unconscious. (p.286).

Projective identification not only functions as a defence, but it is also the psychodynamic basis upon which individuals are able to empathize with another. Projecting parts of self onto the other, then identifying with other allows the person to feel with the other. Yet, excessive identification seeks an autistic, pre-ambivalent state—akin to the life of the neonate.

Laughlin (1970) describes the King David reaction, which is closely related to excessive projective identification. The King David reaction is based upon the Biblical character King David and the Little Ewe Lamb parable (Samuel II, 11-12). Briefly, King David has laid with Bathsheba, the wife of his general Uriah, while Uriah was off at battle. Bathsheba conceived and sent word to David, saying, 'I am with child'. David then sent for Uriah from battle, hoping that he would lay with Bathsheba. Uriah, a committed general, would not lay with Bathsheba because his men could not rest and eat well. Uriah slept at the king's door, refusing to go home. David then sent Uriah back to the front lines so that he might be killed. Uriah was indeed killed. Then the prophet Nathan is sent to David, saying:

(1) There were two men in one city, one rich and the other poor.

(2) The rich man had exceeding many flocks and herds.

(3) But the poor man had nothing, save one little ewe lamb, which he had bought and nourished up and it grew up together with him, and with his children; it did eat of his own meat, and drank of his own cup, and lay in his bosom, and was unto him as a daughter.

(4) And there came a traveller unto the rich man, and he spared to take of his own flock and of his own herd to dress for the wayfaring man that was come to him; but took the poor man's lamb, and dressed it for the man that was come to him.

(5) David's anger was greatly kindled against the man, and he said to Nathan, 'As the Lord liveth, the man that has done this thing shall surely die.

And he shall restore the lamb fourfold, because he did this thing, and he had no pity.

And Nathan said to David, 'Thou art the man'.

David reacted with great contempt for the rich, selfish man. Clearly, he was reacting to a consciously unrecognized and disowned aspect of himself. Nathan poignantly points to this fact with 'Thou art the man'.

The King David reaction is operative when individuals respond to others with excessively strong positive or negative feelings, and evaluate them accordingly. The King David reaction often emerges from scant real data about the other. Powerful unconscious identification occurs with the other through projection of either approved or disapproved aspects of the self. The subject recognizes a part of self in the object.

Laughlin (1970) defines the King David reaction as:

> A complex intrapsychic defensive operation involving the cooperation and mutual interaction of repression, projection and identification; it is usually supported in some measure by rationalization and at times related to denial . . . Through this reaction consciously unrecognized and disowned elements of the self-appraisal which were often ordinarily present to some extent in the other person are also further ascribed to him through projection—and reacted to accordingly. This process has evoked the otherwise unexplained feelings which are experienced toward the other person. The King David Reaction may be negative or positive. (p.238).

As human beings we have a tendency to act in self-serving ways. We eschew parts of ourselves that make us uncomfortable, but readily see those parts in others. Projective identification in general, and the King David reaction in particular, are useful concepts that increase our understanding of interpersonal relations and group behaviour.

Zinner (1976) and Greenspan and Mannis (1974) cogently describe how projective identification operates in the marital relationship. Zinner and Shapiro (1972) articulate how projective identification affects families and their adolescents. Malin and Grotstein (1966) discuss the ramifications of projective identification in therapeutic relationships. Bion (1955, 1956) and Rosenfeld (1952a, 1954) use the concept of projective identification to understand and treat psychosis.

Scheidlinger (1964, 1968), Gibbard (1975), and Bion (1961) postulate that adults employ projective identification to cope with 'the threat of losing one's personal identity in groups'. In using the group-as-mother, individuals employ projective identification and splitting to defend against primitive anxiety and ambivalence that threaten the person's sense of self. Additionally, these writers assert that group members act as proxies in which to deposit disowned (split) parts of themselves. Hence, each group member can become a receptacle for the projected parts of their cohorts. Each group member is likely to elicit a particular kind of projection and is thus symbolized in unique ways. This process of symbolization differentiates group members and thrusts them into specialized roles within the group. Role differentiation results from splitting, projective identification (i.e. unconscious alliance), and symbolization among group members.

In essence, each member is called upon to assume role(s) (given how they are symbolized) that provide a service to the group. These differentiated roles divide and distribute expressive, cognitive, instrumental, mythical, and reparative elements within the group. Fundamentally, roles in groups, in part, serve to manage anxiety, defend against deindividualization or estrangement, structure the group's *élan vital*, and get work done.

Hence, each group member performs important functions on behalf of the group. In this regard all services and functions (i.e. roles) performed in groups are interdependent. This individual role behaviour must always be analysed in the context of the constellation of roles distributed in the group. In short, individual role behaviour is *embedded* in the field of other roles. *All* roles serve meaningful and purposeful functions in groups.

Projective identification motif in groups

The group's projective identification is the precursor for symbolization and role differentiation. The *projective identification motif* refers to the unconscious (tacit) alliance that forms among group members. It describes how individuals are connected to co-members—often in consciously unrecognized ways. Through projective identification group members are connected to each other by passion, indifference, silence, contempt, respect, love, guilt, hate, or other ways. The patterning of projective identification *bonds* group members together.

Myriad and recurrent patterns of projective identification occur within small groups. I ask, technological and environmental demands, and constraints interacting upon group members' valence bonds together with members' willingness to assume roles (although often unconsciously) determine various patterns that emerge in the groups.

The patterning of projective identification in groups is also dependent upon individual groups members' *valence bonds*. Individual group members elicit, introject, and collude with particular kinds of projections ascribed to them. The group member's valence bonds, or tendency to respond to certain types of projections and to adopt special roles, are analogous to the propensity that elements have to combine as in a chemical reaction (Bion, 1961). By definition, projective identification between individuals (subject and object) involves unconscious collusion. This *collusion* is based on a person's valence bonds and their relation to the group.

Valency or the propensity to collude, introject, and respond to projections by others is dependent upon: (1) the individual's object relations (i.e. how the individual relates to himself and to the outside world)—his or her psychological set; (2) the individual's identity based on demographic characteristics, e.g. socio-economic status, race, ethnicity, age and gender, and stereotypic attributions (i.e. projections, symbolizations, and imagoes) ascribed to these demographic characteristics by others. (For example, women are typically affective; men are cognitive and rational. Blacks are hypersexual; whites are non-sexual—see Kovel, 1970.).

These attributions ascribed to a particular demographic identity group make a significant contribution to the valence of the individual. Hence, valency is determined by the person's object relations and attributions ascribed to his or her identity group. Indeed, a person's object relations should involve how he or she responds to skin colour, gender, age, sex. Yet, it has not been extensively discussed in the literature how sociological characteristics affect psychological operations. Stated simply, the propensity to collude, introject, and respond to projections from others and to adopt roles in groups is dependent upon an individual's personal and group identity. This definition of valency includes an individual's psychological and sociological identity. For example, in a mixed-gender group men typically attribute affective-emotional qualitites to women. Women are expected to play caretaking and maintenance roles in groups. Similarly, women often ascribe rational and cognitive qualities to men. Men are expected to play task-oriented aggressive roles. Through projective identification men and women maintain these affective/cognitive, caretaking/rational splits among and within themselves. Although progress is being made on redefining traditional sex role behaviour, the collusive system of projective identification among males and females make it difficult for them to experience themselves as having both affective and cognitive qualities. Indeed, it is difficult to be a *whole* person in this culture.

If a white male executive in banking were to be affectively expressive it is highly probable that he would be limited in advancement or eventually dismissed. To be affectively expressive violates norms governing the behaviour of banking executives. White males (in particular), through projective identification, carry the burden of being simply rational, non-emotional creatures. Given the high correlation between Type A personality and executives, their suppressed affects have health consequences that often result in fatal coronary disease (Jenkins, 1971; Caplan and Jones, 1975).

The excessive use of projective identification to manage interpersonal relations and group situations becomes a major problem and interferes with group effectiveness. For example, Janis' (1972) analysis of the Kennedy cabinet and Bay of Pigs incident clearly indicates how excessive projective identification was used to keep individuals in highly rigid roles. Age and social status dictated that undersecretaries should not speak in cabinet meetings unless they were asked questions by senior cabinet members. A collusive system developed between junior and senior cabinet members that maintained highly rigid roles. It allowed each member to split off parts of himself (the uncertain parts) in each of the others. The 'logic' of this projective identification is:

If senior cabinet members believe that they are most knowledgeable, the most experienced and possessing most insight regarding national security, they then can split the parts of them that may doubt their omniscience, and project their doubts onto the junior cabinet members. Junior cabinet members are then perceived as less knowledgeable and competent. This allows the senior cabinet members to keep the illusion of superior competence in understanding national security matters. In short, senior cabinet members manage to reduce their anxiety by splitting then projecting the doubting parts off in the junior members.

In juxtaposition, junior cabinet members projected their competent parts on the senior members. If the junior members project their competent parts onto the senior members, it allows them to avoid responsibility for taking a definitive stance about national security policies. The junior members could hide behind their lower status. Indeed, senior members were more than willing to have the junior members defer to their greater wisdom. In short, junior members treated senior members like they had *all* the competence. The senior members colluded with this illusion.

Hence, senior and junior members, by excessive use of projective identification, developed a collusive system of illusions and rigid roles that prevented effective problem-solving behaviour.

The cabinet's behaviour in handling the Bay of Pigs incident illustrates how projective identification in groups operates: (1) to protect individuals from threats to their identity (ego-ideal); (2) to maintain highly rigid roles; and (3) to maintain a collusive system. It also demonstrates how valency, in this case based on social status and age, can contribute to role behaviour in groups.

Effective problem-solving and decision-making in groups are related to projective identification that develops among group members. This is a recurrent motif that emerges in groups that hinders or facilitates task accomplishment. Excessive projective identification among group members is more likely to lead to task ineffectiveness, rigid role differentiation, and destructive scapegoating.

Role differentiation in groups

Role differentiation results from the projective identification and symbolization that emerge in groups. Role differentiation is the vehicle by which group members manage their conflicts, ambivalence, and task(s). Gibbard *et al.* (1974) state:

Role differentiation . . . is, in part, a defensive and restitutive effort; and the cost of such differentiation, to the individual and the group, is that splitting, projection and compartmentalization all entail some distortion and simplification of emotional life.

Any specialization limits the individual's range of possibilities—a limitation often compounded by group processes, which seduce or lock the individual into roles that do not meet his emotional requirements. Scapegoating is only the most dramatic manifestation of the group's tendency to exploit the individual. To some degree all group membership is contingent on a conscious or unconscious contract which obligates the individual to sacrifice or suppress one aspect of himself in order to express or develop others. Thus, the individual often finds that groups do not permit him to 'be himself'. (p.250).

Role differentiation also serves an adaptive function for the group. Gibbard *et al.* (1974) assert further:

Rather than becoming flooded with conflicts, the group can make use of individuals (or dyads or subgroups) to circumscribe, localize and isolate conflicts. Through projective identification, a group is divided into 'actors' and 'audience'. Members are recruited to dramatize the central conflicts of the collectivity, and other members are able to participate vicariously in this dramatization.

Thus, role differentiation can serve both defensive and adaptive functions that are intended to protect individuals from anxiety and ambivalence. Roles provide vehicles which bridge and anchor the group. Individuals use roles to find psychological security, often by depositing and exchanging unwanted parts. The matrix of these transactions and their meanings change during the group's life.

Roles are interdependent and distribute the group's *élan vital*. The distribution produces a variety of actors with different scripts. These actors play their 'parts' in service of the group's plot. The group's drama creates myriad 'parts' for individuals to assume. Each member has a 'part' in unfolding the group's drama. Hence, an array of roles emerges in groups based on projective identification (e.g. hero, seducer, silent member, loved object, combatant, scapegoat, pariah, taskmaster, clown, politician, oppressor, victim, patient, conciliator, incompetent, counterdependent, uninvolved, protector, etc.). These roles emerge from the group's plot (i.e. unconscious relationships and aims of the group) and the valency of the members to assume particular 'parts'.

To understand a 'role' in groups we must examine how it is *embedded* in the context of other roles. Embedded role analysis is critical to the socioanalytic approach. The following vignette describes a classroom situation and how roles are embedded and interdependent:

Dave B had been acting out; he was consistently trying the patience of the teacher, Ms T. She was finding Dave's behaviour quite unbearable. She inferred that Dave had poor impulse control, inadequate parental guidance, and poor analytical skills. She essentially used an intrapersonal analysis to understand Dave's behaviour. The conclusion of her analysis was that Dave needed to be put into a special class for emotionally disturbed children. She then made this recommendation to the principal. Dave was sent to the special class.

On the day of Dave's departure from class, Clay, another student in class, began to ask a series of questions of the teacher, spoke when others were speaking, and became 'disruptive'. His behaviour resembled Dave's behaviour. Using an intrapersonal analysis again, the teacher concluded that Clay had 'problems' similar to Dave's. Hence, Clay was finally put into the special class.

As this was occurring, the other class members often giggled; first at Dave, then at Clay. As the teacher would scold the boys, the class would sit back smiling—not at Dave nor Clay, but rather at Ms T. The class seemed to have an investment in seeing Ms T upset and troubled. It also allowed the class task to be abandoned. Clay's and Dave's classmates appeared well behaved and attentive. They seemed to have an agreement to act 'as if' they were good little children, and let two of their members express their discontent with task and contempt towards the teacher.

Additionally, on the day Clay was transferred, John began to behave in a similar way—to play up Dave's and Clay's part. The plot continues.

This illustration shows the power of group-level processes. Ms T. thought that the problem with the classroom was within the characterological structure of the students. She assumed that if she could get rid of the 'troublemakers' things would go quite smoothly. She failed to understand, however, that these students were expressing concerns on behalf of the group. They were only vehicles through which the group expressed its contempt and rage not only for the task but also for the teacher.

It was mentioned that we have ambivalent feelings about authority figures and groups—we both love and hate them simultaneously. However, it is difficult to have conflicting feelings about the same object; hence, we split off our negative feelings into others. Yet, through projective identification we identify with the person who is expressing negative affect by projecting our disowned negative parts. This enables us ('audience') to act 'as if' all of the contempt, rage, and discontent exist in the other ('actor') (Gibbard, 1975). Here is the origin of scapegoating.

We see this phenomenon in work groups and organizations where an individual is symbolized as incompetent or ineffective. Typically, his or her associates secretly discuss the incompetence or the anxiety level of the individual. They act 'as if' this person is the only one who is incompetent or has feelings of anxiety. There seems to be a tacit agreement among them to localize incompetence into this particular person. The manager of the unit evaluates the individual similarly. The person is then put on probation, transferred or dismissed. The manager in this situation acts 'as if' the problems of his unit exist at the intrapersonal level, i.e. within the individual. The manager does not examine the context in which the 'incompetent worker occurred. He or she does not examine why the group has allowed this person to become incompetent. Moreover, he or she does not ask how it serves the unit to *have* this particular person incompetent. It could serve the unit in several ways. It allows the other members to split off their feelings of incompetence (bad parts) into this member, and at the same time, through projective identification, identify with the person's incompetence (because this incompetence is also a part of the member's internal world that he has disowned and externally projected). Hence, the incompetence seen in this particular member represents the projected bad parts of the other group members. Moreover, the projected bad parts are to be destroyed; thus there seems to be an investment in seeing that this member carry incompetence, hoping that it will vanish. Yet we know that it does not solve the problem.

After this person is put on probation, transferred or dismissed, another person may be asked to carry the incompetence on behalf of the unit. In short, if a unit allows one of its group members to carry all of the anxiety or feelings of incompetence, the person will indeed go crazy or get dismissed. Implicit in this conceptual framework is the interdependence of roles.

Role differentiation is, indeed, an imperfect solution for managing the group's problem. This can be seen in the prior illustration. What often results from role differentiation is a compartmentalization of key members who are flooded with anxiety. Winter (1974) describes Redl's (1942) concept of *group psychological role suction* where:

Under certain conditions a specific group situation seems to have an amazing power to 'suck' individuals into performing certain tasks, even though they may not have been strongly inclined in that direction; these tasks which are important for the comfort, or which respond to the motivational or organizational needs of the group.

The group's psychological role suction is a powerful force in the group to keep members in their roles — even if they are not consciously willing to play them. For example, it is rare that a person consciously volunteers to play the scapegoat role. This, however, does not suggest that there is not a collusion to take the role. The scapegoat role appears to be ubiquitous and perhaps the most costly and destructive to the group and individuals. This is not to say that other roles are not important, but rather scapegoating in a group should receive more examination. The following section describes scapegoating in detail.

In sum, role differentiation is essentially a way that individuals cope with the group situation. The emergence of roles serves defensive and adaptative functions. Changing role differentiation is a manifestation of the group's changing pattern of projective identification.

Scapegoating in groups

Scapegoating is a special and destructive form of role differentiation, particularly in the context of work groups. The origin of scapegoating has its roots in myths and rituals of mankind. It emerges from the religious ritual of sacrifice and totemistic practices (Jaffe, 1968; Lieberman *et al.*, 1973).

The ritual of scapegoating is found in the book of Leviticus 16:1-34. Scapegoating was practised by the early Hebrew tribes to atone for their transgressions against their God. Leviticus 16, Verses 7-10, states:

(7)   And he should take the two goats and present them before the Lord at the door of the tabernacle of the congregation.

(8)   And Aa'ron shall cast lots upon the two goats: one lot for the Lord, and the other lot for the scapegoat.

(9)   And Aa'ron shall bring the goat upon which the lot fell, and offer him for a sin offering.

(10) But the goat on which the lot fell to be scapegoat, shall be presented alive before the Lord, to make atonement with him and to let him go for a scapegoat into the wilderness.

The scapegoat represented sins of the tribes that must be separated from themselves and sent into the wilderness. The tribe could project and exorcise their sins through the scapegoat. This act of exorcising the sin (bad parts) on the head of the scapegoat is a mechanism used to cope with their ambivalent relationship to their deity and group. Jaffe (1968) states:

In the process of atonement and purification, the ritual involves, among other things, the disposition of two goats. One is killed and the blood sprinkled upon the arkcover and then upon the altar . . . it (goat) is burnt to make smoke . . . .

The ritual proceeds to dispose of the second goat, which is the 'scapegoat'. *The entire removal of the sin and guilt of the community is symbolized by placing these upon the head of the scapegoat who is then sent away, bearing all of the inequities, into the wilderness or 'land which is cut off' (to prevent the animal's return).*

When later it was no longer possible to send the goat to a place whence it could not return to inhabited parts, the practice became one of casting the animal down a precipice. (p. 66.7) (author's italics)

Groups often search for the scapegoat to represent and repent for their badness (i.e. anxiety, weakness, sins, etc.). The scapegoat role provides the group with an imperfect solution to its felt badness, e.g. incompetence, anxiety, racism, or conflict. By projective identification group members deposit their unwanted parts (their guilt, rage, contempt) in another, then proceed to drive the other into the wilderness or into death. As the Hebrew children used the scapegoat to atone for their sins and to eliminate their guilt, the group uses the scapegoat to cope with its anxiety and badness. Groups create scapegoats to hide every person's self-contempt, self-doubt, weakness, and destructiveness. Miller (1974) states:

The group situation is a particularly salient one for the use of projective identification, a concept introduced by Melanie Klein (1946) to indicate the defensive process whereby aspects of the self are projected onto a person or object which then becomes characterized or controlled by this projected aspect of the self. The manifestation of this defense in groups occurs when members deny a particular feeling, attribute it to someone else, and thus overtly insist that someone else express the feeling for them. Scapegoating is a stereotyped example in groups where shared patterns of denial are focused by the process of projective identificaton on one member. That member is asked and often agrees to express all of the given undesirable attitudes for the group (p. 12)

The *search* for a scapegoat(s) typically begins after the group experiences aggression or frustration. Unconsciously the group members' thought may be: 'Someone is responsible for my anxiety'. This begins the group's search and destroy mission. Typically, people with different demographic characteristics, expressive personalities, and valency for patient or martyr roles become excellent candidates for scapegoating. Groups may even locate a dyad or triad to deposit their denied feelings and then behave in ways to isolate or render them crazy.

Using a scapegoat is an easy (albeit infantile) psychological solution for anxiety and unwanted parts. Excessive projective identification allows group members to deposit all unwanted parts in the scapegoat at the expense of the scapegoat. The scapegoat allows other group members to maintain their self-righteous autistic imagoes. This is why the scapegoat must be separated and sent away; the group cannot stand to look at or face itself seen in the scapegoat. Hence, group members deny any responsibility for making a scapegoat or having any characteristics of the scapegoat.

This cycle of search, isolate, destroy, and denial creates group casualties: to fill a person up with the group's anxiety (psychotic feelings); isolate these feelings in the person as if he or she is the only one who is feeling crazy; exorcise the person from the group; and then deny any responsibility for making a person into a scapegoat is a subtle and dangerous operation. Scapegoating has taken its toll of human life, destroyed work groups, organizations, and families (Lieberman *et al.*, 1973).

Excessive projective identification and rigid role differentiation lead to scapegoating. Role reversal, maintenance discussion, and/or interventions in the group's projective identification motif can alter the scapegoating phenomenon. Comprehending the complexity of the scapegoating phenomenon is essential to the systemic socioanalytic approach. Increasing the awareness of group members may abate the group's tendency to scapegoat. There are indeed other ways groups can cope with their anxiety and frustration.

DIAGNOSTIC HEURISTICS

The group-as-a-whole framework provides a basis for diagnosing organizational behaviour. A variety of heuristics will be given and then applied to a concrete case.

Diagnostic strategies of socioanalytic approach*

(1) Make an initial analysis of the group's processes using all psychological levels of organizational processes (i.e. intrapersonal, interpersonal, group-level, intergroup level, interorganizational).

(2) Develop alternative and competing hypotheses about what is occurring in the group situation.

(3) Give greater emphasis to interpersonal, group-level and intergroup processes than intrapersonal processes. The diagnostician should give individuals in conflict the 'benefit of the doubt' that the reason for the

---

* It is assumed that a diagnostician has been called to consult to a work group where a personality problem exists between Mr/Ms X or Mr/Ms Y. These heuristics and concomitant discussion will by no means prepare the reader to use the socioanalytic approach. They rather highlight major aspects of the approach.

'problems' is not solely dependent on their intrapsychic condition. Too often intrapersonal analyses are made. This often prematurely indicts/blames individuals for an organizational problem. Intrapersonal analysis is quite costly for the individual's life and career and for the organization in terms of turnover. Hence, only make intrapersonal attribution about organizational problems when all of the other process levels have been fully explored.

(4) When analysing organizational processes from a group-level perspective, the diagnostician must raise these questions about the group under examination: (a) What does this conflict represent on behalf of the group-as-a-whole? (b) What does the conflict symbolize for the group? (c) What feelings (*via* projective identification) are being put in these co-actors? (d) Do they express the anxiety, incompetence or hope on behalf of the group? (e) How does it serve the group to have these co-actors take their specialized roles?

(5) The diagnostician must examine him/herself by stepping back and using the 'observing ego' to check out the 'experiencing ego' or the internal experience of being with the client group. The diagnostician aims to use him/herself and his or her experiences as a barometer to understand the group's processes.

(6) The diagnostician must examine ways he or she may be using projective identification to cope with the consulting role. Projective identification can be abated by working on *owning and living with* ambivalence and concomitant anxiety. This reduces the need to split off internal bad/good feelings.

(7) Gather data on the group's unconscious alliances by listening to group themes, the tone of the discussion. Attempt to link and compare the content of the discussion to the 'here and now' group concerns

(8) Diagnosticians must ask themselves what feelings are being put into them. If the diagnostician feels anxious, hopeless, etc., at some levels, the group feels the same and has unconsciously asked the consultant to carry the feelings.

At the same time, if the diagnostician feels powerful, competent, 'able to leap tall buildings at a single bound,' the group *via* projective identification, may be acting 'as if' they are incompetent, deskilled infants in need of protection. To collude with the group's wishes confirms that they are infants (which they actually resent), thus creating a more problematic situation.

With the preceding heuristics in mind, the diagnostician can begin to formulate interventions focused at the group level. Interventions are aimed at the group-as-a-whole. They should be interpretative or demonstrative in nature. Comments should be offered about what the group is doing to the individuals who are the identified problems.

The data used to formulate these interventions should always be presented.

The use of the 'because clause' (Turquet, 1974) is extremely helpful when intervening at the group level. The 'because clause' is a hypothesis about the reason for the group's behaviour and how the co-actors express aspects of the group's *élan vital*.

The diagnostician should discuss the conceptual perspective he or she uses to examine group processes. It should be stated that individual behaviour in groups is assumed to represent the group-as-a-whole. Hence, when a person acts, he or she acts not only on his or her own behalf, but on behalf of the group's life.

Members typically challenge the group-as-a-whole concept. In western society group members like to see themselves as acting always under their own initiatives. This attitude may represent individualistic norms of the western world. To adopt a group-level perspective about individual behaviour in group violates the narcissistic striving of the group members. They are frightened by the possibility that they may be controlled by some force other than themselves. To take the group-level perspective elicits anger and fear in group members. They experience the group-level perspective in itself as a narcissistic blow. It challenges their vanity. Hence, resistance against interventions rapidly grows. A working through of the group's response to the intervention is critical. The diagnostician can request the group to step back and examine the moments when the intervention was made and offer comments about the difficulty in understanding the notion that we exist as interdependent co-actors connected by a covert and unconscious relationship.

The diagnostician should only aim to reduce the pressure on the individuals (i.e. alter the group's projective identification motif) who represents the identified problem. The diagnostician may consult with the individuals separately to discuss how the group may be using them as a repository, etc.

A series of interventions used to reduce the pressure on and conflict between Ms A and Mr K follows as an illustration of the socioanalytic approach.

A case illustration*

A five-day experiential learning laboratory for drug treatment counsellors about the treatment and rehabilitation of minority (coloured) substance abusers was offered in a large northeastern metropolitan city. During this workshop conflict and hostility developed between two participants: Ms A, a black woman, and Mr K, an anglo man. Fifteen participants (eight anglos, five blacks, and two hispanics) comprised the workshop. Three blacks, the staff. The dean of the laboratory was a black man.

The conflict between Ms A and Mr K escalated as the laboratory progressed. In large group sessions they often interrupted and disagreed with one another.

*The author's role was that of the Dean in this case.

While these combatants engaged in their seemingly interpersonal problem, the other group members sat as a silent audience, watching with great interest. The *content* of their disagreement focused on the validity of the material presented by the staff (i.e. black authority). For example:

Mr K (angrily): These theories do not represent my experience. I don't really know if there are any real differences between black and white clients. A lot of these theories is mere abstractions and bullshit!

Ms A (said to Mr K): They are real to me. If you don't like it, or it is not consistent with your experience, you can get out — leave. You don't need to help anybody anyway — except your damn self!

Ms A always defended the validity of the material. Mr K always raised questions about the validity of the material. It was 'as if' a discussion regarding the relative merits or deficiencies of the material presented could not occur without erupting into a conflict. Moreover, when Ms A and Mr K discussed to the point where they might agree, a member of the group would say: 'You really don't listen to each other.' (Other members would nod their heads in agreement.) This would act to rekindle the conflict between Ms A and Mr K. They would accuse each other of not listening and the cycle continued — their conflict roles reinforced.

In spite of their promotion of the conflict between Ms A and Mr K by remaining silently attentive during the interchanges and introducing inflammatory material whenever the two would approach agreement, the other group members were not at all grateful for the services of Ms A and Mr K on their behalf. On the contrary, they complained, both inside and outside the sessions, that Ms A and Mr K were 'too aggressive', 'took up too much air time', and that they were 'tired of listening to them'.

From an intrapersonal perspective, it would appear that Ms A and Mr K have personality problems, e.g. they each lack impulse control, are excessively insecure and competitive, or just 'crazy'. The problem lies *within* Ms A and Mr K. To resolve these 'intrapersonal problems', individual psychotherapy is recommended.

From an interpersonal perspective, the behaviours of Ms A and Mr K suggest that their respective communication styles are incongruent, and that they lack interpersonal competence. The problem lies *between* only Ms A and Mr K. To resolve these interpersonal problems, a 'training' (T) group experience is recommended.

Using the systemic socioanalytic approach (i.e. 'group-as-a-whole' method of analysis), it would appear that Ms A and Mr K are involved in a conflict in which the other group members are intensely interested. Moreover, it also seemed that the participants had a stake in the conflict between Ms A and Mr K. The other group members, through projective identification, forced Ms A and Mr K to confront issues for them that were perceived as difficult and anxiety-laden. Once the opposing positions were assumed, they were scapegoated.

By using Ms A and Mr K as receptacles, the group can simultaneously express its frustration and feel contempt for the dyad. To assume that the problem lies only within Ms A or Mr K, or only between Ms A and Mr K, would be erroneous. Zinner (1976) would say the dyad acted as a 'proxy' in the world (outside the self) which served as a repository for the other group members' wishes.

Moreover, it appears 'as if' Ms A and Mr K represented opposite aspects of the ambivalence that the member group had towards the staff group. The group acted out its ambivalence through the dyad — one black, the other white. It is not coincidental that Ms A, the black woman, expressed the positive side of the ambivalence, and Mr K, an anglo male, expressed the negative side. The group members wanted to simplify their lives; they wanted things clear — in 'black and white' terms.

Through projective identification the group used the dyad to resolve strong, conflicting feelings. It was 'as if' Ms A was in support of the staff without reservation and Mr K was against the staff without reservation. In reality, it was more likely that Ms A had some reservation about the content of the course and the training staff and Mr K had some positive feelings about the course content and the training staff. Yet it was very difficult for either Ms A or Mr K to have appropriately mixed feelings about the course and training staff.

Under the influence of the group's motif of projective identification, the dyad could not 'break out' of their roles without help from other members. They were involved in Redl's (1942) group psychological role suction. The influence of the group's projective identification pattern is revealed in the group members' interest in the pair fighting. They had an unconscious alliance with each other to maintain the pair. At a fantasy level for the group, perhaps, Ms A and Mr K would come together and produce the *answer* (Messiah) to the difficulty in learning by experience and resolve the racial conflicts, but, most of all, they would reduce the overwhelming anxiety generated by participating in this temporary educational enterprise.

This is quite a dangerous situation for the dyads who become the repository for split-off parts of the group. In extreme form, group members in these roles are scapegoated, used, driven crazy, and exorcised from the group or organization. Without a group-level analysis we could assume that the problem lies within the individuals involved. Yet the group projective identification motif reveals that there are forces working to fill up Ms A and Mr K with negative affect and conflict. It is, indeed, this process that drives individuals psychotic in group and organizational contexts.

Through the use of projective identification, group members (the audience) experience vicarious gratifications of their projected impulses as expressed by the conflict in the Black-white dyad. Using Ms A and Mr K to express conflict allowed the release of the group's frustration and anxiety. It also allowed the other group members (audience) to withdraw and stay aloof, as though they had no investment nor internal tension about participating in the laboratory. Projective identification allowed the audience to take an unconscious voyeuristic attitude towards the interaction between Ms A and Mr K. This unconscious voyeuristic posture assumed by the group members provided a vehicle through which they could split off their bad parts and put them into Ms A and Mr K. Splitting and externalizing the bad parts (i.e. anxiety-producing parts) is a defensive manoeuvre to achieve the pre-ambivalent, autistic state of a neonate.

Yet, what of the implicit collusion by Ms A and Mr K to express the group's frustration and anxiety? It appeared that Ms A was predisposed for strong identification with the staff's competence. She wanted to protect the staff from the anger, contempt, and competition of the group. Through the use of projective identification she could positively identify with the black staff. This, therefore, made it more difficult to consciously experience her own competitive, envious, angry, and contemptuous feelings — unconsciously Ms A thought the staff would be destroyed by her badness.

The interaction between Ms A and her predisposition or valence towards identifying with the staff* and the group members' symbolization of and attribution to her sociological characteristics (i.e. black female) extended her identification with the staff to include the function of protecting them. Dumas (1975) suggests that in social systems tremendous pressure is exerted on black women to perform 'nanny' or protective, caretaking roles. Hence, at some level, Ms A was available to protect the staff. Yet the protection of the staff put extreme pressure on her (on leaving the workshop, Ms A and Mr K both complained of headaches and fatigue). From an individual point of view, under the influence of the group's projective identification Ms A's *valence bonds* were exaggerated or extended so that it became psychologically uncomfortable and anxiety-provoking for her. She became swept up in the influence of the group's projective identification, which allowed her to take on scapegoat functions concomitantly with Mr K.

---

*Nobles (1974, 1976) suggests that Afro-Americans have maintained their African connection, or 'Africanity', despite the assertions made by white 'scholars'. This Africanity is clearly seen in the black extended family system (Nobles, 1976; Hayles, 1978).

The oneness of being and survival of the tribe are the principles upon which Africanity is based. Thus, in the ontology of Afro-centric people throughout the black diaspora, there is an existential view that all black people are of the 'same being', of the same 'vital life force' that connects them as one. As an analogue, the spider's web represents the relationships in Africa and throughout the black diaspora, as Ms A's identification with the staff, in part, represents Africanity. There seemed to be an implicit existential connection between Ms A and the black staff. Her identification with the staff was facilitated by her being-black-in-the-world.

Mr K, an anglo male, was also predisposed to collude in the group's projective identification. Mr K reported that he worked in an all-black organization with a black male director. Hence, he had several concerns. First, he had a sincere desire to work with people of colour, and he viewed himself as a sensitive, committed individual who championed social causes. However, he had ambivalence about having a subordinate role working with black people. At work, he was apparently unaware of his negative feeling about working in an all-black organization in his subordinate and minority status. In the laboratory, he projectively identified with other anglos whom he perceived as uninterested in social causes and racist.

In this laboratory situation, Mr K's ambivalence towards his minority working status was triggered by working with an all-black staff who had no 'real world'* authority to affect his employment. Hence, he had a valence, given his ambivalence towards his work situation, to come under the influence of the group's projective identification.

He colluded with the group's wishes to compete with and challenge the staff. He also expressed the group's fantasy that the staff really might be incompetent; and that the only reason they were hired was because of Affirmative Action plans, or 'that they were just running a "good game" without having any skills to teach anything'. The former attitude represented the covert attitudes of the anglo participants, the latter black participants' covert attitudes. Mr K's expressions of admiration and trust for the staff (the other side of his ambivalence) could not be expressed under the influence of the group's projective identification. He developed psychosomatic complaints during the week under the stress of acting as the repository for the negative feeling towards the staff and being scapegoated for it. Yet, like Ms A, Mr K's *valence bonds* were stretched so that he got swept up in his *role* and became a candidate for scapegoating.

This case study and interpretation provide an illustration of how projective identification, role differentiation, and the psychological needs of scapegoating are used in a group setting. A discussion on intervening in interpersonal relations from a 'systemic socioanalytic perspective' follows.

Interventions

On the third day of the laboratory, the staff decided that 'conflict' between Ms A and Mr K had escalated and begun to have a negative impact on the progress of the course. It was thought that the conflict between Ms A and Mr K should be openly discussed in the large group session.

During the large group session the Dean (the author) offered the following comments:

*'Real world' authority meaning that, as trainers, the staff had no relationship with his work organization. The laboratory staff could not affect his employment.

It seems to me that the group has allowed Ms A and Mr K to express mixed feelings and reactions to the relevance of the course content or the competence of the staff that exist inside each and everyone here. Surely, it is much easier to let Ms A and Mr K carry and express each side of the conflicting feelings about the staff on behalf of everyone here.

In response to the Dean's comment, a member replied:

This is Ms A's and Mr K's conflict — it's their trip. I don't have anything to do with it.

The Dean then offered this comment:

Indeed, it would be a simple solution to live under the pretence that the conflict is just Ms A's and Mr K's. Surely, they are willing actors who allow themselves to be used in this way. It seems that Ms A represents the part of each member that may want to protect the staff. Mr K represents the part of everyone that may question the content of the course and the staff's competence. It's quite easy to have Ms A and Mr K simply resolve the group's internal ambivalence.

This intervention* had several purposes: (i) to articulate how the group was using Ms A and Mr K to reduce other group members' internal conflict and tension; (2) to illustrate how Ms A and Mr K colluded with the group's wishes — implicitly suggesting that they should stop the collusion; (3) to uncover 'tacit alliances' that existed among the members. Making explicit by surfacing the group's tacit alliance (the group's projective identification motif) through the intervention renders this particular form of group alliance inoperative. Tacit group alliances can only operate when they are indeed unconscious or covert.

Interventions from a group-level perspective are often resisted and resented by the group members. They experience the intervention, as Tarachow (1963) suggests, as a 'double deprivation'. Firstly, the intervention uncovers the unconscious alliance that exists among the group members, which they experience as being 'found out' or 'caught'. Secondly, there is an implicit statement that staff in this case will not collude with how the group is relating to and using each other. In short, they must change their behaviour towards one another and themselves.

The group's wish to have the conflicting feelings and tension bottled up in two of its members is challenged by the intervention. The *wish* (or the hope) that putting the feelings into Ms A and Mr K can resolve complex feelings and painful anxiety is extinguished.

The message to the group members is that each of them must *own* the parts of themselves that are split off into others *via* projective identification. The intervention invites each member to tolerate his or her ambivalence and

*The group-as-a-whole approach had been discussed with the group members earlier. Hence, the group was familiar with the concepts of projective identification and splitting. If a group is unfamiliar with these concepts, they should be given a lecturette.

anxiety. The intervention requests the members to refrain from using others to carry and express unwanted split parts. The intervention asks members to abandon their neonate coping strategy (i.e. projective identification) to manage the feelings generated by the laboratory experience. The intervention robs the group of its infantile wishes.

The members often respond defensively and with denial to these interventions. To illustrate, a members commented in response to the Dean's interventions:

I don't know what you are talking about. I think the course is OK. I am just waiting to see how you (staff) are going to tie it together. But, I feel all right.

Another group member commented:

Well, I have a number of questions about what has been going on here. Yet, Mr K seemed to have raised them for me. I really didn't want to seem like a smart-ass always asking questions. I might get misinterpreted because I'm white.

A black member commented:

I find the theories presented helpful. Yet, there are questions I don't ask because I think the white members here will use them to criticize you (staff). So, I just keep things to myself and ask you about them after the sessions are over.

There seemed to be an underlaying fear that prevented members from bringing their whole person into the laboratory. It appeared that they needed to keep some of their thoughts and feelings out of the workshop. There seemed a need to 'put a lid on things'. Fantasies of violence and conflict were uppermost in members' minds. Kovel (1970) suggests that even discussing race relations in America elicits primitive and violent fantasies. Hence, there was a concern that things might get out of hand — someone might get hurt. An easy solution to the underlying anxiety was for Ms A and Mr K to carry and hopefully resolve the conflict on behalf of the group by scapegoating the black/white dyad — if the group could fill up Ms A and Mr K with affect and cast them off to atone for the badness (bad feelings) in each member.

Indeed, in ancient Hebrew rituals, the scapegoat was banished to the wilderness — never to return — with the transgressions of the tribes. The banishment of the scapegoat represented atonement. Scapegoating is used to exorcise individual and collective sins (badness) of the tribe.

In the attempted scapegoating of Ms A and Mr K, the staff interfered with this solution by making an intervention from the group level. The group members could no longer ignore how they were using each other and how destructively and violently they were behaving.

In response to the members' comments, the Dean made this intervention:

Denied feelings seek expression. We often split off our feelings and put them into others. Yet, that really does not resolve the feelings; they only get repressed, waiting with greater magnitude for expression.

To deny the truth increases its force a thousandfold. To deny feelings increases them beyond endurance.

It seems then the major question for this group is: 'Can people bring their *whole* selves into the experience of the laboratory — both positive and negative feelings, emotion and intellect?'

A white member responded:

I feel I can't let all of my thoughts out. Things might happen. Conflict, confusion, and hostility may erupt. I don't want to be called a fuckin' racist!

Other members nodded in silent agreement. Then a black group member remarked:

I feel I can't raise questions or say very much because everyone may get into a conflict. I hate confusion and conflict. I'd rather avoid it. And you (the Dean) don't help matters either!

A comment from a Latino member followed:

The conflict in this group is between anglo and black people. I'm just here to learn. I don't say much because I can see both sides of the issue. I have my own special issues. They are not black or anglo; so, I'll let you all fight. But, I feel that the issues of latino clients were not addressed. There aren't any latinos on staff! And, seemingly, nothing can be done about it. So, I'll sit back and let all of this bullshit go on — crazy Americans!

After these members had responded to the Dean's intervention, other group members shared their feelings about the course and each other. As discussion among the group members became more open, exploration of the group's fantasies and fears occurred.

The intervention changed the motif of projective identification among the group members. It robbed the group of its unconscious alliances and thus freed group members to form other types of alliances that were less destructive. Consequently, the group's investment in using Ms A and Mr K to express the conflict abated. They were released from their conflict roles. Their candidacy for scapegoats was relinquished.

To test whether the conflict was interpersonal in nature, the staff asked if Ms A and Mr K wanted to have a third-party (Walton, 1969) consultation to help them resolve their 'interpersonal problem'. There was little interest in this solution by Ms A or Mr K. In subsequent sessions, conflict between them ceased. Other group members became more active and gave feedback. Negative *and* positive feelings were shared.

Critical and positive evaluations were offered. Even greater openness emerged as the session progressed. Group members seemed more able to take responsibility for their feelings (both negative and positive) and for their learning.

At the end of the workshop, Ms A and Mr K did not necessarily adore each other. But they were not engaged in conflict nor scapegoated. Indeed, both had learned a lot about how groups can use individuals and how one can collude. Moreover, they became acutely aware that when one *acts* in a group, the acts may not be the function of one's own intrapersonal conditions, but rather that of the group. Groups can make individuals behave in certain and prescribed ways. Perhaps Ms A and Mr K learned more than other members by being in the entrails of the group.

In evaluating the laboratory, members commented:

Feelings *can* be put *in* you!
A person often uses and is used by other group members to act in a certain way — to assume a particular role.
I don't want to believe that groups can control my behaviour.
When I came here I thought all of that psychoanalytic stuff was bullshit. It really might have some relevance; I have to reconsider.
I have more to learn, all has not sunk in yet.
This was a hard experience. I learned a lot about myself — and the treatment of minorities.

Interventions from a systemic socioanalytic perspective can provide meaningful learning for organization members. They can teach group members that they are all responsible, in part, for what happens in their work group. Often by tacit agreement, through silence and collusion, we determine what people say or how they act in groups and organizations. We can and do fill others with our split, projected parts. Moreover, socioanalytic intervention may teach us that we *are* what we have disdain and contempt for. We are indeed, in part, all of those undesirable traits and behaviours we see in others. Group-level interventions help us to be more empathetic with those whom we would like to kill off. We all, at times, act like King David, author of the *Psalms*.

The underlying intent of the socioanalytic approach is to increase individuals' and groups' understanding of their covert dynamics. It is hoped that individuals exposed to the socioanalytic approach will be more task-effective and humane to each other. Increased consciousness enables individuals to become more competent managers and better leaders and followers. It may also reduce the amount of human wreckage and pathos that occurs in groups and organizations at alarming rates.

Simply stated, the socioanalytic intervention and approach helps individuals understand that we must take individual and collective responsibility for what happens in groups. We are not solipsists, unaffected by others, nor individuals in isolation, but rather connected and driven by collective ties. We are indeed group creatures. The wise poet John Donne (Hayward, 1949) eloquently describes our 'groupishness' and man's identity:

Who bends not his ear to any bell which upon any occasion rings, but who can remove it from that bell which is passing a piece of himself out of this world?
    No man is an island, entire of itself; every man is a piece of the continent, a part of the main . . . .
    Any man's death diminishes me because I am involved in mankind. And therefore never seek to know for whom the bell tolls: it tolls for thee. (from *Devotion XVII*)

SUMMARY AND CONCLUSIONS

This chapter delineates the theoretical and diagnostic aspects of the systemic socioanalytic approach. A number of concepts have been defined and applied to several case illustrations. This is only an introduction to the developing approach, and raises more questions than it answers. Many of the concepts presented here hopefully have heuristic value for scholars and practitioners.

The group-as-a-whole phenomenon is important, but little recognized in determining quality of life in social systems. Phenomena often defined as personality problems or personal incompetence may, in reality, be a manifestation of the group's struggle with its anxiety and tension. Indeed, the group-as-a-whole concept is intellectually challenging and appears to violate western notions of individual uniqueness and autonomy. Nevertheless, it can explain a large portion of variance in individual behaviour within groups. The group-as-a-whole approach also makes it clear that members of Homo sapiens are connected by their 'groupishness', regardless of their contempt for that idea.

ACKNOWLEDGEMENTS

This chapter would have been impossible to produce without the assistance of: *Robert C. Tucker*, who provided me with support and editorial acumen; *Clayton P. Alderfer*, who offered guidance and Socratic priming in helping me develop this 'systemic socioanalytic perspective'; *Earline Houston*, who gave her skills and patience in helping me struggle with this document; *J. Richard Hackman*, who offered his insight and editing; *Graham Gibbard*, whose theoretical advances and earlier discussions provided the springboard for this paper; and *Ella Greene*, my friend, who toiled and carefully prepared this manuscript. To all I am humble indebted. A thousand thanks.

REFERENCES

Albanese, R. (1975) *Management: Toward Accountability for Performance.* Homewood, Ill.: Irwin.

Alderfer, C. P. (1976) 'Change processes in organizations.' In Dunnette, M. (ed.) *Handbook of Industrial and Organizational Psychology.* Chicago: Rand McNally. (1977a).

Alderfer, C. P. (1976) 'Boundary relations and organizational diagnosis.' In Meltzer, H. L. and Wickett, F. (eds) *Humanizing Organizational Behavior.* Springfield, Ill.: Thomas, 1976.

Alderfer, C. P. (1977a) 'Group and intergroup relations.' In Hackman, J. R. and Suttle, J. L. (eds.) *Improving Life and Work: Behavioral Sciences Approaches to Organizational Change.* Santa Monica, California: Goodyear.

Argyris, C. (1962) *Organizational Effectiveness and Interpersonal Competence.* New York: Wiley.

Astrachan, B. M. (1970) 'Toward a social systems model of therapeutic groups', *Social Psychiatry*, **5**, 110-9.

Baker, F. (Ed.) (1973) *Organizational Systems: General System Approaches to Complex Organizations.* Homewood, Ill.: Irwin.

Bion, W. F. (1955) 'Language and the schizophrenic.' In Klein, Heimann and Money-Kyle (eds.) *New Directions in Psychoanalysis.* London: Tavistock.

Bion, W. F. (1956) 'Development of schizophrenic thought', *Int. Jr. of Psycho-Anal.*, **37**.

Bion, W. F. (1961) *Experiences in Groups.* New York: Basic Books.

Caplan, R. D. and Jones, K. W. (1975) 'Effects of workload, role ambiguity, and type A personality on anxiety, depression and heart rate', *Journal of Applied Psychology*, **60**, 6, 713-9.

Cartwright, D. and Zander, A. (1968) *Group Dynamics: Research and Theory.* New York: Harper and Row.

Colman, A. D., and Bexton, W. H. (eds.) (1975) *Group Relations Reader.* Sansalito, California: GREX.

Dicks, H. V. (1963) 'Object relations theory and martial studies', *Br. Jr. Med. Psychol.*, **36**, 125-9.

Dumas, R. (1975) 'The Seed of the Coming Free: An Essay on Black Female Leadership', Dissertation, Union-Antioch Graduate School, Yellow Springs, Ohio.

Emery, F. E. and Trist, E. L. (1973) 'Causal texture of environment.' In Baker, F. (ed.) *Organizational Systems: General Systems Approaches to Complex Organizations.* Homewood, Ill.: Irwin.

Evan, W. M. (1966) 'The organization-set: toward a theory of interorganizational relationships.' In Thompson, J. D. (ed.) *Approaches to Organizational Design.* Pittsburgh, PA: University of Pittsburgh Press, pp. 177-80.

Freud, Anna (1946) *The Ego and the Mechanism of Defense.* New York: International Universities Press.

Freud, S. (1922) *Group Psychology and the Analysis of the Ego.* London: International Psychoanalytical Press.

Gibbard, G. (1975) 'Bion's group psychology: a reconsideration', Unpublished manuscript, West Haven Veterans Administration Hospital, West Haven, Connecticut.

Gibbard, G. S., Hartmann, J. J., and Mann, R. D. (eds.) (1974) *Analysis of Groups.* San Francisco: Jossey-Bass.

Greenspan, I. S. and Mannis, F. W. (1974) 'A model for brief intervention with couples based on projective identification', *Am. J. Psychiatry*, **10**, 131, 1103-6.

Hayles, R. V. (1978) 'Psychological health among culturally different families.' Presented at 4th International Association of Cross Cultural Psychology Congress, Munich, Germany, August 5, 1978.

Hayward, J. (ed.) (1949) *John Donne: Complete Poetry and Selected Prose*. London: Nonesuch; New York: Random House.

Jacques, E. (1955) 'Social system as a defense against persecutory and depressive anxiety.' In Klein, M., Hermann, P. and Money-Kyrle, R. E. (eds.) *New Directions in Psychoanalysis: The Significance of Infant Conflict in the Pattern of Adult Behavior*. New York: Basic Books, pp. 478-98.

Jaffe, D. S. (1968) 'The mechanism of projection: its dual role in object relations', *Int. J. Psycho-Anal.*, **49**, 662-77.

Janis, L. *Victims of Group Think*. (1972) Boston: Houghton, Mifflin.

Jenkins, D. C. (1971) 'Psychologic and social precursors of coronary disease', *New England Journal of Medicine*, **284**, 244-66, 307-17.

Klein, E. B. and Astrachan, B. M. (1972) 'Learning in groups: a comparison of study and T-groups', *Journal of Applied Behavioral Science*, December.

Klein, M. (1932) *The Psycho Analysis of Children*. New York: Delta.

Klein, M. (1946) 'Notes on some schizoid mechanisms', *Int. J. Psycho-Anal.*, **27**, 99-110.

Klein, M. (1955) 'On identification'. In *New Direction in Psychoanalysis*. London: Tavistock.

Klein, M. (1959) 'Our adult world and its infancy', *Human Relations*, **12**, 291-303.

Klein, M. and Riviere, J. (1964) *Love, Hate and Reparation*. New York: Norton.

Kovel, J. (1970) *White Racism: A Psychohistory*. New York: Pantheon.

Kretch, D., Crutchfield, R. S., and Ballachey, E. L. (1962) *Individual in Society*: A Textbook of Social Psychology. New York: McGraw-Hill.

Laughlin, H. P. (1970) *The Ego and Its Defenses*. New York: Appleton-Century-Crofts.

Lieberman, M. A., Yalom, I. D., and Miles, M. B. (1973) *Encounter Groups: First Facts*. New York: Basic Books.

Lott, A. J. and Lott, B. E. (1965) 'Group cohesiveness as interpersonal attraction: a review of relationships with antecedent and consequent variables', *Psychological Bulletin*, **64**, 259-302.

Mahler, M. S. (1972) 'On the first three subphases of the separation-individuation process', *International Journal of Psychoanalysis*, **53**, 333-8.

Malin, A. and Grotstein, J. S. (1966) 'Projective identification in the therapeutic process', *Int. J. Psycho-Anal.*, **47**, 26-31.

Mant, A. (1976) 'How to analyze management', *Management Today*, Oct.

Miller, E. J. and Rice, A. K. (1967) *System of Organization: The Control of Task and Sentient Boundaries*. London: Tavistock.

Miller, J. C. (1974) 'Aspects of Tavistock consultation' Unpublished, Yale University, Dept. of Psychiatry.

Newcomb, T. M. (1961) *The Acquaintance Process*. New York: Holt, Rinehart and Winston.

Nobles, W. W. (1974) 'Africanity: its role in Black families', *The Black Scholar*, **5** (9), 10-17.

Nobles, W. W. (1976) 'Formulative and empirical study of Black families', *Black Family Project*. San Francisco: Westside Community Health Center.

Oshry, B. (1978) *Power and Systems Laboratory in Organization Behavior*. Boston: Power & Systems Inc.

Perls, F. (1970) *Gestalt Therapy*. New York: Basic Books.

Redl, F. (1942) 'Group emotion and leadership', *Psychiatry*, **5**, 573-96.

Reed, B., Hutton, J. and Bazulgette, J. (1978) *Freedom to Study: Requirements of Overseas Students in the United Kingdom*. London: Overseas Student Trust.

Rice, A. K. (1965) *Learning for Leadership: Interpersonal and Intergroup Relations*. London: Tavistock.

Rioch, M. J. (1970) 'The work of Wilfred Bion on groups', *Psychiatry*, 33, 2/70, 55-66.

Rosenfeld, H. W. (1952a) 'Notes on the psychoanalysis of the super-ego conflict of an acute schizophrenic patient', *International J. Psycho-Anal.*, 33.

Rosenfeld, H. W. (1952b) 'Transference-phenomena and transference-analysis in an acute catatonic patient', *Int. J. Psycho-Anal.*, 33.

Rosenfeld, H. W. (1954) 'Considerations regarding the psycho-analytic approach to acute and chronic schizophrenia', *Int. J. Psycho-Anal.*, 35.

Scheidlinger, S. (1964) 'Identification, the sense of belonging and of identity in small groups', *International Journal of Group Psychotherapy*, 14, 291-306.

Scheidlinger, S. (1968) 'The concept of regression in group psychotherapy', *International Journal of Group Psychotherapy*, 18, 13-20.

Segal, H. (1964) *Introduction to Works of Melanie Klein*. New York: Basic Books.

Sherwood, M. (1964) 'Bion's experiences in groups: a critical evaluation', *Human Relations*, 17, 114-30.

Singer, D., Astrachan, B. and Gould, L. (1975) In Klein, E. 'Boundary management in psychological work in groups', *Journal of Applied Behavioral Science*, 2, 2, 137-76.

Smith, K. K. (1977) 'An intergroup perspective on individual behavior.' In Hackman, R. J., Lawler, E. E., and Porter, L. W. (eds.) *Perspective on Behavior in Organizations*. New York: McGraw-Hill, pp. 359-72.

Sullivan, H. S. (1970) *The Psychiatric Interview*. New York: Norton.

Tarachow, S. (1963) *Introduction to Psychotherapy*. New York: International Universities Press.

Thibaut, J. W. and Kelly, H. H. (1959) *The Social Psychology of Groups*. New York: Wiley.

Turquet, P. M. (1974) 'Leadership: the individual and the group.' In Gibbard, G. S., Hartman, J. J. and Mann, R. D. (eds.) *Analysis of Groups*. San Francisco: Jossey-Bass, pp. 349-71.

Walton, R. E. (1969) *Interpersonal Peacemaking: Confrontation and Third Party Consultation*. Reading, Pa: Addison-Wesley.

Weir, J. and Weir, S. (1978) Personal communication.

Wells, L. (1978a) 'Assessing the quality of student life: a new model', Working Paper §18, Yale University School of Organization and Management.

Wells, L. (1978b) 'Open system theory applied to the management of organizations: special application to drug prevention programs.' In Bauman, A. (ed.) *Prevention: A Course for Local Program Survival — Resource Manual*. Rosslyn, Va: National Drug Abuse Training Center.

Wells, L. (1978c) 'CARS — (class, age, race and sex) study dynamics of a microcosm: A group-level in intergroup laboratory.' Working paper, Yale University.

Winter, S. (1974) 'Interracial dynamics in self-analytic groups.' In Gibbard, G. S., Hartman, J. J. and Mann, R. D. (eds.) *Analysis of Groups*. San Francisco: Jossey-Bass, pp. 197-219.

Yalom, I. D. (1970) *The Theory and Practice of Group Psychotherapy*. New York: Basic Books.

Zinner, J. and Shapiro, R. (1972) 'Projective identification as a mode of projection and behavior in families of adolescents', *Int. J. Psycho-Anal.*, 53, 523-30.

Zinner, J. (1976) 'Projective identification in marital interaction.' In Grunebaum, H. (ed.) *Contemporary Marriage: The Structure and Dynamics of Marriage*. Boston: Little, Brown.

Advances in Experiential Social Processes, Volume 2
Edited by C. P. Alderfer and C. L. Cooper

Chapter **8**

Planning for Black Human Interaction Groups

Robert C. Tucker

Yale University, U.S.A.

BACKGROUND

The first question the reader may ask is: 'Why is a separate chapter on group experiences for black people necessary? After all, the needs and problems of blacks in this area should not be appreciably different from those of whites.' This may be true, but being black in the U.S. brings with it certain inescapable problems that are peculiar to black people. These are pervasive problems which become infused within and confound black interpersonal and hetero-sexual relations. Being among those who occupy the lowest rung of the American survival ladder, blacks are engaged in a major struggle for economic and psychological survival. Consequently, they must not only deal with ordinary interpersonal and cross-sexual conflicts, but also with extensions and variations of those conflicts that derive from status and economic deprivation.

One area of particular concern is the current state of relations between black men and black women. Since 1975 black media (popular journals, radio, and television) have given increasingly broad coverage to the 'deterioration' in black male-female relations, and many black social and scholarly groups have conducted public forums to create greater public awareness of the situation; but despite extensive delineation of the problem and discussion of the issues, nothing of substance has been proposed to correct the problems that underlie the condition. Thus far ameliorative efforts have been more *expressive* than *instrumental*, and have been largely ineffectual.

What follow are perspectives on two salient but ignored behavioural science questions: how do black people respond to (and in) human interaction (experiential) groups; and how central are male-female relations as a theme for black human interaction groups.* These perspectives include: (1) discussion of

---

*The term 'human interaction groups', as used here, refers to the wide variety of experiential group events whose major goals are study and/or modification of human behaviour as it occurs. Specific reference is made to so-called sensitivity, encounter, gestalt, Tavistock, psychodrama, and bio-energetic groups.

the applicability of extant experiential group models for black people; (2) exploration of the dynamics underlying black male-female interactions; and (3) delineation of a viable experiential group model for black people. This chapter is not presented as a definitive statement on experiential group methods for black people, but is offered as an informational and conceptual base upon which others are encouraged to build and experiment further.

BLACK PEOPLE AND GROUPS

The issue of *black behaviour in groups* has received little or no coverage in the popular media, and has not been systematically examined in scholarly literature. Since the quality, dimensions, and determinants of black behaviour in groups are issues that have been virtually ignored, there is no body of empirical or clinical data upon which a discussion of black behaviour in groups can be based. This chapter, therefore, is largely and necessarily based upon the observations, professional experiences, and intellectual constructions of the writer.

Information available to the writer includes his personal experiences as a member in various types of groups; reports from associates; observation of negative response among black high-school students; casual negative reports of black athletes, street people, and working people; and study of the limited literature (Winter, 1971; Steele and Nash, 1972). Data derived from these observations and experiences suggest that black people generally do not respond positively to human interaction groups of any kind. This assumption is supported by survey data on the opinions of a limited number of individuals who *did not join*, *did not attend* or *dropped out of* three separate human interaction groups led by the writer and his wife. Reasons given for non-participation in these groups varied, but the most consistently reported reason was lack of confidence in the group method.

Those who were most negative.described human interaction groups as 'mind games', 'mental masturbation', 'punk rapping', or 'structured white bullshit'. Among these individuals, group discussions were viewed as abstract, escapist irrelevancies that provide evidence of basic weakness and craziness among *white* people: *craziness* because members reveal their hidden fantasies and secrets ('putting your business in the street'); and *weakness* because members 'shamelessly' ask for help. Black *men* who participate in groups are often viewed as 'brainwashed punks', and black women are often viewed as 'white-oriented bitches'. The substance of these beliefs did not appear to vary with education or income, only the terms used to describe the beliefs were different.

The predominance of this belief system may be partly explained by the fact that the openness and honesty expectations within human interaction groups run directly counter to the long-standing secretive and 'slick' survival orientation of ghettoized blacks. Underlying this proposition is the belief that even though open and honest people may survive in the suburbs, they would not last very long on the 'neo-plantation' or within the black ghetto.* When one is struggling to survive physically and psychologically and is competing with others for scarce resources, openness and honesty would appear to be of limited utility — would occupy a lower position on the hierarchy of needs.

This appears to be true even in light of the black tradition of 'testifying' in church: admitting one's sins publicly and asking for forgiveness. *Testifying*, however, differs from 'open and honest' disclosure in many ways: (1) it deals primarily with *acts* rather than feelings or covert desires; (2) it occurs among people who are known to the individual and who are culturally and racially related to him; (3) it occurs in a setting in which the testimony is (at least overtly) accepted at face value without confrontation; (4) the testifier is free to give as much or as little detail as he chooses; and (5) often the content of testimony is ritualistic, i.e., is the same for different individuals and is usually repeated over time (English and Griffith, 1979). In other words, the *act* of testifying is more important than the *content* of the testimony.

Under these conditions there is little likelihood that the individual will present information related to emotionally charged secrets, and little chance that he will present information that can be used against him. On the contrary, by relating minor transgressions he establishes the relative sanctity of other aspects of his life. He is reasonably safe and relatively undisclosed.

It is also important to note that the self-disclosure expectations of human interaction groups run counter to the 'cool' tradition that is a prominent feature of ghetto life.† Being 'cool' serves the same purpose for ghetto blacks as it did for gunfighters in the Old West. One cannot show weakness, fear or dependency because to do so would be to invite others to take advantage of one (Tucker, 1978). To ask ghettoized blacks to be open and honest with strangers is tantamount to asking the gunfighter to check his gun at the sheriff's office.

Most black Americans live in the urban ghetto or on the neo-plantation. Those who have escaped urban or rural ghettoes are usually no more than one generation removed, and many view their present position as tentative at least and precarious at best. Given the uncertainty and lack of security that marks life in the ghetto, its inhabitants develop coping styles that help them to deal

---

*Neo-plantation as used here refers to rural ghettoes marked by poverty, poor health care, and extraordinarily low economic, educational, and social opportunities. Black sharecroppers, tenant farmers, small-scale marginal farmers, and rural farmhands comprise the neo-plantation population.

†Robert Thomson (1978) has found evidence of a cool tradition in Nigeria dating as far back as the fifteenth century. The term *tebere* is literally translated as calm, cool, and composed, which approximates the idiomatic definition of the term in the black and hispanic ghettoes.

with an inhospitable environment (Clark, 1965). Fearing that their economic and social advances may be temporary, many upward mobile blacks tend to retain a large number of the habits and responses that helped them survive witnin and escape from the ghetto. These response patterns are heavily ingrained and will yield only to new behaviours that are clearly and demonstrably supportive of their present position.

Thus a major component of group life is at odds with a survival style that (over time) has been embedded in the consciousness of most black Americans. The problem is exacerbated by the fact that many blacks have little respect and low tolerance for abstraction, personal disclosure, or public display of weakness; and, therefore, tend to avoid and disparage formal human interaction experiences. Consequently, the extent to which a black person can fully participate in human interaction groups (as they are presently formulated) is largely a function of the extent to which the individual is acculturated to white middle-class norms.

This revelation should surprise no one, because virtually all extant group work models are based upon middle-class, Euro-centric norms, experiences, and needs. Those models were not designed with black people in mind, and make no acceptable provisions for the needs and sensitivities of culturally different people. Instead, they appear to be generally oriented towards the specific needs of economically secure people who are struggling with emotional rather than physical survival issues. Economically secure white people do not worry about adequate housing, but about whether their house is consonant with their aspired status; do not worry about having *enough* to eat, but about how tasty their food is. Physical survival is assured for them, but when the stomach is full often the spirits are empty. Consequently, group experience may be a vehicle through which white middle-class people (WMCP) may learn to fill the void, and enrich the emotional and spiritual aspects of their lives.

Living within a milieu in which status and power are the major stakes and in which competition for life *essentials* is not a prominent feature; a pervasive 'win-lose' frame of reference is not necessary for many WMCPs. They, therefore, can *afford* to luxuriate and take time away from economic struggling to experiment with structured openness and honesty; to seek wholeness; and to explore life's meaning. This is a luxury which most blacks cannot afford.

The primary struggle for most black people is economic and physical survival, and there is little evidence that group learning facilitates either of these. Further, since guaranteed biological survival and economic comfort appear to be preconditions for awareness of higher-order needs, such as the need for group experience (Tolman, 1942), there is little reason to expect the modal black person to actively seek membership in a human interaction group. Indeed, it would be inappropriate to even encourage most black people to participate in extant human interaction groups because these groups do not minister to their primary psycho-biological survival needs.*

The fact that human interaction groups are not really responsive to the human welfare needs of most black people confounds and inhibits the 'group movement' attempts to be all-inclusive. Since black people are a large and highly visible minority in the U.S., group behaviour theorists realize that their presence in groups is vital to assure *heterogeneity*. Heterogeneity is needed to foster member growth, and blacks are needed to provide broad heterogeneity. Thus far, however, no means have been found to *satisfactorily* include black people as full members of predominantly white groups.

HETEROGENEITY IN GROUPS

Group interaction can be viewed as a phenomenon that is energized by the dynamic interplay of opposing elements within a group. The extent to which the task of the group can be efficiently and effectively pursued is a measure of the extent to which differences among individual group members can be compromised, harmonized or mediated. Hence, learning in groups is optimized in the very process of conflict resolution, and the differences among group members provide the base for the learning process.

It is possible for all group members to learn in this process, but certain members learn more or 'better' than others. This difference can be explained partly by differences in intellect and/or receptivity among group members, and partly by the differential effect group members and group structure have on different members, affecting their ability to participate and learn at the same rate or in the same areas as others (Winter, 1971). Sex, age, race, ethnicity, education, social class, and personal experiences are all relevant variables that affect how an individual responds to a group and how group members respond to the individual. The extent to which group members are heterogeneous and homogeneous in respect to these variables always affects the quality, quantity, and types of interactions that occur.

Since heterogeneity is expected, and in many ways the *raison d'être* for the group's existence, little attention has been given to the impact of these differences on the individual. Instead, attention has been given to the impact the differences have on group development. The level of analysis is the group rather than the individual, the fact of heterogeneity rather than the differential impact resulting from the *ways* in which the group is heterogeneous. In other

*What is presented here does not permit us to make accurate predictions or cogent arguments about the needs, behaviour or motivation of any black *individual*. Variation between and among black people is virtually infinite, and no single explanation or principle would apply for *all* black people. Explanations and predictions presented here refer to the behavioural consequences of individual and institutional racism (Carmichael and Hamilton, 1967) on the *collective* black personality.

words, an assumption is made that age, race, ethnicity, and sexual differences make equal contributions to group heterogeneity. Advocates of this view appear to be saying: 'We need older people, young people, men, ethnics, women, and blacks to create a viable microcosm of U.S. society, and everyone will be equally effected by the differences between them and others.'

This is an assumption that must be questioned. Perhaps the telling measure is the extent to which one's membership in one or the other category marks the individual as different from the group, impedes communication between the individual and the group, and prevents the individual from getting important needs met by the group. The question is, what is the *hierarchy of loyalty*, and what types of similarities or differences are most desirable or least acceptable. Is there a greater bond of community between women (despite their race) than between white people of both sexes; than between black people of both sexes; than between old people of all sexes and races; than between men of all races and ages, etc.? Since these questions have not been adequately addressed by behavioural scientists, we must work from a base of speculation and assumption.

Within extant group methodology this ticklish problem is dealt with by venerating the task of *inclusion* (leadership techniques for mitigating group action to exclude deviant members, or for helping a deviant member to feel accepted and as one with the group). The possibility that this might be easier for an individual who is different in terms of sex or age than it would be for a person who is racially different is a consideration that should not be ignored. Within the context of U.S. society, we are not primarily split on sexual lines, age lines or ethnic lines, but on racial lines.* Men and women, young and old, Irish and German, tend to live together, go to school together, work together, and intermarry. Certainly, there are men's clubs, senior citizen centres, Irish parishes, women's schools, etc., but essentially, the diverse factions of white society intermingle with much more regularity and with less conflict than do black and white or brown and white or black and brown factions.

In the U.S. white people of all ages, sexes, and ethnicities are inexorably linked as a people — as Americans. Then there are others who are assimilation-resistant by virtue of their unacceptability within the prevailing cultural milieu. These deviant people join the counterculture by choice (those who would be accepted if they changed their life-styles or philosophy) or because they have no other choice (those who can never be fully accepted because their differences are inherent and unchangeable). This suggests that racial differences are more prominent, more distressing, and much more potent than

---

*Class divisions are also powerful, but (with the minor exception of patrician groups) these divisions yield to economic and political change. Thus a poor white boy could conceivably parlay economic success into social success, and could conceivably become President of the U.S. On the other hand, because of racial antipathy among the white majority, this would be virtually impossible for a black person.

sex or age differences within U.S. society. The world view, problems, prospects, and experiences of black and white people within the U.S. are so different that the differences themselves can become the primary focus of interaction. This confounds group process and makes the course of group development difficult to predict.*

Since racial antagonism and antipathy remain as an ongoing, bitterly fought, consuming, ever-present issue in the larger society, there is no reason to believe that they can be easily disposed of through catharsis or inclusion exercises in groups. Racial antagonisms have deep economic and historical as well as psychosocial roots, and cannot be *substantively* mediated within a microcosm. Consequently, identifying ways to effectively and appropriately deal with these problems within groups is an impossible task for the leader of the racially integrated group.

Through inclusion exercises the leader can smooth over differences by noting racial differences and encouraging group members to 'own' their biases, announce their willingness to change, and state their acceptance of the deviant member(s). In this process 'sin' is confessed, penance is made, forgiveness is solicited, and catharsis occurs. The group then proceeds 'as if' this problem has been solved. The deviant member(s) is left to deal with his differences on his own. He can choose to continually speak out when he detects overt or covert racism in the proceedings, or he can sit back and attempt to forget his blackness — attempt to merge with the group in order to lose his deviant identification.

BLACKS IN PREDOMINANTLY WHITE GROUPS

Little has been written about the difficulties that blacks experience in predominantly white groups, but it is suggested here that the latter (intentionally or unintentionally) place serious learning constraints on black members. Blacks may learn a great deal about how whites behave in groups, how whites respond to blacks, and how individual blacks respond to how whites respond to blacks; but they learn little about their own behaviour as it would manifest itself in the absence of racial stress. Black people may respond quite differently in predominantly black groups from how they would in predominantly white groups.

Within integrated groups, black-white differences are probably more (or at least equally) apparent and significant, as are sexual differences. It is virtually impossible for a black person to function as 'just another member of the

---

*Racially integrated groups whose primary task is to explore or resolve intergroup/interracial conflict would not fall under this rubric. For these groups another set of related problems obtains.

group' because he *is* different and is viewed as deviant.* Consequently, a number of difficulties may occur, including at least the following:

(1) Members may use him to explore their racial biases and/or ambivalences, viewing him as representative of *all* black people.

(2) Members may ingratiate themselves to prove that they like him — or that they are colour-blind.

(3) He may use his blackness to gain influence or to elicit sympathy, guilt, and contrition from other members.

(4) He (specifically the black male) can be used to carry and express all the rage and anger for the group, thus permitting other members to avoid dealing with their own anger/rage and the consequences of expressing these feelings.

(5) He may use the group to vent his anger at whites; but since his presence in the group is evidence of ambivalence, his angry tirades should be interpreted as a combination of legitimate expression of rage and a *sub-rosa* yearning for acceptance by whites.

(6) He may use the group to investigate the bases for black-white conflict and to explore ameliorative approaches. In the process he offers himself as an embodiment of the feelings and aspirations of black people.

(7) Variations of (1)-(6) above.

These phenomena do not differ greatly from what is expected in ordinary group experience, but the white group leader's own unresolved feeling about blacks, combined with his feelings of guilt or rage at the black member, often makes it difficult or impossible for him to deal properly with the issues. As a consequence, he often becomes as immobilized, apologetic or as non-responsive as the other white group members. Often the choice before him is to either bog down in unresolvable conflict or to ignore the issue and go on.

When faced with a hostile, recalcitrant or immobilized white group leader (and white group), the black member is often left with only two viable choices: he may choose to continue his protest in order to receive some measure of satisfaction, or he may attempt to mute his feelings 'for the good of the group'. Regardless of what he does, however, he is clearly marked as deviant and his individuality is submerged by his blackness. Consequently, learning

---

*The male pronoun is used here to refer to both male and female black people. It should be noted, however, that integration of black women into predominantly white groups tends to be less problematic than the integration of black men into those groups. It is not clear why this is so, but one would suspect that black women present less of a threat to white membership than do black men. When the black member is female, it is possible for whites to feel less fearful of violent confrontation, and for white men to be less fearful of sexual competition for female group members. It is also possible to neutralize the black female by putting her into a nurturant, 'mammy' role.

opportunities for blacks in predominantly white groups are somewhat limited. Indeed, learning may be limited to certain aspects of interracial relations and may include little opportunity for personal and interpersonal learning in other spheres.*

Learning opportunities for whites are much greater because they are more likely to be responded to as *individuals*. Even in interracial interactions whites have greater learning opportunities because (generally) whites know little about black people beyond stereotyped notions. As whites are the dominant group in the U.S., their survival is not dependent upon an understanding of black culture. Whites, therefore, can afford to ignore black culture, while blacks must come to terms with white culture in order to function within the U.S. socioeconomic system.

Blacks are in a subordinate position and their survival is closely linked to their ability to understand the *man* who makes the rules and referees the game. Moreover, blacks are immersed in a culture dominated by white tastes and white concerns; work in the homes of white people; and are exposed to the intimate details of white life in movies, television, and books. They, therefore, have much *less* to learn in interracial encounters, and enter predominantly white groups with excess baggage that severely delimits their learning.

On the other hand, opportunities to participate in a *black group* with black facilitators may be welcomed by a select group of middle-class black people whose life-styles, education, professional affiliations, and experiences have made them more open to human interaction experimentation. These appear to be blacks who are involved in the helping professions, blacks who are involved in industry, blacks who are alienated from black culture, *avant garde* blacks, and blacks who for other reasons have adopted white middle-class norms.

BLACK PEOPLE IN BLACK GROUPS

Though the civil rights movement, national poverty programmes, and affirmative action programmes have done little to change the lives of the *majority* of poor black people, they have provided opportunities for numerous black *individuals* to attend major universities, and to move into the professions. Many of these individuals feel rather insecure in their new status, but others now appear to feel 'successful' and confident that they 'have it made'. These blacks still suffer from discrimination and (many) retain their black identity, but in many ways they have more in common with their white middle-class counterparts than with other blacks.

*One might argue that these same dynamics obtain for other minority groups and, to a lesser extent, for women in groups. The writer neither confirms nor denies that argument. Black people are the issue here, and the inclusion or exclusion of other 'underdog' groups is not viewed as a really relevant consideration.

They, too, can afford to get in touch with spiritual emptiness, existential dilemmas, intimacy needs, and the search for meaning. They have achieved economic and social success, but find that *striving* is as valuable as an *end* as it was as a *means*. Now they have gotten 'there', and like their white counterparts, find that *getting there* was more rewarding than *being there*. At this point they are confronted with the same adult development issues (described by Levinson, 1977) that confront their white counterparts, and they wonder if group experience could provide helpful growth opportunities. Given their lifestyle, education, economic position, and experience, one would expect that they would function with competence and reasonable comfort in human interaction groups.

Ordinarily, these individuals would be desirable candidates for recruitment into predominantly white groups, but given the predictable racial issues, their 'best bet' would be black groups. This is so because black groups provide a setting in which black individuals can function as individuals rather than as stereotyped curios. In this milieu, members can fully explore themselves; can learn how they behave in groups; can learn how they relate to other black people; and can learn how they relate to members of the opposite sex — without invidious racial complications and without being constantly placed in a 'one-down' position.

At this point the reader may speculate that this support for totally or predominantly black groups is a 'cop-out' — an elaborate ruse designed to free blacks from the painful confrontations with whites that are necessary concomitants of life in a multiracial society. This may be a reasonable concern but (as mentioned earlier) predominantly white groups tend to provide more learning for whites than for blacks. Blacks have a greater need to come to terms with themselves as *individuals* than to reach rapprochement with a microcosm of white society. Interracial issues might be better explored in racially balanced groups set up specifically for that purpose.

In group many whites simply see black configurations and assign characteristics to the person based upon prior notions. These white members do not respond to the black member as an individual, but as a composite of their stereotypes. The black member must, therefore, expand most of his energy helping whites to overcome their stereotypes and fighting for his own identity. In a black group this type of struggle is unnecessary and the individual can devote more energy to learning about *himself* and his relationship with the people who occupy his primary life-space.

If we accept the assertion that black groups are important for black people, the question that must be considered at this point is: 'How does one organize and conduct a black human interaction group, and how would it differ from white human interaction groups?' The writer suggests that the major differences would be found in the race of the participants and the facilitator — racial heterogeneity is *not* a group organization goal. Further, the group work model used should not be radically different from models currently used for white and integrated audiences, but should be selected with great care.

SELECTING A MODEL FOR PREDOMINANTLY BLACK
HUMAN INTERACTION GROUPS

The first task in designing special group experiences for black people is to select a specific group work model, a work format, and a theme.* Singer (Singer *et al.*, 1975) identifies six categories under which most small group events may be subsumed: (1) interpersonal learning groups; (2) group process learning groups; (3) personal growth learning groups; (4) independently oriented change groups; (5) group process oriented change groups; and (6) focused criterion change groups. One might choose one or a combination of these models for work with black people. In considering the proper format one might choose to run all-male groups, all-female groups or male-female groups. One might choose a theme that is general or a theme that is related to some specific topic, depending upon group goals.

From the information presented earlier in this chapter, one would anticipate that the greatest demand would be for heterosexual groups with a male-female relations theme. Based upon the writer's experiences, the *interpersonal learning group*, as exemplified by the sensitivity ('T') group, is the preferred model because it offers numerous options that make possible the selection of techniques and exercises that closely match the needs, sensitivities, and proclivities of specific groups.

EVALUATION OF EXTANT GROUP METHODS

Traditional *group process learning groups* (such as Tavistock 'study groups') are not appropriate because they are primarily concerned with group *process* and make no provisions for meeting the sentient needs of group members. 'Tavi' is best suited for examining covert and overt processes (that occur in groups) which impede or facilitate pursuit of the group's primary task. Learnings are essentially intellectual and are largely derived from insight — the 'ah-hah' principle. For our purposes the Tavistock method is inappropriate because the process does not encourage group cohesion, mutual support, or compassion. Certain elements of Tavistock encourage development of self-reliance and independence, but the model's deficits (for our purposes) overshadow its benefits.

The goal of black male-female groups is to provide a setting in which members will feel safe and secure enough to discuss their feelings and to

---

*These decisions should be based upon the goals of the interaction, the needs of potential group members, and the skills of the group leader.

experiment with new behaviours. This is difficult to do in a setting where one's revelations are analysed and dissected, and in which supportive behaviour is not modelled by the facilitator. Black men and women come together in groups seeking empathy rather than analysis. The need is for emotional growth rather than intellectual exploration — intimacy rather than insight (Tucker, 1977).

At the other end of the spectrum one could consider *focused criterion groups*, such as encounter or Esalen type groups. Groups run in this style centre on individual member issues, on specific self-destructive behaviours, and on processes that underlie maladaptive individual behaviour. Unlike the Tavistock method, which focuses on group-level processes, the encounter group focuses on intrapsychic processes and often even ignores group-level processes. Encounter groups tend to cut through conventional masking behaviours and dig into the raw inner core of the individual exposing the primitive underpinnings of the personality (as do Tavistock groups in different ways).

In contrast to 'Tavi' groups, which depend primarily on insight and intellectual constructions for learning, learning in encounter groups derives primarily from 'gut level' confrontation which yields 'gut level' response — catharsis through facing up to feelings of guilt and shame and being absolved by a non-condemning and supportive group. Growth occurs as the individual sheds his emotional garbage; confronts his shortcomings; clarifies his values; and develops constructive life responses and a life-style that is supportive of his emotional needs.

The most serious problems with encounter methods for our purposes are as follows: (1) methods are individual oriented and inadequate attention is given to group-level processes; (2) members are pressured to conform to group definitions of what authentic feelings or behaviour are; and (3) methods include delving into areas of protected personal information, and often unconscious material may be uncovered that cannot be adequately dealt with in a time-limited temporary group.

In encounter groups the leader models behaviours he expects of group members. He presents himself as the epitome of openness and honesty, and encourages members to emulate his behaviour (Klein and Astrachan, 1971). Those who successfully emulate him are rewarded with praise and acceptance. Those who display deviant behaviour or different views of emotional reality are pressured to conform — it is not really very different from behaviour modification. Expressions of beliefs or feelings that are dissonant with the leader's prior notions of what constitutes 'authentic' feelings and beliefs are often met with derision, scorn, and ultimately the confrontations:

I can't buy that! I think you're bullshitting!

Let me hear what you really feel.
Now I know you're human.
Now I can feel your pain.
I get disgusted when I see you slumping over like a coward.
etc.

Confrontation methods can be quite helpful to certain people in certain settings; but can also be quite dangerous with other people in other settings. If the goal is therapy or radical personal change, encounter methods may be useful; but with 'so-called' normal groups their utility is at least questionable. In the experience of the writer, confrontation clearly has a role in normal (non-sociopathic) black groups, but must, of necessity, be softer and less intimidating than in the modal encounter group.

Individually oriented change groups (as the name suggests) do not deal with group-level issues at all, and are too clinical for our purposes. The level of analysis is the *individual* in these groups, while our interests lie primarily at the level of *group* interaction. *Group process oriented change groups* do pay attention to group-level phenomena but are essentially clinical in orientation, while the orientation here is towards 'normal' groups. For these reasons, and others, it would appear that neither of these models would be appropriate for our purposes.

A variety of more exotic, esoteric, and/or more specialized group methods (each of which may have elements of one or more of the six categories) might also be considered. These include gestalt, bio-energetics, primal therapy, reality therapy, and others. In the opinion of the writer, these methods would be more useful in formal psychotherapies than in normal black groups. Moreover, the *avant garde* principles that underlie them are not congruent with the more conservative proclivities of black people.

Since the writer has suggested that the T-group, developed by the National Training Laboratories (NTL), is the model with greatest promise, we should discuss why it might be selected. One reason is that volumes of literature, innumerable exercises, and numerous practical guides are available that help the individual leader to develop a style and a set of experiences that match the needs of his groups and which set well with his own personal style and philosophy. The model also permits broad experimentation with new methods and techniques.

Further, one can run T-groups that closely resemble encounter or gestalt groups, or groups that are infused with Tavistock, bio-energetics or other elements. More importantly, this model permits competent pursuit of specific goals, and it is particularly crucial that groups for black people have very clear goals. Blacks are wary of ethereal group experiences, and have low tolerance for vagueness, esoteria, and confusion in groups.

GOALS FOR BLACK GROUPS

The goals of a given group may be best expressed in terms of behavioural expectations, and (in the writer's experience) the primary goals for black male-female groups should include (at least) the following:

(1) *High investment* — the participant should demonstrate commitment by consistent attendance and high participation.

(2) *Self-disclosure* — the participant should be willing to share information about his personal life in order to receive feedback and to contribute to the learning of others.*

(3) *Commitment to change* — the participant should be willing to clarify his values and goals; assess the congruence between his values/goals and his present behaviour; and take action to change maladaptive and non-constructive aspects of his behaviour.

(4) *Risk-taking* — the participant should be willing to take risks to improve his life situation.

(5) *Support* — the participant should provide emotional support and demonstrate concern for the welfare of other participants; and should demonstrate an ability to accept support and concern from others.

(6) *Interpersonal competence* — the participant should learn to establish authentic, mutually rewarding relationships with others, without ignoring his own needs — an ability to give and receive love and support, and an ability to establish and deal with intimacy.

(7) *Develop personal competence* — the participant should develop an ability to handle his personal affairs competently: to give, receive, and evaluate advice, and to take appropriate action to attain goals.

These behavioural expectations (outcomes) are, of course, not appreciably different from those that might be set forth for a 'themeless' white group. The important difference is in the setting. What is being suggested is that black people may achieve these goals more readily in an all-black group, and that high-quality male-female relations are predicated on the same principles as high-quality person-person relations.

One caveat should be kept in mind, however: the programme should be goal oriented rather than process oriented. One should organize around group needs rather than method demands, and the facilitator should have a broad repertoire of skills and knowledge at his command. The model is the modified

---

*The process is facilitated when the group is predominantly black, but is still problematic because of black life-styles which run counter to the demands of group disclosure. 'Openness and honesty' should remain as goals but the facilitator should be aware of the roadblocks that prevent disclosure.

T-group and the facilitator should be prepared to make further modifications when needed.

PLANNING BLACK HUMAN INTERACTION GROUPS

As with ordinary groups, the first step in designing a group experience for black people should be *contract setting* with the proposed group or with a representative subgroup. These negotiations and discussions will help the facilitator and the group to set realistic expectations for the interaction. Initial negotiations should include standard questions such as, but not limited to, the following:

(1) What is the purpose for the group? What do members hope to achieve?

(2) What are members willing to invest to achieve those goals? What is the extent of their interest and commitment to pursue identified goals?

(3) What will be the scope of the contract? How many meetings? How often? How many hours? Where and when?

(4) What will the costs be and how will they be handled? — facilitator fee, coffee, materials, space, etc.

(5) Who are the potential members and how many people will be involved?

The second step is to brainstorm types of experiences that the group would benefit from. This process should be initiated at the first group meeting, and should follow a presentation (by the facilitator) of activities or exercises he has in mind. This is an extremely important step because it not only demonstrates consumer consciousness, but takes into consideration the deficits in our understanding of how black people will respond to various group activities. The brainstorming activity provides an opportunity for members to explore their needs, interests and wishes, and provides rich data for planning and design. The facilitator should translate the results of the brainstorming session into questions for discussion, exercises for further exploration of issues, and activities that encourage growth in desired areas.

The third step is to construct an incremental design that permits the group to move from stage one, which is where members are at the outset, to stage three, which is where they want to be at the conclusion of the experience.

GROUP DEVELOPMENT

The stages in black group development do not differ markedly from those of predominantly white groups as described by Bennis and Shepard (1965), in that they tend to move from the *dependence* to the *interdependence* phase. These stages essentially fit Benet's (1976) linear model in that there is clear movement in one direction, even though forward movement is not constant and regression does occur. During the early periods of group life members engage in a variety of non-work oriented activities in an attempt to ward off anxiety and to gain security. Successful groups then move to the interdependence phase, during which time they focus less on role and power and more on personality and affection, and finally to the *bonding* phase which precedes termination.

Phase I is essentially *cognitive* (dependence); Phase II is *affective* (inter-dependence); and Phase III is *spiritual* (bonding). This final phase is crucial for black groups because the circumstances of their lives discourage positive group identification (Tucker, 1978). Achievement of the final phase is possible because black people seek solidarity and loving *bonding* with other black people — to avoid being alone, and to feel a fully acceptable part of a sustaining group. These are feelings that most black people cannot experience in a white world or in a white group.

Bonding involves mutual respect, affection, and a feeling of being spiritually linked with others. It is a precursor for trust and love and a necessary precondition for open, honest, and caring interactions. When bonding is present a feeling of group potency and group cohesion is pervasive, but bonding occurs only after cognitive and affective needs and conflicts have been adequately met and dealt with. This is not to suggest that bonding can only occur in the *absence* of conflict, but it is to suggest that it cannot occur until the roots of conflict are uncovered and members are committed to work *towards* resolution of conflict — to prevent conflict from escalating into hostility.

Pseudo-bonding can occur quite early in the life of the group, but is usually an expression of anxiety rather than an expression of love or concern. When this occurs the group will behave as if its purpose is to have a love affair rather than to explore and build interpersonal relations. During this period issues will be ignored and conflict will be avoided at all cost. The competent group facilitator should be prepared to interpret this behaviour and should encourage the group to deal with the issues that their pseudo-bonding activity attempts to mask.

Most of the skills utilized, and caveats that obtain, for normal heterogeneous groups would apply for heterosexual black groups; but there are certain dynamics that are peculiar to and/or prominent within black groups that should be anticipated:*

(1) Black men tend to dominate the early sessions and tend to offer alternative leadership for the group. This is achieved by dominating discussion or by

---

*The group considered is a male-female relations group. Attention is focused on this type of interaction because it is the type for which there is the greatest apparent demand. Principles delineated, however, would have broad application for other types of black or minority groups.

withdrawal. Through non-participation a black man can draw attention to himself rather than group issues. By dominating the conversation the member can make alternative activity proposals and can shift attention from areas of group concern to areas in which he feels most comfortable. In either case (negative or positive), he exercises leadership.

Since both the facilitator and female group members are usually aware of how difficult it is to recruit enough men to provide the desired sexual balance, both are hesitant to reject the male member's proposals out of hand. The astute facilitator understands that these proposals should be interpreted and discussed, both in terms of their practicality and in terms of the underlying motivation of the individual.

(2) Male resistance to the formation of structured heterosexual subgroups or to separate male-female caucuses should be anticipated. More aggressive black men tend to object whenever they are denied access to the entire group. This should be interpreted as a desire to compete and wield influence over as large a group as possible and/or as a means by which they may avoid dealing with intimacy.

(3) Often single women are stifled in heterosexual groups. They are fully aware of the fact that single black men are at a premium, and fear being labelled as castrating, domineering or argumentative.

They are aware of the fact that they are in competition with other female members for the attention of the men, and are reluctant to do or say anything that would adversely affect their competitive position. Consequently, they avoid saying or doing anything that would antagonize the men, and tend to be non-supportive of other women.

Since this is the case, separate male-female caucuses may be necessary to permit the women to explore these issues, work with these problems, and develop mutual support systems. Having dealt with these problems in caucus, the women will be better prepared to enter into authentic exchanges with each other and with the men.

(4) Men are often stifled in groups because of their need to be 'cool', their inclination to compete with one another for dominance (over the herd), and their fears of intimacy. Separate male caucuses provide an opportunity for men to explore these issues and prepare them to enter into more authentic exchanges among themselves and with the women.

(5) Married couples tend to be stifled when participating in groups composed primarily of single people. The costs of disclosure are much greater for them because their most intimate other is present to hear disclosures that may hurt. Consequently, they often find it necessary to negotiate with one another about what they will reveal in group, and they often agree to be constantly aware of the impact of disclosure on the other.

Though it is possible to work these difficulties out, it is wiser to work with couples only when the group is comprised exclusively of couples, or in settings where one or the other partner is not present. Which alternative would be best for any given couple varies with the individuals involved, but it is clear that the participation of couples in groups comprised primarily of singles is problematic at best and unwise at least.

(6) Facilitators can be blinded by limitations in their own experiences. For the same reasons that white facilitators have difficulty in dealing appropriately with black members, male or female facilitators have difficulty in understanding and appreciating the problems and issues of the other sex.

It is, therefore, wise to work with a co-facilitator of the opposite sex. The writer has found that the presence of his wife as co-facilitator is invaluable in understanding issues, diagnosing problems, and planning interventions. In general, women tend to have less difficulty in empathizing with men than men do with women, but both have difficulty in fully understanding the motivation and experiences of the other.

Appropriate activity for black groups should be identified in initial negotiation sessions, but the model delineated below might serve as a useful framework. This model approximates Benet's (1976) *linear model* in that it seeks to move participants from Phase I (dependence) to Phase III (bonding) in an orderly, sequential way.

Phase I — dependence (cognition)

During this phase members are uncertain about their role in the group, how they are perceived by others, and what is going to happen to them in the group. To ward off anxiety members centre their energy on the leader and tend to be silent or highly intellectual in their responses. They are testing out the waters slowly to assess the risks, and look to the facilitator to lead them in the right direction (see Bennis and Shepard, 1956).

As Schutz (1973) suggests, the issue of *inclusion* is also very important during this phase. Members explore issues such as who is a member, who should be a member, whether the sexual balance is appropriate, what is expected of them, and what their commitment to the group is. At this point members feel competent to respond to the *cognitive* demands of group membership, but are not ready to deal with emotional or spiritual issues. Activities, therefore, should be geared towards meeting members 'where they are' in order to prepare them to move to the next phase.* The following activities may help in that process:

---

*At this point directed and structured activities are better received by members than indirect and unstructured activities.

(1) *Contract setting* — to relieve anxiety and to set goals.

(2) *Inclusion* — introductions (name, residence, profession, and astrological sign) in large group. [+]

Mill to dyads. Make contact with each person in the room through a non-verbal salute (nod, touch, smile, hug, kiss, etc.), and then link up with another member. Introduce yourself, discuss why you decided to join the group, discuss how and/or why you picked your partner, and discuss each other's life-style, likes, and dislikes.

Mill to quartets, and eventually to octets, discussing different issues at each step until all members have been introduced to each of the other members.

(3) *Lecturette* — at this point a brief lecture can be helpful to stimulate interaction. The lecturette should address the problems inherent in intra-racial relations, and should lay the groundwork for group discussion.

In the act of giving a lecture the facilitator could be criticized for 'feeding' into the group's dependent stance, bus since the group *is* also in a 'cognitive' phase, this activity meets members where they are and makes it safe to begin movement towards the next phase. Discussion following the lecture should include two separate sets of questions: what members *think* about the issues; and how they *feel* about discussing the issues. Discussion of feelings is preparation for moving to Phase II, and the facilitator should move the group along as it demonstrates readiness.

Phase II — interdependence (affective)

This phase in group development is marked by decreased antagonism and increased empathy and affection. Members' comments increasingly centre on issues of boundaries and group integrity, which reflect an increased sense of commitment to the group. At this point members also begin to focus on individual behaviour, indicate greater willingness to give and receive feedback, and demonstrate increased readiness to deal with issues such as attractions and antipathies. Most importantly, the sense of increased trust makes authentic discussion of controversial, conflict-laden material more possible.

Issues that arise during this phase overlap with Phase I issues, are predictable, and usually include a number of the following topics:[*]

[+] Increasingly, astrological signs are being used by blacks and whites as a measure of identity. To what extent this is a *fad* is not clear at the moment.

[*] In dealing with all these issues, the facilitator should anticipate member tendencies to make black-white (racial) comparisons and parallels. He must use good judgement in determining how long he waits before making an interpretation or taking action to bring discussion back to the 'here and now'.

(1) *Sex-linked differences* — What are the ways in which men and women differ in terms of emotionality, roles, empathy, openness, and honesty?

(2) *Monogamy* — Is monogamy practical? Is it a preferred relational pattern between men and women? How justifiable are double standards?

(3) *Life-styles* — How functional is the traditional nuclear family and traditional domestic roles? How functional are common-law marriages? How desirable is it for couples to have separate bedrooms or separate apartments? How much freedom should one give up in marriage?

(4) *Communications* — What are the primary causes of communications difficulties between people, especially between men and women?

(5) *Friendships* — What is friendship and what are its dimensions? Can men and women have sustaining non-sexual friendships?

(6) *Love* — What does it mean? What are its philosophical roots? What are its behavioural demands, and how is it experienced?

(7) *Attractions* — How do physical or sexual attractions differ from love? How should they be handled in groups and in life? How should the issue of competition be handled within the group?

(8) *Support* — What is a personal support system? How important is it to maintain a support system in life? How are support systems developed within the group?

(9) *Feedback* — How can members give each other accurate feedback on changeable behaviour?

These issues do lend themselves to intellectualization, but this difficulty can be avoided if the facilitators deal with issues in context as they arise in the life of the group. During the cognitive phase these issues are simply talked about in the abstract, but during the affective phase they gain reality as members work with their real-life problems. At this point in group life authentic relations are developing among members, together with genuine affectional bonds. Many conflicts remain unresolved, but a sense of group belonging, mutual concern, and tolerance facilitate compromise. The group behaves as if it hopes to merge all the individual members into one undifferentiated corporate body.

At the overt level the purpose of this merging of individuals is to preserve intimacy, but at the covert level there is a wish to avoid conflict that may destroy the euphoric fantasy. Being part of a harmonious, sustaining whole (especially among black people) is often valued as an end in itself rather than as a means for achieving a more realistic end. However, relational patterns are developing that are requisite for movement to the next phase.

Phase III — bonding (spiritual)

The group is now prepared to move on to Phase III (spiritual bonding), and the facilitators are faced with a four-part task: (1) they must encourage thoughtful movement towards bonding; (2) they must discourage and challenge pseudo-bonding posturing among members; (3) they must encourage members to experiment with new behaviours that are congruent with group learnings; and (4) they must move members towards termination of the laboratory experience and towards real-life application of learnings. This is a crucial period in black group development because bonding can lead to regressive denial and self-congratulatory activity that retard group learning. When handled properly, however, bonding can lead to accelerated learning and development of constructive, new behaviours among members.

Since it is currently in vogue to profess commitment and pride in one's Southern (U.S.) and African roots, facilitators should anticipate a certain amount of rhetoric about black love and racial solidarity. Members should be challenged to examine how much of this is real and the extent to which fantasy can *actually* be converted into fact within the context of the group experience. At this point additional structured exercises may be useful for analysis and exploration of new behaviours.* At each step, however, members should evaluate their current behavioural patterns, experiment with new patterns, and evaluate the relative effectiveness/propriety of each of these.

Group members, at this point, should also assess the extent to which *specific* goals have been met (these will vary from group to group) and should prepare for termination of the group. Standard expressions of interest in continuing the group beyond the contracted time period or for informal continuation of the group should be expected here. The facilitator should interpret these suggestions as resistance to termination, and should counter them with a challenge to the group, e.g., for members to develop new friendships and establish new relations in the real world that are based upon group learnings.

SUMMARY

Black behaviour in human interaction/laboratory groups is a topic that has been largely ignored by behavioural scientists. Consequently, we know little about the subject and are restricted here to reconstructed interpretations of a limited number of experiences. We do know, however, that there are major roadblocks that delimit learning and growth for black participants in predominantly white group.

These difficulties stem in part from difficulties in integrating black

---

*These would include trust exercises, massage, relaxation, poetry, swaying, and positive feedback (stroking).

experience into group life, and in part from the incongruence between modal group expectations and the survival demands of modal black life-styles (ghetto and neo-plantation). It is suggested that middle and professional class blacks have life-styles that are more congruent with group life demands, and that these individuals *could* learn optimally in predominantly black groups led by black facilitators.

The T-group, with its many options, is recommended as the preferred modality (or conceptual base), and 'male-female relations' is identified as the most relevant theme. A contract clearly delineating the goals, demands, and scope of the experience should be negotiated with members as early as possible. Male and female co-facilitators should be employed to ensure that both points of view are understood and appreciated.

Black group development should be progressive: beginning with a phase marked by dependence and cognitive interaction, proceeding through a phase in which affective interaction predominates, and terminating with a phase in which spiritual bonding is pervasive. These phases engage the members 'where they are' and move them to where they want to be at termination. Success is a measure of the extent to which members develop new understandings, experiment with and adopt new behaviours, and develop constructive relational patterns that are congruent with their original and derived goals.

REFERENCES

Benet, A. J. (1976) 'Yin yang: a perspective on theories of group development.' In *The 1976 Annual Handbook for Group Facilitators*. San Diego: University Associates, pp. 179-88.

Bennis, W. G. and Shepard, H. A. (1956) 'A theory of group development', *Human Relations*, 4, 415-36.

Carmichael, S. and Hamilton, C. V. (1965) *Black Power: The Politics of Liberation in America*. New York: Vintage.

Clark, K. (1965) *Dark Ghetto*. New York: Harper & Row.

English, T. E. and Griffith, E. (1979) 'Possession, prayer, and testimony: cornerstones in the self-help group', Unpublished manuscript, Yale University.

Klein, E. B. and Astrachan, B. M. (1971) 'Learning in groups: a comparison of study and T groups', *Journal of Applied Behavioural Science*, 7, Issue 6.

Levinson, D. J. (1977) 'The mid-life transition: a period in adult psycho-social development', *Psychiatry*, 40, 99-112.

Schutz, W. C. (1973) *Elements of Encounter*. Big Sur: Joy Press.

Singer, D., Astrachan, B., Gould, L., and Klein, E. *et al.* (1975) 'Boundary management in psychological work with groups', *Journal of Applied Behavioural Science*, 2, 137-76.

Steele, R. and Nash, K. (1972) 'Sensitivity training in the black community', *American Journal of Orthopsychiatry*, 42, 424-30.

Thomson, R. F. (1978) 'Black ideographic writing: Calabar to Cuba', *Yale Alumni Magazine*, November, 29-33.

Tolman, E. C. (1942) *Drives Toward War*. New York: Appleton-Century-Crofts.

Tucker, L. M. (1977) 'Loneliness and the black woman: implications for primary prevention', Unpublished Doctoral Dissertation, Union Graduate School.

Tucker, R. C. (1979) 'Love, Let It Be', *Essence Magazine*.

Tucker, R. C. (1979) 'Why Black men hide their feelings', *Essence Magazine*.

Winter, S. K. (1971) 'Black man's bluff', *Psychology Today*, September, 39-43, 78-81.

Advances in Experiential Social Processes, Volume 2
Edited by C. P. Alderfer and C. L. Cooper
© 1980 John Wiley & Sons, Ltd.

Chapter 9

Defining and Developing Environmental Competence

Fritz Steele

Development Research Associates, Boston, Massachusetts, U.S.A.

As can be seen from the variety of topics covered in this volume, the use of experience-based social processes as a method for training and development has been applied to many different types of populations with many different desired outcomes. Some programmes seek to develop awareness or skills in the general public, while others are aimed at more specific populations such as executives, managers, people in the helping professions, students, school children, and so on. The methods aim for outcomes such as increased self-awareness, improved interpersonal competence, developed management skills, a more empathic helping style, improved problem-solving skills, better tennis strokes, or whatever can be learned through trials and patterned experiences.

There is, however, a relatively undeveloped learning area which has been under-represented in the development of experiential training methods: *environmental competence,* or people's ability to deal with their immediate surroundings in an effective and stimulating manner. Apart from research concern for how children learn about their spatial world and how to cope with it (e.g. Piaget, 1929), the behavioural sciences have done very little for the continuing development of environmental competence in adolescents and adults. (Some reasons for this neglect will be suggested later.)

This chapter, therefore, will attempt to explore the nature, range, and possibilities and problems of using experiential methods for training in environmental competence. I hope to expand readers' awareness of the need for such development, and in addition suggest methods, media, and various roles that could be played in stimulating environmental competence. The chapter is organized into four topic areas: (1) the definition of environmental competence and the practical skills which can be the outcomes of training; (2) methods for developing environmental competence; (3) special problems and possibilities associated with this area; and (4) some general conclusions about the learning processes involved in expanding environmental competence.

THE NATURE OF ENVIRONMENTAL COMPETENCE

In an earlier book (Steele, 1973), I used a simple definition of environmental competence: a person's ability (a) to be aware of social and physical surroundings and their impact and (b) to use or change these settings to attain goals or enjoyment without inappropriately degenerating the setting or reducing effectiveness. Within this broad definition, environmental competence falls roughly into three subcategories:

(1) Personal style, attitudes, and awareness factors.

(2) Knowledge about one's surroundings and how to influence them.

(3) Action skills/behaviour patterns.

(1) Personal style, attitudes, and awareness

There are a number of obvious personal style factors which help to determine a particular person's level of environmental competence.

Self-awareness

Having a sense of one's own needs, identity, values, interests, and skills.

Perceptual skills

Being able to perceive one's surroundings relatively accurately with neither too much distortion nor systematic 'blind' areas which are consistently difficult to perceive and therefore create a pattern of incompetence in dealing with particular kinds of problems.

Sense of self-worth

The feeling that one has value in the world and deserves to have high-quality interaction with one's settings, *versus* a conscious or unconscious assumption that one is unworthy and therefore deserves to have poor environmental experiences.

Tolerance for ambiguity

Being comfortable in situations which are not completely structured or defined, so that one can take action or risks in relation to the setting without having to be sure in advance about the 'rules' or the outcome. Also related to this is the tendency to initiate interactions with the environment, as opposed to having a reactive style of generally responding to demands from the environment.

Curiosity

An interest in how things happen in the world and a desire to discover more about one's self, the surrounding world, and the interactions between the two. A curious person is not necessarily high on environmental competence, but an incurious one is more likely to be low over the long run, since he or she is unlikely to learn very much from experiences.

(2) Knowledge about one's surroundings

People obviously differ in the extent to which they have available to them particular information with which to deal with their settings. The following are a few of the knowledge areas which can have a large impact on ability to use and influence settings.

Content knowledge about people in settings

Having useful information about the ways settings influence humans and *vice versa*, and having concepts which allow one to describe the mix of costs and gains as opposed to simple overall evaluations such as 'good' or 'bad'. An important related skill here is the ability to notice effects and patterns caused by what is *not* there (missing elements in a setting) as well as by what is.

Technical knowledge about physical settings

Knowing how natural and man-made environments are constructed and can be used; having alternatives available for consideration when influencing one's own settings in terms of materials, form, layout, linking systems, and so on. Architects and other designers would naturally tend to be potentially more knowledgeable in this area, and it is not accidental that many innovations in home and office design are first carried out by designers for their own use.

Mental maps

A technical term for having useable mental pictures of where different parts of one's settings are located (such as areas of a city), how they are related to each other, and how to get to them. This includes knowing about available resources, transportation systems, and walking routes, plus where to obtain basic resources if one's usual sources fail (Gould and White, 1974).

Social system understanding

Knowing how to influence the structure, norms, and policies of groups or organizations so that one can influence the 'feel' of one's social and physical environment together. It is also very helpful here to have social sensing skills: to be able to perceive and understand the norms and values of other groups and cultures and to do this relatively quickly, before major errors are made which cut one off from useful relations with that group.

(2a) Environmental competence in social systems

The areas of competence described above were primarily attributed to individuals. We could also think of social systems as being more or less competent to deal with their physical and social environments. This competence is a function not only of the competencies of individual members, but also of system characteristics which tend to increase the environmental competence of the members or to encourage it to be used. This is too large a topic to be fully explored here, but I will briefly suggest a few of the social system features which tend to lead to an 'environmentally competent system' (and therefore could be set as training goals for group training activities).

Shared information

Having patterns of relatively high disclosure within the system, so that there is a shared pool of timely information about the goals of the system, who the members are, necessary activities and their effects, and personal preferences of members. Decisions about settings based on accurate information are more likely to produce a good match between the members of the system and their settings (Steele, 1975).

Problem-solving methods and effective interaction processes

A social system that generally deals with problems and decisions in an effective manner will tend to do the same with environmental issues. A key factor here is the system's encouragement (through both formal and informal rewards) of members describing the problem and its causes before jumping to solutions. Many group discussions tend to be solution-oriented rather than problem-oriented.

Facilitative rules

Having policies, rules, and procedures that facilitate full use of the system's settings is very important, and can be contrasted with the constricting administrative processes of many groups and organizations. Management of settings is typically controlled from the top authority levels and tends to enforce a narrowing of alternatives rather than provide a wide range of options as tasks and needs change.

Norms which support environmental awareness

All social systems develop informal norms, or 'rules of the game', about what their members should do and not do in order to be acceptable to the system. If these rules include a positive concern for settings and how they influence members (and *vice versa*), people in the system are more likely to be able to practise environmental skills and to learn new ones. Allowing energy to be put into environmental concerns (*versus* defining them as 'unimportant') promotes competent settings management, which can, in turn, reduce energy drains such as always having to search for meeting space because the rooms in an office building are each labelled as available for only one use so that many of them sit empty much of the time.

(3) Environmental competence in action: some practical skill areas

The previous discussion simply presented some subcategories of environmental competence for individuals and groups. This kind of listing tends to make it sound like a rather dry concept — an impression that does not do justice to the exciting possibilities which exist when one is effective in influencing one's surroundings. This excitement can be sensed through considering some practical behavioural skills found to be present in those people who are competent in dealings with their settings. They are in no particular order, but considering them as a group will communicate a stronger flavour of environmental competence as a dynamic ability to relate to the world, not just as an area of 'knowledge'.

Exploration and scouting

This is the ability to learn quickly about the structure, resources, possibilities, surprises, and threats contained in an unfamiliar setting. It includes having good strategies for finding out about available sources, special spots, power distribution and other social system features, transportation systems, and how the setting relates to other settings.

Some people seem to have a natural knack for this sort of scouting. Patrick Geddes, one of the fathers of modern city planning, used to be able to get the 'feel' of a town through simply walking the streets for two or three days plus studying official maps of the town (Kitchen, 1975, p. 256). In his scouting process, he noticed details such as the number of doorbells on the fronts of houses (an indicator of the density of a residential area) which most visitors would not see.

Exploring can be done in a number of ways: predetermined, *systematic canvassing* of an area after studying a map or obtaining a description of the area from a resident; *unplanned wandering* with no set route and an openness to see and feel whatever is there; *focused searching* for some particular location or resource (such as trying to find out as much as possible about textile sources in a particular city, or where people spend their leisure hours in the evenings); and so on. These processes can be used in many different types of settings: cities, towns, countryside, universities, etc.

There is also a sequencing influence related to *when* one explores. Those who are effective at scouting/exploring tend to do it early in their contact with a new setting rather than later. Doing it early allows the information and new views of the setting to influence a larger proportion of one's experiences there and open up other experiences that would not occur otherwise.

Making contact quickly

The test of this skill is whether one is usually aware of one's self in one's immediate surroundings. It includes personal observational skills facilitated by asking such questions as: What do I feel right now? What am I trying to do here? What are the dominant features of this setting? What other settings are being recalled by my experiences here? What feelings are these memories causing in me? What kind of a mood am I in right now, and how is that affecting the way I see and use this setting? How is this setting helping and hindering what I am trying to do?

Taking the time to practise asking and answering these (and similar) questions can be a great help in developing a sense of being in contact with one's place. As mentioned in the first part of this chapter, it is very useful to be competent at describing your own state and the impact of the setting before jumping to a simplistic evaluation of whether the setting is 'good' or 'bad'.

Matching self and setting

This is the ability to choose appropriate settings for different activities, moods, and needs for information, stimulation or seclusion. It is literally the skill of doing the right thing in the right spot, and usually requires two steps: a *diagnostic* step of consciously identifying what one wants to do; and a *matching* step where one considers the characteristics of various alternative settings and chooses one which provides a good fit with one's needs. The process is not always this tidy and rational, of course: one may also choose to alter a setting to fit one's needs better after starting to use it, and one may change one's mind about what one wants to do when one sees that a setting provides a particular opportunity (such as wading in a city fountain on a hot day, when the original purpose of going to the site was to eat lunch).

This skill sometimes includes a flair for choosing special sites for special events, as well as being able to 'move on' without guilt feelings about having chosen a site in the first place.

Quick Personalization

People differ in the extent to which they are able (or likely) to alter new or temporary settings so that they feel some sense of ownership and personal place in them. This skill includes being willing to change locations of furniture, to bring personal items such as pictures or posters into the space, and to reorganize the ways different elements are used.

When visiting a new town, city or region, one may also personalize the setting, not by altering it, but by using it in a certain way which makes the user feel more at home than he or she would otherwise. For example, when my wife and I recently spent a week in Flagstaff, Arizona, we found that playing tennis on public courts early in the visit gave us a quick feeling of belonging, of doing something with residents, which in turn made us both feel that the town was a bit more 'ours' than just a site for a brief visit.

Quick personalization skills are particularly useful for people who travel a great deal and need to make transient settings reflect themselves if they are ever to feel at home anywhere, for families who move frequently (for job relocation or whatever reasons), and for white-collar workers whose office assignments are frequently changed. For all of these, as well as many other types of people, quick personalization can reduce the likelihood of always feeling out of place and transient.

Non-degeneration of settings

This skill area might also be called 'creative custodianship'. It is a competence demonstrated by using one's settings well without destroying their essence or character in the process. It includes an awareness of systemic influences and the importance of ecological systems (including the need to consider pollution effects very carefully), an understanding of the historical, thematic, and fantasy-producing qualities of certain settings (so that one does not, for example, 'modernize' an early Georgian house with photographed woodgrain plastic panelling), and a sense of oneself as a 'custodian' for settings that one may temporarily control (lease, own, use, etc.), but which have had and will have a much longer history than any individual user.

An example of a custodial approach to one's settings is the development of 'low impact camping', which stresses wilderness camping experiences which leave no trace of man's presence once the camper has moved on. Although certainly not a new idea, it has achieved considerable acceptance among American outdoor and forest service groups as a means for people to avoid crowded campsites and still preserve fragile wilderness settings that are in danger of deterioration through overuse.

Two types of skills

The practical skills discussed here can be grouped into two large categories of knowledge. One is *knowledge about a particular setting or system of settings*: technical knowledge about it, what resources it contains, how to use it, how to gain access to the resources, and so on. The second type of knowledge is more general and consists of *the processes for finding out about settings quickly and effectively*. Examples of this type of knowledge included scouting/exploring and making contact with one's self and the environment. The second type of environmental competence is particularly useful over the longrun, since it allows people to transfer their skills to use of whatever settings they choose. Knowledge about a particular setting is also important; but it can be very limiting if people stay in well-known but no longer useful settings because they are not confident of their ability to make a move to an unfamiliar setting. In other words, if the process is solid, the content knowledge will tend to follow, while the reverse is not necessarily true.

METHODS FOR DEVELOPING ENVIRONMENTAL COMPETENCE

From the preceding discussion the reader will see that I consider environmental competence to include a large number of observable skill areas. It is not surprising, then, that there would also be a large number of experiential methods which could enhance a person's environmental competence. I will now describe a fairly comprehensive range of methods for such development. As will soon become clear, a number of these methods will not sound like the usual definition of 'experiential learning', and this is intentional. I believe that many inputs to environmental competence are unplanned patterns, as opposed to designed programmes. We need to understand these inputs in order to give us clues about how to design more powerful experiences, as well as which experience patterns to try to influence in people's day-to-day surroundings.

As people develop from children to adults, their environmental competence is heavily shaped by the pattern of life experiences in their culture. This pattern has a number of components, including: the society's formal educational processes; other alternative educational experiences which are available in the society; the common leisure-time activities; the form and content of what they see and hear in various mass media; the availability of materials and experiences which are designed specifically to enhance environmental competence; and prevailing norms and rules about sites and how they can be used.

In the following discussion of each of these types of influence, my comments are based primarily on the patterns and resources of American society, since that is the one I know best. I see the current general level of environmental competence in the United States as being relatively low: Americans have the technology to profoundly influence their environment, but relatively low competence in (a) setting standards for what are better and worse influences, and (b) knowing how to use the potential of existing settings. I see Britain as ahead of the US in these areas, and the Scandinavian countries and oriental cultures such as Japan and China as being still further advanced. Scandinavian culture has developed a highly valued skill area around man-created settings, while oriental cultures tend to produce citizens who are competent in their relations with their natural surroundings. The United States, unfortunately, has tended to produce neither design consciousness nor natural consciousness in very large quantities. The following are some of the areas which could contribute to the development of these competencies in the US, as well as in other cultures such as the UK where there are still many people who have relative difficulty in using their settings well.

Formal education

Although very early school experiences tend to help a child to learn about space, perspective, houses, and the like, attention to this area falls off rapidly until it is almost non-existent in secondary schools and beyond. As one professor of architecture put it:

Seeing the world clearly and completely is a unique ability of the young . . . .
    In most education, these visual activities are abandoned as soon as verbal skills are developed. Visual skills are replaced as a means of communicating and organizing. Since this transition is generally complete by the sixth grade, visual studies at this time become 'art' — the school's way of saying they aren't very important.
    The result of this transition is that as soon as Johnny can read and write, he stops being trained to see. All the mess of the visual environment can now be rationalized, explained away and ignored . . . . (Bennett, 1973)

There are already some formal educational antidotes to this trained blindness, and they should be encouraged and expanded. They include:

— An experimental architectural studies programme at New York University designed to teach the non-architect how to evaluate the physical appearance of cities.

— High school geography courses such as the innovative 'High School Geography Project', which uses games where students take specific roles such as pioneer farmer in nineteenth century western Kansas and attempt to cope with all aspects of that environment (Gould and White, 1974, p.45). Gould and White have also suggested specific training in the nature of 'mental maps' (the ways in which we form images of different areas) as a means to breaking down parochialism (Gould and White, 1974, pp. 80-1).

— A project called the Urban Awareness Program, in which professional designers, such as architects, landscape architects, and planners, work with the primary grades in the Cambridge (Mass.) public schools with the goal of bringing the children an improved sensitivity to the built and natural environment around them (*Architectural Record*, 1975).

— A programme in 'Organic Architecture' at Goddard College, Plainfield, Vermont. Students in the design course have designed, engineered, and built several new buildings on the campus, under the supervision of the faculty (*Progressive Architecture*, 1971). This use of the College itself as a design laboratory for obtaining practical experience is in sharp contrast to the pattern at most colleges and universities, where new facilities are usually designed by outside professionals (and rich learning opportunities are thereby irretrievably lost).

— Formal military education in most parts of the world has probably been the most advanced type of experiential environmental education, since there has always been a strong emphasis on understanding new settings quickly and developing practical skills at using settings well. Survival has been correctly seen as depending on having soldiers with high environmental competence. The Outward Bound Programs, designed to teach survival skills, come from this tradition in military education.

There should be specific courses in environmental perception, evaluation, and use at each level of the formal educational process; and they should go beyond current models such as low-status industrial arts or home economics courses. These courses should be designed to promote the sharing of experiences among participants, so that they can evaluate the extent to which their outcomes are a function of a particular setting and the extent to which they are a function of personal preferences, skills, and habitual ways of dealing with the environment. My guess is that many of the above examples have been designed with relatively little thought about the social processes involved and most emphasis given to the places or things being studied.

It would also be a help if societal reward systems were altered to reflect an increased valuing of environmental competence, such as including related areas in tests of achievement and college entrance examinations. Basic concepts of systems theory and interdependence should be taught as an encouragement to thinking of one's surroundings as interdependent systems that affect one another rather than isolated entities.

Alternative education experiences

The last 20 years have seen a great upsurge in the 'learning business'. Many new educational opportunities now exist that are not sponsored by the more traditional, official educational institutions; and this pattern is likely to increase as the US and other cultures emphasize lifelong learning rather than just childhood education. The variety of alternative educational experiences in environmental competence is as broad as the imagination's ability to generate new forms of experience. The following are a few examples.

— A very interesting historical precedent for specially designed settings to promote environmental competence was provided by the pioneering city planner Patrick Geddes in the nineteenth and early twentieth centuries. For instance, he created a setting in Edinburgh called the 'Outlook Tower', a learning museum open to the public (but not frequented by them the way it should have been) which visually and verbally depicted the history and interdependence of the various subsystems of the city — geographic, economic, and social systems. He also created a large number of conferences on environment and planning, often using Edinburgh as a living laboratory which conference attendees would observe and discuss (Kitchen, 1975, p. 140).

— A 'Pride Program' was developed in a study of vandalism in the Boston public schools. Based on both education and competitive awards, the goal is to develop a sense of custodianship — that is, an awareness of the problems caused by damage and the advantages of beauty in the school setting (Zeisel, 1976).

— The Shelter Institute was founded in Maine in 1974, providing practice-based courses with the goal of presenting 'the alternative methods of dealing with all home building problems, and the implications, long and short term, of each alternative, so that the individual can make reasonable decisions based on engineering fact, not Madison Avenue fancy' (Aley, 1975). (This is not a bad definition of practical competence in dealing with one's own shelter needs.)

— Some government authorities in the US and the UK have begun to provide public educational experiences which can result in citizens helping to renew or preserve their neighbourhoods rather than being only a force for degeneration. Nan Fairbrother described a number of programmes which are concerned with the revitalization of derelict land, such as Lancashire's courses on methods for planting spoil heaps (Fairbrother, 1970).

The need for such public educational events is quite large, and could cover practical maintenance of high-quality urban and rural areas as well as reclamation of unused spaces.

In addition to these examples, I think that a relatively neglected but high-payoff area would be environmental and architectural awareness training for non-designers who make design decisions that affect the general environment: town planning council members, facilities managers in private organizations, and the like. Many of these types of decision-makers have little appreciation of the consequences of their decisions, or of the range of possibilities for creating high-quality settings.

As my last example of designed programmes, I must mention the application of gestalt therapy, the area of the applied behavioural sciences which is most directly relevant for experiential training in environmental competence. Gestalt training is particularly useful for helping a participant become aware of him or herself in the present, in the immediate environment, and combine that awareness with the personal responsibility for being and acting in that situation. This process has been particularly advanced by an architect become gestalt therapist, Donald Busch, who turned from designing places to the creation of gestalt learning experiences to help people use their places (and their own energy) in richer ways. He created the Entayant Institute near New York City as a vehicle for this training (Jablons, 1977).

Self-administering materials

Besides programmes of one sort or another, the last few years have seen an increase in the production of books, pamphlets, maps, lists, games, etc., which provide help in dealing with settings and can be used without the aid of an instructor. The advantage of these types of materials is that they can be used in one's own setting and at one's own preferred pace.

— Resources summaries such as *Alternative London* or *The Whole Earth Catalogue* provide a large amount of information about resources, products, locations, communication modes (telephone numbers, underground stops, etc.), and the like for a particular city or region. This information is often inaccessible or too scattered to be found out piecemeal. Besides providing useful specific bits of information, these guides affect users' competence by suggesting new *categories* of information about a city — categories that they may not have ever considered, but which suggest new possible uses for the setting.

— Another common aid book is more focused: the 'walking tour' guide to cities or country regions. I have seen many of these in the past few years, including ones for London, Paris, Geneva, New York City, Chicago, Boston, Cleveland, and San Francisco. One of the most interesting ones is called *Man-Made Philadelphia* (Wurman and Gallery, 1972). It begins with the routes or 'bone structure' of the city. It then describes various elements in the city, but it deliberately does not stick just to typical sights and tourist attractions such as Independence Hall. It includes the ordinary, gritty features that make a city a city — different housing and commercial areas, the docks, typical traffic-jam points, and so on. The authors' goal was explicitly to improve users' environmental competence, to provide enough information for citizens to understand the structure and systems of the city and therefore be more informed on key decisions.

Mass media patterns

Citizens receive many of their concepts about settings and how to use them from the society's mass media: newspapers, television, radio, and magazines. An increased emphasis on environmental issues in the past few years has undoubtedly made people more aware of environmental relations, although the emphasis has tended to be less on improving citizens' competence and more on decrying what 'they' (industries, politicians, the highway lobby, etc.) are doing to pollute the environment. This theme needs to be augmented by more inputs which would help citizens to develop their own competence in dealing with their own settings.

— Regular newspaper columns dealing with architecture and design can develop a regular audience and help them to be able to see their surroundings on a greater variety of evaluative dimensions. In the United States, the major share of work in this area has been done by the *New York Times*' architecture critic, Ada Louise Huxtable (Huxtable, 1975) It is a measure of how far we have to go in this area that Robert Campbell (another excellent architecture critic) could report in the Boston *Globe* in February 1975 (and reconfirm in 1977) that there were only six regular architecture critics writing in newspapers in the US, compared with hundreds in film, art, theatre, and music. The proportions are probably not much different in Britain.

— Television has been used very little in the US as a medium for educating the public in concepts of design and environmental competence; and what little has been done is generally on the Public Broadcast System, not the major networks. My observations suggest that television in Britain has made much more of a contribution to environmental competence than it has in the US through series such as those done by Sir John Betjeman. Much more could be done in both societies to take advantage of the visual potential of television for demonstrating differences between low- and high-quality settings.

— Commercial films also help to establish cultural patterns of environmental awareness or blindness. The ways in which settings are depicted and used by actors are subliminal suggestions which may be unconsciously absorbed by cinemagoers and applied in their own lives. Certain directors, such as Michelangelo Antonioni, have been particularly concerned with settings and how they can be used richly.

Leisure activity patterns

A society's members learn about life from the inputs of all their experiences (both planned and unplanned), including the ways they play. For instance, do-it-yourself projects can promote environmental competence, as do field trips, vacations to new settings, and hiking and camping experiences. A few other examples:

— A number of games have been created to help children have fun and develop environmental skills at the same time. An example is 'Citygames', developed by the Boston Children's Museum, which raises consciousness about the many hidden facets and patterns of the city.

— Supervised wilderness experiences have become available in a wide variety of forms, from Outward Bound programmes to float trips down scenic North American rivers such as the Colorado, the Rogue, and the Salmon. The director of group trips down Idaho's Salmon River has as one of his specific goals (besides people's enjoyment of the trip) the sensitization of people to the values of wild rivers and wilderness country (Norton, 1975).

— Perhaps the fastest-growing example of a leisure activity which promotes enhanced environmental skills is the sport of orienteering, a game originating in Europe. The contestants use only maps, compasses, and their own observations to reach a series of designated stations as quickly as possible in a particular wilderness area. The process could be and probably already has been extended to urban areas as well.

The point of the orienteering example is not really whether one learns better from wilderness or urban navigation, but simply that a pastime that encourages route-planning, data generation, use of maps and compass, quick observation of relevant features of a setting, and post-meet discussions of tactics and experiences can improve players' general environmental competence as well as provide exercise, amusement, and the challenge of competition.

Special problems and opportunities

I have defined experiential methods very broadly in order to sensitize us to the variety of methods that can be used to enhance environmental competence. Some of these methods are designed and planned workshops, courses, active museums, etc.; others are patterns of media inputs: newspaper coverage or columns, films, television, etc,; while still others are leisure-time pursuits such as games, travel experiences, and wilderness activities. I believe that each of these activities can be a spur to environmental learning, but their very variety represents a challenge, since people also can engage in many activities from which very little learning results. This is probably most true of the environmental area, which has several rather special problems or patterns which can make experience-based learning difficult. In the following sections I will describe some of these problems, together with several positive opportunities which can be used to enhance environmental competence.

Problems in environmental competence development

The first problem stems from the history of blindness to spatial/environmental influences in our society. Because this has traditionally been treated as an unimportant, 'peripheral' area which should not take priority over task or social concerns, people have tended not to discuss spatial experiences with one another, either at work or in home and social settings. There is relatively little sharing of experiences of categories for comparing them, so relatively little learning tends to take place. This pattern is similar to the effect of the taboo against discussing personal salaries with colleagues or friends, which results in many people not learning very much from those around them about how to manage personal financial affairs (Steele, 1975).

This social climate factor of low discussability is often amplified by the person's relatively low ability to focus on immediate feelings and perceptions triggered by a setting. As a society Americans are overdependent on sight as a sensing input, and tend to ignore the cumulative impact of sounds, smells, tastes, and tactile messages. Thus, environmental training must break into the circle by first getting the person's attention and focusing it on self, surroundings, and especially the interaction between the two. This is why I consider the gestalt therapy approach to have such high promise as a method of unfreezing.

In addition to a lack of discussion of spatial experiences among individuals, there is a lack of feedback loops in people's experiences in public or quasi-public settings. When one walks through a bleak public space, even if this is recognized as a poor experience who does one tell? There are very few clear mechanisms for giving reactions to buildings, shops, squares, etc., and therefore very few ways to follow up on one's vague feelings so that new learning can occur. For instance, if I could complain to someone about my experiences in Boston's Government Center Plaza, they might agree with me and say 'too bad', but they might also point out what criteria were used in the design process and how I was not making use of the full potential by the kinds of choices I was making while using the Plaza. In other words, the total process could expand from a simple gripe to a confrontation and learning experience. (And, if the designated feedback process were designed right, the cumulative reactions of users of the Plaza could lead to some alterations in the design, such as the inclusion of more trees and more benches for sitting or sleeping.)

The fact that this last possibility probably sounds far-fetched to most readers is indicative of a second major problem in the area of training in environmental competence. Simply put, there is a lack of natural, accepted settings for engaging in this sort of training, plus a general lack of institutional supports for it. To see what I mean, consider the supports for more accepted experiential training methods, such as those in interpersonal skills and awareness. Individuals often see the need to improve this area of their functioning; and institutional leaders recognize the potential pay-off to their organizations and are willing to support such training with both money and time off for their members to participate. We may tend to take these supports for granted, but they are the patterns which have allowed interpersonal and group training to grow and mature — we have had a natural context for trying new designs and learning from the research which has accompanied them.

By contrast, the logistics and politics of environmental development are much less clear. Companies do not particularly value the development of this skill area in their members, nor do their leaders see this development as relevant for themselves. There are relatively few public programmes providing a choice of experiences that individuals can use for their own development.

On top of this lack of support, I believe that there may well be active *blocking* of training in environmental competence, by people and groups that have a vested interest in maintaining low skill levels. For instance, local politicians seem to avoid such development for themselves and others, possibly out of a fear of reduced degrees of freedom to make unilateral planning decisions without the hassle of informed opinions from their constituents. Similarly, upper management in work organizations has traditionally held almost complete power concerning facilities decisions, and is unlikely to be uniformly delighted by the development of environmental skills and awareness in its workforce (Steele, 1973, p. 95). The point is simply that training in environmental competence tends to run up against some fairly strong vested interests in addition to an historical pattern of apathy or blindness towards the area.

A third major problem concerns the complexity and cost of engaging in experiential training in environmental competence. In order to create varied conditions and settings which can generate feelings, perceptions, actions, and so on, one needs to have a fairly rich and flexible training setting. Most conference centres do not serve this purpose well, having been designed for more social, interactive types of learning. Hotel-type settings are even worse, since they usually contain only a very outdated model of what a 'conference' should look like (usually a big horseshoe-shaped table with pitchers of water and a speaker's rostrum in front). All of these can be used to some degree, since a trainer can design events which heighten awareness of any setting, but they are not very rich as settings for a variety of training experiences.

Ideally, one would want a setting with a variety of spaces, lighting, materials, etc., including some parts that can be manipulated by the participants so they can experiment with consciously creating suitable settings for different activities. This set-up should also be located in a fairly rich area in terms of variety or quality of nearby places (*versus* in a mall on Route 1 in Saugas, Mass., for example). This allows the use of training designs related to touring, exploring, and testing the impact of existing settings. I have found training programmes carried out in Central London hotels to be very good for this purpose, though not for the participant-tinkering dimension.

All of these considerations suggest that environmental competence programmes can be quite costly to stage compared with other training areas. This may be another reason why there are fewer of them being carried out today, and why such large-scale measures as Paolo Soleri's Arcosanti (an emerging city megastructure being built as a participative learning experience in the southwestern desert) sometimes seem like the only alternative. I believe that there are a number of less grandiose ways of making such training feasible and affordable. One is simply the good choice of location for training, so that rich surroundings provide good alternative examples. Another is to take advantage of activities that people are engaged in anyway. An example would be to design daily debriefing/processing sessions for travelling tour groups, so that they could share their experiences with one another and hopefully learn about the *process* of using their travel well. A third approach is to create training designs which use models of larger environments. There is some research evidence that people can identify with working with scale-model environments and can make translations to their choices in real settings. They seem to experience vicariously many of the same emotions that they would in a full-scale setting (Kleeman, 1978). This offers a lot of promise in terms of learning about home, work, and public settings and how to shape them better.

Special opportunities

The future for experiential environmental training is not all problems, of course. (If it were, I probably would not have bothered to write this chapter.) The area also has some inherent opportunities because of some of its special qualities. One is the fact that there is a larger number of potential change agents who can be involved in some sort of environmental development than for more traditional social training areas such as interpersonal behaviour. Possible contributors include those in many different types of roles: psychologists, therapists, educators, government planners, developers, newspaper columnists, architects, interior designers, and so on. All of these can contribute something to the development of environmental competence, given the right context and some support.

Another advantage is that environmental learning, if it is done well, can be built on wherever one is — the opportunities for follow-up activities are almost limitless, since people are always in some type of setting or surroundings. They are always practising, or having the opportunities to practise, skills in dealing with these settings, whether it be at home, work, play, or in public settings. This may seem obvious, but the seeds for taking advantage of follow-up practice opportunities need to be sown during training or it tends not to happen. Most people learn very little from their experiences in settings except for the rudiments of how to get by from day to day.

One final opportunity is the potential impact that can result from influencing a large-scale pattern which in turn influences the environmental competence of a whole culture or segment of society. For instance, if one could design ways to use television news media to make regular inputs on how to use (and demand) high-quality public spaces in one's city, a new feedback loop would be developed over time as citizens learned to be more pro-active, and the shape of cities would begin to change as well. This is a scale of impact which is considerably larger than that which we expect with more traditional types of training methods.

CONCLUSIONS

Since the preceding discussion has ranged over a wide number of topics, I will briefly summarize the main patterns which lie behind the specific examples. These patterns can suggest new approaches to design, new research possibilities, and new ways in which readers can use their own settings for greater learning and enjoyment.

As a way of thinking about experiential environmental training, the methods described in this chapter can be compared with social process training. In interpersonal learning laboratories, the primary purpose is to create structures and processes that promote people's sharing of their internal experiences, in order *to make hidden data visible*. In this way, participants can compare both the similarities and differences in their experiences, as well as seeing the consequences of their actions. With environmental experiences, there are two rather different goals. One is to help people be *aware of their own internal experiences* (i.e. of their reactions to settings); the other is *to make visible data relevant* — that is, to reduce staring and increase participants' awareness of consequences of their own choices on how well they get by in their environments. In the past they have tended to know that they use some settings better than others, but not to feel that it makes much difference.

I have also defined 'experiential methods' very broadly. They include not only group exercises, simulations, and the like, but also certain types of reading (e.g. regular newspaper columns, which provide a pattern for sensing societal values) and tinkering, such as working with models or remaking places with materials provided by the training designer. Experiential methods have also included simply helping people look at activities they are engaged in anyway, such as experience-sharing sessions during a travel tour.

These varied experiential methods have equally varied goals in terms of what kinds of environmental skills or competence they are trying to encourage. Techniques such as the gestalt workshops are primarily aimed at increasing *personal awareness* of oneself in settings, and possibly at promoting freer *attitudes* towards various settings and the possibilities they might hold. Specific workshops on environmental problems such as pollution or resource utilization are trying to change *attitudes* plus hopefully influence *behaviour* in directions that will have a positive effect on patterns of environmental relationships for society as a whole (e.g. less pollution, less waste).

Many of the specific school courses or workshops mentioned earlier and also the outward-bound type programmes are trying to develop *specific environmental skills*, such as diagnosing and repairing problems in one's dwelling, or identifying and preparing edible plants in the wild. I would like to see this type of training expanded to include day-to-day life in our urban areas, and to see it provided for people who need it most but are now least likely to get it. For example, vagrants could use training in how to relieve oneself in an American city (notably short on public lavatories compared with European cities) without being hassled or arrested; or elderly, handicapped, and absent-minded people could be trained to deal with changing/dangerous patterns of automobile traffic when walking in the city. I would even like to see general training for office workers in how to walk as a group at lunchtime without blocking the sidewalk for everyone else.

The general thrust of most of my examples has been to develop *competence plus caring* — that is, to develop people's perceptions, attitudes, behaviours, and skills so that they can use their own settings richly and also not mess them up for other people: to be both good users and good custodians. The other theme was the need to also train them to be *good learners*: to develop skills in quickly scouting a new setting and learning how to use it well, so that one's competency is not dependent on being always rooted to one particular spot. Being an effective environmental learner puts one in the position of being adaptive rather than situation-bound.

I have one final recommendation. If this is an interesting area for you, by all means become more involved in the design, implementation, and evaluation of methods for expanding environmental competence. As I have described here, the opportunities to do this exist at a variety of scales of effort, from small workshops for a few people, to large planned programmes in school systems, to attempts to change whole societal patterns such as leisure activities or the rate of inclusion of architectural news in major news media. Each of these approaches can produce important benefits for the level of environmental competence in society, and each attempt can also provide us with information about what we do not know and need to explore further.

REFERENCES

Aley, J. (1975) 'Housing school students inform as well as learn', *The Boston Globe*, Dec. 25, 32.

Architectural Record (1975) October, 35.

Bennett, R. (1973) 'Why Johnny can't see', *The Boston Globe*, Sept. 2, A-5.

Fairbrother, N. (1970) *New Lives, New Landscapes*. London: The Architectural Press (Penguin edition, 1972).

Gould, P. and White, R. (1974) *Mental Maps*. Harmondsworth: Pelican.

Huxtable, A. L. (1975) *Will They Ever Finish Bruckner Boulevard?* New York: Macmillan.

Jablons, P. (1977) 'Interior decorating by gestalt?', *The New York Times*, Aug. 18, 27.

Kitchen, P. (1975) *A Most Unsettling Person*. New York: Saturday Review Press.

Kleeman, W. (1978) 'Does working with models save time?', *The Designer*, **21**, 4, 14.

Norton, B. (1975) *Rivers of the Rockies*. Chicago: Rand McNally, p.132.

Piaget, J. (1929) *The Child's Conception of the World*. New York: Harcourt Brace.

Progressive Architecture (1971) 'Organic architecture at Goddard College', November.

Steele, F. (1973) *Physical Settings and Organization Development*. Reading, Mass.: Addison-Wesley.

Steele, F. (1975) *The Open Organization: The Impact of Secrecy and Disclosure on People and Organizations*. Reading, Mass.: Addison-Wesley.

Steele, F. (1976) 'Humanizing the physical setting at work.' In Meltzer, H. and Wickert, F. (eds.) *Humanizing Organizational Behaviour*. Springfield: Thomas, pp. 357-69.

Wurman, R. S. and Gallery, J. (1972) *Man-Made Philadephia*. Cambridge, Mass.: MIT Press.

Zeisel, J. (1976) *Stopping School Property Damage*. Arlington, Virginia: American Association of School Adminstrators.

Advances in Experiential Social Processes, Volume 2
Edited by C. P. Alderfer and C. L. Cooper
© 1980 John Wiley & Sons Ltd.

Chapter **10**

Experiencing Organizational Structure

Barry A. Stein

Goodmeasure, Cambridge, Massachusetts, U.S.A.

and

Rosabeth Moss Kanter

Yale University, U.S.A.

INTRODUCTION

The use of experiential social techniques for learning has become widespread in the last 30 years. Initially, these techniques focused largely on learning about issues on a microlevel, and particularly on the interaction between the individual and the social setting. Thus social psychology, the field that is concerned with the interaction of individuals in social systems, has quite appropriately seen the use of experiential techniques as a valid and useful extension of its area of relevance. What is less clear is the particular utility of experiential techniques for learning about broader organizational phenomena, even though there have been claims that such techniques are highly relevant to learning about organizations and social systems, particularly through simulations. Some of these latter are, of course, well known — for example SIMSOC (Gamson, 1972), or the Power and Systems Laboratory (Oshry, 1976). Related claims have been made for more episodic or partial activities, beginning with T-groups (Schein and Bennis, 1965) and extending to groups brought together to facilitate learning and change for entire communities (Schindler-Rainman and Lippitt, 1978). There is no doubt that people learn things about social systems in these settings. What we wish to explore, however, is whether and how experiential techniques help people learn about structural features of organizations in a way that is enhanced by the use of experiential methods.

Structure in a certain sense has always been critical to experiential techniques, insofar as an important element is the design of a format — that is, a structure — that helps induce certain perceptions, that enables certain learning, or that focuses attention on the impacts on individuals that arise because of that setting. The issue in using experiential techniques to learn about structure itself is just the reverse. The focus is on using the perceptions to elucidate the structural character of the setting, rather than using the structure as a device to bring about certain perceptions or enable certain experiences. Clearly, structures help people learn about processes — this is the principle behind simulations. The question is whether the reverse is also true.

In this chapter we explore the extent to which experiential techniques can be used to help people to learn about organizational structure, taking note of possible limits intrinsic in the nature of experiential learning as it interacts with characteristics of structure.

To do this, we propose initially to define and describe structure in a particular way, to define a range of experiential methods, and to look at two experiential methods that we have found useful in teaching about it: a reflective and a game process. In both cases, theories of structure are necessary. We have used Kanter's (1977) framework, which provides a coherent analysis of certain key structural elements with implications both for understanding organizations and social systems and for the design of experiential processes. We illustrate these points by showing how Kanter's framework can be utilized experientially and by describing our experience in its use.

THE NATURE OF ORGANIZATIONAL STRUCTURE

The word 'structure' is used to refer to many different things. Popularly, it usually suggests characteristics of the formal organization chart. This concept is certainly too narrow; it mistakes certain aspects of structure for the idea of structure itself. Even in the professional literature, however, the word 'structure' is used very differently (or, more often than not, defined only implicitly). Blau (1974, p. 12) defines it as '. . . the distributions, along various lines, of people among social positions that influence the role relations among these people', and (1977, pp. 4-5), somewhat more formally, as 'a multidimensional space of different (and interrelated) social positions among which a population is distributed'. Thompson (1967) defines structure slightly less atomistically:

Invariably (the major components of a complex organization) are . . . segmented or departmentalized, and connections are established within and between departments. It is this internal differentiation and patterning that we will refer to as structure.

Galbraith (1977) sees structure as the domain of 'organizing modes' related to the division of labour, departmentalization, distribution of power, and hierarchical configuration (e.g. arrangements of the formal organization chart).

Operationally, however, what is implied in all ideas of structure is order, regularity, and predictability. Structures are organizational frameworks or skeletons that provide coherence and continuity over time, often differentiated from processes, which are more fluid, occasional, temporary or changeable. (A recent text is titled *Organization: Structure and Process* (Hall, 1977).) However, all *definitions* of structure are abstractions focusing on this or that aspect of the skeleton. The experienced reality of structure in organizations resides in its impact, in the patterns and regularities that it imparts to the behaviour of the organization and its members.

This is what we mean by structure: elements that show coherence and continuity over time; that represent the sources of relative predictability in any organization or social unit; and that therefore both constrain and enable the behaviour of participants in the system, whether they are aware of it or not. Learning about structure by direct experience therefore properly begins with awareness of the existence of these patterns and recognition of their sources, followed by analysis and identification of the elements that compose them. (Bringing about awareness is, of course, a crucial issue in experiential learning.) This definition is consistent with that arrived at by Meyer (1977, p.44): 'Organizational structure . . . refers to patterned behavior in the fairly large groups which have goals and have boundaries separating them from environments.'

Every group, organization or social system exhibits and continues to develop patterns so that certain things become easier, more acceptable, more likely,·and more rewarded, while others become less so. These patterns, whether formalized or not, whether made explicit or not, whether described publicly or not, constitute the directly perceptible structure of the organization.

The patterns are coherent, and exhibit momentum and continuity; they account for the tendency of organizations and other social units to maintain the *status quo*. This characteristic of structure underlies much of organizational behaviour. The very process of transforming mere assemblages of individuals into such social units as groups or organizations lies in the creation of patterns — structure — but those same patterns, once in place, resist other change. This fact, that structure is difficult to change, is also its greatest strength.

We can therefore speak of structure in two senses: (1) the behavioural regularities in an organization, its components or its members; and (2) the elements of the organization that are responsible for producing those regularities. Thus, it includes informal understandings as well as organization charts; formal procedures as well as behavioural norms; and informal roles as well as formal positions with explicit occupancy. Moreover, structure has both a long-term and short-term dimension. Some patterns are readily observed in the short run: hours of work and attendance, for example. Others, such as career patterns, are long-term in nature and not usually as visible. These distinctions and others are important in setting the limits of experiential learning and are discussed at length below.

EXPERIENTIAL LEARNING AND STRUCTURE

Given this understanding of organizational structure, what is meant by experiential learning about it? Does it differ from experiential learning about other things, and if so, in what way?

Experiential learning of any sort requires at least two things: (1) conscious awareness of the experience; and (2) transformation of the awareness into a cognitive lesson. As to the first, for learning to take place, participants must be explicitly aware, in the sense that their attention is directed to certain aspects of the experience. This leads in turn to two conditions that must be met: (1) the experience must offer appropriate potential for attention (the key design issue); and (2) that attention must be appropriately directed (the key staff role). Mere awareness is not enough, however, because learning does not just consist of simple self-consciousness; rather, it requires recognition of the relevance and significance of the perception — a cognitive act transforming experienced but otherwise isolated data into a generalizable conclusion. In one form or another, this requires a theory. (For a more complete discussion of experiential learning, see Kolb *et al.*, 1971).

In the case of experiential learning about oneself, these conditions are easily met. In the T-group, to take the most obvious formal setting, trainers provide the directing of awareness; the theories are often implicit, personal, and idiosyncratic. In learning about self, this is satisfactory and perhaps necessary. As participants apply conclusions from this experience to other times and situations, individual differences are interesting but not central (except as sources of still other learning).

Experiential learning about structure raises some very different issues. First, individual or isolated perceptions are not in themselves adequate when the focus is on patterns. An individual can always learn from an experience in the sense of making use of personal reactions and conclusions. But patterns mean, by definition, regular effects repeated over some period of time. Moreover, whereas individual perceptions are arguably valid for the person, regardless of their relevance to anyone else, the impact of structure — the reality of structure — necessarily extends beyond an individual or a single occasion. Structure, that is, exists apart from individuals. Thus, experiential learning about structure requires a shared and externally focused perspective in addition to the initial individual perceptions. Finally, since the actual *experience* of structure must be related to patterned effects rather than root causes, a different kind of theory is needed for the mapping of perception in that realm; that is, a theory about the impact of specific structural elements on individuals.

Experiential learning about structure, then, is both a more complex process and more difficult to achieve than experimental learning about self. It incorporates and begins with self-learning, but goes beyond this to incorporate other persons and experiences, based on a more abstract and general theory. T-groups can also be used in this way, as when attention is directed to generalizable effects of groups so composed and arranged. This was, of course, the original purpose of 'laboratory' groups.

THE DESIGN OF EXPERIENCES
FOR LEARNING ABOUT STRUCTURE

Most experiential learning takes place in natural settings; that is, as people go through their normal activities. On the other hand, the label as ordinarily used refers to activities designed deliberately to promote learning, in classes, workshop, seminars or planned activities. There are, however, a limited number of discrete approaches, with different advantages and limitations. Starting with the least contrived approach, the four alternatives are as follows.

Natural. This is what is ordinarily referred to as learning from experience. With conscious awareness of patterns, which can be gained by self-reflection, didactic instruction, reading, or guidance and coaching, people can use their reactions and perceptions as data from which influences about surrounding structures can be gained. The more sophisticated their theories, the more powerful and focused the learning.

The major advantage is that all data are potentially available in their pristine state: there are no explicit biases or distortions. (Any patterned biases or distortions that do exist are, of course, actually reflections of existing structures.) The major disadvantages are: (1) too many data, selection among which requires an *a priori* theory (see the March and Simon, 1958, discussion of bounded rationality); and (2) patterns may take very long to reveal themselves, or may be masked by too great complexity in the environment.

Simulated. This attempts to overcome both major disadvantages of the natural experience without doing excessive violence to the major advantage. By designing an experience which contains the essential elements of the natural, usually in time-compressed form, while eliminating extraneous features, participants are said to learn faster and with greater clarity. The accuracy of these claims depends on the operational meanings of 'essential' and 'extraneous', as manifested in the design. Others have written extensively on formal simulations of this kind (Abt, 1970; Boocock and Schild, 1968; Jubor and Stoll, 1972). Under these circumstances, less sophisticated theories are needed by 'learners', but more sophisticated ones by 'teachers'. There is, therefore, a trade-off: some responsibility for learning is shifted from the learner (where it largely resides in the natural case) to the designer.

The major advantages are: (1) compression of time permits relatively rapid learning about a variety of structures, especially those of long-term character; (2) reasonable reproducibility and repeatability facilitate reinforcement of learning through discussion and interchange; and (3) the limited context helps highlight the patterns. The major disadvantages are: (1) the possibility that the 'essential' elements are incomplete or distorted (so that the learning does not really apply to the natural situation); and (2) there is little possibility of learning something entirely new, since the environment is, by definition, limited in richness. In sum, "garbage in, garbage out", as computer programmers say.

Games. We use this word to describe experiences built around deliberately fragmented or partial activities. Whereas simulations attempt to create a reasonable, if abbreviated, replica of a natural experience, games deliberately focus on an aspect of that experience. Often, these are designed to test hypotheses — much experimental social psychology involves exploration of behaviour in such settings. In other circumstances, as in the example we offer below, they are designed not to test a hypothesis but to demonstrate a proposition. In either case, the quality of the result depends on the power of the hypothesis/proposition and the sharpness/precision of the theory underlying the design.

The major advantages are: (1) the very high leverage gained by sharp focus (games or experiments can usually be brief, yet with powerful results, because of the concentration on a limited point); and (2) the predictability of the range of effects, thus facilitating deliberate learning about particular points. The major disadvantage is the obverse: the target may be missed entirely if the theoretical framework and the design are not sufficiently accurate. A game is a good tool for teaching a particular lesson; it is not good for general learning, such as about organizations. An example from our own practice is described at length later in the chapter.

Reflective. The fourth and last variant we have found particularly useful. It takes advantage of people's *past* experience, in which structural patterns may be discerned even though they were not noticed at the time. Reflective processes provide people with new theory that is relevant to some aspect of their experience, that offers alternative explanations for that experience, and that engages them in reflecting on the meaning of selected experiences and the patterns observable in them. We discuss an example later.

The major advantages are: (1) it permits people to draw on a large body of experience retroactively (and therefore to compress it in both time and space); and (2) it is easy and straightforward in application. The major disadvantages are: (1) the remembered data are of uncertain accuracy (which is why this method is much better for discussion in groups than for individuals); and (2) the immediacy and affect associated with other forms of experiential learning (and that account for some of their power) are missing.

Several points are suggested by this list. First, theory is always important —

the better the theory, the better the learning — but it becomes steadily more so as the purely experiential quality of the process decreases. Second, control of learning shifts more and more from the learner to the teacher/facilitator/ designer, in the same direction. Third, the efficiency of the learning process, meaning (potential) learning gained per unit of time invested, is likely to increase in that direction. And fourth, the precision with which lessons can be put also increases. Overall, the design of experiential processes for learning about structure (as about other things) is complex and offers much scope for designers/teachers. We stress that the most important thing is an adequate theory, one that relates particular structures to perceptible effects.

In designing specific activities, we draw on Kanter's (1977) theory of structure and its impact on behaviour. The use of the theory will become clear in the examples of reflective and game processes in learning about structure that follow. This theory identifies three key elements of organizational structure — power, opportunity, and social composition (relative numbers) — and relates them to individual and organizational patterns of behaviour. *Power* refers not to formal authority or hierarchical position but, rather, to the capacity to take action or to get things done. It is a composite of formal and informal elements, the latter accounting for the fact that people in similar positions of authority often have very different amounts of influence and power in this sense. *Opportunity* refers to the general potential for individual challenge, growth and development, rewards, and contribution to the important goals of the organization.

Both power and opportunity are structured — that is, patterned — so that access to either differs with individual locations in the organization's structure. Kanter shows how these two key structural elements have specific impacts on people, both in terms of their actions and in connection with self-image, motivation, aspiration, achievement orientation, and competence. For example, much stereotypical behaviour associated with, for example, women in clerical/secretarial roles can be explained by this framework without relying on explanations rooted in individual propensities, social background or biological characteristics.

In addition to power and opportunity, another element — *social composition or relative numbers* — completes the Kanter framework. It applies specifically to situations in which there are persons of different types in terms of highly salient social characteristics. This is an important structural element in such situations as a few women in a group of men, a few whites in a group of blacks, or an obviously handicapped person among the non-handicapped. This variable, particularly when one social type is very scarce or is numerically a token with respect to the majority, also has an important effect on behaviour. For example, the person in a token situation feels strong pressures to perform, is under disproportionately close observation, and is relatively easily stereotyped.

TEACHING ABOUT STRUCTURE: A REFLECTIVE PROCESS

We have developed a variety of questions and instruments for measuring and analysing aspects of organizational structure and individual positions as structurally defined (Kanter, 1979; Goodmeasure, 1978). These derive clearly from theory and are easily applied in practice. The issue from an experiential standpoint is how people can come not only to see and test the validity of such concepts, but also to incorporate them into their own modes of interpreting their experience. Since people tend to have already well-developed frameworks for interpretation, an important educational goal is to find efficient ways to teach people to 'look for' structure and structural explanations without appearing to deny their experience itself.

Our primary strategy is a simple one. First, we ground all discussion in events and incidents with which participants are familiar — we distinguish conceptually between the experiences themselves, data from which have been observed or experienced, and interpretive framework used to transform them. This often helps confirm participants in the accuracy of their own impressions; a confirmation that builds legitimacy for alternative interpretations and a supportive atmosphere for listening and exploring.

The second step, by contrast, is to vary the possible *interpretation* of such events, as suggested by Kanter's theory, so that participants can see the difference between structural and individual or interpersonal explanations for the same events. The critical element is the mutual discovery that a variety of idiosyncratic perceptions can be effectively subsumed under a common explanation. A pattern has been noted. For many people, this involves a major and profound 'paradigm shift', and not merely a new definition or idea.

An example of the reflective strategy, which we have found especially applicable to short-term programmes, involves prepared vignettes briefly describing familiar organizational situations that illustrate structural variables but that also lend themselves to individual or interpersonal explanations. Participants are asked to diagnose these situations both before and after a presentation of the structural theory in some detail. They thus have an opportunity for immediate comparison between the conclusions drawn from the same data but based on alternative theories. The vignettes themselves are extremely brief; they serve actually to evoke participants' own experiences. In this, they differ entirely from teaching cases, which are intended to be sufficiently complete to be useful to people *without* relevant experience.

The two vignettes that follow are typical of those that contrast structural and individual models, with sex as one relevant variable. They were written after enough interviews in the particular organization to make sure they were typical situations. These were used in an in-house programme where participants shared a great deal of knowledge about the organization. (It is not necessary that people have all the facts at hand; an alternative use is to raise diagnostic issues, e.g. to understand the data that need to be gathered for more complete understanding. But this is no longer experiential in character.)

Vignette 1

Andy Merton, one of the most respected personnel managers in the Bank, has been developing a new program to help more tellers eventually become administrative rather than loan officers (a job with greater growth potential). He'd hoped that many of the women tellers would be interested, but, so far, the tellers that have been interested are almost all men. Somewhat concerned, he's gone to some of the women that he thinks would make good candidates, to see why they're not volunteering. These are some typical responses.
— 'I like the work I'm doing now.'
— 'I don't think I have what it takes.'
— 'I just wouldn't feel comfortable.'
— 'Other people need those jobs more than I do.'
— 'I don't want to leave my friends.'

Vignette 2

Martha Cotton, Manager of a Head Office staff group, had worked for the Bank for 26 years, starting as a secretary and gaining her present job about five years ago. The department she manages contains a substantial number of women, including several of high potential who report directly to her.

Lately, some of these women have been complaining about her management style, first to her and then, more delicately, to her manager, Alan Fox. They've told him that she's always looking over their shoulder, second-guessing their decisions, and is endlessly critical. They wonder, in fact, if a woman boss can really do the job.

Alan, concerned, has asked Martha about this, of course without identifying the women involved. She explains that the job requires close attention to detail, the work is simply too important to take any chances, and that, in any event, her subordinates aren't as competent as they think. Although she doesn't say so, he also senses that she is very angry.

In Vignette 1, opportunity is the primary structural variable; in 2, it is power, with numbers (minority status) as a second issue.

Questions put to participants in analysing these vignettes include:

(1) For what reasons might this problem exist? How might it have come about in general?

(2) What further questions would you ask to gather more information about this situation? What else would you like to know about it?

(3) What actions might you suggest for helping managers resolve the problem? What possibilities would you explore?

(4) What advice would you give to the individual persons involved? What might they be able to do themselves?

We have not systematically documented 'before' and 'after' responses — i.e. before and after hearing the opportunity-power-numbers framework in depth — because we have been using this material for educational rather than research purposes. But we and other colleagues have noted some striking differences. The before-theory discussions tend to involve quick answers and simple solutions that accept the situation as inevitable and unchangeable. Participants want to move immediately from explanations into problem-solving without gathering more data (examples are marked P). Stereotyping and 'blaming the victim' are common (S). Other responses are defensive or hopeless; 'nothing can be done' (D).

About 1

'We can't expect all the tellers to be administrative officers.' (D)

'Not everyone aspires to management.' (D)

'Women need encouragement; men are better gamblers.' (S)

'Give them career counselling.' (P)

'We can't promise everybody promotions anyway.' (D)

About 2

'Explore Martha's background. Give her training.' (P)

'Does she have problems at home?' (S)

'She assumes everybody needs some supervision. She doesn't know how to manage.' (S)

'She is approaching retirement.' (S)

'Help her change her style. Identify priorities.' (P)

'As a secretary she was used to details. She can't change.' (D)

The after-theory discussions have a quite different flavour. Participants do not necessarily *reject* their earlier interpretations, but they spend more time exploring the issues in depth before going on to possible solutions. They see situations in more complexity, and they raise more hypotheses and questions. They also minimize 'blaming' of the individuals involved and show more understanding that *anyone* might behave that way in that situation. Sex, race, and other stereotypes tend to disappear. Furthermore, participants do not merely parrot key concepts from the theory; they extend them as their own experience suggests. Perhaps most significantly, they see a greater variety of action options and possibilities for change than they did before.

About 1

Our current counselling programs are "doing things wholesale". How do the women know we mean *them*? Maybe we have to drag them "kicking and screaming" into the administrative jobs so they see they can do them.' (Looking for new options)

'People don't have to *accept* opportunity because they might not move on, but it is our responsibility to do all we can to see it is *available*.' (Shift in assumed responsibility)

How can we add other opportunities to the teller and loan jobs? We don't want to lose people who could contribute more.' (Expanding options)

'A stuck job lowers a person's self-evaluation. They stop feeling they can do any more.' (Structural explanation)

About 2

'Martha has reached a job ceiling. Stuck people devalue people under them as a way to solidify their own position. This ignores the power to be gained by having dynamic subordinates.' (Consequences of structure; possible options)

'Alan is just trying to make her a "nice guy". He could consider how to make Martha's job have more opportunity or to reward her for development of subordinates.' (Shift from 'Martha as problem' to her manager)

'Martha is bitter because "high potential" people are getting opportunities she didn't. She should get something out of getting her people promoted — some reward, some recognition.' (New structural option and hypothesis)

'We could get Martha involved in more "powerful" things. We need to build up her supervisors' confidence in her.' (New options)

'Give Martha the feeling she's a "kingmaker".' (Seek new options)

'Get Alan to delegate more to Martha, share power with her.' (Structural option for manager)

One key point here is that people's own experience *alone* would rarely lead them to search for structural explanations or intervention possibilities. One's most common direct perception tends to be related to characteristics of other people, and thus it is conceptually 'efficient' to locate explanations first in those characteristics. A coherent structural theory, on the other hand, helps enrich experience by suggesting additional — and perhaps more powerful and useful — ways of interpreting it through recognition of patterns. Moreover, a theory of *organizational* structure and its impact permits people to recognize the patterns that specifically derive from *organizational* structures and not generic social or cultural ones (Meyer, 1977).

A STRUCTURAL GAME EXAMPLE

A game for teaching about organizational structure and its impact was suggested to us by a classic laboratory experiment conducted by Cohen (1958). Unlike most experiments of that era, which focused on interpersonal or isolated small group dynamics, Cohen's research attempted to model some of the more complex aspects of hierarchical structures that occur simultaneously — and thus to approximate actual organizations more closely.

Other researchers, Cohen argued, tended to use two basic approaches to defining hierarchies when investigating communications within them. Some considered hierarchy in terms of social status, observing how low-status persons strive to communicate with those of high status in an effort to achieve either real or imagined mobility. In the second approach, researchers defined hierarchy in terms of power; low-status persons tailor their communication to high-status persons so as to establish good relations with those who control their opportunities for advancement.

Cohen combined these two approaches to create a more complete conception of the hierarchical environment. His experiment was designed to examine the communication behaviour of low-ranking persons in a predefined hierarchy. Cohen was especially interested in the differences between low-power groups that had no chance for upward mobility and those that did. Thus, he wanted to manipulate two of the three key structural variables in Kanter's theory: opportunity and power.

The experiment was arranged as follows. Small groups of subjects were divided into equal subgroups, sent to separate rooms, and given a task which required communication among them. The groups were *told* that the experiment was to test task performance in situations where only written communication was permitted. Half the groups would be directing the task by sending written instructions, and half would be attempting to complete it, communicating back to the directors and among themselves in writing. In fact, all the groups were attempting to perform the task, with Cohen and his staff sending them a predesigned series of written communications.

To instill a motivation to perform, the experimenters urged the subjects to apply themselves to the task involved (the planning and construction of a model city), saying that good performance was highly correlated with sensitivity, intelligence, and the ability to work well with others. After informing the subjects that the job of sending the messages was more prestigious and important (to establish the low status of the subject groups), the experimenters added powerlessness by telling them that those sending the messages — the directors — would be the sole evaluators of successful performance. Finally, half the groups were told that, no matter how well they performed, they would have to stay in their jobs (the no-opportunity condition); half were given the possibility of moving up to the directing groups at any time as a reward for good performance (the high-opportunity condition).

The groups then applied themselves for the allotted time period, after which the experimenters, on the pretext of preparing for a second phase, handed out a questionnaire asking about the subjects' desires to continue in the same job, to switch to issuing the written instructions, or to leave the experiment. Then the second phase was 'cancelled', and all subjects filled out the main post-experiment questionnaire. This instrument gathered data on: the degree of support/rejection of their ideas that subjects felt they received from their group and from the directing group; the subjects' desires to meet and work with their group members again; and the degree to which subjects saw alternative ways of organizing to accomplish the task.

As expected, the results were consistent with the behaviour patterns of low-status persons in hierarchies formed in other experiments. The introduction of the mobile/non-mobile (chance/no chance for advancement) distinction, however, produced some striking differences in the behaviour of low-status persons. While the groups of both mobile and non-mobile subjects sent almost identical volumes of communication to the directing groups, the content of the mobiles' messages was significantly more task-oriented. The mobiles sent fewer critical comments about the directors to others in their group and sent fewer to the directors themselves than the non-mobiles. The mobiles felt that they received much more support and attention from the directors than did the non-mobiles, who turned inward to their own groups.

These results show that the mobiles behaved in ways that increased their chances of being favourably rated by the directors: they were task-oriented, were careful about criticism, and were less focused on their own group. The non-mobiles, with no chance to advance, behaved otherwise: they worked sporadically, were openly critical of the directors, and were centred on their own group because of a sense of threat from above. Thus, Cohen provided a clear and simple demonstration, confirmed by numerous field observations, that employee behaviour on the job is strongly influenced by the structural characteristics of that job, particularly power and possibilities for advancement.

We transformed this laboratory experiment into an occasion for experiential learning. We wished to provide direct data for personal exploration about the effects on individual motivation and effectiveness and on group dynamics of (1) opportunity structures (presence or absence of potential upward mobility); and (2) power structures (differences in the capacity to control events to effect desired outcomes).

From our own organizational research, it was clear that 'opportunity' was relatively more straightforward, linear, objective, and easily measured than 'power' (see Kanter, 1979). Indeed, for most conventionally structured complex organizations opportunity is readily visualized in terms of ladders, paths, and tracks leading from one position to another, with directions such as upward and downward at least potentially specifiable. But power in our sense is more elusive, since it does not necessarily correspond to formal hierarchical position (and thus is not automatically linear). For example, it is better visualized in terms of partially overlapping concentric circles (as in 'inner circles').

This difference in the two aspects of structure shows up in the game itself. Whereas the degree of opportunity tends to be set by boundary conditions that define paths of upward mobility, the degree of power any group experiences will depend in part on such boundary conditions as resource control and information centrality, but also in part on informal and emergent issues such as group norms, interpersonal relations, and power attributed by others (see Kanter, 1977). There is generally a strong dependency character in power relations (Blau, 1964); this is also built into the game. The 'top' group that controls rewards is dependent on the 'bottom' group that engages in production; the degree of power or powerlessness experienced by the 'top' group in part depends on its capacity to ensure that anything gets done, as well as its greater ability to reward or punish (Kanter and Stein, 1979). Thus, whereas opportunity is easily established by the 'rules of the game', the power structure is more variable and emergent, even though we begin with a formal distribution of authority.

The game concerns a manufacturing organization; the product can vary. We have used greeting cards, fortunes from Chinese fortune cookies, and advertising slogans in the example that follows. Participants, divided into at least two 'divisions' of at least six people each, are given instructions and a position in an established organization (by random assignment):

You are members of divisions A and B (number of divisions depends upon number of participants) of United Advertisers, Inc. Your product is advertising slogans for _____ (relatively close to the group's true product, if the programme is done in-house).

We, the staff, represent corporate management. We judge the quality of your product, market it, provide links between your division and the clients. We also make personal decisions, such as promotion, outplacement, transfers, and raises. In the next quarter, we expect a slot at the corporate level to open up. Our policy is to hire from within. During this quarter we will be carefully evaluating divisional performance in order to decide from which division to promote someone. Divisions compete with each other in this firm. At the conclusion of the second quarter, we will pay each division one cent for each acceptable (to us) fortune.

Divisional organization consists of three hierarchical levels, as shown in Figure 1. The staff bring together the three participants defined as managers for

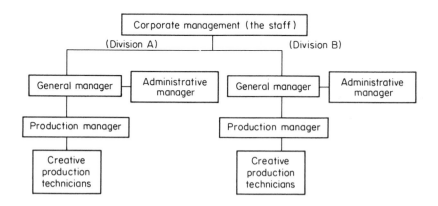

Figure 1   Divisional organization for opportunity and power game

a briefing before the actual game-playing begins. In this briefing the staff define the task and the criteria for acceptance of the product, and also the functions of the three managerial roles.

(1) General manager: has overall responsibility and accountability for marketing.

(2) Administrative manager: staff functions and resource management (including human).

(3) Production manager: direct product quantity and quality responsibility.

The groups then go to work, after a defined planning period. At the end of one work session (the 'first quarter'), the staff announces promotions, and the groups go back to work for a second quarter or more. Debriefing and discussion follow.

The entire game can be carried out in two and a half hours:

Introduction of activity and random role assignments	10 minutes
Briefing management groups	10 minutes
Group planning	15 minutes
First quarter production session	20 minutes
— Corporate announcement: promotions —	5 minutes
Group planning and rearrangement because of promotions	10 minutes
Second quarter production	20 minutes
Processing and debriefing	60 minutes
	150 minutes

Debriefing can be done in a variety of ways:

(1) Division by division, members report their 'individual reactions and thoughts' in response to stimulus questions, verbally and in writing. For example:
(a) What were your thoughts when the promotional announcement came?
(b) What were your hopes (if any) before the announcement? After the announcement? If they changed, why?
(c) How did the announcement of promotion possibilities affect your behaviour? The behaviour of the other group members? Your feelings towards other group members?
(d) Did your feelings about management change after the announcement?
(e) Did your *feelings* about your skills and your own performance change after the announcement? Did the *quantity* and *quality* of your production change?

All of these questions are designed to tap key dimensions of behaviour and attitudes hypothesized to be affected by patterns of opportunity and power: aspirations; self-esteem; engagement with work; desire to model oneself after and to please higher-level groups; development of protective, anti-'success' peer groups; passive resistance and sabotage; hostility; territorial protection and turf-mindedness (Kanter, 1977)

(2) Assigned observer's report, based on an observation checklist containing similar questions.

(3) In the total group, participants discuss and conceptualize the experience — the relation of experiential data to theory; new insights; qualifications or extensions of structural concepts; the relation of the experience to reality; alternative responses possible in situations of blocked mobility, etc.

Typically, reactions to the two opportunity conditions differ. People in the *low-opportunity* group tend to become disappointed and rebellious, consider changing the rules or stopping the game. They are relatively uncreative, and their 'product' tends to involve a great deal of aggressive and sexually abusive imagery (e.g. 'kiss my R's'). They tend to have less internal role differentiation than the high-opportunity group, to be more rules and process oriented, and to argue over ownership of ideas. They tend to be less active, and their tone more subdued. Like many people in jobs with low promotion prospects, they tend to be more concerned about their 'pay' (how the money will be allocated after the game) than the task. Finally, they make negative assumptions about each other's commitment to the task, and are concerned about their own competence. Even though they realize they are 'set up' by the game, they often nevertheless get caught up in feeling 'down'.

Things are different for the *high-opportunity* group. There is generally considerable creativity, a high level of activity, and a strong task orientation. There is a great deal of commitment; people build on each other's ideas. They tend to lose track of participating in a game and become enamoured of their own success, sometimes seeing their ideas as actually useable.

In this game, power interacts with opportunity in a number of ways. Perhaps most striking, as predicted by the theory, is the difference in style of the newly-promoted manager (with high attributed power) and the relatively lower-power managers left behind in the 'stuck' (no-promotion) group. The high-power managers in the game tend to be quite clear about their roles, easily gain the cooperation of their groups, and are perceived as helpful. The *low-power* managers, on the other hand, are seen as intrusive and autocratic and face a group resistant to the task; thus they tend to become even more autocratic and intrusive, partly just to get a hearing, and partly out of frustration that their (low-mobility) group is uncooperative.

Thus, this game not only provides for participants a rich experience of some of the dimensions of life in a complex organization, and one that rings true to most members of them; it also provides direct data that tend to validate the theory and its potential for more general application.

LONG-TERM AND POLICY-RELATED STRUCTURES

So far we have discussed structure in terms of its patterned impact on individuals. But organizational structures also have impact on longer-term and more intrinsically organizational entities. For example, patterns of decision-making about such matters as future goals, operational strategies, and resource utilization are embedded in the fabric of the organization, with complex origins in the past. It is precisely such macro-patterns that generate organizational momentum and resistance to change. Yet these patterns, though they certainly affect people, cannot be experienced in their entirety by individuals.

What any one individual experiences about, for example, decision-making in this larger sense is but a fragment of the whole, and by no means necessarily representative. The patterns created by such structures operate on systems of people, and on such organizational entities as functions, offices, or work groups. Individual perceptions are not even as discrete as those associated with the fable of the seven blind men and the elephant. There, at least, once it is known that, say, it is the elephant's trunk being experienced, conflicts disappear and unambiguous learning becomes possible. Rather, what individuals experience from these macro-structures are epiphenomena; temporary artifacts of complex interactions between individuals and the organization. This is not to say that people cannot appreciate and learn about macro-structures; merely that doing so involves largely non-experiential processes.

Using the individual's own perceptual apparatus as a measuring rod or indicator permits more awareness of certain patterns than of others. But this is a function not merely of individual sensibility, but also of organizational position. One's location in the structure has a systematic effect on the nature of the patterns to which one is exposed — differing in kind, mix, and relative importance — and therefore on the possibilities for experiential learning about structure. (This is one systematic source of distortion in communication. Two people, in very different positions, are not really experiencing the same organization.) For a variety of reasons, then, experiential learning about macro-structures is difficult or impossible.

To illustrate some of these points, consider an organization that is growing in size (numbers of peoples). This change will, in general, be associated with other changes in both formal and informal structures. Depending on: (1) the pre-existing size and structure of the organization, (2) the position of certain individuals within it, and (3) the relationship of both of those to the actual changes, those individuals will experience very different things related to that growth. If the organization is already very large and complex, or if the individual observed is in a unit not centrally involved in the growth, the *experience* of the change (as against what is read in memos) is likely to be limited or non-existent. If the organization is relatively small or is relatively loose in its formal structure, or if the individual is part of a unit within which the growth is occurring, the experience of that growth is likely to be powerful and extensive. Note, however, that *all* of these perceptions are accurate in one sense and fragmentary in another. No one person can experience the growth of the organization *per se*; that is an institutional, extra-individual phenomenon.

Related issues arise in terms of time; that is, the time over which patterned effects occur. (This can be very long indeed; historians like Toynbee have sought patterns in the rise and fall of civilizations.) It is clear, at least, that one is not limited to experiential learning only about the immediate present, even in terms of available theory; Kanter's framework explicitly incorporates time. Opportunity is not merely a reflection of the situation at a given moment, but rather a dynamic variable that involves expectation effects as well as actual position changes over time. Similarly, power is more than a present reality; it is related to future behaviour and options, outcomes associated with present options. As illustrated before, the processes used to help teach about these structures themselves take account of the flow of time, as do most organizational simulations and games.

It is easy enough to set up simulations and games that compress time — ones, that is, that simulate the passage of long periods of real time — but that does not address the real issue. Under what circumstances is such an experience plausibly equivalent to the experience of real time? With respect to experiencing structure, there are two different cases.

In the first case, individuals suspend their disbelief (operate as if the time-scale were different than in fact it is), but are able to relate the subjective experience in the simulation to the subjective experience that would occur in reality because the experience are in fact similar. This is the assumption underlying the game described earlier. In principle, it is accurate when the subjective experiences are essentially independent of the rate of experiencing.

The second case involves a sequence of discrete experiences that can easily and accurately be reproduced. The difference is that in reality they would be separated by large amounts of time. Nevertheless, it might be argued that the impact of those structures on individuals would be identical and independent of spacing, at least to a first approximation.

There are many simulations and games built on this latter principle; for example those that require participants to make a decision in concert with others, taking account of changes that are said to have occurred since the previous decision. Whether this accurately reflects reality depends on the assumption that the time between rounds of the game is not critical to later decisions. This is probably at best a half-truth in most cases, but it is a less important restriction than a second assumption that underlies both cases.

There is an implicit assumption that internal standards, perceptions, and levels of awareness of the individual are not importantly changed by the passage of real time in an experience-rich environment. This is certainly not obvious. What *feels* the same way may not at all *be* the same, and the more remote in time or circumstance are the experiences being compared, the more likely it is that feelings will not hold constant for the comparison. A particularly elusive quality of structure is that its effect may mask itself; e.g. it may be having an effect, but part of that effect is on perception itself, which changes the perceived effect.

The extent to which time and space can be either experienced or compressed must be therefore limited. The longer the time (or the broader the sort of organizational structure explored), the more difficult it is either to model accurately or to link direct experience to the reality of the organization itself. Thus here, too, theory becomes even more important or, rather, needs to become more powerful, if present measures, perceptions, behaviours, and impacts are to lead to conclusions about long-term effects and potential larger-scale outcomes. However, to restate an earlier conclusion, the more the learning depends on the power of theory to enable conclusions from a limited experiential base, the less the label 'experiential learning' applies. But, of course, the more powerful the theory, the more possibly erroneous the conclusions. We are here confronting a larger issue: the limits of experiential social psychology.

THE LIMITS OF
EXPERIENTIAL SOCIAL PROCESSES AND LEARNING

This is an issue not easily addressed on the basis of our present knowledge, nor is it an area that has been addressed extensively in the past. We can, however, summarize some key issues. We have shown the importance of theory for permitting people to apply experiential learning to situations that differ from that experienced, and to draw more generalizable conclusions. But as the distance to be bridged increases — that is, as the difference between the experiential situation and relevant other situations increases — the theory becomes more important, the experience itself less. At some point in this process, the value of the *experiential* component becomes insignificant in the sense that the learning is more purely cognitive. There may still be value, of course, but the special qualities of *experiential* learning disappear in the process.

The counterargument is that, even though the cognitive component of learning becomes relatively greater, there will remain an irreducible distinction in the way the person learns, or in the things learned, because of the presence of an experiential component. These issues are too complex to be explored in depth here. We suggest, however, that the latter argument confuses the idea of experiential learning in general, which we grant has unique qualities, with *particular* experiential learning that needs to be assessed in terms of its contribution to the learner's understanding of the phenomenon being addressed.

The mere fact that people feel as though they learned something valid certainly does not assure it. Where experiential learning addresses individual psychological matters — where, in short, the focus is on learning something about oneself — this is more likely to be true, and it is here that experiential learning has been most utilized and explored. However, where the learning concerns external, non-individual matters, such as organization structure, the same conclusion does not follow. One of the traps in experiential learning is its invitation to solipsism — the belief that what I sense, feel, and understand represents the only reality — because of the powerful claim of experience on the person as experiencer.

Even more, however, we cannot be sure that even genuinely held feelings drawn from aware experiences have either external *or* internal validity. Data gained from direct perception are subject to distortion and error quite as much as data from any other sort of instrument. Some sources of distortion apply to experience-based data in general — for example some people have limited sensitivity to some phenomena — but these can also be seen as properties of the person and therefore valid in learning about self.

This argument does not apply to experiential learning about organizational structure which, as we pointed out before, has external extra-individual reality. In this case, inaccurate or distorted perception directly reduces the validity of the learning. And although we can correct for some of those errors by being aware of them, this is itself a cognitive, not an experiential process. For example, consider changes over time. There is no reason to believe that one's internal standards, sensibilities, and levels of awareness stay constant over time — indeed, the notion of growth and development virtually requires that they do not. Experience at one time, then, is not necessarily the same as that at another, even though subjective judgement evaluates them equivalently. We may then infer a pattern where one does not exist. The same point can be made about other dimensions than time. Experience, in short, changes the experiencer.

We are treading on complex philosophical territory. These issues are related to, among others, the distinction between phenomena and essence. To a phenomenalist (e.g. Hume or Mill) an experience necessarily captures the truth of the situation; theories are mere convenient devices to help make sense out of (i.e. reduce to apparent order) those experiences, which are otherwise too complex. From this perspective, more extensive structures exist only to the extent that they are in fact sources of perceptible phenomena. To the extent they are not, then the idea of 'structure' is merely an abstraction.

To essentialists (e.g. Descartes or Wittgenstein) the situation is quite different. Phenomena are in themselves merely glimpses of an external reality, mediated by our necessarily limited ability to apprehend them in their entirety. Since these realities can *only* be imperfectly perceived, they can only be truly understood and accurately represented by theory.

This issue is obviously not susceptible to resolution, since it is not a simple matter of right or wrong. It is, rather, a perspective with which one looks at the world. Our view of the application of experiential techniques to learning about structure assumes some truth to the phenomenalist position, but does not assume pure phenomenalism. We believe that organizational structures are objective realities, which can be understood less by direct experience as they become broader, concern longer time horizons or involve whole organizations. Even here, however, there will be elements or aspects that can be directly experienced. We should utilize experiential processes, just as we should pay attention to our actual experience in organizations or social systems, because these experiential data link different frames of reference. With the addition of theory and cognition, we can understand larger structural elements. Individuals need always to integrate these two sources of information — internal/subjective and external/objective. Experiential processes for learning are therefore essential for appreciating social or organizational phenomena, but their real strength comes in combination with more cognitive approaches.

ACKNOWLEDGEMENTS

We are grateful to Gerhard Friedrich and Daniel Isenberg for colleagueship in developing a better variant of the game and to Derick Brinkerhoff for research help.

REFERENCES

Abt, C. C. (1970) *Serious Games*. New York: Viking Press.
Blau, P. M. (1964) *Exchange and Power in Social Life*. New York: Wiley.
Blau, P. M. (1974) *On the Nature of Organization*. New York: Wiley.
Blau, P. M. (1977) *Inequality and Heterogeneity: A Primitive Theory of Social Structure*. New York: Free Press.
Boocock, S. S. and Schild, E. O. (1968) *Simulation Games in Learning*. Beverly Hills, Cal.: Sage.
Cohen, A. R. (1958) 'Upward communication in experimentally created hierarchies', *Human Relations*, **11**, 41-53.
Galbraith, J. R. (1977) *Organization Design*. Reading, Mass.: Addison-Wesley.
Gamson, W. A. (1972) *SIMSOC: Simulated Society*, Participant's Manual and Instructor's Manual. Second Edition. New York: Free Press.
Goodmeasure (1978) *Conditions for Work Effectiveness: A Goodmeasure Survey*. Cambridge, Mass.: Goodmeasure.
Hall, R. H. (1977) *Organizations: Structure and Process*, 2nd edition. Englewood N.J.: Prentice-Hall.

Jubor, M. and Stoll, C. S. (eds.) (1972) *Simulations and Gaming in Social Science*. New York: Free Press.

Kanter, R. M. (1977) *Men and Women of the Corporation*. New York: Basic Books.

Kanter, R. M. (1979) 'Access to opportunity and power: measuring institutional sexism/racism in organizations.' In Alvarez, R. (ed.) *Measuring Institutional Discrimination: Management and Research Tools*. San Francisco: Jossey-Bass.

Kanter, R. M. and Stein, B. A. (1979) 'Introduction to life at the top: the struggle for power.' In Kanter, R. M. and Stein, B. A. (eds.) *Life in Organizations: Workplaces as People Experience Them*. New York: Basic Books.

Kolb, D. A., Rubin, I. M. and McIntyre, J. M. (1971) *Organizational Psychology: An Experiential Approach*. Englewood Cliffs, N.J.: Prentice-Hall.

March, J. G. and Simon, H. (1958) *Organizations*. New York: Wiley.

Meyer, M. W. (1977) *Theory of Organizational Structure*. Indianapolis: Bobbs-Merrill.

Oshry, B. (1976) *Notes on the Power and Systems Perspective*. Boston, Mass.: Power and Systems.

Schein, E. H. and Bennis, W. G. (1965) *Personal and Organizational Change Through Group Methods: The Laboratory Approach*. New York: Wiley.

Schindler-Rainman, E. and Lippitt, R. (1978) 'Toward improving the quality of community life.' In Cooper, C. L. and Alderfer, C. P. (eds.) *Advances in Experiential Social Processes*, Vol. I New York: Wiley.

Thompson, J. D. (1967) *Organizations in Action*. New York: McGraw-Hill.

Advances in Experiential Social Processes, Volume 2
Edited by C. P. Alderfer and C. L. Cooper
© 1980 John Wiley & Sons, Ltd.

Chapter **11**

Consulting to Underbounded Systems

Clayton P. Alderfer

Yale School of Organization and Management, U.S.A.

A small black girl who appeared to be no more than nine years old lay sleeping on the step of the main entryway to the Harmon School. It was 2.45 on a warm spring sunny Tuesday afternoon. School for that day had just ended. Students, teachers, and parents were talking excitedly in small groups clustered on the sidewalk in front of the school. Anyone wishing to enter the school had to step over the child or risk waking her. Someone leaving the school from inside might actually step on her because it would be practically impossible to see her without opening the door. Yet no-one seemed to notice her. A rush of thoughts and feelings surged into the consultant's awareness as he approached the school.

Harmon was an 'outer, inner-city school', located in a 'boundary region'. To the south and east were predominantly black lower income families, and to the north and west were predominantly white middle and upper middle income households. The neighbourhood immediately surrounding Harmon was populated by black and white families of middle income. One teacher in 11 at Harmon was black; about 35 per cent of the 250 children were black; and the principal was a white male noted for his openness and 'liberal' philosophy.

At the time of this event a white male external consultant was beginning to establish a working relationship with the Harmon staff. On the whole the group seemed fearful of him: 50 per cent of them were attending voluntary meetings to see whether a consulting relationship could be established. Although deeply disturbed by the sight of the sleeping child, the consultant felt that he would damage the tenuous signs of trust that were just beginning if he showed evidence of strong feelings at this moment. Catching the eye of one of the teachers with whom he sensed a firmer relationship, he asked, 'Does this happen often?' She explained that it did and that the child's family life was very stressful. 'Dorie probably didn't sleep at all last night. I tried to call her mother earlier but no one answered,' she explained. The consultant asked if there was not a better place for Dorie to sleep while they searched for her mother. The teacher answered that there was a bed in the school nurse's office. She then gently woke Dorie and led her to the more comfortable setting. The consultant entered the building to attend a faculty meeting.

The scene changes . . .

An experienced internal OD consultant was called by the co-chairmen of The Area Operating Team (AOT), a high-level peer group of operating managers for a 13,000 person corporation providing electronic communication services to more than three million customers. The clients told the consultant that the high-level corporate committee was having a great deal of difficulty working together effectively. In the group's last three meetings nothing had been accomplished. Everyone on the committee was 'frosted'. At least one member was known for coming late to meetings and leaving early. Standard operating ·procedure was for individual managers to make presentations to the committee, and for several side conversations to occur while the planned reports were in progress.

From information available to him outside the client relationship, the internal consultant also knew that AOT was about to confront leadership succession. One of the co-chairmen was about to be replaced. The consultant thought this issue was known but not discussable among AOT members. Indeed, there were probably many factors, inside and outside AOT, to explain why the group's behaviour would be so chaotic, despite the crucial role it played in the corporation. The internal consultant agreed to meet with the co-chairmen to explore how he might be helpful to the group.

On the surface, these two case fragments could hardly be more dissimilar. Nevertheless this chapter proposes that they share important system properties. Interventions derived from a common conceptual framework were helpful in both cases. The case fragments were presented to illustrate the kinds of information available to a behavioural science consultant early in a client relationship. For those who know the theory, the data identify the two situations as 'underbounded' systems (Alderfer, 1976a; Brown, 1979). Normal interventions devised to aid 'overbounded' systems probably would not work in either case.

The following section presents a theory of underbounded and overbounded systems that distinguishes the organization problems found in Harmon and AOT from those to which organization development technology is more frequently applied. The next two sections give descriptive accounts of work with Harmon and AOT to show how the theory applies to them. The final section is a comparison of the two cases, including some preliminary generalizations about group and organizational consultation with underbounded systems.

A THEORY OF UNDERBOUNDED AND OVERBOUNDED SYSTEMS

A system is a set of units with interdependent relationships among them. All human systems are open systems with boundaries to regulate transactions between the system and its environment and to determine what is inside and outside the system. Boundaries are the defining characteristic of systems. Permeability is a crucial property of system boundaries. Because open systems depend on transactions with their environments for survival and growth, there is an 'optimal' degree of boundary permeability for each system-environment relationship (Alderfer, 1976a,b; Skynner, 1976). 'Overbounded' systems show *less* boundary permeability than is optimal for the system's relationship to its environment, and 'underbounded' systems show *more* boundary permeability than is optimal for the system's relationship to its environment. The primary threat to overbounded systems is that they become closed off to their environments and lose the capacity to respond adaptively to environmental changes and to reverse the build-up of entropy. The primary threat to underbounded systems is that they will become totally caught up in their environmental turbulence and lose a consistent sense of their own identity and coherence. Thus, being extremely underbounded is a greater threat to a system's survival, especially in the short run, than being overbounded.

System boundaries are both physical and psychological. In the long run, if steady states occur, physical and psychological boundaries tend to become congruent (Alderfer, 1976b). In the short run, however, the congruence may be imperfect. Psychological boundaries tell more about the 'here-and-now' of a system, but their condition is harder to detect than physical boundaries — especially for an outsider. Interdependence among parts and among the attributes of parts is characteristic of all systems. The condition of system boundaries therefore strongly influences other system properties. When a system departs from optimal boundary permeability it begins to show a variety of 'symptoms', which may be easier to identify initially than the actual boundary condition. Consulting work with a variety of underbounded and overbounded systems has led to the identification of 11 interdependent variables whose values differentiate underbounded and overbounded systems from optimally bounded systems. An applied behavioural scientist may use these indicators rather than hard-to-detect boundary relations in order to determine in which direction, if in either, a system departs from optimal boundary permeability. The variables are:

(1) Goals
(2) Authority relations
(3) Economic conditions
(4) Role definitions
(5) Communication patterns
(6) Human energy

(7) Affect distribution
(8) Intergroup dynamics
(9) Unconscious basic assumptions
(10) Time-span
(11) Cognitive work

Goals

The typical definition of organizations makes reference to organizational goals (Porter *et al.*, 1975). At some level and for some purposes, organizational goals provide the major source of legitimacy for organizations. Miller and Rice (1967) define the primary task (goal) of an organization as that work the organization must do to survive in its environment. Yet the analysis of organizational goals from either a conceptual (e.g. Simon, 1964) or an empirical (e.g. Perrow, 1961) perspective is not a simple process. The goal structure of an organization refers to the clarity with which organizational goals can be stated and to the degree of organization-wide consensus on the priority of organizational goals. Underbounded and overbounded systems differ in their goal structure.

Underbounded systems have neither the clarity nor the degree of consensus in their goal structure that can be observed in overbounded systems. A sense of 'meaninglessness' is not uncommon in underbounded systems. Participants may experience their system as floundering without a sense of direction. This lack of direction may arise either because people genuinely do not know what they are doing or because the conflict about goal priority is so severe that no direction among many competing orientations can be sustained long enough to bring any genuine achievement. Overbounded systems, on the other hand, tend to show an unequivocal clarity about goals and their priority. Executives in business firms are prone to say 'We are in business to make money', or 'The ultimate test is the effect on the "bottom-line" (of the profit and loss statement)'. Increasing the clarity of organizational goals or the degree of consensus about goal priority is associated with decreasing boundary permeability, and decreasing the clarity of organizational goals or increasing the disputes about goal priority is associated with increasing boundary permeability.

Authority relations

The crucial place of boundaries in the survival and growth of human systems has led a number of theorists to link boundary management with authority (Miller and Rice, 1967; Astrachan, 1970). According to this view, the major work of system leaders and managers is to define and adjust key organizational boundaries in order to promote the work of the system.

In being a leader, teaching leadership or consulting to leadership it is useful to conceptualize leadership, in part, as boundary management. But causality in human systems is rarely unidirectional; associations between variables are usually based on mutual causality (Buckley, 1967). Therefore, the condition of system boundaries influences the nature of authority relations within the system as well as *vice versa*. The nature of the authority available to leaders and/or the effort they must expend to increase their authority depends on boundary permeability.

Authority relations in overbounded systems are typically highly centralized and monolithic. Most resources are controlled from a single locus of authority, usually at the top of the organization. There is a unity of purpose, of direction, and of control that forms the basis of the traditional pyramidal organization (Gulick and Urwick, 1937). Much of the early work in organizational behaviour identified the dysfunctions of the traditional pyramidal form (Argyris, 1957; March and Simon, 1958; McGregor, 1960); and the first organizational development interventions were also designed to improve systems of this kind (Jaques, 1952; Argyris, 1962). The problems of overbounded systems are now reasonably well known, and there is increasing evidence that behavioural science interventions have been designed to deal with the pathologies of such systems (Friedlander and Brown, 1974; Alderfer, 1977b).

Authority relations in underbounded systems are typically fragmented and unclear. Instead of a single authority source to whom all must ultimately answer, there are multiple authorities and/or none to whom some people intermittently report. Responsibility for work may rest with several individuals and groups or with no-one. There is less systematic research on underbounded systems (e.g. Brown and Brown, 1973) and far less consensus on how to conceptualize and evaluate the phenomena (Weick, 1976). Within the organization development literature there is a growing list of 'failures', which may be understood, in part, as the result of applying interventions designed for overbounded systems to underbounded problems (cf. Brown *et al.*, 1974; Firestone, 1977; Berg, 1977).

Economic conditions

Changes in the territory or technolgy of open systems, often brought on by economic changes, have effects on psychological boundaries (Trist *et al.*, 1963.) If the economic condition of a system significantly worsens, its territory and technology will be threatened. It may be less able to attract people, or it may have to eliminate people from the system in order to survive. Conversely, if the economic position of a system improves it has the potential for improving its territory and technology and for heightening its attractiveness to members and potential members.

As a result of these dynamics, underbounded systems are more likely to be facing economic difficulties than overbounded systems. Underboundedness may 'cause' financial problems, or *vice versa*. A system unable to organize itself for sustained work is likely to miss opportunities for economic gain or to waste resources it already has. A system confronted with economic hardship from outside will find its psychological boundaries threatened as it struggles for survival. The effects of a poor financial condition make it increasingly difficult for organization members to cooperate in order to solve financial problems because they anticipate being asked to leave or they feel they must seek alternative forms of compensation and therefore choose to leave.

Role definitions

Individuals in organizations develop patterns of role behaviour based on the expectations placed upon them by the organization modified by their own personal values, beliefs, abilities, and group memberships (Levinson, 1959; Alderfer, 1977a; Katz and Kahn, 1978). The clarity and consistency of organization expectations'is in part a function of boundary permeability. Role expectations in overbounded systems tend to be highly precise, detailed, and restrictive. Role expectations in underbounded systems tend to be unclear and conflicting.

Thus the psychological costs to individuals for occupying organizational positions in overbounded and underbounded systems are different. In overbounded systems people feel confined, constrained, and restricted. Incumbents experience lack of creativity and stimulation, especially at lower levels in the organization where the full force of the organizational structure affects the individual (Argyris, 1957). In underbounded systems people feel fragmented, conflicted, and isolated. Incumbents lack a clear sense of direction in their work and may seem immobilized. There may be a lack of explicit expectations from others or a great diversity of conflicting demands from multiple uncoordinated sources. The different dynamics of authority relations in underbounded and overbounded systems are directly related to the different kinds of problems with role definition in each type of system.

Communication patterns

Communication problems are ubiquitous to organizations that are functioning suboptimally. The issue common to all communication problems is that valid information is not being given and received as needed to do the organization's work. Information may be distorted by the sender or receiver, or there may simply be no exchange at all between senders and receivers.

Overbounded and underbounded organizations differ in the nature of their communication problems. The authority and role relations among individuals and groups in overbounded systems are designed to establish communication links among parties and to make it possible for people to meet together when necessary. Typical problems in overbounded systems arise because people distort the information that is exchanged in order to present their own position in the best possible perspective. Criticism of one's own position tends to be minimized. Bad news is with-held from senior officials as much as possible.

Communication problems in underbounded systems arise from difficulties in identifying who should talk with whom, in establishing communication links among key parties, and in bringing people together to discuss issues of common concern. When it is possible to solve these problems, which then permits exchange of information to take place, the quality of exchange is also different in underbounded systems. Interaction patterns in general are more varied. Withdrawal and lack of exchange may alternate with outbreaks of simultaneous talking. Conflict is never far below the surface and may show in extreme form when elements of an underbounded system meet.

Human energy

All open systems rely on human energy for a significant portion of their work. The power of a system and of the individuals and groups within a system depends on the state of human energy in the system. System boundaries provide a means for confining or releasing human energy and/or effectively channelling or ineffectually diffusing it. In overbounded systems human energy is often confined waiting to be released into well-established channels to do organizational work. In underbounded systems human energy is more diffuse and difficult to channel towards system goals.

In overbounded systems, the effect of increasing boundary permeability is to release human energy for work, while the consequence of decreasing boundary permeability is further to restrict available energy. In underbounded systems, the effect of increasing boundary permeability is to diffuse available human resources, while the effect of decreasing boundary permeability is to harness energy for organizational objectives. The process of increasing boundary permeability usually takes less energy than the process of decreasing boundary permeability.

Affect distribution

Individuals and groups, as open human systems themselves and as subsystems within larger organizational systems, have affective lives. People have feelings about the conditions in which they find themselves, and they are influenced by the emotions of others with whom they interact. Human beings experience a variety of emotions, including anxiety, joy, fear, love, anger, contentment, despair, and so on. People may withhold or explicitly exchange their feelings.

Whether spoken or not, signs of the feelings within a system are usually apparent to a trained observer. Although human affairs typically involve a mix of emotions — both favourable and unpleasant — there is usually a detectable balance of feeling within a system, and overbounded and underbounded systems differ in their respective affective balances.

The balance of feeling within an overbounded system is typically positive. In part this is because the short-term future of an overbounded system tends to be favourable. The system is not facing imminent chaos; its survival is not threatened. But a positive affective balance in overbounded systems is also partially the result of repressive forces within the system. The effect of a monolithic authority structure mutes interval criticism and tends to direct negative affect outward rather than inward.

The balance of feeling within an underbounded system is typically less favourable. Chaos and disorganization are immediately observable. People usually do not have much confidence in themselves or in the system, and there is often a significant underlying feeling of futility. In general, a decided lack of observable positive feeling is characteristic of underbounded systems.

Increasing boundary permeability in overbounded systems permits the emergence of negative feelings that had been previously hidden. Depending on how this process is managed, people may feel released and euphoric or guilty and depressed (Slater, 1966). Typically, change towards a fuller balance of positive and negative emotions increases the available energy in a system. Decreasing boundary permeability in underbounded systems helps positive feelings to emerge. People learn that they share common concerns, are influenced by common processes, and can cooperate to control the chaos that previously threatened to overwhelm their system. Decreasing boundary permeability in an underbounded system, like increasing boundary permeability in an overbounded system, results in the system as a whole being one where both positive and negative emotions can be observed. Conversely, allowing negative feelings to emerge in an overbounded system will increase boundary permeability, and promoting the discovery of positive feelings in an underbounded system will decrease boundary permeability.

Intergroup dynamics

Intergroup dynamics in an organization refer to the relations among the various groups within the system, which are generally of two classes: (1) task groups, and (2) identity groups (Alderfer, 1977a). Task groups are defined by the kinds of work they perform (e.g. production, marketing, physician, teacher) and by the level in the hierarchy in which they are located (e.g. foreman, department head, dean, vice president). Identity groups refer to the group affiliations that help individuals to shape their personal identities. These groups consist of generation groups (young, middle-aged, old), gender groups (men and women), ethnic groups (English, African, Irish, etc.), and others determined by the life experiences of members before they enter the organization. Conflict is inevitable in a system complex enough to have several well-defined sets of groups. But organizations differ in terms of whether the primary conflict is rooted in task or identity groups.

Overbounded systems tend to have their primary intergroup conflicts among task groups, and underbounded systems to have their primary conflicts among identity groups. When organizational structure can significantly shape environmental dynamics, task group boundaries are more powerful than identity group boundaries. When environmental forces overwhelm organizational boundaries, identity group conflicts dominate task group conflict. In the former situation the organization loses the richness available from cultural diversity and individuals find significant portions of their identities denied. In the latter case struggles among identity groups prevent the organization from achieving a sustained sense of direction; its task effectiveness suffers; and individuals lose the gratifications of real achievement. Thus, strengthening the boundaries of identity groups in overbounded systems provides a useful counterforce to the suppression of group identities in these organizations. Conversely, strengthening the boundaries of task groups in underbounded systems permits a clearer sense of purpose to be obtained and a greater degree of task accomplishment to be achieved. Because of the interdependence between task and identity groups in most organizations, change in the boundaries of one type of group will have implications for the boundaries of the other (Alderfer, 1977a).

Unconscious basic assumptions

Individuals in groups may be observed to be acting *as if* certain relationships existed among themselves or between them and the group leader (Bion, 1961). The term to conceptualize the prevailing state of a group's 'as if' life is 'basic assumption'. Basic assumptions operate outside the explicit awareness of group members and are useful in explaining why a group seems to act at variance with its stated mission. Why does a school fail to educate children? Why does an integrating group fail to come together?

The basic assumptions of groups in overbounded systems are different from the basic assumptions of groups in underbounded systems. Deriving from the authority structure, basic assumption dependence tends to be prevalent in overbounded systems. Members act as if they have come together to have their needs gratified by an all-powerful leader. Basic assumption flight-fight tends to be prominent in underbounded systems. Members act as if they must flee from the threats they represent for each other or they engage in persistent unproductive conflict. Observers can detect which basic assumption seems to be prevalent in a group by observing their own emotions. Changes in the boundary permeability of a group are accompanied by change in the basic assumption life of the group.

Time-span

Systems vary in the span of time over which they concern themselves. Some organizations are capable of thinking and planning ahead, while others are much more short-term oriented. Overbounded and underbounded systems vary in the time perspective of their management. Because of their more certain authority relations and their more secure economic condition, overbounded systems tend to have longer time perspectives than underbounded systems. Because the threat of dissolution regularly confronts underbounded systems, they tend to have a much shorter time perspective. As the boundaries of a system become more secure, the time perspective of members tends to lengthen. But organizations whose boundaries are too secure risk difficulties from the build-up of unsolved short-term problems because members focus excessively on the future.

Cognitive work

All organization members face the problem of understanding why things happen as they do in their system. People need a set of beliefs, or a rudimentary theory, to explain what they experience in an organization, to help them interpret events that occur, and to aid them in deciding how to behave. Without such a framework they would be overwhelmed by confusion and become beset by meaninglessness. Their personal theory may come from a variety of sources and may be more or less conscious and explicit. The organization may attempt to play a major or minor role in influencing members' personal theories of how the system works. It has been demonstrated that these theories often have common themes across different types of people in a wide variety of organizations (Argyris and Schön, 1978).

Overbounded and underbounded systems differ in the nature of the cognitive work done by members. Overbounded systems are more likely to have a single coherent body of theory (or ideology) that members are expected to master and to use in their work for the system. Typically, new members are taught 'the company line' early in their careers. As people remain in the organization and move upward in the hierarchy they are expected to teach others about the organization's theory. Innovations in the organization must be worked through the existing theory or the theory must be modified to allow for the innovation. Usually both processes happen. One way to bring about change in an overbounded system is to act in new ways and later explain that the system's theory must be changed because 'we actually behave differently around here'.

Underbounded systems often have no theory at all, or else multiple theories prevail without adequate mechanisms for identifying or resolving differences among them. When there is no theory to teach new members, the system lacks an integrating framework and change may require the development of a coherent statement of mission or policy. When there are multiple theories, the system needs mechanisms for dealing with the differences in order for a greater sense of intellectual understanding to emerge. Usually the multiple theories are associated with the various warring groups whose conflict keeps the system in constant turmoil. Finding means to deal with the theoretical differences also reduces boundary permeability and aids the system to establish a greater sense of wholeness.

The 11 dimensions distinguishing overbounded and underbounded systems shown in Table 1 are conceptually distinct but dynamically interdependent. Each is directly related to the physical or psychological boundaries of human systems. Furthermore, particular dimensions are also directly related to each other. For an applied behavioural science consultant the dimensions are useful for diagnosis and for intervention (Alderfer, 1976a). During diagnosis they provide a means to determine whether a system departs from optimal boundary permeability and, if so, in which way. The more clearly the signs on several dimensions point in the direction of overbounded or underbounded conditions, the more sure a diagnostician can be that he is seeing pathology. If intervention becomes appropriate, the dimensions also provide targets or levers for change. The realities of most organizations usually provide more opportunities to change some variables than others. The list of variables provides a number of alternative routes to change. We return now to the Harmon and AOT case fragments to demonstrate how they were underbounded systems and what was done to intervene.

HARMON AND AOT AS UNDERBOUNDED SYSTEMS

Open systems theory assumes that each unit is both a system in its own right, containing subsystems within it, and a subsystem within a larger suprasystem (Miller, 1978). Harmon was one elementary school in the public school system of Elm Town, a New England city of over 100,000 people; AOT was one corporate committee within an organization employing more than 10,000 people. Within Harmon and AOT there were significant subsystems, both individuals and groups. Outside both systems there were also significant individuals and groups who, seperately and together, made up the external environment of these systems.

The suprasystems of Harmon and AOT may also be analysed in terms of their boundary properties. Were they overbounded, underbounded or optimally bounded? Although the primary focus of the consultation with Harmon and AOT was on the school and the committee, information was

Table 1   Properties of overbounded and underbounded systems

Overbounded systems	Variable	Underbounded Systems
goals clear; priority unequivocal	Goals	goals unclear; priorities equivocal
monolithic	Authority relations	multiple and competing
minimal short-term stress	Economic conditions	impending economic crisis
precise, detailed, restrictive	Role definitions	imprecise, incomplete, overlapping
difficulties with openness when people meet	Communication patterns	difficulties in determining who can and should meet
constrained, blocked	Human energy	diffuse, exhausting
positive inside; negative outside	Affect distribution	negative inside; negative outside
organizational groups dominate	Intergroup dynamics	identity groups dominate
dependency	Unconscious basic assumptions	flight-fight
long	Time span	short
single theory-ideology	Cognitive work	multiple or no theory-ideologies

available to form working hypotheses regarding the suprasystem properties of both clients. Indeed, it is essential for the consultant to form some working hypotheses about supersystem properties in order to work with any system by using open system concepts. The working hypotheses regarding suprasystem properties were different for Harmon and AOT. Harmon was an underbounded system within an underbounded suprasystem, and AOT was an underbounded system within an overbounded suprasystem. These differences will become apparent as more detail about the two systems is presented. They decidedly affect the consultation provided to the two systems, the results of that consultation, and the prospects for change from behavioural science intervention.

The Harmon School

Intervention with the Harmon School began when the consultant was invited to attend a meeting of the Harmon Steering Committee (HSC). The HSC was formed by John Smith, Harmon principal, when he decided to join the Davison Project, an independently funded enterprise designed to promote improved leadership by elementary school principals through more effective cooperation between parents, teachers, and administrators. The consultant had met the principal of Harmon when both men had served on the citywide task force for the Davison Project.

Prior to meeting with the HSC the consultant had received a copy of the HSC minutes defining the work they wished to undertake. The document was unusually explicit in identifying the many and diverse forms of conflict plaguing the Harmon School:

... there appears to be a power struggle between the two existing parents' organizations
....
It is difficult to build up trust among the staff, parents, and administration when communication is not functioning adequately ....

Impressed with the openness of the committee's document, the consultant arrived at the first steering committee meeting with a favourable attitude towards the group. Except for the principal, all members of the HSC were female, one of whom was black. Three members were Harmon teachers, and the other three were parents of Harmon children. The teachers represented grade levels from K to 5, and the parents had had associations with both Harmon parent groups.

All of the elementary schools in Elm City could potentially have had two parent organizations. PTAs were the older organizations and included state and national affiliations. During an era of urban unrest that influenced Elm City in the late 1960s, the School District had established 'school-community councils' as a major structural innovation to promote mutual influence among members of the school community and school staff. At Harmon these two organizations had different traditions and periodically engaged in rivalrous conflict with one another.

To a significant degree the two parent organizations at Harmon represented the different socioeconomic groups that lived in Harmon neighbourhoods. Members of the PTA tended to be white middle and upper middle class people who were concerned about college preparation for their children. Their values about education tended to be primarily academic. Members of the PTA were also very active in developing and maintaining after-school programmes to provide children with additional extra-curricular enrichment opportunities. Members of the Council tended to be more diverse, including black and white people of a wide range of socioeconomic backgrounds. The educational philosophy of the Council tended to emphasize the whole child, including value and behavioural goals as well as academic performance.

Tension and conflict between the two parent organizations reflected the changing nature of Elm City. Effects of the disputes did not stop outside the school boundaries. Several years before the project began both white and black teachers had been persuaded to leave Harmon by parental pressure. More recently a white teacher had been the subject of parental protest and a classroom 'visit' because her teaching about the family was disturbing to a significant number of Harmon parents who were divorced singles living cooperatively. Overall Harmon's dynamics were the product of many diverse forces, and the school's location in a 'boundary region' of the city made it especially susceptible to conflict. Observation of the parent-school relationship over the duration of this project strongly suggested that the emotional fuel for the fire between PTA and the Council was deeply rooted and quite difficult to uncover or to change.

One effect of the various forms of parental pressure at Harmon was a divided and frightened teaching staff. After lengthy discussion, the HSC recommended that systematic intervention begin with the professional staff alone rather than with parents and teachers together. This proposal was made by a parent member of the HSC and strongly endorsed by the teachers and principal. The HSC believed that the teachers had been so frightened by parental influence at Harmon that they would be very reluctant to engage in direct parent-teacher exchanges without first developing greater confidence and trust among themselves and with the principal. In the preceding years formal teacher participation in the PTA and the Council had markedly diminished for similar reasons.

At this point in history Harmon was also facing other threats to its external boundaries. Like many cities throughout the Northeast, Elm City's population was declining. As a result Harmon's enrolment was becoming smaller, and for economic reasons the central administration decided that a teacher had to be transferred from Harmon. When community groups learned of the excess space at Harmon, they began a petition process to obtain rights to use Harmon rooms. Eventually Harmon parents went to court to prevent the school from being used by outside groups.

Working with the HSC, the consultant decided to pursue separate tracks of consultation with the school. The first would be with the professional staff and the second with the parent organizations.

Staff consultation

After the HSC agreed that formal consultation should begin with the Harmon staff there were a number of meetings to discuss the conditions of their participation. Initially as few as five staff (three of whom were the HSC) attended these voluntary sessions.* Eventually the groups agreed that everyone who was willing would be interviewed. After completing the interviews, the consultant would provide an analysis of what people said without identifying individuals. Both the HSC and the whole of the Harmon staff participated in the design of the interview questions. Since the project was originally aimed to help principals improve their leadership style, the consultant suggested that specific questions might be asked about this topic. Feedback of these results would be to the principal on a one-on-one basis and later to the group as a whole if he wished. The principal readily agreed to this suggestion, and the interviews were begun. As the process of establishing the contract for this part of the project proceeded, attendance at staff meetings gradually increased. Eventually all of the teachers except one participated in the interviews. Feedback sessions were attended by everyone.

There was a total of four feedback meetings to deal with the data from the interviews. The sessions extended over an entire calendar year, with the first occurring at the close of the 1976-7 academic year. At the first session the consultant provided an overview of the entire Harmon School as he had learned to understand it from the interviews. The findings were grouped according to 'internal' and 'external' factors. The external factors described the forces acting on Harmon from without, and the internal factors dealt with relations among the staff and the principal's style. This initial session was designed to provide some intellectual understanding of the Harmon system, not to promote working through of the data. Material on the principal, for example, was in the form of a series of dimensions on which people chose to describe his style, not the kind of concrete quotations frequently used in team-building sessions. The dimensions were his: values, use of authority, relationship to subgroups in the school, and relationships to children. This session concluded with the faculty agreeing to meet again in the fall to decide whether they wished to pursue a more complete analysis of the data. After the group meeting the consultant met with the principal to provide him with more concrete data on his style as perceived by the Harmon staff. The form of this feedback was a series of 35 statements, edited to preserve confidentiality, taken from the staff interviews. For the most part the statements had both a positive tone to them and stimulating possibilities for growth by the principal. He found the session worthwhile and agreed to have a similar discussion with the staff in the fall if they wanted to continue to work as a group.

In the fall, the faculty did decide to work as a group and to spend the first session discussing the principal's style with him. As input to this session the consultant wrote 35 statements on newsprint and posted them. With concrete material before them, either the principal or a staff member could select an

---

*It was about this time that the episode described at the outset of this chapter took place.

item to explore in detail with the whole group. Beginning with substantial anxiety and discomfort, the session eventually transformed itself into an exciting and fruitful exchange. Although the principal felt stressed at various times throughout the session, he emerged with a strong conviction of having learned about his behaviour and with a sense of direction about how to be more effective.

As the session drew to a close and the fruitful outcome was clear, the principal indicated that he was interested in additional work if the staff were willing to confront some of their issues in the same manner that he had faced his. The staff agreed and an additional date was set. As it turned out, this session had to be rescheduled several times because of citywide meetings called by the central administration. When the staff session was eventually held several months later, important momentum had been lost.

Harmon teachers were organized as three 'education centres' according to groupings of grade levels. Cooperation among teachers from different grade levels provided the opportunity for children to have lessons fitting their development. For example, a child might be in an advanced reading group and a moderate maths programme. The learning centres were not as cooperative in practice as in design. One group of teachers worked especially well together, but the other two groups showed varying degrees of isolation from each other and from the other learning centres. The staff session on internal issues identified these dynamics more clearly than the interviews had done, but the teachers decided not to risk additional working through of their differences.

As the academic year drew to a close, the principal reconvened the staff to see whether they had seen changes in his behaviour based on the discussions they had had at the beginning of the year. People commented that they had noticed improvements on a variety of dimensions, and there was consensus among the staff about these changes. Moreover, the staff seemed to feel that the academic year as a whole had gone well. One year earlier, at the time of interviews, seven out of 10 staff interviewed indicated that Harmon 'was not a fun place to be, not a healthy atmosphere'. The staff atmosphere at Harmon seemed to have changed for the better from one year to the next.

Parent intervention

While work among the staff and principal was proceeding as described above, efforts to develop more effective relations with the parent organizations began with the start of the new academic year. Members of the HSC discussed ways to convene the leadership of the two organizations in order to explore the nature of the differences and difficulties between them. In addition, it became apparent that a substantial proportion of parents were untouched by either organization, and their energy and influence in the school was lost. The HSC took upon itself the further task of understanding why a substantial proportion of parents at Harmon were active in neither organization.

A series of meetings to explore these issues was scheduled during the fall and winter. Parent members of the HSC contacted the officers of the two parent organizations and unaffiliated parents who they thought would become more involved in the school if conditions changed. The first of these meetings took place in November. The session was attended by four unaffiliated parents — two black and two white — and by one officer from the PTA. Neither officer of the Council attended despite extensive efforts to encourage them. A detailed history and explanation of the Davison Project was provided for the people attending. It was not possible to explore the differences and relationships between the parent organizations when only one group was represented. All people present agreed to meet again, and it was decided to make additional efforts to attract Council officers to future sessions. At the next HSC meeting it was reported that the Council people had explicitly decided not to attend the joint meeting. While attending a subsequent Council meeting, the principal was asked to defend the HSC and its role in relation to the two parent organizations. During this same meeting the Council leaders suggested that perhaps the Council should be disbanded.

Another joint meeting of the HSC, PTA, and Council was held in January. This time there were three PTA representatives, one Council officer, the parent members of the HSC, and a city councilman from the neighbourhood. No unaffiliated parents were present. The Councilman was not a parent but apparently had been invited by one of the PTA people as a means of confronting the authority issues raised by discussing the relationship between the two parent organizations. Members of the HSC dealt explicitly with the councilman's relevance to the meeting and after a short and amicable discussion he decided to leave. At this point severe conflict among the remaining participants emerged. One of the PTA people charged the consultant with attempting to divide the group, and another PTA member attacked an HSC member who historically had been associated with the Council. The mood of the meeting eventually became more calm, and it was possible to explore the conditions under which more cooperative relations between the two parent organizations might be possible. Throughout the discussion it was clear that the two organizations were quite wary of each other and of the HSC as a mediator of the conflict. PTA members made it very clear that their state and national affiliations prevented a merger of the two organizations, but some were willing to consider the possibility of 'joint' meetings between the two groups when common concerns arose. Despite explicit agreements among all present that PTA boundaries would be respected, PTA officers continued to act as if their organization was under attack from the HSC for sometime thereafter.

A third PTA, Council, and HSC meeting was held several weeks later. This time *two* Council people, *one* PTA person, and one unaffiliated parent joined the HSC parents to plan further steps regarding the two parent organizations. In advance of this meeting the teacher members of the HSC were invited to attend but decided not to join because 'they might become separated from other teachers'. This meeting showed evidence of greater commitment to the joint exploration by Council representatives but some pulling back by PTA people. Both PTA and Council representatives agreed to consult with their respective organizations to determine how a mechanism for planning a joint PTA-Council meeting might be established. A withdrawal period of several months by both organizations followed this commitment, and then, as the academic year was drawing to a close, a major large-scale session to explore the relationships between the two organizations was staged.

In a letter to Harmon parents, the principal characterized this meeting as an opportunity for 'open discussion on such topics as the pros and cons of each organization . . . and how the organizations separately and working together can contribute to a vital school-community relationship.' Present at the meeting were officers from the two Harmon organizations, city and statewide representatives from the Council and PTA, Harmon parents, and the parent members of the HSC. The meeting provided representatives from both organizations with the opportunity to describe the larger environments in which the parent organizations operated. The similarities and differences between both parent groups were examined, and opportunities for discussion by the parents was provided. Some question about the trustworthiness of the HSC's intentions was raised by a male associated with the PTA. It was clear from the meeting that while differences in objectives and legitimacy existed, the two organizations did have a significant tendency to share/compete for the right to do similar work. As anticipated, their struggles did tend to keep unaffiliated parents from joining either group and to cause teachers to be wary lest they be 'caught' taking sides with one organization against the other. Because of the struggle, both 'parent-teacher community' organizations tended to be primarily parent organizations, as others tended to stay away in order to avoid being hit in the crossfire. The large-scale community meeting was a success for problem identification; after this event it would be difficult for anyone to maintain that the existing relationship between the two parent organizations was not harmful to the Harmon School and its community. The meeting also indicated again that the HSC was a source of concern for the PTA and that the relationship between these two groups needed attention if the HSC was not to become part of the problem rather than a force for improvement at Harmon.

In subsequent sessions the HSC acted to change its relationship to the PTA and the Council by altering its membership to include those who were liaison people from the HSC to the two parent organizations. Initially, this process seemed clumsy. At the first meeting of the reconstructed HSC neither of the new members was present. Following that there was some dispute with the

PTA regarding whether the new members was an HSC members acting as liaison to the PTA or a PTA officer acting as liaison to the HSC. Individual members of the HSC spoke to the new member, however, and eventually the HSC was reconstituted as intended. With its recomposed structure, the HSC was in a position to take the next step in changing the Council-PTA relationship. That occurred during the fall of the subsequent academic year.

Council had been showing increasing signs of being a collapsing organization. Even the PTA insisted that before they would talk about improving relations with Council they wanted to deal with a revitalized organization. Otherwise, what would be the point of expending the energy? The HSC, with the full knowledge and support of the PTA, took on the task of reviving Council or of ascertaining that Council did not have enough support to continue to exist. Along the way, the HSC learned that municipal funding for Council had collapsed at the close of the preceding academic year. As a consequence Council's major basis for legitimacy as a link to city government also ended. This discovery did not close the matter, however, because the Harmon community might nevertheless wish to support the organization for its own purposes. Through advertising in a neighbourhood newsheet and sending notices to Harmon parents, the HSC sponsored another community meeting, this time to decide the fate of the Council. The meeting was chaired by two members of the HSC, a parent and a teacher, known for their evenhandedness and interest in Council matters. The meeting drew sparse attendance but included two PTA officers and four former Council activists, two of whom were black. In a meeting noteworthy for its orderliness and rationality, the group decided that there was not enough interest to sustain a Council at Harmon and that two key functions unique to Council would either be adopted by the PTA if they wished or be maintained independently by the principal if the PTA did not wish to take on the additional work. With the Council gone as an organization, the conflict between the two parent organizations could no longer plague the principal, the teachers, or the unaffiliated parents of Harmon School.

Conclusion to the Harmon case

This report concludes with the decision to eliminate one of the two Harmon parent organizations. Over a two-year period consultation with the Harmon School was associated with moving the school towards more optimal boundary permeability and away from severe underboundedness. Intervention targets were the authority of the principal, the small group dynamics of the Harmon staff (including the basic of assumptions of this group), and the intergroup dynamics of the parent organizations. Related to the intervention programme were a more positive feeling among the Harmon teachers, largely derived from greater openness between principal and teachers, and a more stable, less crisis-oriented external environment, mainly achieved through the elimination of severe conflict between two parent organizations. Boundary permeability of the Harmon School was thus altered through both internally and externally oriented interventions. If the project continued there would be an expectation of further improvement in peer relations among the teachers because they would have less reason to define roles that promoted withdrawal from meaningful contact with one another in order to avoid being played off against each other by the competing parent organizations.

The project was provided with unexpected influence when the economic conditions of one parent organization severely worsened. A problematic feature of the newly structured Harmon system pertains to its impact on black families in the Harmon neighbourhood. Although the HSC and the various community meetings included the participation of strong, articulate black members, the net effect of eliminating Council was to remove an organization whose values seemed to speak more clearly to minority concerns than the PTA had. Unresolved questions are whether the PTA will expand its value base under the new structure and whether black families will become an important force in the single parent-teacher organization at the Harmon School.

The AOT executive committee

AOT was a committee of nine regular members and two quasi-members. Seven regular members held line responsibility for the corporation's major geographical regions. The co-chairman headed staff units, and the two quasi-members were also leaders of staff groups. The line managers differed from one another by the type of geographical region they served. Four of the line managers headed 'urban' regions where service was provided primarily for commercial and residential customers within medium-sized cities. The three other line managers headed 'suburban' regions where the geographic areas were larger and the distance between customers was greater. Inevitably, different managerial problems arose because of the customer conditions.

Cutting across the differences between staff and line and the differences within staff and within line managers was another important variable influencing relations among the committee members. Although all members of the committee were 'peers' by virtue of being at the same organizational level, there was an important difference between the men in terms of their mobility potential in the corporation. For some their present job was as high as they would go, while others could expect future promotions. Competition among the managers — particularly among those holding line positions — was further enhanced by a company indicator system that compared managers on a variety of performance dimensions.

Work with the AOT committee can be divided into two phases. During the first period the consultant attempted a series of 'one-shot' interventions. Individually these efforts varied in their effectiveness, but cumulatively they had no positive impact except to set the stage for a more comprehensive second phase. In the second period the consultant developed a clear contract with the group and executed a planned change programme that substantially reduced AOT's boundary permeability.

Phase 1: three strikes and you're in

There were three separate intervention attempts during the first phase. Each seemed to be rooted in the assumption that a minor adjustment could restore the committee to effective functioning. All were based on well-known organization development technologies. And each one was flawed to a greater or lesser extent by the consultant's becoming enmeshed in the committee's own underbounded dynamics.

The first strike was focused on helping the committee develop its own set of objectives. AOT was part of an organization that maintained its own corporatewide management-by-objectives (MBO) programme. At the time when the intervention with AOT began, it was 'fashionable' to develop committee MBOs. The internal consultant's first assignment with the committee was to help the group to develop a series of MBOs.

On the first attempt to conduct individual and group brainstorming in a meeting set aside for this purpose, the internal consultant did not even get on the group's agenda. He attended the session as planned and observed the group become diverted from its stated objective by an emergent discussion about the reorganization of a major portion of the company. As time passed in this session the chairman became increasingly concerned lest the consultant be prohibited from working with the group on their planned agenda. On three separate occasions, the committee simply refused to permit the consultant to speak after he had been introduced by the chairman. This session ended without their being able to do the work that he entered the meeting to accomplish. However, as the meeting ended, the group reaffirmed its commitment to work with the consultant, and they scheduled another meeting two weeks hence to try again.

The second strike took place as planned two weeks later. At the start of this session a new leader for AOT was announced, and a new member was added to the group. Both of these changes seemed to add stability to the group, and the consultant was able to execute a new design for group problem-solving he had planned for the group. Although the group worked efficiently and enthusiastically with the consultant, they were unable to complete their problem-solving within the time allotted. Nonetheless all responded favourably to the activity, and the consultant received many positive comments for his contribution. Reflecting on the episode some time later, however, the consultant indicated that despite the satisfactory evaluation, he remained uncertain about the effects of the consultation. His intuition was subsequently verified when the group attempted to finish the work several weeks later. At this meeting the consultant's work was first on the agenda. But the underbounded nature of the group once again took its toll. As the consultant was beginning his work, an outside presenter who was scheduled to be sixth on the agenda arrived, and the group deferred to his wishes to speak. After this work was completed, an unscheduled request to speak by a staff member from outside the committee arrived unexpectedly and was permitted to proceed. The session continued in this manner and ended without the consultant being able to work. In reviewing the meeting, the managers acknowledged that they were decidedly unable to control their fate as a group. The consultant experienced disbelief about what had happened to him and to the group. Nonetheless, the process was still not at an end.

The third strike occurred in response to an intervention planned jointly by the consultant and the committee co-chairmen. As a means to achieve some common basis for discussion within the group, the three decided to ask the group to develop a common job description for the seven line manager members of the committee. These seven men had the same job title, a position of extreme importance and usual challenge within the corporation, but there was no common statement of their responsibilities. In fact, they prided themselves, not only on the concrete differences in the assignments they faced, but also on their unique styles in solving their management problems. One of the co-chairmen had recently occupied one of these line positions and during his tenure had developed his own job description. As homework for the next committee meeting, each member was asked to take this one job description and use it as a starting point for writing his own. The hope was that from the seven separate job descriptions the group could identify common themes and use them to develop a single (universal) statement of responsibilities, which in turn would help to unite the group. Once again the committee dynamics did not allow the consultant to get on the agenda. By this time it was clear to all that serious problems were preventing the consultant from being effective and that it was time either to terminate the relationship or to develop a substantially different approach. The impetus was to continue working with the group because the consultant's problems to this point, at worst, were no different than those of the individual group members. Moreover, AOT was a tremendously important corporate group, and stories about its working difficulties were a continuing embarrassment to members within the upper corporate strata.

Phase 2: three steps to coherence

The second phase of intervention with the committee was deeply rooted in an explicit acknowledgement of the difficulties — indeed failures — of the first phase. Yet the emotional tone of this situation was not one of blaming, scapegoating or denial. Serious problems existed; all parties shared in their making; and everyone had a stake in improving the condition of AOT. In contrast to the first phase, the members of AOT no longer shared the illusion that short, quick intervention could help. They had had three painful episodes to demonstrate the contrary. Now they were ready for more sustained, intensive work, and the consultant was no longer willing to do less.

The first step in the second phase actually began outside the committee meetings. During the first phase of the AOT work, the consultant, as well as the AOT committee members, had been participating in a leadership succession experience. His own supervisor had been reassigned and became a *member* of AOT as a result. As a result, the consultant had been working several months without a boss until his new supervisor completed his former assignment and moved to become the consultant's full-time supervisor. The new supervisor was a former member of AOT who had stopped attending their meetings because the efforts were so unproductive.

Once on the job the consultant's new supervisor took a major role in developing the Phase 2 activities. He contacted all members of AOT individually to determine whether they wished to stop the consultation or to continue in a new mode. Receiving positive responses from all committee members, the consultant's supervisor thereby helped to set the stage for an explicit contract between the consultant and the group. The remaining step was to determine who should participate in the intensive work. AOT, after all, had several 'quasi-members' as well as their regular members. AOT members were themselves split on this issue. Because the quasi-members were staff managers, there was some tendency for the staff members of AOT to want them included. In the end, the group decided that they should not be part of Phase 2. With that decision, the group reduced the permeability of its own external boundaries and more clearly established the roles of group members in relation to one another.

Step 1 ended with an explicit contract with the consultant regarding his interviewing each regular committee member about three major topics: the committee itself, the roles of the individual managers, and the nature of staff/line relationships among committee members. These data were to be analysed and fed back to the committee in group sessions. The consultant agreed to work with the committee to make changes if the data indicated clear directions to take.

Step 2 in this process consisted of the interviews and data feedback. It took one month for the consultant to arrange appointments and to interview the nine committee members. Data from the interviews were transcribed anonymously and recorded under the three major topics of the interviews (i.e. the committee itself, the managers' jobs, and staff/line relationships). Feedback was organized around the same three topics. As it turned out, one complete day was devoted to discussing the managers' roles and staff/line relationships. A second day was used for reviewing the data about the committee itself. In designing this feedback a decision was taken to deal with the more external (and slightly less threatening) data first and then to address the internal dynamics of the committee. This approach added further strength to the group boundary by addressing the external forces affecting the group in advance of (and as preparation for) dealing with the more disturbing internal consequences. This strategic choice in feedback follows directly from the consequences of working with an underbounded system. In this kind of situation, introducing the more conflict-laden material pulling the group apart initially would have only accelerated its already existing chaos. For an underbounded group to deal with internal conflict, it is necessary to strengthen the external group boundary so that, when the internal conflict arises, the group boundary is not as easily threatened. The consultant's interviews with individual managers in the data collection phase also served to bond the group together through the relationship each committee member developed with the consultant. Relationship building of this sort is essential for any group intervention. In an overbounded group, the aim of relationship building is to aid information flow, while in an underbounded group the purpose is to strengthen member ties to the group as a whole.

Step 3 in the intervention process was for the committee members to achieve agreement about a set of explicitly stated operating procedures for the committee. To aid this activity, the consultant prepared a theoretical analysis of the committee as an open system with inputs, internal processes, and outputs. The feedback data became the stimulus for committee decisions about how to structure itself in order to work more effectively. In the end the committee produced a statement about the role and operating procedure for the AOT committee that consisted of five parts: (1) functions; (2) membership; (3) leadership; (4) process; and (5) external relations. The statement of functions defined the goals of the committee. With this statement the intervention resulted in a clarified goal structure for the committee. The section on membership determined who was and was not a committee member definitively. It solidified the group's boundary. The statement on leadership legitimized the leader's role in executing and maintaining the structure agreed upon by the members. Especially significant in the section on leadership, however, was also a statement about followership, 'All members share responsibility for orderly conduct of meetings'. As might have been anticipated, the portion on group process was the most extensive and detailed of all. This section included items regarding both external processes (e.g. screening of agenda items) and internal processes (e.g. provision for 'conscientious dissent' by members in relation to majority opinions). Finally, there was a statement about the group's external relationships with superior, peer, and subordinate groups in the corporation.

Conclusion to the AOT case.

After a period of sustained chaos, order had been restored to AOT. The committee members expressed satisfaction with their own work and with the help that had been provided by the consultant. Many organization development interventions aim towards 'unfreezing' tightly controlled groups. But AOT did not suffer from conventional symptoms. Maintaining the metaphor, one would say AOT needed 'freezing', not unfreezing. The Phase 2 interventions helped to move the group from unproductive disorder to sophisticated group effectiveness. The forces for disorder and for change came from outside AOT as well as from inside, and the actions that brought about change addressed the external forces on AOT as well as the internal dynamics characteristic of the committee. The revised and consensually adopted operating procedures made an important difference by providing a greater sense of control of AOT by its members. Nonetheless, AOT was located at a point in the corporation where many important, often conflicting, issues has to be resolved. The external forces influencing AOT members did not go away because the members had learned to manage themselves more effectively. The group would continue to struggle with the 'pulls' towards being an underbounded system even after the successful intervention was completed.

COMPARISON OF HARMON AND AOT
AS UNDERBOUNDED SYSTEMS

The Harmon and AOT cases illustrate the special dynamics of consulting to underbounded systems. Differences between the two systems included their size, purpose, and suprasystem properties. Harmon was an organization of several hundred people and several major groups. AOT eventually became a group of nine individuals. Harmon was a school whose primary mission was to educate elementary school children. AOT was a coordinating committee whose dual purposes became to process information and to make decisions. Harmon's suprasystem was diffuse and extremely underbounded. AOT's immediate environment was a conventionally structured, overbounded business corporation. Similarities between the systems included their initial underbounded conditions on most of the 11 dimensions defined to diagnose system pathology:

Goals

Harmon seemed clear about its primary goal of educating elementary school children. AOT was without a clear goal structure.

Authority

The Harmon principal's authority was regularly in danger of being undermined by the warring parent groups. AOT had co-chairmen whose leadership was not legitimized by committee members.

Economic conditions

Harmon was facing increasingly difficult economic conditions. AOT operated within a relatively prosperous corporation.

Role definitions

Harmon teachers and parents as a whole did not have a common agreement about their roles, especially in relation to each other. AOT members were unable to meet each other's expectations with regard to running effective meetings.

Communication

Harmon teachers were reluctant to attend voluntary meetings to improve their relationships. Harmon parents who identified with the two warring organizations were extremely reluctant to appear in meetings with each other. Some AOT members were irregular attenders of committee meetings.

Energy

Harmon teachers, in particular, felt that their efforts to influence the direction of their school did not seem to make a difference. The AOT managers felt decidedly out of control of their meetings.

Affect

Both Harmon and AOT members showed primarily negative feelings about their system.

Intergroups

Harmon teachers and parents were feeling the pulls of different ethnic and social class groups in shaping the school. AOT managers were experiencing the struggles of upward mobility and competitiveness influencing their relationships with each other.

Unconscious basic assumptions

Harmon teachers and parents showed a marked tendency to vacillate between fighting and avoiding each other. AOT members attended meetings irregularly, permitted inside and outside interruptions to their planned agenda, and repeatedly demonstrated dysfunctional conflict in their meetings.

Time-span

Harmon parents and teachers reported several incidents where the school was influenced by crises rooted in the community (e.g. demands for space in the school by a local day-care group) or in the city (e.g. bussing of students from another school that had been closed for economic reasons). AOT managers saw their meetings changed by unplanned outside speakers and by emotional demands to discuss issues surrounding corporate reorganization. They literally were unable to plan ahead as much as a year in advance in terms of major objectives.

Cognitive work

Neither Harmon nor AOT seemed to have a common intellectual framework for understanding their systems.

Thus, Harmon's and AOT's underboundedness differed substantially only in goal structures and economic conditions when consultation began. Both systems were severely underbounded and seemed to benefit from organizational consultation. In each setting consultation was directed towards both external and internal dynamics. The attention to factors inside *and* outside the system's boundary differentiates underbounded consultation from more conventional organization development. It recognizes and utilizes the environment as an important ingredient in producing system change (Pfeffer and Salancik, 1978). Affecting the external environment requires less energy and can be more clearly focused when the suprasystem is overbounded than when the suprasystem is underbounded. In fact, consultation to underbounded systems may demand more from professionals than work with comparable overbounded systems.

NOTE

After an early draft of this chapter was completed the author received a draft of L. Dave Brown's forthcoming paper 'Planned change in underorganized systems', in T. G. Cummings (ed.), *Systems Theory for Organization Development*, Wiley, 1979. The two papers have similar conceptual roots, developed in our work together, but they focus on different case studies and elaborate different theoretical points. We cite each other's work when it is relevant, but the papers were in fact independently developed even though they have much in common.

REFERENCES

Alderfer, C. P. (1976a) 'Boundary relations and organizational diagnosis.' In Meltzer, H. and Wickert, F. R. (eds.) *Humanizing Organizational Behavior*. Springfield, Ill.: Thomas, pp. 109-33.

Alderfer, C. P. (1976b) 'Change processes in organizations.' In Dunnette, M. D. (ed.) *Handbook of Industrial and Organizational Psychology*. Chicago: Rand-McNally, pp. 1591-638.

Alderfer, C. P. (1977a) 'Group and intergroup relations.' In Hackman, J. R. and Suttle, J. L. (eds.) *Improving Life at Work*. Santa Monica, California: Goodyear, pp. 227-96.

Alderfer, C. P. (1977b) ''Organization development', *Annual Review of Psychology*, **28**, 197-225.

Argyris, C. (1957) *Personality and Organization*. New York: Harper and Row.

Argyris, C. (1962) *Interpersonal Competence and Organizational Effectiveness*. Homewood, Ill.: Dorsey.

Argyris, C. and Schön, D. (1978) *Organizational Learning: A Theory of Action Perspective*. Reading, Mass.: Addison-Wesley.

Astrachan, B. (1970) 'Towards a social systems model of therapeutic groups', *Social Psychiatry*, **5**, 110-9.

Berg, D. (1977) 'Failure at entry.' In Mirvis, P. H. and Berg, D. N. *Failures in Organization Development and Change*. New York: Wiley, pp. 33-56.

Bion, W. R. (1961) *Experiences in Groups*. New York: Basic Books.

Brown, L. D. (1979) 'Planned change in underorganized systems.' In Cummings, T. G. (ed.) *Systems Theory for Organization Development*. New York: Wiley.

Brown, L. D., Aram, J. and Bachner, J. (1974) 'Interorganizational information sharing: a successful intervention that failed', *Journal of Applied Behavioral Science*, **10**, 533-54.

Brown, L. D. and Brown, J. C. (1973) 'The struggle for an alternative: a case study of a commune', *Human Organization*, **32**, 257-66.

Buckley, W. (1967) *Sociology and Modern Systems Theory*. Englewood Cliffs, N.J.: Prentice-Hall.

Campbell, D. T., Kruskal, W. H. and Wallace, W. (1966) 'Seating aggregation as an index of attitude', *Sociometry*, **29**, 1-15.

Firestone, W. A. (1977) 'Participation and influence in the planning of educational change', *Journal of Applied Behavioral Science*, **13**, 167-83.

Friedlander, F. and Brown, L. D. (1974) 'Organization development', *Annual Review of Psychology*, **25**, 313-41.

Gulick, L. and Urwick, L. (1937) *Papers on the Science of Administration*. New York: Papers on the Science of Administration.

Jaques, E. (1952) *The Changing Culture of a Factory*. London: Tavistock.

Katz, D. and Kahn, L. (1978) *The Social Psychology of Organizations*, 2nd edition. New York: Wiley.

Lett, E. E., Clark, W. and Altman, I. A. (1969) *A Propositional Inventory of Research on Interpersonal Distance*. Bethesda, Maryland: Naval Medical Research Institute.

Levinson, D. J. (1959) 'Role, personality, and social structure in the organizational setting', *Journal of Abnormal and Social Psychology*, **58**, 170-80.

March, J. G. and Simon, H. (1958) *Organizations*. New York: Wiley.

McGregor, D. (1960) *The Humanside of Enterprise*. New York: McGraw-Hill.

Mehrabian, A. (1968) 'Relationship of attitude to seated posture orientation, and distance', *Journal of Personality and Social Psychology*, **10**, 26-30.

Miller, E. and Rice, A. K. (1967) *Systems of Organization*. London: Tavistock.

Miller, J. G. *Living Systems*. New York: McGraw-Hill.

Pearce, J. L. (1978) 'Something for nothing: an empirical examination of the structures and norms of volunteer organizations', Unpublished Doctoral Dissertation, Yale University.

Perrow, C. (1961) 'The analysis of goals in complex organizations', *American Sociological Review*, **26**, 854-66.

Pfeffer, J. and Salancik, G. (1978) *The External Control of Organizations*. New York: Harper and Row.

Porter, L. W., Lawler, E. E. and Hackman, J. R. (1975) *Behavior in Organizations*. New York: McGraw-Hill.

Simon, H. A. (1964) 'On the concept of organizational goal', *Administrative Science Quarterly*, **9**, 1-21.

Slater, P. E. (1966) *Microcosm*. New York: Wiley.

Skynner, A. C. R. (1976) *Systems of Family and Marital Psychotherpy*. New York: Brunner/Mazel.

Truit, E. L., Higgin, G. W., Murray, H. and Pollack, A. B. (1963) *Organizational Choice*. London: Tavistock.

Weick, E. (1976) 'Educational organizations as loosely coupled systems', *Administrative Science Quarterly*, **21**, 1-19.

Zubek, J. P. (1969) (ed.) *Sensory Deprivation: Fifteen Years of Research*. New York: Appleton-Century-Crofts.

Advances in Experiential Social Processes, Volume 2
Edited by C. P. Alderfer and C. L. Cooper
© 1980 John Wiley & Sons, Ltd.

Chapter **12**

The Manifesto of Existential Training

Max Pagès

Université Paris IX, France

and

Burkhard Müller

Universität Tübingen, West Germany

INTRODUCTION

The following 'Manifesto' emerged within the setting of an Action Research Project which was assigned the task of experimentally developing methods of training and group work for facilitating 'individual and group initiative' within the International Youth Exchange. The project was established by the Franco-German Youth Organization (FGYO) which was founded in 1963 and mutually financed by the French and German Governments with the aim of 'forming closer ties between the youth of both countries and deepening their understanding of one another'. The FGYO primarily subsidizes the exchange programme of other organizations whose aims correspond to its own, but also organizes experimental programmes and research projects.

Our project evolved out of the work of an 'Innovation Group' which, in addition to ourselves, consisted of members of the FGYO and its Franco German partner organizations. Each member of the group had had experience — often extensive — on the administrative and/or educational side of international youth exchange programme as well as in the training of group advisers. It was assumed that this group, which had held one-week workshops about three times a year over a period of two and a half years, had the potential experience at its disposal to solve the task of our project. Potential experience has here a twofold meaning: in one sense it signifies previously acquired expert knowledge, and in another sense it suggests that having worked and lived together in these international groups presented in itself a varied field of experience for our problem. The concept developed in the following theses has guided our collaboration with this group from the beginning, at first more as a vague idea, then as an increasingly clear one. It is simultaneously the product of the work of the group and with the group, which does not mean that all group members had agreed on fundamentals.

Perhaps it might lead to better understanding of our procedure if we state what we have not attempted: we have never endeavoured to contribute to the methodology of international youth meetings by carrying over already developed group methods in this field, insofar as they stood at our disposal, in order to explore the possibilities and difficulties of this transference. We have not chosen this relatively secure course, because it promised to obscure rather than clarify our greatest problem. This problem was not the application of the methods themselves, but the clarification of the meaning and goals of this application.

It is clear that, in regard to their methodology, international meetings should not be viewed in isolation. Repertoires of methods from the most diverse fields such as free-time formation, group pedagogy and dynamics, gestalt therapy, the didactic of political education, institutional analysis, etc. . . . flow into these meetings according to the ability and previous experience of trainers and participants. It should, however, not be overlooked that frequently the *context* from which these repertoires emerge is simultaneously carried over with the methods — often unintentionally. This means, for example, that methods which originated within the context of 'therapy' turn the international meetings into (pseudo)-therapy; methods which originated within the context of 'free-time formation' turn the international meetings into a mere form of leisure-time activity; methods which originated within the context of 'training' (*Ausbildung*) turn the international meetings into a school-like situation; etc. . . . This occurs all the more because a specific definition of what an 'international meeting' actually is and should be has been scarcely attempted — if at all. Thus neither the individual representatives of the various nationalities which 'meet' there are challenged to define the meaning of their 'meeting' (as it corresponds to our conception), nor the institutions that organize and support it. On the contrary, the meaning is defined by the applied methods, rather than being measured the other way round according to a predetermined direction and goal.

This relationship becomes particularly confused when the original context of the accepted repertoire of methods has fallen into uncertainty or oblivion. The latter applies especially to the repertoire of methods of American origin which are still dominating the market: the arsenal of methods of group pedagogy and group dynamics. Their ideological context and moral-political impetus can be characterized by the keyword 'reeducation'. All of these methods are strongly rooted in the reaction of the American social sciences to the experience of fascim. In this respect they represent an attempt to reeducate a society whose small group structures are partially or completely undemocratic, and to firmly establish democratic conduct within its social and organizational basis, so that the microstructure would not support a disturbance in the democratic macrostructure but hinder it if necessary. This type of programme and methodology, developed by Dewey, Lewin, and Lippitt among others, still dominates the field of 'international meetings', even if implicitly. This becomes apparent when the meaning of the meeting, if it is discussed at all, is defined by such concepts as 'elimination of prejudices' or 'exercise in the forms of peaceful conflict settlement'.

But who should actually reeducate whom? and who should be freed from their prejudices and be instructed in the 'correct' forms of conflict settlement? Should the French guide the Germans, or should it be the other way around? Or are the internationally minded, 'European'-thinking, multilingual individuals the prototype of an unprejudiced attitude? We venture to doubt this.

We are strengthened in this doubt by the fact that our special experimental field, the Innovation Group, offered to all appearances particularly favourable conditions. In this group there was certainly *more* awareness of problems relating to prejudice, *more* understanding of the cultural and political situation of the other country, more bilingual members, and more competence in verbal conflict settlement than is the case in 'normal' meetings between German and French youths. This group succeeded more easily than other groups, especially in the beginning, in giving the impression of being generally free from prejudices. But only so long as the one did not come too close to the other — somewhat in the same way as the users of an international airport remain free from prejudice. In the moment, however, in which real interests and convictions came into play, massive communicative and cooperative difficulties arose in the group distinctly following the lines of nationality. All attempts at mutual reeducation, which were continually made at such points, failed drastically. Perhaps it was due to these miscarried attempts that many members of this group experienced it as particularly hard and intolerant (and this implies that it was also burdened by prejudice). Perhaps this was also due to the fact that the real working through of living together first *begins* when people give up trying to mutually free themselves from their prejudices.

Thus one conviction reinforced itself within the course of this work: predetermined methods of training, with the operational and power structure necessary to implement them, do hinder rather than foster a meaningful training process. The latter can be developed more completely when the latent potentialities and conflicts of individuals in the concrete historical situation of their encounter are confronted more directly, using all the intellectual tools they have at their disposal. The following methodological text attempts to present a general formulation of this thesis. We are aware of its somewhat utopian character in the present social institutional situation of training, but we hope it could stimulate a desire to look at training activities, including the more institutionalized ones, from a somewhat different perspective.

I. THE EXISTENTIAL PROJECT: BASIS: IMPULSE AND GOAL
OF THE TRAINING SITUATION

1. We believe that every participant in every training situation pursues a project concerning his own existence.

2. This project is something specific for each individual and for the particular moment in which he finds himself in the course of his personal history.

3. It is to an extent an unconscious* project in which the individual's wish to work out the contradictions which confront him in his personal and social life is expressed. The project leads to precise actions, which effect a provisional synthesis of these contradictions at this particular point in the individual history.

4. The conscious, so to speak manifest 'project' that every one pursues in training is only partially an expression of the unconscious project; it also partially serves to mask it.

5. The goal of existential training is to make it possible for each individual to work out the contradictions that he reveals during the process of training and to allow him to develop and realize his project.

II. THE EXISTENTIAL INVOLVEMENT OF THE TRAINER

6. The trainers (insofar as such a differentiation between roles exists inside a group) are placed in the same situation as the participants with regard to the project. They also are pursuing an unconscious project, which is to an extent hidden and masked by their official roles, but nevertheless specific for each trainer and bound to his personal history.

7. The trainer is confronted with the same task as the participants: to become aware of the existant unconscious project that is behind the mask of his official 'project'; to effectively bring his own contradictions into play within the group; and to share with participants contradictions and objectives as well as the partial syntheses which he is discovering.

8. It is not illegitimate from this point of view — as it basically would be in other conceptions of training — for the trainer to concentrate on his own problems and projects, and to then use the group in order to develop these and

---

*In this Manifesto the word 'unconscious' should not be understood within the limits of the traditional psychoanalytic connotation. This and other psychoanalytic concepts will be applied within a broader context which will include action dimensions and relations to social institutions. The traditional notion of unconscious usually refers only to unconscious personal ties; it does not include the unconscious ties to institutions: the identifications, projections, fears, and conflicts which are related *to collective objects* (see thesis 53).

search for an answer. This is, on the contrary, necessary, just as it is necessary for the trainer to be prepared to share with the participants at any point during his or their work. The refusal of the trainer to allow himself to be brought into the group in this way is an obstacle to the training situation.

9. Insofar as the trainer has a special role or position in the group (as the result of a mandate, payment, or his responsibility for method and organization stemming either from an external institution, the participants or both of these) it is necessary that his status be considered as a part of his personal history, as a place where his own contradictions come into play, and not as an impersonal, professional, occupational, ethical, or social necessity that is imposed upon him or the participants as a fact.

III. DEPROFESSIONALIZATION OF TRAINING WORK

10. This concept involves radical structural changes in the relationship between trainers and participants, and signifies for the ones as well as the others overcoming the break dividing the 'working' sphere from the sphere of so-called 'private' life. These two aspects are bound to one another: the separation of the trainers from the participants would allow the participants' 'private' desires to be utilized and alienated within the forms of 'work' suggested by the trainers.

11. Traditional training is based on a more or less implicit *contract of dependence* between trainers and participants. This contract reads when considered schematically as follows: the participants grant power to the trainers with the guarantee that the trainers (trainer, teacher, therapist, etc. . . .) worry about them and not about themselves. The participants expect that their salvation will be achieved through the knowledge and methods of the trainers as well as by the personal relationships that they will be able to maintain with them. This remains true independent of the training methodology, even when that involves a good dose of frustration (as in psychoanalysis and the methods inspired by it or in new therapies such as bio-energetics . . .). In exchange for the power that is entrusted to them the trainers renounce their claim on possibly bringing their own problems into play within the group. Thus the power of the trainers can be seen as an *equivalent* to their own repressed desires.

12. The power of the trainers resides foremost in their professional status and social role, which characterize and distinguish them as 'those who are there in order to worry about the others and not about themselves'. This distinction becomes apparent *economically* (the trainers are paid whereas the participants are not), *politically* (the trainers decide about the programme or its aims, about material and organizational arrangements, they structure the time and deal with the external authorities), and, even more important, *ideologically*

(the theories and methods of the trainers serve as the dominant ideology of the group). It is the power to give meaning to the participants' experiences. The decisive work for the trainer according to the traditional view is codification: the task of translating the participants' desires into a socially acceptable language which gives them meaning.

13. This relationship of dependence is both conscious and unconscious. That which the trainers are able to do by virtue of their competence serves to justify the unconscious irrational dependence that the participants feel towards them. The trainers allow the awareness of that which they are able to do for the participants to mask the obscure transaction which is effected when they accept or make a claim to power. Their power is equivalent to and is a substitute for an entire 'unspoken' (*non-dit*) complex, for unsolved emotional and social contradictions (feelings of inferiority and loss, search for affection, social humiliations, etc. . . .).

14. The dependence of the participants on the trainers is accompanied by the dependence of the entire training group, trainers included, on the institutions which support the training — sponsoring organizations, professional groups to which trainers or participants either belong or to which they refer, etc. . . .

The power of the institutions is manifested in the selection and definition of the problems dealt with, the choice of the trainers, the composition of the training group, the financing, and in the criteria of work utilized. The trainers are the mediators between the institutions and the participants. Their codification work is embedded in the broader social codification of the institutions, which they are relaying. The contract of dependence with the institutions ensures — in exchange for the power granted to them — the material and moral protection of the group, as well as of the individuals who make up the group, and above all the protection of the trainers.

15. The consequences of this situation of twofold dependence are:
— the obligatory codification of the participants' desires within the prevailing social codes;
— the alienation of participants who consciously and unconsciously identify themselves with personal and impersonal collective objects, i.e. trainers, institutions, rules, prevailing ideologies and methodologies . . .;
— the exemption of the participants from responsibility, not only in the area of the organization of group activities, but also in the more important area of their unconscious projects; the participants *give up their project, their power to search and give meaning to their experience*, which they hand out to others.
— the sterilization of the trainers, who deprive both themselves and the participants of the active interest which they could personally bring into the training activity.

16. It is consequently clear that a necessary bond exists between the existential involvement of the trainers and the existential involvement of the participants,

since the trainers, in their roles and their professional status, shield and hinder the existential involvement of the participants — independent of the ideology and methodology to which they refer.

17. The concept of existential training leads, at least in utopian terms, to a radical deprofessionalization of the work involved in training. It leads to a dissolution of the trainer's *occupation* and to the recognition of a training *function* which can be filled by everybody. The aim is to create a training community based upon mutual as opposed to one-sided help, with a view towards developing each individual's responsibility for the clarification and realization of his project. Then the training situation becomes a collective effort in which one can turn to the other in order to develop the special personal project that is rooted in each individual's existence.

18. We in no way intend to deny the reality of social or emotional dependence on authorities and powers. Nor do we allege that the former can be immediately eliminated. We only maintain that structural conditions of every type must be sought — economic, political, ideological, psychological — which avoid their strengthening and make it possible to work on them effectively.

19. We also intend to think about those cases which are seemingly very far removed from the utopia that we are presenting, as well as about the relevance of our conception in relation to traditional training situations.

IV. CHANGING THE TYPES AND SOURCES OF SECURITY

20. We assume that it is far more the wish for security than the wish for power as an end in itself which allows the twofold relationship of dependence described to function in manifold variations. The contract of dependence is in its conscious and unconscious elements nothing other than a system of security which functions with regard to all sides concerned:
— the side of the trainers;
— the side of the participants;
— the side of institutions.

21. This security function, which will be more closely designated in the following, is what makes it so difficult to overcome the relation of dependence. Merely denying dependence only creates an unproductive form of insecurity. On the other hand, this contract of dependence is a decisive hindrance to opening up other sources of security. This mutual relation between protection and hindrance will be made clear by an isolated but not too remote example: package vacations.

22. Tourist arrangements in a developed form (i.e. club vacations) are clear contracts of dependence. Their aim is to offer the tourist a premium on novel,

alluring, exotic experiences, and at the same time a premium on relaxation through material and psychological security. Both of these aims are, however, only compatible when the tourists are externally and internally *ghettoized* within the land they are visiting; in other words, when they are cut off from a real encounter with foreign life and culture and put off with surrogates. The perfect tourist arrangement destroys the possibility for real positive experiences precisely because it systematically eliminates the possibility for negative disturbing experiences with foreign life and culture. The only way to really experience local hospitality, for example, is to risk breaking externally and internally out of the tourist ghetto. Local hospitality is in itself a source of security, but in principle one of another quality than the security offered by tourist arrangements. This alternative type of security can only be experienced by one who has previously gone through the experience of insecurity; that is, the experience that one can *become open* to local hospitality (which cannot be purchased) and must at the same time bear the risk that one will *not* be invited.

23. The contract of dependence has a similar isolating effect for the participants of international youth meetings, providing protection on the one side and hindering new experiences on the other. As long as it is assumed — openly or implicitly — that the arrangements of the organizers and trainers are responsible for the success or failure of the meeting, then the participants are protected:
— from the necessity of having to find out the meaning of their participation at any given time;
— from conflicts with others which grow out of this necessity;
— from the anxiety of not being able to succeed or not being accepted;
— from having to attribute their own lack of experience and their boredom to themselves, and from not having a scapegoat for this.

24. The need for such protection becomes increasingly stronger as foreign elements collide with one another in a meeting: different languages, lifelong habits, political convictions, unfamiliar surroundings, etc. . . . As long as fears of these sorts govern a meeting, insecurity inevitably increases in individual behaviour, as does consequently the wish for capsulization, withdrawal into familiar groups, dependence on a common programme, arrangements, etc. . . ., whereby the conflict is neutralized.

25. It would be fatal to ignore such fears or to denounce them as weaknesses. They can on the contrary turn into an important element of the meeting if they are accepted and communicable. The danger of *previously* arranged security through contracts of dependence lies, however, in the fact that on the one hand it hinders the awareness and articulation of the aforementioned needs, and on the other obstructs access to other sources of security:
— the security that grows out of the experience of being able to advocate a position and way of living without having to cover up breaches or contradictions;

— the security of being accepted by people who are different and think differently;
— the security of being able to function independently in foreign territories and speak a foreign language;
— the security of being able to stand one's ground in conflicts with institutions, etc. . . . .

26. We do not believe that the trainers help the participants to such a new form of security by seeking to procure security for them or, conversely, by creating educational arrangements in order to provoke ostensibly productive insecurity. On the contrary, they can only help the participants find a new form of security by personally risking that which they expect the participants to risk. This risk thus involves breaking out of the professional role in which the trainers, with the help of the participants and the organizing institutions, keep themselves imprisoned.

27. The contract of dependence that assigns this role to the trainers protects them in various ways:
— it makes it possible for the trainers to orient their actions to the norms of the university culture, leading political and educational notions, professional rules, standards of research, etc. . . . ;
— it protects them from the supporting institutions, in that it legitimizes their activity as 'serious work' or 'serious research'. Generally speaking, it is much easier to make clear to an outsider what the trainers do or should do when the *particular* or their activities is contrasted with that of the participants: that is, when the contents of the contract of dependence are described;
— it legitimizes the trainers' salary;
— it enables the trainers to retreat behind their formal roles in the face of unpleasant challenges made by the participants, and it sustains at the same time the fiction that such retreats occur in the best interest of the participants;
— it protects the trainers from conflicts within themselves, and keeps them from doubting their own spontaneity, ability to communicate, ideological steadfastness, etc. . . . .

28. This security built on dependence, however, simultaneously blocks for the trainers themselves all of the alternative sources of security enumerated above (see 23) with regard to the participants. This implies once again that the trainers themselves are not in the position to experience (out of fear that they will come into conflict with their role) what they expect the participants to experience. Their aims, such as:
— opening themselves to foreign norms and ways of living;
— teaching conflict settlement;
— clarifying their own positions, attitudes, special interests, needs, etc. . . . .
fall into conflict with their behaviour. The resulting failure of the work (for example stemming from the participants' passive resistance) makes the trainers

in turn insecure and induces them to seek their well-being in still better educational arrangements: an endless cycle.

29. The supporting institutions also have security needs which exert a pressure in the direction of strengthening and lengthening contract of dependence. These needs express themselves in built-in possibilities of control at different levels:
— at the level of the appropriate application of funds and the calculability of financial and insurance risks;
— at the level of norms and values (moral standards, political norms) which if infringed could endanger an institution's legitimacy before other institutions;
— at the level of controlling the success of goals which institutions have set for themselves (i.e. French-German understanding, European integration, etc. ...).
   Such controls become above all controls on the responsible individual (organizers, trainers) who, if necessary, can be called to account. In order for these 'answerable' individuals to be controlled, they must for their part have their work under control, which means that they must have the participants under control through contracts of dependence.

30. As the strength of these needs for assurance and legitimacy grows, it becomes increasingly more difficult for institutions to acquire access to other sources of security and legitimacy. This applies for example to the work field of the FGYO. The most important of these sources would be the readiness of French and German youths to look at the FGYO and its partners as 'their' institutions and to defend them if necessary. The lack of such readiness indicates the decisive weakness in the legitimacy of most institutions of youth cooperation — the FGYO included.
   The bureaucratization of youth meetings (together with the internally corresponding development of a school-like atmosphere on the one hand and a tourist atmosphere on the other) is clearly both the *consequence* and the *cause* of this lack of readiness. This is also a circle, because the responsibility for the success of the work remains individually and bureaucratically controlled ; for the same reason the 'preparation, execution and utilization' by the youths themselves (Guiding Principle of FGYO) remains largely only on paper.

31. If this circle is to be broken, it is fundamental for the institutions to recognize collective responsibility on the financial level, as well as on method and content levels. That will lead without doubt to conflicts and will compel the bureaucratic apparatus to step out of its shadow. But how else shall the gap between democratic claims and a controlled reality, in international youth meetings for example, be overcome?

V. DESPECIALIZATION OF THE TRAINING SITUATION

32. A difficulty in making this concept of training understandable stems from the fact that it systematically attempts to undermine a principle that is deeply rooted in the structure of our everyday life and consequently in ourselves: the principle of the specialization and clean division of different areas of life. *Work* is one thing, as was already stated, and *free time* is another (it is above all not work). To learn in school is one thing and to pursue personal interests is another. What I accomplish in school or in my occupation is one thing, but what I personally gain from this and what it personally costs me is an entirely different matter. Other divisions are woven into this structure:
— the division of the political public life from the private sphere;
— the division of cognitive reflection from emotional self-expression;
— the division of reflection from action.

33. All professional methods of training are based on specialization, even if the lines of division take slightly different courses. They focus on one area of human experience, while consciously neglecting another. Thus there are methods of corporal expression as well as didactic methods, methods to stimulate play and creative activity as well as methods of organizational development, methods of group process analysis as well as methods of political and institutional analysis. The consequence of this specialization is that at times particular dimensions of experience and self-expression are suppressed in the life of the groups. This is then justified by the assumption that effective work is only possible when concentrating on the existing chosen dimensions. As a result, however, the activities of the groups are mutilated and hierarchically structured. Specialization cuts up the groups' experience into so many professional markets controlled by the experts whose 'scientific' labels are trademarks.

34. The most well-known form of this restriction is carried out in the interest of intellectual-mental work. It is allegedly sensible in performing effective mental work to sit on a chair, to reduce physical and playful possibilities of expression to a minimum, and to protect oneself from becoming too emotional. We have found on the contrary that exactly this supposedly necessary discipline can make intellectual discourses sterile and at the same time an arena of hidden power struggles; whereas, conversely, very often alleged disturbances provide a productive impulse and first allow recognition of what the participants in the discussion actually have at stake and what they do not.

35. Specialization in other dimensions can, however, equally well lead to sterility:
— in group dynamics self-experience and the clarification of personal relations

frequently get isolated from the context of the life (particularly as regards economic and practical dimensions, which should in theory attain more clarity) and become an aim in themselves;

— specialization in physical expression leads frequently to rituals of self-portrayal, to the reproduction of theatrics as an aim in itself, whereas political dimensions or work on problems of authority remain excluded;

— specialization in the dimension of self-organization of collective living frequently turns concern with organizational problems into a fetish which does not leave any room for the question of what needs should be met by a form of organization at any given time.

36. We are not arguing here against experimenting in all of these directions any more than against allowing one of these dimensions to obtain particular emphasis at different points of group living — although that which is relevant for a group and that which is relevant for particular individuals in the group can be thoroughly different and should be permitted to be so in our opinion. We believe that a group becomes all the more animated, the more these dimensions mutually penetrate one another without being hindered in this by external discipline.

37. There is a specialization related to the aforementioned directions which plays a large role in the experimental programmes of the FGYO as well as other groups and frequently leads to frustrations and wars between the divided camps. This is the specialization or division between those who consider work on themes, problems, and educational matters to be the 'essential' thing, and those who hold living together within the group and its requirements (the organization of living quarters, meals, administration of funds, time distribution, intervals, surroundings, personal relations, etc. . . .) to be the decisive experience and learning field of the group. The former see the latter merely as agreeable or burdensome marginal issues, which frequently consitute hindrances in coming to the 'essential' thing; whereas the others seem to think that what has been lived in the group has also already been grasped and assimilated as a meaningful experience for the life outside. We believe that all movements of group living are productive and progressive which bring both of the above perspectives together and mutually illuminate them: the distancing consideration of objects 'outside' and the immediate involvement in the process of living together in all its dimensions.

38. Another aspect of this despecialization is the overcoming of the division between work on institutional and political structures on the one hand, and the handling of emotional relations between individuals and groups on the other. We believe that institutional and emotional structures are tightly bound to one another and form a 'social-mental' system, for both areas overlap one another in individuals. As was said in the Innovation Group, people are involved as 'representatives' as well as 'persons'. As representatives they are French,

German, members of youth organizations, university people, students, apprentices, unemployed, union members, Christians, etc. . . . who are intent on experiencing, learning, and enjoying 'something' specific which has to do with this representative = institutional = political existence (even if it is only that they want to flee what above all reminds them of their status).

At the same time they are, however, people directly entangled in a process of life 'here and now' which they can deny for themselves and which they can pronounce irrelevant, but which they cannot withdraw from. We believe that people will learn to think both 'the personal' and 'the political' in a situation in which the conscious experience of 'what happens with me here and now' collides with the 'something' which I as a representative expected from a meeting with other representatives. At such points it becomes apparent what is and is not at stake for individuals who want to change the institutional and social structures in which they live.

39. Finally: the despecialization of the training situation is therefore (amongst other things) difficult, because it makes it hard to define and label what occurs in training. Pedagogical patterns of thinking do not make it easy to grasp what one learns when one learns to live in open situations.

VI. METHODS AND TECHNIQUES IN TRAINING

40. What has been said up to now should not be misunderstood as our wishing to speak out against the use of pedagogical methods and techniques in training. We do, however, stand opposed:
— to the ritualized and repetitive use of methods;
— to methods which are no longer a means of expressing individual and collective interests and wishes, methods which become an end in themselves;
— to methods which can only be applied by specialists or with high technical expenditure;
— to methods which cannot be creatively varied according to given situations and needs;
— to methods which only function when their 'rules' are strictly adhered to.

41. The methods of training have been in our opinion falsely defined if they only designate the particular skills and knowledge of the trainer. On the contrary, every participant has a repertoire of particular abilities and knowledge that is at the same time an expression of his person and his specific interests, culture, social circumstances, etc. . . . . . All such abilities contribute to the development of a group's life and are also a point of departure for confrontation and conflict. There is no difference in principle whether it is thereby a question of argumentative abilities, the capacity to express emotions, familiarity in artistic and/or technical media, organizational abilities, or cooking skills.

42. The problem is that at this point hierarchies and authority relationships are formed and that recognized and less acknowledged abilities reveal themselves, as do stars and outsiders, talkers and non-talkers, etc. . . . . This cannot be resolved by the trainers attempting to take on the roles of arbiters and distributors of the equality of chance. We believe that the loss here would be greater than the gain, because in this way the contradiction is once again constructed, i.e.: intending to overcome the contract of dependence by introducing a new exclusive role means a new contract of dependence. Instead of this the trainers should examine for themselves the extent of their own interests in regard to such less acknowledged abilities and aspects of life and then make this the theme of a discussion. It also makes a difference whether the trainers themselves are models for a way of conduct that primarily demonstrates professional skills, or whether they have an experiential relation to their own life within the group: whether or not they risk moving on a stretch of ground that is new and unfamiliar to them, try doing things they have not yet attempted, etc. . . . .

43. In this work we hold all methods to be questionable which in any way lead to turning the participants into clients and objects of treatment. The best defence against this — often unintentionally produced — tendency is for the trainer to apply his repertoire of methods only in order to make particular interests and needs of his own communicable to others. This is both the best protection against employing methods in sterile and ritualized ways and the dynamic impulse for transforming methods creatively and discovering new ones.

44. In the Innovation Group we found that it is a false reduction to limit oneself to those methods which require a particular scenic arrangement (almost every compilation and handbook on group methods and games limits itself in this manner). Far more life is often generated by methods which do not presuppose previously declared preparedness to 'take part', but are, rather, impulses within communal life, play, and discussion, like:
— a sudden idea or a physical activity which interrupts a discussion that has become sterile and ritualized (for example, one method devised by the women of the Innovation Group was that they simply sat themselves in the middle and placed their heads together if they had the feeling that the men had again begun to soliloquize amongst themselves);
— attempting to make oneself heard by using other than verbal means of communication;
— changes in the places and arrangements of common meals;
— wall bulletins which provide a permanent topic for discussion also outside the 'official' mutual rounds of discussion. With regard to such impulses, as with all group methods, it is important that it is still a matter of creating a means for the expression of own interests and wishes, and not principally of

manipulative impulses ('I just wanted to be the initiator for once', 'I wanted to see what it was like', 'I wanted to show the others how they would react', etc. . . .).

45. Training following this conception resembles a research process. Neither the goals and methods nor the relation between them can be conclusively laid down in advance. As in a research process, the relation of goals and methods is dynamic; this happens when there is a constant new definition of goals and a permanent process of adaptation or a new development in methods. It is the task of the trainers as well as the participants to collaborate in this searching process.

VII. THE STRUCTURAL CONDITIONS OF EXISTENTIAL TRAINING SITUATIONS: A CONCEPTION OF SELF-ORGANIZATION (AUTOGESTION)

46. The fundamental stipulation is that the initiator of a training project forgoes thinking, planning or deciding for the others. Instead, he must orient himself to what he personally strives for and fully accept from the beginning the personal and situationally bound character of his desires, and his status as participant.

47. The usual structural division between 'trainers' and 'participants' is eliminated from the start at the economic, political, ideological, and psychological levels.

48. At the economic level there is no longer a definite position for a professional trainer who is paid to 'animate' the group, before the group is composed and has defined any project. The tasks carried out in training, regardless of who executes them are either paid or left unpaid according to available and mobilizable funds, according to actually felt needs and recognized competences. The amount of the payment (if any) is the sole responsibility of the group and should be decided by collective negotiations.

49. For the same reason nobody controls, at the political level, in a status-determined manner, the important decisions of group living, particularly those concerning the group's composition, the form and rhythm of its work, and its eventual relations to external powers.

50. At the ideological level there is no dominating official theory, ideology or methodology, to which the existence of the group is bound by definition and statute (i.e. a psychoanalytical group, a group for institutional analysis, group dynamics, bio-energetic, tennis, English . . .). The initiators of a project renounce their roles as direction-giving authorities for the participant. They accept equally theories, ideologies, and methodologies which differ from their

own and which others outside themselves bring into the group. That should not imply that they are neutral and have neither wishes nor suggestions for the group. On the contrary, but at the same time it is not a question of a wish 'for the other's well-being', whereby one puts oneself in another's place; rather it involves a wish which they have for themselves with regard to the others. At this point they come into conflict with other group members and possibly retreat when the conflict is not productive, that is to say when it does not lead to an acceptable synthesis for them. They do not attempt to compress the group into a single conception or style of learning.

51. *Psychologically* seen, the most favourable prerequisite is a renunciation of thinking and deciding for the others, identifying oneself with them or expecting one's salvation or downfall to come from them, which involves a definite acceptance of separation, loneliness, and failure. This presupposes — on an internal level — the recognition of the problematical and conflicting character of personal motives and wishes, as well as an actual wish to be confronted with these contradictions and open oneself to them as opposed to confining them within a formula. It also presupposes a relative dissolution of the unconscious identification structures with others. This leads in mutual relationships to a partial dissolution of the 'stingy' forms of relations (W. Reich) based upon reciprocal identification and projection — this in the direction of a basic openness towards the unforeseeable.

52. Stipulations 50 and 51 distinguish our project from the customary procedure of self-organization (autogestion). Often the self-organization of a group is limited to collective determination of the programmes and time. Even when one goes beyond 'pedagogical self-organization'* and jointly administers money and relations with external powers, *the ideological ascendancy of the initiators of the project normally remains untouched.* On the other hand, self-organization cannot be based upon psychological power relationships. The ideological and psychological predominance of the initiators is thus the innermost core of power relationships in training groups and the main source of the alienation that hinders the process of ownership (appropriation) of aims and meanings by participants. Economic-political self-organization is a necessary though not sufficient prerequisite for the elimination of alienation. For this reason the personal implication of the initiator of the training project is necessary, for it creates the prerequisites for eliminating ideological and psychological alienation, in that it allows the initiators to renounce their roles as those who give meaning and their close relationships based on identification with the others. Economic and political self-organization does not go far enough, since it turns to individuals who are structurally not in the position to do anything but to carry out a project for the

*Georges Lapassade (1967) distinguishes between the self-organization of the inner institution (pedagogical self-organization) and the self-organization of the outer/external institution.

initiator. They exist *for and through* the 'initiators of self-organization'. The collective which should be organized is a myth under these circumstances; it remains the ideological property of the initiators, and at another level it consists of the personal unconscious relationships of identification which are maintained with them. Many of the difficulties which are encountered in the practice of self-organization and form the mockery of reactionary circles (difficulties in coming to an agreement, sterile and endless conflicts) are a consequence of this. It is not a matter of genuine interindividual conflicts: the participants fight for scraps of the ideological and psychological possessions of the initiators. The same observation accounts in our opinion for many conflicts in revolutionary groups.

53. These prerequisites could be characterized in other words as such: the aim is to eliminate as much as possible everything which could operate as *collective objects* (persons, rules, symbols, ideologies, institutions) which are set apart from the participants and the interindividual relationships which they are able to maintain — collective objects which reinforce their alienation. The self-organization that we propose is not the organization of a mythical collective which merely replaces the myth of a boss or an institution, and that like these myths conceals actual domination and exploitation. Rather, we propose dealing with interindividual relationships which themselves are based on the dealing with the individual's relation to himself. The collective training situation depends on self-training* and should make this easier. The first prerequisite to this is that the initiator of the project himself assumes a stance of self-training.

VIII. THE GENESIS AND INCOMPLETENESS OF THE TRAINING PROJECT

54. Another important aspect is the genesis of a training project. The usual training situation can be described as a premature forced birth situation. An anonymous group of individuals finds itself gathered, determined, and constrained by an individual's or institution's project, which for their sake have not defined their own project for themselves. This is a situation in which alienating and constricting relations to collective objects immediately arise, and in which a mythical pseudo-collective establishes itself — a situation which codifies and blocks the genesis of individual projects, the ripening of interpersonal relations, and the emergence of collective objects brought forth by the individuals themselves (goals, programmes, methods, ideas . . .). Other conditions could be envisioned under which individuals motivated by a personal training project (by a project which above all concerns them personally) are striving to establish non-anonymous situationally bound

*A concept developed in the Innovation Group by Hinrich Schnack (personal communication).

relationships with others and patiently testing with them the compatibility of the projects, the working conditions, and the wish to associate with various persons. In this way complex and decentralized networks of relations could join together from the beginning. This would prevent constricting and standardized structures. These networks would be receptive to changes and alterations of everykind (differentiation of tasks, changes in the group's composition, variations in methods . . .). From this perspective each individual's project as well as the collective project remain constantly open. It is regarded as being in a state of permanent maturation, passing through a process of continuous definition and redifinition. This means that the project is accepted as *incomplete* by nature (Lapassade, 1963) and that emphasis is placed more on its genesis and permanent transformation than on its conclusion and completion. Here an affinity can be seen between our understanding of training on the one hand and research and creation on the other.

IX. TRADITIONAL SITUATIONS AND THE PROCESSES OF CHANGE

55. But, people will say, your project is utopian. It is not realizable in practice, or at best only under privileged circumstances. For example, it could be practised by those who have free time at their disposal which they can invest in training activities without expecting honour or social position. This does not include the large majority of professional group leaders. Our answer to this objection is twofold. On the one hand this Utopia is already to an extent realizable. Free time already exists in part, depending on occupations and persons. And for the so-called 'free' professions the amount of free time depends to a large extent on the degree of the individual's self-alienation and on his ability and will to free himself from alienating models of work and social success, which is exactly where existential training could be of assistance. This free time is, at least in part, used, so to speak, to escape and recover in various ways — for better or worse (and rather worse than better) — from the aggression and mental damage originating in 'work'. Could this time not be better filled with activities which might really restore the energy, activities outside the money and power struggles of professional training? Individuals would freely engage in these in order to think about and reorganize their own existence, to play out the contradictions which they sense, to retrace their start and origins inside and outside themselves, to test new types of relationships with others, allow their projects to ripen, deliberate amongst themselves, and mutually help one another with the realization of their projects.

56. So far as the traditional situations are concerned, defined by trainers whose wages and status depend on their work, which is in turn determined socially by the institutions to which they belong, a dependency from which

they will not or cannot free themselves, we believe that the position developed here can help to indicate a direction. It is a matter of detaching oneself from the repetition of a professional anonymous project executed by an interchangeable trainer for an interchangeable participant in order to come closer to a personal and situational approach. This involves the group leader asking himself:

— why he is doing this work, not his work as group leader in general, rather the particular work which he is now beginning at this point in his life, for the institution that is paying him, exactly under the conditions which he finds himself, and precisely with these participants. What pleasures and what aversions does he have with regard to this work? What conflicts, what influences, is he subject to at this moment in this situation?

— what particular relations link him at this moment to the institution which is employing him and under whose provisions he now stands. What binds him to it and what separates him from it? What other kinds of relationship to it does he desire, and what hinders him from implementing them, inside and outside himself? What keeps him from changing the provisions under which he works? What fears, what pleasures, are active for him in his role as initiator as he practises it in this group?

57. As can be seen, it is a matter of maintaining an open attitude and not being satisfied with a standardizing formula or a rationalization which merely justifies the role that one is playing. It is also a question of becoming responsive to the conflict dimension in which this role is probably being lived and opening oneself to working on the personal contradictions which one encounters as trainer. It is equally important for the trainer to come to terms with the concrete emerging project that he is carrying inside himself, to change both himself and his situation, and not to withdraw into a capsule in order to provide the participants with a polished facade of personal competence, seriousness, and efficiency.

58. By following this procedure the trainer's role is not denied or magically annulled, which is without doubt worse than fulfilling it naively. On the contrary, it is considered from a distance and becomes problematical. The trainer ceases to be the voice of power in the group, a voice that is in actuality simply a reproduction of the voice of social power coloured by the initiator's personal timbre. He asks himself: Why am I a trainer? How much compelled am I, how much do I adhere to it? Why precisely these methods or principles? What exactly do I want from these people? What do I want to do that I cannot do? Why am I not able to do it?

59. It is thus a matter of opening oneself to the conflict and the project; with regard to oneself as well as to the others and the relations with them. The participants cease to be enemies who must be defeated, or objects which must be brought up and made normal according to one's own particular educational

plan ('freeing' them from their ignorance, fantasies, corporal blockages, and who knows what else). These are people who are filled with the same confusion and contradictory plans as oneself. The conflicts with them undoubtedly reflect on the one hand various dependencies and infantile attitudes which they have carried over from childhood, but on the other hand they also reflect the absurd situation of dependency into which the trainer has brought them and within which he also suffers, this *papier mâché* pedestal which he has been placed upon and which pleases him though at the same time bores him to death. These conflicts are not only productive for the participants but also for the trainer himself, in a dialectical way, in that they betray the absurdity of his position and his resistance to changing it.

60. Openness also involves accepting working through conflicts as a way for change. We are by no means maintaining that social and psychological dependence can be eliminated without strain and conflict, not even under the privileged conditions of self-organization. In every instance it is a matter of a *process* of change and not of a situation which can be attained at once. We are simply saying that conflict concerns the trainers just as much as the participants. The contradictions on *both* sides must be perceived. The wishes for change and the obstacles preventing their realization, the manner in which these obstacles mutually reinforce one another, all involve patient work in which recognizing resistance to change within oneself and within others is just as important as identifying the wishes for change themselves. Being open to change does not oppose but on the contrary is related to seeing the aversions to change and recognizing one's own resistance as well as that of others. It is a matter of approaching a new starting point where the mutually struggling energies can evaluate themselves in their true forms and the scales can conclusively tip in one direction or the other without being forced. Believing the opposite is based on a magical attitude, a magical denial of resistances by the trainers, above all of their own, and conceals in reality a seizure of power. Certain militant training practices, particularly institutional analysis, fall under this critique: action on the principle of all or nothing and indeed at once, the rejection of resistances, the reproduction of power by the trainer, etc. . . . . . We mistrust the professional liberators as much as the others when they will not simultaneously engage in a process of personal self-liberation within the group in which they are working.

X. WORKING THROUGH CONFLICTS

61. Existential training presupposes working through conflicts, which means coming to an awareness of the conflicts with oneself and others is necessary for maturation and for engaging in a personal project.

62. This work on the conflicts is realized and becomes apparent at several levels simultaneously:

— at the level of imaginary mutual relations between the representatives of authority and power (professional trainers or privileged persons in the case of a self-organized group, institutions or their representatives) and the participants;
— at the level of power relationships between these two;
— at the level of the relations between the participants;
— at the level of the individual's relation to himself;
— at the level of expressing and elaborating the project. This process goes through several stages, which we will call submission, challenge *(contestation)*, revendication, confrontation, and generalized confrontation. These stages overlap one another without a fixed boundary, and there are also differences between the development of different individuals.

63. The initial situation, *submission*, is characterized by the *repression* of conflict and personal objectives *(enjeux)*. What the participants expect from the group is determined by what the trainers and institutions expect from it. This expectation is codified in the trainer's language, which exempts the participants from having to formulate a personal project. The individual's relation to himself is experienced as conflict-free and unproblematical, or else the personal contradictions are clothed in socially acceptable desires which are directed towards the trainers and which they will fulfill. The authorities and powers are unconsciously built up to be protective and beneficent deities, from whom a mythical protection is expected. They exercise an absolute power over the group which is recognized and submitted to. Aggression against them or conflict with them is fully repressed. They pursue unobstructed a dream of omnipotence in their relations with the participants. The contract of dependence applies reciprocally in full effect. The relations between the participants are entirely dominated by the relations with the trainers. They are characterized by indifference or mistrust and an unconscious rivalry for the attention and favour of the trainers.

64. When the conflicts with the authorities and powers begin making themselves noticeable, they first assume the form of *challenge (contestation)*: for example often through passivity, obstruction, absence, leaving, or simply remaining silent; or they can take on the form of vague and undefined demands that still have an abstract character. The authorities and powers respond to the challenge with various power manoeuvres (formal recognition of the demand, feigned satisfaction, 'good relations' with the participants . . .), none of which actually brings their power and its psychological basis into question.

During this period the attitude towards the authorities and powers is ambivalent: protection is expected from them and yet they are detested because of the dependence they create. But the conflict with them remains latent. It is blocked by the dependence on them which the individual unconsciously feels but does not admit to himself.

This situation is characterized by the *confusion of objectives* (*enjeux*) and the risks involved. Personal and collective projects begin to find expression, but each individual imagines, without admitting it to himself, that he can receive what he wants without risking conflict with himself or with others. This means, for example, that those fighting for self-organization want to get to a point where the group organizes itself without risking loss of sympathy from the group's institutionalized trainers and the protection of the institution which is supporting the project; or women want to abandon submissive conduct towards masculine forms of behaviour without risking loss of the masculine group members' support; or a professional trainer imagines that he can realize his didactic concept of the autonomy of the participants without risking losing the narcissistic pleasures derived from his position of power. In this situation unconscious objectives (*enjeux*) and risks counterbalance the conscious ones. Unconscious objectives for the participants are the gratifications which they derive from the relations of identification with the trainers and the controlling institution — the protection offered to them against their doubts, feelings of insufficiency, and problems of identity. In the same way, the trainers and the representatives of power cannot question the gratifications which they derive from their position of psychological and social control. What is at stake for both of them (the unconscious risk which nobody is really prepared to take) is the preservation or dissolution of the implicit contrast of dependence. Because the contract of dependence cannot be acknowledged, let alone placed in question, the individual and collective goals cannot be brought into play within a real conflict that inevitably makes the position of each individual and the basis of his security questionable. It is a pseudo-conflict for both sides, a game of conflict but not a real conflict.

For the same reason the individual masks the conflicts with himself, particularly the ambivalence towards authority and power (simultaneously seen as sources of self-realization and obstacles to it); this is also the case with the corresponding ambivalence which the authorities and powers feel towards the participants.

Also for this reason the individual and collective projects remain vague and abstract. These are dreams of change and Utopia, radical and absolute but not wishes for change directed towards specific aims which could be attained now in this situation. They are *imaginary* plans (projects) for change. The imaginary gratification of the wish for change makes it possible to avoid engagement in a real conflict with oneself or with authority and power. Change is expected to result from a magical manipulation which will be brought about by the others (indeed, without admitting it, by authority and power).

During this period attempts at cooperation between participants can arise in connection with projects of change, but without the concrete solidarity needed for changing the situation, because the unconscious fundamental relations based on submission persist in such a way that they bind the participants to the authorities and place the latter as a third party between the participants. This is shown in the difficulty involved in taking part in a common stand against authority and power.

65. Usually challenge is either followed or accompanied by *revendication*. Participants complain, demand, personally seize hold of authority and power, often quite forcibly, but their demands possess as little precise form in this instance as they did in the case of the challenge: they thus run the risk of failure. They neither engage in a real conflict with authority and power nor with themselves, that is with the fear they have of losing their protection.

The attitude towards authority and power remains ambivalent, but this ambivalence is complicated by another unrecognized ambivalence which the participants feel towards themselves. The enmity towards authority and power finds increasingly more direct expression, but there is more internal personal conflict concealed behind the conflict with authority which remains unconscious. Authorities are hated because of the dependence they create, but the individual's disdain for his own attitude of dependence is behind this hatred, an attitude which he is neither able to admit to himself nor free himself from. They are blamed for demanding dependence, but also at the same time for not having understood how to maintain it and for not being able to meet the mythical expectations which were initially placed on them. This is the phase of disappointment and embitterment, the phase of a disappointment which cannot be acknowledged because it would expose the dependence. The participants hate and regret their dependence, they deplore the mythical identity which it offered and for which they do not have a substitute. Change is experienced as destructive and devastating to the identity of the individual. They unconsciously build up authority and power as demonic deities which they equip with powers of destruction, because they cannot recognize their own potency to change: potency which is conceived of as the destroyer of the lost and lamented identity.

The confusion of objectives (*enjeux*) continues, but it changes its character in a definite way. What is now unconsciously feared is not so much losing the relationship of dependence as falling back into it, and the risk of this is projected into authority and power. Thus the participants lie in wait for the trainers and are on the watch for their attempts to dominate, which are perceived as destructive, because the participants are not sure of themselves. The wishes for change which are proclaimed are ambiguous. They are personal wishes for change, but are also simultaneously directed towards authority and power. The participants expect the representatives of authority and power to stand up for change, to hasten it, or possibly even to bring it about, for the participants themselves are not really prepared to do so.

The participants' ambivalence has its counterpart in the ambivalence of the representatives of authority and power. The submissive children who were confidently used by the trainers as the objects of their own wish to dominate have become disobedient demons who oppose this wish and undermine the basis of their own security. They are hated for this reason and at the same time the trainers mourn the lost relationships of dependence, which they attempt to preserve or reestablish. The actual process fluctuates between power manoeuvres, which are part of an attempt to win back the opposition to the side of the trainers, and methods involving active suppression, authoritarian conduct, and force.

66. *Confrontation* with the representatives of authority and power is something entirely different from challenge (*contestation*) and revendications. This time it is a matter of a personal engaged and concrete act of the will, of a 'citizen's initiative' (*Bürgerinitiative*). It is a personal act which emerges out of the anonymity and expresses itself with an 'I will' or 'we intend to'. It is an engaged act: this time the conflict is real, the possibility of a break with the authorities and powers has been accepted. It is a concrete act: a precise objective (*enjeux*) is identified around which the struggle will revolve and which carries a precise position within the group's space and time. It is aimed at the power of the trainers and institutions and involves enlarging the economic-political-ideological-psychological sphere that the group can control.

Accepting the possibility of the break with authority and power is a fundamental prerequisite to confrontation. It means that the individual simultaneously begins to confront himself and resolutely faces the internal personal conflicts that were repressed in his relationship with authorities and powers; he faces his ambivalence and risks losing their protection and love.

The break with authority and power is not sought, which would again be a way of reproducing dependence, but rather it is accepted. The connections with the authorities and powers are still desired insofar as they can constructively contribute to the group's project. What is rejected is the totalitarian power which they claim for themselves, and at the same time the individual renounces the mythical protection which he had expected from them. It could be said that a differentiation is effected between the actual persons who possess authority and power and the actual services which one expects from them on the one hand, and the *imaginary authority and power* on the other. By the latter we mean the totalitarian power which satisfies the illusion of omnipotence of those ruling and the mythical protection which corresponds to the wish for dependence of those being ruled. The bargain is quite clearly put in the hands of the authority and power: 'Either renounce your totalitarian power and we will be prepared to work with you, or we will get along without you.'

This new position with regard to the intrapersonal conflicts and the conflicts with the possessors of authority and power makes it possible to enter into a real conflict with them, but it also opens up the possibility for negotiations and compromises, since they are no longer seen as deities or totalitarian demons who are good or evil, but rather as simultaneously useful and dangerous realities with whom it can be advantageous to come to terms. The attitude towards authority and power ceases to be repetitious and determined in a coercive manner by the unconscious in the sense of submission or revolt. A new starting point is approached in the relations to them. The attitude which is taken towards them depends on their answer.

A step is taken outside the confusion of objectives (*enjeux*). A hierarchy of objectives can be established. The imaginary objectives in the relations to authority and power, that is the need for mythical protection, vanish or become effaced. The goals of collective development have priority. Collaboration with the authorities and powers falls into second place, provided that the primary goals can be pursued. At the same time the goals of collective development come out of the imaginary. One ceases to simply dream of salvation and to expect it to come from a magical manipulation by the authority. Intentions fasten themselves to concrete goals which can and will be reached here and now, in the present situation — or in the near future. This marks the emergence of an until now latent, now conscious and precise *collective project*.

The relations between the participants are based on a real solidarity. A negotiating collective arises, a group that fights and negotiates with the representatives of authority and power.

67. In other respects, however, the individual and/or subgroup projects remain vague and undefined. They are confined within the collective project, which is conceived of as the inescapable prerequisite to their existence. Precedence is given to changing the socio-emotional situation of the entire group in its relationship with the trainers and institutions, and to eliminating their totalitarian power and the irrational dependence on them.

But a new fantasy arises, this time at the level of the entire group, which is unconsciously conceived of as a mythical collectivity that *guarantees* the realization of individual and/or subgroup projects before they have even been formulated. This is a fresh source of mythical protection and the origin of a new confusion of objectives. The mythical collective conceals the power conflicts within the group and the dependence that is connected to them — conflicts which were up until now dominated by the conflicts with authority and power. The mythical collective persistently prevents each individual from confronting his own inner contradictions (which are obscured by dependence on others) and also prevents the search for a personal project and personal identity. The guarantee which the collective offers is simultaneously real and imaginary. It is real insofar as it protects the individuals from actual danger, namely, against the threat posed by the institutionalized authorities and powers. It is imaginary insofar as it allows individuals to avoid conflicts

Table 1 Working through conflicts

	Submission	Challenge	Revendication	Confrontation	Generalized confrontation
Imaginary relations Of representative of authority and power potence with participants	Dreams of omni-potence	Ambivalence	Ambivalence; repression of the dependence on participants	Dismantling unconscious images, accepting the possibility of a break; reality-oriented relations	
Of participants with representative of authority and power	Protective images, wish for mythical protection	Ambivalence Need for protection/ enmity	Demoniac images, repression of dependence on authority		
Power relations Of representatives of authority and power with participants	Totalitarian power	Manoeuvres to regain control	Repression	Struggle, negotiations, compromises	
Of participants with representatives of authority and power	Submission	Obstruction	Demands, complaints, assaults		
The individual's relation to himself	Unproblematical; repression of the enmity felt towards images of authority	Repression of the ambivalence felt towards images of authority	Repression of the enmity and ambivalence felt towards oneself	Confronting ambivalence towards authority and towards oneself	Confronting the conflicts stemming from dependence on other images of authority. Confrontation with internal contradictions

Relations between participants	Indifference, mistrust, unconscious competition for the authority's favours	Attempts at cooperation, instability, lack of solidarity	Collective of revendications	Collective of negotiations, solidarity	Confrontation between the subgroups and the individual participants; dismantling the local centres of dependence and power
Development of the projects	Repression of personal objectives; codification of desires	Confusion of objectives; imaginary, impersonal, and Utopianistic projects of change of individuals	Confusion of objectives (*enjeux*); projects of change concrete but opposed to one another	Dismantling the imaginary objectives with regard to the representatives of authority and power; clarification of the issues; concrete collective project	Emergence of the projects of subgroups groups and individuals duals
Influence	One-sided influence of representatives of authority and power on participants	Domination of the conflicts with the representatives and images of authority and power over the conflicts between the participants. Refusal of mutual influence		Reciprocal influences	
Repetition/change	Predominance of repetition and re-production			Predominance of change	

amongst themselves and with themselves. It is like a provisional protective veil, necessary for the growth of the individual in his internal and external struggle with authority and power.

68. The representatives of authority and power can continue to perpetuate repression, in which case the break will take place (with the risk that the group will fall back into the stage of making challenges), or they also can engage in confrontation. In this case their way is parallel to that of the group. It implies accepting a possible break with the participants, renouncing the totalitarian power and imaginary gratification that it offers, making compromises and negotiations accessible, without looking for them at all costs, and allowing for the clarification and regulation of that which is at stake. The primary objective is no longer a power one, an objective — for the group — confused with personal aims (their original training project). Rather, it is a personal goal, still vague and unformulated, something which they could pursue without the group or with other people, but whose optimal realization for them is bound up with an agreement on collective work. Confrontation is the antithesis of repression, just as it is the antithesis of revendication. It is *a conflict that demands internal change within both parties*.

69. In the case of a self-organized group an analogous process develops in relation to privileged persons, particularly regarding the initiators of the project, for we repeat that neither power nor dependence can be immediately eliminated; they can only be reduced in the course of a process of conflict. What is brought into question in this case is above all the ideological and psychological power of the privileged persons and the dependence tied up with it, and the power which stands at their disposal and which they often abuse with the help of their intellectual and social prestige, charisma, charm, and seductive manoeuvres.

70. Confrontation with the representatives of authority and power creates a completely new situation in the group. It changes the group's socio-mental space in that it simultaneously changes the power relations and the imaginary reciprocal relationships between the possessors of authority and power and the participants. It allows all who have taken part to become involved in a concrete collective project. Finally, it opens the way to dealing with the conflicts between the subgroups and between the individual participants which up until now were hidden by the central conflict with the authorities and powers.

71. From this point on the group can engage in a process of *generalized confrontation*. This involves tearing up the protective mask of the mythical collective, engaging in the conflicts between the subgroups and individuals, dismantling the centres of local power and dependence, and coming to terms with each individual's deeper inner conflicts. Dependence always refers back

to internal contradictions, to the impossibility of coming to terms with a contradictory identity that is experienced as a lack of identity and reconciled in a dependent relationship with someone else. The possibility for personal projects to emerge or, rather, to gradually become clearer is — through confrontation with others — bound to the possibility for breaking the ties of dependence to them, confronting internal contradictions, and, lastly, confronting loneliness and death. The personal project then emerges as a provisional synthesis of one's own contradictions, a synthesis which is found in a desirable, but not necessary, relationship with the others on the basis of mutual freedom.

72. The various stages of this evolution can be schematically summarized as in Table 1.

73. In our opinion it is important to grasp the connections between these different dimensions, particularly the following;
— the connection between the imaginary relations between the representatives of authority and power and the participants and the real power relations between them. The development of both phenomena is linked and results in a change of the social-mental space. This concept precisely designates the connection between social power and fantasmatic constructions;
— the connection between the changes in the real and imaginary power relations and the working out of the projects. Limiting the real and imaginary power relations is precisely what makes it possible for the projects to emerge from the purely imaginary (that is, from the realm of the magical gratification expected from the possessors of power). This limitation also makes it possible for the participants to leave the confusion of the projects behind them and allows collective projects and the projects of the subgroups and individuals to gradually crystallize.

The same applies to the connection between the external conflicts with others and the individual's internal conflicts. The confrontation is productive because it is both an external and internal conflict. It makes a change in the environment and psychological change possible and results in a change in the social-mental space. The other forms of conflict — challenge, demand, repression — as powerful as they might be, are pseudo-conflicts, since they are based on flight from internal conflicts and on their displacement. In our opinion a real conflict between two parties supposes a reciprocal relationship whereby the conflict with the other party brings about a conflict with oneself.

74. This concept and this approach of ours are distinguished from *political* approaches of change, in the usual sense of the word political, in that the latter primarily looks at the external conflict without necessarily seeing the connection between it and the struggle with internal conflicts. A *political* approach can call forth changes in the social structures, but it also leads (in

new forms) to the reproduction of power relations which closely resemble the earlier ones, based on the action of untouched unconscious relationships.

75. Our approach also distinguishes itself from the various *therapeutic* approaches which reject the coupling of work on the imaginary with work on effecting a change in the power structures with which it is closely connected. Existential training is psychosociological. It does not separate these two aspects. It aims at local changes, but deep and real changes in the social-mental space of each person engaged in the situation, regardless of his status. It is premature to discuss its political significance at the global-social level. It could be possible that, if it were to find general expansion, it would evoke the dissolution and downfall of the organized power apparatuses through a local and decentralized action on all places of power, and through a personal transforming influence on the local possessors of power, involving them in their institutional role. This perhaps would be more efficient than a frontal attack, which damages the aggressors just as much as those being attacked. Although existential training does not free us from the necessity of making global political changes, it should, so it seems to us, definitely accompany them.

REFERENCES

Lapassade, G. (1967) *Groupes, Organisations, Institutions.* Paris: Gauthier-Villars.
Lapassade, G. (19--) *L'Entrée dans la Vie.*

Index

Action perspective
  case, 27–49
  defined, 51
  event sequence, 56
  implications, 60–61
  objectives, 53–54
  vis-à-vis other approaches, 56–60
Apprenticeship model
  conceptual work, 159–160
  identity development, 22–23
  implications, 161
  joint activities, 159
  multiple learners/teacher, 158
  sequencing, 160
  teacher–learner relationship, 157–158

Behavioural change, 33–35
Black group development, 215–221
  bonding, 221
  dependence, 218–219
  especially unique dynamics, 215–216
  interdependence, 219–220
Black human interaction groups (*see also* Black group development), 211–215
  evaluation of existent group methods, 211–214
    encounter, 212–214
    Tavistock, 211
  goals, 214–215
  planning for, 215
Black people and groups (*see also* Black group development and Black human interaction groups), 202–205, 207–211
  black groups, 209–211
  experiential groups, 202–205
  predominantly white groups, 207–209

Clinical field skills (*see also* Apprenticeship model)
  description, 148
  diagnostic, 151–153
  need for, 144–145
  personal/emotional, 148–149
  relationship management, 149–151
  skill hierarchy, 153–154, 160
Conflict, existential group, 316–326
  challenge, 317
  confrontation, 320–324
  confusion of objectives, 318–319
  generalized confrontation, 324–325
  revendication, 319
  summary, 325–326
Change, 314–316
  after experiential learning (literature review), 63–69
    early studies, 64–65
    recent studies, 65–68
  attributing causes, 84–86
  enhancing personal causality, 86–89
  types, 81–84
Coping behaviour (*see also* Skilful behaviour), 50

Defence Behaviour, 49, 51–53

Environmental competence
  definition, 226
  development, 232–242
    alternative education, 235–236
    formal education, 233–234
    leisure activity, 238
    mass media, 237
    opportunities for, 241–242
    problems, 239–241
    self-administered, 236–237
  skills
    exploring, 229–230
    making contact, 230
    non-degradation of setting, 231–232
    personalization, 231
    types, 232

Fieldwork
  academics, 145–147
  internal OD consultants, 147–148

Group-as-a-whole, 169–170, 196
Group-as-mother, 170–174

Heterogeneity in groups, 205–207

Learning person model, 4

Opportunity, 251, 260–262
Organizational processes, 166–169
  group, 168
  intergroup, 169
  interorganizational, 169
  interpersonal, 168
  intrapersonal, 167
Organizational structure, 243–265
  experiential learning (see also Teaching,
      organizational structure), 248–252,
      263–265
    design, 249–252
      analysis, 248
      games, 250
      natural, 249
      reflective, 250
      simulated, 249–250
    limits, 263–265
    nature, 249–251
  long-term effect, 261–263
    experiential learning, 263–265
    real world, 261–265

Personal growth workshop
  aims, 1
  design rationale, 2–3
  phases
    I: towards self-understanding and
        self-respect exercises (descriptive,
        sequence, criteria for choice, aims,
        summary), 8–21
    II: exploring interpersonal space
        group process, 23–33
        grouping, 21–23
    III: consolidation and closing off 33–
        35
Personal learning, 69–76
  comparison of models, 75–76
  models, 69–75
    how to learn, 70–73
    individual skill, 69–70

personal responsibility, 73–75
Power, 251, 260–262
Projective identification, 174–178
  in groups, 178–180

Role differentiation, 180–183

Scapegoating, 183–185
Self
  as cause, 79–80
  as object, 76–79
Self-defeating person model, 5
Skilful behaviour (see also Coping beha-
    viour), 53–55
System (boundaries, overbounded, under-
    bounded), 269, 277
System variables
  affect distribution, 273, 292
  authority relations, 270, 292
  cognitive work, 276, 293
  communication patterns, 272–273, 292
  economic conditions, 271, 292
  goals, 270, 291
  human energy, 273, 292
  intergroup dynamics, 274–275, 292
  role definitions, 272, 292
  summary, 278
  time span, 276, 293
  unconscious basic assumptions, 275–
      276, 293
Systemic socio-analytic perspective (see
    also Projective identification; Role
    differentiation; Scapegoating'')
  definition, 165–166
  diagnostic heuristics
    case, 187–191
    interventions, 191–196
    strategies, 185–187

Teaching, organizational structure, 249–
    251
  game, 255–261
  vignettes (examples), 253–255
T-group,
  inquiry v. skill training, 95–96
T-group design, 125–133, 139
  assumptions, 132–133
  debriefing, 131–132
  effectiveness, 129–131
  establishing collaboration, 126–127
  initial activities, 126
  maintaining energy, 128
  minimaxing psychic name/resistance,
      128–129

participation levels, 127–128
time allotment, 131
T-group exercise selection, 122
T-group staff intervention roles, 133–140
  block identifier, 136–137
  director of design events, 135–136
  norm sender, 137–138
  process intervenor, 136
  role models, 138
  teacher-guide, 133–134
Three-dimensional model of interpersonal
    behaviour (*see also* Personal Growth
    workshop, phases), 6–8
Trainer
  health
  selection, 117–119
Trainer development (model)
  implications (of model), 155
  training as being (Stage 2), 102–109
    problems, 106–109
  training as a role (Stage 1), 96–104

benefits, 99–100
  problems, 101–102
  training as process (stage 3), 110–115
    difficulties 112–115
    transition to 109
Trainers
  deprofessionalization, 301–303
  involvement, 300–301
Training groups
  dependence, 301–306
  goals, 300
  incompleteness, 313–334
  methods and techniques, 309–311
Training situation
  despecializing, 307–339
  existential, 311–326

Underbounded systems (*see also* System;
    System variable)
  Harmon, 267–268, 279–286
  ADT, 268, 286–291